A HISTORY OF RUSSIA

A
HISTORY *of* RUSSIA

BY

V. O. KLUCHEVSKY

LATE PROFESSOR OF RUSSIAN HISTORY IN THE UNIVERSITY OF MOSCOW

TRANSLATED BY

C. J. HOGARTH

Shadows we are and
Like shadows depart

VOLUME FOUR

LONDON: J. M. DENT & SONS LTD.
NEW YORK: E. P. DUTTON & CO.   1926

CONTENTS

CHAPTER I

v

CONTENTS

CONTENTS

CHAPTER XII

CHAPTER XIII

CHAPTER XIV

CHAPTER XV

CHAPTER XVI

A HISTORY OF RUSSIA

CHAPTER I

The life of Peter the Great up to the beginning of the Northern War—His early manhood
—His court tutor—His primary education—The events of 1682—His pursuits at
Preobrazhensköe—His "toy" soldiers—His secondary education—His moral
development—The Regency of the Tsaritsa Natalia—Peter's military "Company"
—That "Company's" significance—Peter's first tour abroad—His return thence.

PETER THE GREAT, the fourteenth child of Tsar Alexis, that father of many
children, and the first issue of Alexis' second union, was born in the Kremlin
on 30 May, 1672. His mother, the Tsaritsa Natalia Kirillovna Narishkin,
was come of the household of A. S. Matveiev the "Westerner"; and since
Matveiev's establishment was organised strictly on the European model,
we may conceive that it was thence that Natalia imbibed the foreign tastes
which later she took with her to court. At all events, no sooner did Peter
open his eyes than he found his playroom filled with articles of foreign
manufacture, and was reminded by his whole environment of what was
German. Even at the age of two he is seen diverting himself with German-
made musical-boxes, "strikers of cymbals," and "large cymbals"; whilst
in his nursery there stood also a sort of copper-stringed harpsichord of
Teutonic manufacture. The items afford us a vivid picture of the Alexeian
court; they show us, more than anything else could do, how greatly that
court leaned towards *objets d'art* of alien origin. And later, we see Peter's
nursery filled with appurtenances of mimic warfare; there dawns upon our
vision a whole arsenal of toy weapons, with heavy artillery predominating,
but accompanied with horse-drawn field-pieces and wooden arquebuses
—all of them clear evidence of the preoccupation that was most engaging
his elders' attention at the time.

When four years old Peter lost his father, and the nature of the *régime*
initiated under Theodor, the son of Maria Miloslavski, and the successor of
that father, caused new-comers to obtain the ascendancy at Court, to assume
public control, and to place Peter's mother and her kinsfolk in a very difficult
position. The real cause was the fact that in his time Tsar Alexis had
contracted two marriages, and left behind him two separate cliques

I

of adherents and connections who hated one another with a deadly hatred, and were prepared to stick at nothing to gratify their mutual animosity. Eventually the Miloslavskis won the day, and Matveiev, the Narishkins' leading spirit, was banished to the remote northern settlement of Pustozersk, and the young Widow-Tsaritsa retired into the background.

By some writers it has been suggested that Peter was brought up according to a system of court education other than that which had obtained with his father and elder brothers: that is to say, that he was brought up with much greater stringency. But an objection to this view is the fact that there are chroniclers of the early eighteenth century who aver that, up to at least the age of ten, Peter acquired his letters precisely as his father and his elder brothers acquired them, and that the only difference was that he displayed much greater proficiency. In particular, we have from a chronicler named Krekshin, a junior contemporary of Peter's and a man who spent thirty years in industriously (albeit indiscriminately) collecting every possible item, document, tradition and report which bore upon the Reformer's career, a detailed account of Peter's induction to learning which, whilst not wholly reliable as a documentary source, at least gives us a graphic word-picture, and is of the greater interest in that the writer cherished for the Reformer a respect amounting almost to reverence. According to Krekshin, Peter's tutelage at least followed old Russian custom in that Peter entered upon it just before he attained the age of five. The immediate cause was that, in consequence of Tsar Theodor, Peter's elder half-brother and godfather, having more than once said to the Tsaritsa Natalia, Theodor's stepmother and fellow-sponsor: "Your Imperial Majesty, it is high time that our godson were instructed," the Tsaritsa at length consented to the step, and commissioned her mentor to find a pedagogue who should be "peace-loving and kind," and "skilled in Holy Writ." The final choice, however, Theodor delegated to a *boyarin* named Theodor Prokofovitch Sokovnin, a man who savoured of ancient Russian piety throughout, as well as was come of a household which from the first had afforded asylum to Old Believers, and dissented from the Nikonian innovations —so much so that, under Alexis, two of Sokovnin's sisters, Theodosia Morozov and Avdotia Urussov, had sealed their godliness with martyrdom (the Tsar had punished their stubborn attachment to the Archpriest Abbakum and the ancient faith by immuring them in a subterranean dungeon at Borovsk), and later Alexis, a brother of the family, yielded his life upon the scaffold for having taken part in an Old Orthodox conspiracy against Peter himself. So, on being asked to nominate a man for the Tsarevitch's education, Sokovnin nominated Nikita Zotov, a benevolent, easy-going, virtuous scholar and ex-clerk of the *Prikaz Bolshogo Prichoda,* or Office of Principal Revenue; and Krekshin's account of Zotov's introduction to the post has about it such a smack of old Russian simplicity that the mere recital of it should help us to determine the manner in which Zotov performed his duties.[1] First of all, Sokovnin led Zotov to the Tsar's private chambers, and then, leaving him in the ante-room, entered the Presence to report arrival. Upon that a *dvorianin* issued from the chambers with the enquiry: "Which of you here is Nikita Zotov?"; and this plunged the future Court tutor into such a fit of nervousness that for some little while he could move neither hand nor foot, and the *dvorianin* had to take him by the arm, or he would have fallen outright. Only when he had begged for a moment's respite, and then withdrawn a little, and made the sign of the cross, could Zotov enter the Imperial Chamber. Upon that the Tsar extended to him his hand, and put him through a literary examination in the presence of the Patriarch, Simeon Polotski; and as soon as the Tsar's learned guardian had expressed approval of Zotov's manner of reading and writing, Sokovnin led away the now duly-attested Court Tutor to the widowed Tsaritsa, who, receiving him with little Peter held by the hand, said: "Inasmuch as I know thee to be a man of godly life, and one skilled in Holy Writ, I do entrust unto thee mine only son," and, when Zotov burst into tears, and, trembling with emotion, flung himself at her feet with a cry of "O Empress Mother, I am not worthy to accept of thee such a charge," raised him, reassured him, and bade him begin his labours on the following morning. And to that opening lesson came also the Tsar and the Patriarch; and when the latter had con- secrated water, and aspersed those present with a brand-new bushel, and blessed the bushel, and laid it upon the hornbook, Zotov, after a low obeis- ance to his young charge, entered upon the task of the day; during the per- formance of which, incidentally, the Patriarch presented him with a hundred roubles (in modern currency, a thousand), the Tsar with a *dvor,* or suite of apartments, and elevation to the rank of *dvorianin,* and the Tsaritsa with "two sumptuous sets of clothing both upper and under, and all proper furnishings for the same," though, of course, Zotov did not presume to don the garments until both the Tsar and the Patriarch had left him the chamber to himself. Krekshin ascribes this initiation of the young Tsar to culture to 12 March, 1677, when Peter would be just under five years old; and since that age was the age which old Russian custom prescribed for the ceremony, it is the less credible (in view of the foregoing tale) that Zotov ever at any later period put his pupil to "new learning" and "flights of Greek and Latin."

---

[1] That is to say, should show us that those duties were performed on the ancient and stereotyped lines, and not (as some allege) according to new tutorial methods.

Kotoshikhin gives us the item that the young Tsarevitch likewise had selected for his instruction "certain learned men" who, ex-secretaries of *Prikazi*, "were neither turbulent nor revellers." But though the foregoing story would seem to show that, like them, Zotov was studious rather than "turbulent" or "a reveller," presumptive evidence exists that eventually he proved wanting in this respect, since he developed such a weakness for liquor as to lead Peter to dub him his "Prince Priest," and appoint him "President" of his mock "College of Drunkards." Chroniclers, too, there are who accuse Zotov outright of having exercised a bad educational influence over his pupil; but if that was the case, at least let us remember that Zotov was summoned to court less for the purpose of educating Peter in the full sense of the term than merely for the purpose of putting him through his letters, and that he may well have performed that task at least as efficiently as had been done by his official predecessors. Of course, Zotov began with the "teaching by word," that is to say, he accompanied Peter through the hornbook, the Breviary, the Psalter, the Gospels, and the Acts, and, on each occasion of the task, conformed with the pedagogic rule of the times by making his pupil repeat by heart what had just been studied. Also, Peter came to acquit himself manfully in the Court choir—to sing and intone in his youthful baritone voice as well as any cantor, and to be capable of reciting the whole of the Liturgy from memory. In short, he received his education precisely as his father had done, and as Alexis' elder sons had at least begun theirs. At the same time, Zotov's course of instruction was not confined solely to letters, since the improvised pedagogue from the *Prikaz Bolshogo Prichoda* so far felt the influence of the new ideas as to follow Morozov's (Alexis' tutor's) example by adopting also the ocular method. The immediate cause was as follows. From the first the young Tsar imparted such zeal and rapidity of assimilation to his studies as to spend even his leisure hours in being told tales by his tutor, and shown *kunshti* (books of illustrations); and when this circumstance was reported to the Tsaritsa she bade the tutor procure also "books of history" (illuminated manuscripts) from the Court library, and likewise commissioned some of the engravers of the *Oruzheinaia Palata*, or Ordnance Office, to execute other such works, until Peter's chambers had come to have in them a whole collection of "diverting copybooks," that is to say, of manuscripts depicting towns, buildings, ships, soldiers, and warlike armaments in gold and colours. Further, the boy had given him "tales of persons with proper inscriptions" (that is to say, illustrated stories, or annotated drawings), which the best available talent had executed, and which Zotov so arranged in the young Peter's chambers that, whenever his pupil seemed to tire of books of the ordinary kind, these others could be substituted, and their illustrations displayed and explained. Also, Krekshin says that Zotov so far adhered to old Russian custom as sometimes to relate to his pupil the great deeds of his father and Ivan IV., or even the earlier achievements of Donskoi, Alexander Nevski and Vladimir. And though Peter, in his later days, came to have little leisure for Russian history, it never wholly lost its interest for him, and to the end he asserted its importance in popular education, and advocated the compilation of historical primers. And to this result who shall say that Zotov's early lessons did not contribute—who shall refuse to the ex-Government clerk the credit of that achievement?

Unfortunately, Peter had not even attained his tenth year before his elementary education ended—more correctly, became temporarily broken off. This was because Tsar Theodor died on the 27th of April, 1682, and there followed upon his death the usual stormy happenings, with Peter proclaimed Tsar over the head of his elder brother Ivan, and the Tsarevna Sophia and her Miloslavskis organising an intrigue which, in May, led to a revolt of the *Strieltzi*, to wholesale massacres of *boyaré*, and to the establishment of the Imperial half-brothers as joint rulers, and culminated, on 5 July, in a demonstration of Old Believers in the Hall of Angles itself. Peter was an eye-witness of these sanguinary scenes, and though his self-possession surprised everyone—there is a story that, as he stood beside his mother on the steps of the Red Square, and saw Matveiev and his adherents falling pierced with the *Strieltzi's* spears, he moved not a muscle of his face— there can be no doubt that the horrors in question bit deeply into his memory, and were bound the more to do so in that he was a lad beyond his years (even at the age of eleven, he was mistaken by a foreign ambassador for sixteen), and capable of understanding the affair better than might have been supposed. Those scenes were the outcome of centuries: centuries had brought it about that for days the Kremlin stood ringed with the menace of the hangman and the torture-chamber, and infuriated *Strieltzi* turned it into a shambles, and everywhere men rushed to and fro in search of members of the Narishkin faction, and drank, and rioted, and squandered the loot which they had seized from wealthy *boyarin* and mercantile mansions—the clergy, meanwhile, meekly obeying the insurgents' every behest, and eventually sanctioning the joint Tsarship with their benediction. Only some of the *boyaré's* slaves threatened to interfere on behalf of the system which they could see being trampled under foot. In vain did the *Strieltzi* beguile those slaves with promises of their freedom, and with tearings up, and scatterings about the Red Square, of *kabala* deeds and serf indentures, and, alternatively, with retribution at the hands of the *Kholopii Prikaz*, or

Office of Bonded Servitude. To these promises the slaves merely retorted: "See ye that soon it be not your heads, and not our bonds, that shall be lying on the Red Square! For to what end rebel ye? Large is the Russian Land: but not large enough is it for you and our masters alike to exercise dominion therein." And for a long while the slaves (who, in that *boyarstvo*-owned capital, outnumbered the *Strieltzi* by two to one) stood waiting for a signal to quell the riot. But the signal never came.

Thence onward, therefore, the Kremlin repelled Peter, and, with its store of antiquities, its maze of Court suites, its bevies of ex-Sovereigns' sisters and daughters and aunts, its hundreds of choristers and cross-bearers and "men of the higher *chini*" in attendance upon the Kremlin ladies, sank to the status of a deserted *château*. And this it did the more because, as another result of the events of 1682, the widowed Tsaritsa was banished to the suburban village of Preobrazhensköe (once Alexis' favourite country seat, and later, owing to its position on the St. Petersburg road, the principal residence of the Imperial Court), and, with her son, made to live divorced from the work of government, and to subsist upon what Prince Kurakin calls "nought save what she did receive of the hands of the Tsarevna Sophia." In fact, there were times when her straits forced her covertly to seek help of the Patriarch, of the Troitski Monastery, and of the Metropolitan of Rostov. On the other hand, although, owing to the conspiracies of his half-sister, Peter now was a Tsar under a ban, and banished from his own Kremlin, he at least found more room for growth at Preobrazhensköe than had been the case in Moscow, since, through being thrown upon his own resources at Preobrazhensköe, and transferred, at the early age of ten, from the discipline of the schoolroom to the licence of the servants' hall, and having little to interest him in his mother's apartments (where he could see only mournful faces, and hear only the diatribes of ex-courtiers against the cruelty and injustice of humanity in general, and the cruelty and injustice of Sophia and her counsellors in particular), the high-spirited boy from 1683 onwards, daily left this depressing *milieu* made his way into the grounds of the Palace, or into the wooded country beyond them, and indulged in lonely, wandering excursions. And another effect of his having no hand to guide him was that he invented for himself a sport, and then converted that sport into a permanent school of self-education. That is to say, he, like many observant children, took to mentally counterfeiting what his elders most made the subject of their thoughts and colloquies. At that period the subject was war; and though some of Peter's contemporaries attributed his early leaning towards the military art to innate, natural promptings, whilst certainly he was of a temperament calculated easily to fan that leaning to a flame, more probable causes of what was at first only a boyish diversion becoming, later, a pursuit with a definite purpose are to be found in the talk about foreign armies which he would hear everywhere about him, and in the tales concerning his forefathers' armies which Zotov had told him earlier. Besides, we may reasonably assume that insensibly Peter's youthful instinct for diversion drew reinforcement from his poignant impressions of the rising of 1682, and thence added to itself at once the instinct of self-preservation and a yearning to be revenged upon *Strieltzi* who had dowered the Tsarevna Sophia with a measure of illegal authority, and, by doing so, forced his mother to defend herself, and to set up an opposition army. At all events, we have at our disposal court documents which enable us to follow Peter's early military pursuits at every step, to note how they increased in number as the years went on, and to mark how complex they grew in proportion as new forms were added to them, and fresh branches of the military art were tackled. One result of it all was that there now set in between the *Oruzheinaia Palata,* or Ordnance Office, at Moscow and Peter's quarters at Preobrazhensköe a regular stream of articles in general, and of weapons in particular, required for the young Tsar's sport, with a corresponding return stream of articles returned for repairs—these ranging from a shattered arquebus to a cracked drum. Thus Peter requisitions a figure of the Saviour, a dining-room clock, an Arab statuette, and a German carbine. Again, he calls for gunpowder, lead, standards, halberts and pistols in such quantities that almost it is as though the Court Arsenal were taking the road *en masse.* Meanwhile his life was anything but sedentary. Darting hither and thither, he would visit the villages of Vorobievo and Kolomensköe, call at the Troitski Monastery or the Monastery of Savva-Storozhevski, and traverse the neighbouring court and monasterial hamlets with military trains. Study of his proceedings at this period also shows us what company he kept when he was not militarily employed, and what sort of *entourage* customarily surrounded him. What we do *not* see, however, is how far he continued his purely scholastic studies. True, in 1688, he sends to the Ordnance Office for a "large globe" and a Kalmuk saddle; but as to the precise purpose for which he required the former we remain in ignorance. All that we know is that that purpose must have been one of a vigorous rather than of a scientific character, since soon afterwards we see the globe being dispatched to a clockmaker for repairs! Similarly, though, on another occasion, he calls for "a book on fire weapons," he demands, with it, "a diverting ape"!

These requisitionings for private delectation were accompanied with musterings of sharers in the sport. In this respect Peter had a rich field of choice to hand. To begin with, it was required by old Russian custom that as soon as a Tsarevitch of Moscow attained the age of five he should have appointed to his service a number of valets and butlers and equerries drawn from "sons of Court gentry meet to be chamber-men." From the first the Tsars of the pre-Petrine era maintained uniformly grandiose establishments and retinues. Alexis' taste for falconry alone had led to over 3000 hawks and falcons and other birds of prey figuring as registered members of the Venery Department, and being fed upon the produce of 100,000 dove-cots, and trapped, reared, and trained by over 200 hawkers and falconers, whilst in his stables department there had been 40,000 horses,[1] and, to attend upon these animals' wants, 600 officials, not of plebeian origin, but of an origin qualifying them to rank as "honourable men," as men of birth, as men in receipt of money, of clothing, of either *pomiestia* or *otchini*, and of a "licence to eat and to drink of all of the Tsar's substance." But after Alexis' time these departments had dwindled and expired, since Theodor was too weakly to go hunting, and the same with the Tsarevitch Ivan, and Peter, for his part, detested falconry and the chase, and public opinion would not let an Imperial Princess ride afield; and as, of course, a result of this extinction of departments was to throw many court and household dependents out of work, it was pre-eminently these unemployed whom Peter now selected for the more onerous tasks which he had in mind. That is to say, he recruited a number of these young chamberlains and grooms and falconers into his private service, and, forming them into two squads, augmented their body with volunteers from the *boyarstvo*, the *dvorianstvo*, and the boyaral slaves, until two battalions of 300 men each had been mustered. At first these men were known merely as Peter's "*potieshnie liudi*," or "men of diversion," or "men of sport" ("toy soldiers," as we should say), but the description is not altogether accurate, since, though as yet the Tsar was only "playing at soldiers," his companions in the sport did perform actual military service, and receive payment as much as though they had been in Government employ. Later, also, the title "*potieshni*" came to connote a *chin* or grade to itself. A petition runs: "I am a paid man equal unto thy great lords, for I am one of thy *potieshnie koniuchi*." [2] Moreover, recruitment of the corps was carried out strictly in official and departmental style—in 1686 the *Koniushenni Prikaz*, or Office of Horse, is seen receiving orders that seven court equerries should be sent to Preobrazhensköe "for enrolment of *potieshnie* artillerymen": and though the ranks of Peter's "toy" soldiers began by being made up solely of such warriors as Alexander Menshikov (a man whom Prince Kurakin describes as "only lowly by birth"

---

[1] The translator hazards that in the original this figure is a misprint for 4000.
[2] Horsemen.

—though at least his father was a court equerry), later the corps was entered by youths from higher walks of life, and in 1687, in particular, by Prince I. I. Buturlin and Prince M. M. Golitzin, of whom the latter was one day to rise to be the well-known field-marshal of that name, but for the present was taken on only "for a learning of the drum," since as yet his paucity of years forbade of his being appointed to a higher post. Naturally, the corps kept Preobrazhensköe in a constant state of racket, and for its benefit Peter built barracks, staff-offices, and stables, and made the Department of Horse furnish it with artillery harness and equipment, and organised the whole into an institution having its own staff and budget and treasury. Also, so determined was he to become a full-fledged warrior, and to convert his fellows into the same, that he clad both them and himself in uniforms dark green in hue, armed them with muskets, chose certain of his "chamber-men" (though "persons of choice name only," it will be noted), to act as staff- and over- and under-officers, subjected his command to a daily course of training amongst the neighbouring fastnesses, and himself traversed all the military grades, beginning with drummer. Moreover, for the better instruction of his "toy soldiers" in the art of besieging and storming fortresses he built a "*potieshnaia fortetzia*" on the river Yäuza, dubbed it "Pless-burg," and periodically bombarded it with mortars and other offensive weapons. But such advanced martial exercises called for a high degree of technical skill, and Peter would never have made the progress that he did but for outside help: unaided homegrown knowledge would never have achieved such results. He obtained that help through the fact that near Preobrazhensköe there existed an eccentric Bohemian settlement which, though eyed askance by the directors of the Muscovite Empire, had come to be known as the *Niemetskaia Sloboda,* or German Suburb,[1] and, though begun, during Alexis' time, as a colony only for the foreign military men whom that Sovereign engaged for the organisation of his Russian regiments of the Foreign Contingent, had since come to include amongst its *personnel* as many as two foreign generals, nearly a hundred foreign colonels, and a great number of foreign under-officers. And though Peter began by resorting to this settlement only when he needed one or another foreign inven-tion or appliance which the engineering resources of his own *potieshnie* were unable to produce (for example, in 1684 he induced a foreign mechanic named Zömmer to show him an instrument for discharging grenades which later became his favourite plaything), he later invited some of the foreign officers concerned to remove from the settlement to Preobrazhensköe itself, that they might drill his mimic regiments there, and make them equal to

[1] See vol. iii. p. 279.

the professional forces maintained by the State proper. In this manner it resulted that by the early nineties of the seventeenth century the mimic regiments themselves had come to be professional corps, and, through the fact that they were quartered in the villages of Preobrazhensköe and Semenovo, derived thence their regimental titles, and were compounded definitely into formations having attached to them foreign colonels, majors, and captains, a few Russian sergeants, and a Russian colonel-in-chief, a man named Avtamon Golovin, and described by Kurakin, Peter's brother-in-law and crony, as "a man gross of wit, but at least skilled in the exercise of soldiers."

Another result of Peter's passion for foreign marvels was that he received a secondary education which none of the Tsarevitchi, his predecessors, had ever enjoyed. Prince Y. T. Dolgoruki relates an example of this. When that Prince was setting forth, in 1687, to act as Russian Ambassador in France, he happened to mention to the Tsar that recently he had possessed an instrument "which can reckon spaces and distances without any need of approaching the spot," but that someone had stolen the instrument; and upon that Peter besought him to purchase a device of the same kind as soon as he reached Paris, and this the Prince promised to do, and in time sent home to Russia an astrolabe. Unfortunately, Peter found himself at a loss what to do with his prize: his one idea was to take it to the usual ubiquitous, inevitable, and omniscient German *Doktor*. True, the *Doktor* himself had to confess that he had no knowledge of the instrument, but at least he promised that he would unearth someone who had, and, "on Peter again and again, and with great earnestness, constraining him," brought to light a Dutchman named Timmermann, "with whom Peter did mightily, and with great zeal, apply himself unto" study, not only of the astrolabe, but also of the sciences of arithmetic, geometry, ballistics, and fortification. Now, some of Peter's note-books on these subjects have come down to us in Peter's own handwriting, so that we are able to scrutinise some of the mathematical problems which he resolved, and to mark some of the explanations with which these resolutions were accompanied; and be it at once said that perusal of the notebooks leaves us aghast at the poverty of Peter's literacy, at the execrableness of his handwriting, at the carelessness with which he observed the rules of orthography, and at the difficulty and the painfulness of the inscription of his characters. Thus, in some places he fails to divide words; in others he spells words purely on the phonetical system; and he can even insert a *yare*[1] between two conson-

---

[1] The *yare*, or hard sign (in reality, a hard mute vowel which has become obsolete of the Russian alphabet, is a terminal character only, save in one case alone. But even in that case it ought not to be inserted between two consonants.

ants! The note-books also make it clear that during his boyhood he paid little attention to any mathematical term which he found puzzling, for he is seen to write for the Latin word *additio* both *"aditsoe"* and *"voditsia."* Nor can his tutor himself have been very strong in his mathematics, since sums which he worked out, and especially sums of multiplication, exhibit more than one error of working. At the same time, we gain from the note-books a good idea of the zest which Peter imparted to his mathematico-military avocations, and of the swiftness with which he traversed successively arithmetic, geometry, ballistics, and fortification, mastered the astro-labe, and learnt how to demolish fortresses, and how to calculate the trajectory of cannon balls. Also, there came a day when, as he and Timmermann were inspecting some storehouses erected by Nikita Ivanovitch Romanov in the village of Izmailovo, he discovered a battered old English boat. Ever afterwards he averred that the boat had fathered the Russian Fleet, since it had been the first cause of his conceiving the passion for navigation which subsequently led him to build his Archangel and Periaslavl flotillas. Yet though he seems to have thought it unnecessary to mention that that beloved "father of the Russian Fleet" had had collateral ancestors, those collateral ancestors had nevertheless existed, since quite two years before the discovery of the boat at Izmailovo he is seen sending to the Ordnance Office for "small ships" (probably these were models preserved from the building of the *Orel* on the Oka),[1] whilst Court documents of 1686 mention construction of toy vessels at Peter's own Preobrazhensköe, and in any case Alexis' Government more than once agitated for the organisation of a Russian Fleet. Wherefore behind Peter's aspirations towards sea power there lay both tradition and heredity.

We have now at our disposal sufficient data of Peter's boyhood and youth for a reconstruction of his early spiritual development. Up to the age of ten he traversed merely the stereotyped ecclesiastico-literary educational course of the day—though he did so amongst scenes and phenomena which an older Russia had never known: and, the age of ten attained, he was, owing to a series of sanguinary events and painful impressions, driven from the Kremlin, and had his mode of life deflected from the usual Court round, and remembered the Kremlin only with the bitterest of memories and the most unlovely of sentiments. Then, prematurely left to his own devices, he betook himself to toys of war, and, aided by them, and by Zotov's earlier picture-books, pursued, about and around the palace of Preobrazhensköe and the neighbouring woodlands, a sport which had first occurred to his fancy in the days when Moscow had been his home. Next,

See vol. iii. p. 276.

he discarded his foreign-made dolls—he took to himself real, live soldiers, and real, useable guns: and as he had no expert assistant to guide him, and no definite system to go by, he added to these, as companions in his sport, a number of his "chamber-men," and, with them, pursued, until he attained the age of seventeen, quasi-martial diversions which had the effect of completely divorcing him from the ideas—more correctly, the customs and the traditions—hitherto constituting the whole political outlook and governmental science of a Muscovite Tsar. Nor did he develop any new political ideas to replace the old, since no longer was there a source at hand for such ideas, nor anything to give them shape. True, though prematurely interrupted, the teaching begun by Zotov was eventually renewed; but when it was renewed it was renewed under very different guidance, and in a very different direction, from before, seeing that, whereas his elder brothers had passed straight from being taught their Church letters by a Government *diak* into the hands of more advanced preceptors whose methods may have differed according to the individual, but at least had inculcated moral and political notions of a type superior to those of the ordinary Muscovite purview (since they had included citizenship, the science of government, and the duties of a Sovereign towards the subject), no secondary tutor of the sort ever fell to Peter's lot, for Simeon Polotski and Rtistchev were succeeded only by a Dutch artisan with an educational armament limited to a course of mathematico-military training. True, this course may, from the mechanico-technical standpoint, at least have been as efficient as Zotov's had been from the standpoint of letters; but undoubtedly the two courses differed in import, since under Zotov it had been the memory chiefly that had been taxed, whereas Timmermann brought into play only the eye, the sense of adaptation, and the faculty of proportion, whilst leaving the reasoning power and the heart dormant. All this communicated to Peter's ideas and tastes the one-sided tendency that, whilst his political mentality remained absorbed in the struggle with his half-sister and the Miloslavskis, his civic attitude developed only into a general antipathy to ecclesiastics, to *boyaré*, to *Strieltzi*, and to Old Believers, and soldiers, guns, fortresses, and ships were allowed to fill the intellectual space which should have been occupied by citizens, political institutions, popular needs, and civil relations. In fact, in Peter's spiritual household, all that province which concerns the community, and duties to the community, and represents the sphere of ethics, and is indispensable to every right-thinking human being, remained to the end so much a neglected corner that the community ceased to figure in that household before yet the household had realised its relation to the community.

During the August of 1689 the Tsarevna Sophia and Shaklovit, her latest gallant, organised a new rising of *Strieltzi*, a new movement against the Tsaritsa's kinsfolk; and though, on the midnight alarm sounding, Peter fled into the forest, and made his way to the Troitski Monastery, without considering for a moment his mother and his pregnant wife, this was the only occasion when he displayed such pusillanimity, and the fact shows us how completely he, in time, became inured to apprehension of injury from his kinswoman. And since the conspiracy proved a failure, there came an end to the three-fold system of rule which had never failed to excite derision abroad, and had been approved of at home by none but a few patrician families; and inasmuch as the household at Preobrazhensköe was not one of those families, "the third and the most shameless member of that rule" (to quote a letter which Peter sent to his brother Ivan at this period) was sent to be confined in a convent, Ivan was retained to serve as a ceremonial, figurehead Tsar, Peter returned to his military sports, and the ex-Tsaritsa resumed the ruling power. Unfortunately, says Kurakin, she proved "in nowise fitted to rule, in that she was small of mind"; wherefore the work of administration next became parcelled out amongst her retainers, of whom the most talented was Prince B. A. Golitzin, a man who at least had shown skill in fighting the conspiracy, and was well-educated enough to be able to make a speech in Latin, but "did tipple without ceasing," and exercised such unchecked authority over his Department (the "Court of Kazan," [1]) as eventually, to bring the whole of the *Povolzhie* [2] to ruin. Two other such time-servers were Lvov Narishkin, brother to the Tsaritsa, and Tikhon Strieshnev, a relative of the young Tsars through their maternal grandmother: of whom Kurakin says that the former was a fool, a drunkard, a wastrel, and "a man who, even in his good deeds, did compass those deeds less through any power of reason than through a mere drollery of humour," and that the latter was as wanton as Lvov, and, to boot, "a cunning and cruel Court intriguer." At the same time, the pair did at least contrive to administer the country for a while, even though they did so, "with an exceeding great disorderliness" (that is to say, with innumerable legal wrongs and injustices), "and with many arrangings of recompensings, and many robbings of the State." More: they contrived to get the *Boyarskaia Duma* so completely under their thumb that "the chief *boyaré* did sit in the Council Chamber without voices, and appear but as onlookers." Of course, such an abasement of the great *boyarin* families, and especially of families of princely rank, caused the aristocratic Kurakin searchings of heart, and brought him to the conclusion that the Narishkin-Strieshnev faction were "lords of the

[1] See vol. ii. p. 256.   [2] The region of the Lower Volga.

poorest and the meanest gentility"; whilst when Peter made a second
marriage the result was to bring to Court yet another clique, in the shape of
three score or so Lopukhins. And even though these Lopukhins were received
by the native aristocracy with polite distaste, and had their leading members
(for the most part *Prikaz* officials) stigmatised as "men of malice, and mean
slanderers, and fellows of the basest soul," they succeeded in rivalling even
the preceding administrative ring in their power of overriding the capital's
Governmental-official-clerical community, and of rendering that capital so
abundantly fertile of official scandals that some memoirs written by an
okolnich named Zheliabuzhki (a close observer of, and an active participator
in, the affairs of his day) bring before us a whole procession of *boyaré,
dvoriané, dumnie liudi*, and *prostie diaki* who had to be sentenced variously to
torture, to loss of salary, to the *knut*, to flagellation with rods, to exile, to confiscation of property, and even to death, for such crimes and misdemeanours
as "brawlings at Court," "utterings of furious words in the presence of the
Tsar," putting their wives to death, violating women's honour, forging
documents, and purloining Government funds—in one case even with
the help of the wife of the Finance Minister himself, when the culprit
who had to be sentenced to the *knut* was a Prince Lebanov Rostovski,
and the offence that of having laid violent hands upon coffers belonging
to the Treasury whilst in transit along the Troitski road, although
the culprit himself was the owner of hundreds of peasant homesteads,
and, six years later, is seen figuring as a captain in Peter's *potieshnie*
corps. Naturally, such a Court *milieu* permits of our drawing no fine
distinctions between an old party and a new, or between a conservative and a liberal. No, the conflict then taking place at Court was
one between two rival sets of barbarous morals and instincts rather
than a contest between barbarism and more enlightened tendencies and
ideas.

It is not to be wondered at that, such being the setting in which Peter
found himself placed after the deposition of Sophia, the impressions which
he derived from current events scarcely induced him to take an increased
interest in Governmental and social affairs. No, they only increased his
absorption in his own pursuits, and added to the energy which he devoted to
martial diversions, and brought him into ever closer and closer touch with the
German Suburb, and led him with growing frequency to borrow thence
officers for instruction of his "toy" infantry and "toy" artillery during
ordinary times, and for the command of those forces during times of
manœuvres—favours acknowledged with personal visits, and with unceremonious acceptance of invitations—especially if they came from

General Gordon—to dinner or supper. Further, this strengthening of ties with the *Niemetskaia Sloboda* led to his enlarging his "toy" army, or "Company," with such soldiers of fortune as "Alexashka" Menshikov and Franz Yakovlevitch Lefort: the former of whom was a bombardier of obscure origin, and so illiterate as scarcely to be able to sign his own name, though also one who loved a hearty laugh and jest, so that he became his patron's prime favourite, and the latter, Lefort, was a Genevan adventurer who had travelled half the world over before alighting upon Moscow, and was nearly as illiterate as Menshikov, but, withal, cheerful, keen-witted, convivial, optimistic, a staunch friend, an indefatigable ballroom cavalier, a good companion whenever a bottle was toward, an adept in the art of merrymaking, a skilled organiser of banquets added to music, dancing, and fair society, and, in general, a fellow whom Kurakin, the "Company's" Imperial Chamberlain, dubs "a French *débauchant*." Lastly must we reckon old General Patrick Gordon, a canny, punctilious Scotch adventurer whom a contemporary *bylina* [1] averred to have "fought in seven hosts, and under seven kings." Thus Peter recruited into his "Company" foreign and Russian officers in about equal numbers, though he took care to give the latter twice as important a standing in it as the foreign element. Amongst the Russian officers there were included the Generalissimo, Prince T. U. Romodanovski (but known also as "Frederick"); the King of Pressburg, a man whom Peter armed with extensive police powers, and made director of the "Company's" intelligence department, and his chief inflicter of the *knut* and the torture-chamber (we find the fellow described as "like unto a monster in guise, and tyrannical, and evil of mind, and wishful at no time to do good unto any man, but drunken all his days"—though also we know that he was as devoted to Peter as a dog might have been); and I. I. Buturlin, King of Poland, and known in his own capital as Tsar Semenovski—a man who had formerly been in command of the *Strieltzi*, and was "both cruel and drunken and mercenary." And as no love was lost between the *Strieltzi*, as the older force, and the new *potieshnie*, this sometimes led to outbreaks that were very much actual, and in no degree "toy." In short, the "Company" was composed of such a hotchpotch of races and dialects and social grades that, really to understand the difficulties encountered by any member who wished to communicate with a colleague, we must turn to a two-lined letter of Lefort's which the latter sent to Peter in 1696, that is to say, as long as twenty years after Lefort's arrival in the country. The letter is couched in the "Russian" language, but inscribed in Latin characters, and runs: "*Slavou Bogh sto ti prechol sdorova ou gorrod voronetz. Daj boc ifso*

[1] Ancient folk-song.

dobro sauersit i che Moscva sdorovou buit!" [1] Similarly does Peter himself
begin letters to Menshikov with the Anglo-German address (transliterated
into Russian characters), "Mein liebster Kamarat, mein best frient"; whilst
T. M. Apraxin, *Voevoda* of Archangel, is invoked by him as "Min Her
Guverneur Archangel." As a rule, however, the "Company" dispensed
altogether with marks of compliment, and once Peter is found roundly
upbraiding Apraxin for having written him "with such an excess of praise
as I like not, and the less in that thou, being of our own Company,
shouldst the more have known how it is meet to write." And when Peter
married Eudoxia Lopukhin the lure of the "Company" came more than ever
to exceed the calls of the domestic hearth, for the marriage was a marriage
born merely of intrigues on the part of the Narishkin-Strieshnev faction,
and the dull, quarrelsome, superstitious Eudoxia was no fit mate for a man
like Peter. In fact, it was only so long as the pair remained in ignorance of
one another, and Peter's mother (who, like everyone else, had little love
for her daughter-in-law) forbore to hasten the inevitable rupture, that
harmony reigned between them. And in proportion as the home *régime*
rendered Peter's absences more and more protracted, those absences increasingly augmented the coolness that subsisted between him and Eudoxia,
and that coolness, again, both the frequency and the duration of the absences.
Thus Peter's life, at this period, ended by becoming the life of a wandering
military student pure and simple, as he prepared, and let off, ingenious, but
dangerous, fireworks, held reviews, trained his infantry, supervised military
expeditions, conducted military manœuvres and engagements at least
serious enough to leave an appreciable number of wounded, and even of
killed, in their wake, experimented with new guns, built a yacht on the
Yäuza, complete to the last detail, borrowed textbooks on ballistics from
Gordon, induced Gordon to procure such textbooks from abroad, studied
all things, observed all things, tested all things, catechised foreign officers
on European topics and the art of war, and dined and slept wherever he
might happen to alight—whether at the quarters of the officers of the
German Suburb, or at the "Company's" mess in Preobrazhensköe (where
he had for host a Sergeant Buzhenin), or, in fact, anywhere save in his own
home, a place to which he repaired only when he wished to dine with his
mother. In 1691, for example, he invited himself to a supper-party at Gordon's,
and eighty-five guests assembled to meet him, and bivouacked, after the
meal was over, in their chairs, and, next day, moved on to Lefort's for dinner.

---

[1] The "Russian" is full of orthographical and grammatical errors, and the "ifso"
appears to have been borrowed from the English language. In sense it runs: "Thank
God that thou hast reached the town of Voronetz in safety! God keep thee, and bring
thee as safely back to Moscow!"

In the corps Lefort held a sort of compound post both as "Generalissimo" and as "Grand Admiral," but above all things as Peter's "Minister of Banquets and Revels," and used the villa which Peter built for him on the Yäuza for such day-and-night debauches as, says Kurakin, gave rise to "drunkenness exceeding description," to drunkenness "whence many did die." Yet though such carousals under "Ivashka Misrule" would affect Peter's fellow survivors for days afterwards, Peter himself always arose betimes, and set about his tasks as though nothing had happened.

So, until he reached the age of twenty-four, Peter occupied himself with convivialities with his officers, and with military sports. In particular, he led military expeditions to Alexandrovskaia Sloboda, to Periaslavl, and to Archangel, and, in the process, had his "playing at soldiers" converted into a pursuit with a purpose (perhaps, the more so because at that time military affairs were the pre-occupation also of his elders), and his immaturities mellowed with the approach of manhood, and his "toy" soldiers transformed into real regiments, and his "toy" cannon into real artillery. True, Gordon, the expert supervisor of his "toy" expeditions, describes these expeditions, in his memoirs, as "military ballet-dances"; but at least one effect of those expeditions, added to cruises in the flotilla which Peter built at Periaslavl, was to create the country's first *cadres* of a regular army and a regular fleet. For the rest, Peter's warlike diversions exercised upon him a high military-educational influence, and he developed their scope until we have it from Kurakin that some manœuvres carried out by Kozhukov on the Moskva in 1694 occupied three weeks in performance, gave employment to 30,000 men, and were conducted according to a regular plan previously drawn up by Gordon. Also, the "Company" kept a daily register of its doings: and that register, adorned with sketches of camps and baggage trains and battles and similar devices, we still possess. In fact, at last the cautious Kurakin himself had to admit that one result of the exercises had been to furnish the country with a reserve stock of trained soldiery, and that few contemporary European rulers could have mustered a force equal to Kozhukov's, a force which, "by reason of waddings and other mischances," had left behind it a trail of twenty-four slain and fifty wounded. True, Peter's own version of the exercises is that he wished, through them, merely to gratify his idea of sport; but, however that may be, they at least seem to account (as having acted as a preparation for real war-making) for the ease with which the Azov expeditions of 1695 and 1696 achieved their designed objects. And even if, on the other hand, the plan of the Azov expeditions was retrospective, and intended to act as a justification of the preliminary sham manœuvres, at least Azov was captured with the aid of an artillery trained through means of such mimic exercises, and of a flotilla built in a single winter at Voronezh as a result of the Tsar having acquired the necessary artisan ability and experience through personal labour on his wharves at Periaslavl.

Not until 1697 did the then twenty-five-year-old Peter first set eyes upon the Western Europe of which his friends of the German Suburb had told him so much, and whither Lefort had so often urged him to go. Nevertheless Peter's idea of touring the West arose spontaneously, and was, indeed, an idea bound, sooner or later, to spring from such a bent and setting as his, and not the less so in that he had spent the last few years amongst Western European immigrants, and learnt their crafts and languages at least sufficiently to, in 1689, sign letters to his mother, "Petrus," and to christen his flagship at Voronezh *The Principium*. Besides, he had, from his first entry into "toy" military service, made it his business, both ashore and afloat, to assimilate every possible detail of every possible novelty, and to induce his companions to do the same: and how should the man who had bidden his Russian youths proceed abroad for scientific study not eventually follow suit? Indeed, it was not so much in the capacity of an intelligent traveller desirous of inspecting the marvels of alien culture that Peter undertook his first foreign tour as in the capacity of a workman anxious to familiarise himself with mechanical craftsmanship which he both lacked and needed. That is to say, Peter went westward less for civilisation than for technique, and over the seal upon some of his letters written at this period there appear the words, "From one who fain would be of those who do learn and do partake." For the same reason was it that the Tsar of All the Russias became merely a plain member, a mere "Peter Mikhailov," of a State Mission which he ordered to visit some of the courts of Europe in connection with a struggle then in progress between Turkey and a Coalition of European Powers. But though this Mission's ostensible task was to strengthen the existing ties between Russia and the Powers concerned, and to form new ones, its real task was (as we see from secret instructions given to the Mission's "Grand Ambassadors," Lefort, Golovin, and Voznitsin—the latter a *dumni diak*) a ransacking of every country visited for "able naval commanders who shall have attained unto their present rank through service alone," and for "lieutenants and craftsmen who shall be meet for all the labour of ships." Meanwhile the Mission's members were to be free to assume naval service under a foreign flag, and to "render themselves skilled in marine charts and maps, and in the compass, and in all such devices of the sea," and to acquire navigation both through warlike cruises and through ordinary voyages, and to familiarise their hand with any and every species of ship's instrument and tackle, and to seize every possible opportunity of being present on a foreign war vessel during the progress of hostilities. But, above all things, they were to round off any foreign service, firstly, by obtaining a certificate of proficiency from their nautical instructors, and secondly, by bringing home with them two foreign naval artificers on the understanding that those artificers should have their out-of-pocket expenses repaid them on the conclusion of their Russian contract. Moreover, the Government offered any *dvorianin* who would undertake to send one or more serfs abroad for nautical study a bonus of one hundred roubles (one thousand modern): and *dvoriané* themselves were to be permitted to volunteer to receive a Western education. Thus we learn from Prince Kurakin who, accompanied a party of nineteen young *dvoriané* to Venice (*dvoriané* described, in their letter of recommendation to the Doge, as "gentry minded to take cognisance of all that may be new in the conduct of the military art of Europe"), that its members in due course applied themselves to mathematics, to astronomy, to navigation, to mechanics, to fortification both offensive and defensive, and to trips afloat. In short, the real aim of the "Grand Embassy" and its huge suite was, for all its pretext of a diplomatic commission, observation and examination and assimilation of the craftsmanship of Western Europe, and inveiglement to Russia of skilled Western artificers.

The first thing in the matter of business that "Volunteer Member of Embassy Peter Mikhailov" did when he found himself abroad was to apply himself to the study of gunnery. And so rapidly did he acquire his skill in this respect as fairly to astound the Prussian colonel who acted as his tutor in Königsberg, and to lead that officer to set down in the agreed certificate that "in all things may Peter Mikhailov now be deemed, and be accepted as, a skilled, learned, and experienced master of fire weapons." But the scene of his actual entry into the world of Europe was the Dutch town of Koppenburg, where he was accorded a banquet by the Electors of Hanover and Brandenburg, and, though at first perplexed as to proper comportment at table, soon recovered his self-possession, and delighted his hosts by drinking their healths *à la Moscovie*, whilst confessing that, whereas he cared nothing for music or the chase, he loved navigation, naval architecture, and pyrotechnical invention; in proof of which statement he exhibited his toil-worn hands. And when the banquet was over he joined the company in the recreation of dancing; during which his Muscovite cavaliers mistook their German partners' corset-stays for ribs, and he himself caught hold of the ten-year-old Princess who was one day to become the mother of Frederick the Great, lifted her up by the ears (so that her headdress was utterly ruined), and kissed her. Next followed "spectacles" arranged by two stars of the

German theatrical firmament, for the Muscovite strangers' bewilderment; and when the "spectacles" had attained their object in full, the guests departed, and the German Princesses found themselves free to comment upon their impressions of Peter. He was, they said, one who possessed both outward comeliness and a measure of wit, but, unfortunately, mingled with these qualities an excess of *gaucherie*, and was lamentably unable to consume his victuals with *aplomb*. Then, growing still more equivocal, the ladies added that, though undoubtedly he was handsome, he bore himself so ill, and was in all things such a typical representative of his country, that one need not have come all the way from Hanover to Koppenburg, and spent a whole fortnight there, just to entertain such a fellow as that!

It was natural that Peter's bent should lead him to desire to make the acquaintance, first and foremost, of Holland and England, since those were the two countries where, as yet, naval, military, and industrial technique had attained its highest development. Wherefore, travelling ahead of the rest of the Mission, and taking with him only a few companions, he worked for a week as a plain carpenter in a private shipyard at Saardam, and meanwhile rented a garret, amongst the full hubbub of a Dutch shipbuilding town, from a blacksmith whom he had met in Moscow. During that time he spent even his moments of respite from toil in visiting sawyards, factories, business houses, and spinning mills, or in calling upon the relatives of some Dutch carpenters who, he knew, had emigrated to Moscow. Yet even the red frieze jacket and white canvas breeches of a Dutch *ouvrier* failed to preserve his incognito intact, and it became scarcely possible for him to move save in the presence of a crowd of persons eager to gape at the Tsar-shipwright. On the 16th Lefort and the rest of the Mission reached Amsterdam; and when the party had attended a play in that city on the 17th, and, on the 19th, a municipal dinner and fireworks display, Peter, on the 20th, made a night journey to Saardam for his tools and then accompanied his companions to the wharf of the Dutch East India Company, a place which the Burgomaster of the city, one Witzen or Witzin, a man who had lived for a while in Moscow, had specially recommended to Peter for purposes of work. And at that wharf "Peter Mikhailov" and his colleagues, being students specially despatched abroad for technical acquisition, were each of them assigned, as a letter of Peter's phrases it, "places according unto each man's willingness" —the Tsar and Menshikov and eleven others setting about carpentering, and the remaining eighteen sail-making, work as sea-going hands, and mast-manufacture. Moreover, Peter tells us that "our men did have a frigate put down only for their own building," and that the vessel was launched within nine weeks of the laying of its keel. Thus the Tsar spent his every day at work, and seldom was at home even during his leisure hours, since his every thought was bent upon inspecting the city's resources, and he kept rushing from spot to spot with feverish haste. In Utrecht also, where he was greeted by the King of England (*Stadtholder* of Holland), he, with Witzen for his companion, went everywhere, and, amongst other things, attended a lecture by Ruisch, the well-known anatomical expert, and saw the Professor perform a few operations, and, on entering the great man's study, and seeing lying there the body of a child so beautifully laid out as to seem still to be alive and smiling, bent down and kissed the infant. Similarly, at Leyden he looked in upon the great Doctor Boerhaave in his anatomical theatre, and, on noticing that some of his Russian suite seemed to be viewing a dead body with distaste, bade them sever the corpse's muscles with their teeth. In short, ever on the move, he inspected rarities and curiosities; visited factories, workshops, hospitals, educational institutions, and military and industrial establishments; made his way into an observatory; entertained and called upon foreigners; and concluded contracts with marine artificers. Nevertheless, though he himself says that his four months' labours in Holland taught him "all that it behoveth a good carpenter to know," we know that he deemed both the theory and the practice of Dutch shipbuilding to contain shortcomings. At all events, early in 1698, he moved on to England, where marine architecture had already attained a very high standard of development; and when the King of England had extended him a friendly welcome, and given him his best royal yacht, and Peter had visited the rooms of the Royal Society of Arts ("where I did behold all manner of things marvellous"), the Russian ruler repaired to quarters near the King's Wharf at Deptford, that he might complete his knowledge of shipbuilding, and blossom from a plain ship's carpenter into a fully-fledged naval artisan. Thence he made excursions to London and Oxford, and several times visited Woolwich; in which town he witnessed shell-preparation in a laboratory, and "himself did essay the casting of bombs." Also, he reviewed warships at Portsmouth, and noted the number of the vessels' guns, and the calibre and weight of shot of those guns, and witnessed a sham fight that was held specially for his benefit off the Isle of Wight, and had all these events recorded in a daily "Journal" kept by the party, together with entries concerning theatres visited, churches inspected, a reception accorded to the English bishops (at which the dignitaries remained for half an hour), and an invitation extended to a giantess whose four *arshini*[1] of stature allowed Peter to walk under her outstretched arm without bending his head. Further, the party toured the Royal Observatory, dined out (and sometimes returned home

---

[1] Approximately 9 feet, 4 inches.

"very merry"), inspected the Tower (where they were much taken with the Mint and the political dungeons "wherein it is customary to lodge the more honourable men of England"), and, lastly, paid a "privy" visit to Parliament. In connection with this last a particularly interesting item has come down to us. Evidently the Chamber visited by the party was the Upper one, for Peter says that there he beheld the King on his throne, and the Lords of the Realm disposed on benches about him; and the interesting item in question is that, after Peter had listened for a while with the help of an interpreter, he turned to his companions, and said: "When subjects thus do speak the truth unto their Sovereign, it is goodly hearing. Let us learn in this of the English." Unfortunately, there are occasions also when the "Journal" remarks: "We did spend this day at home, and make merry": and it is to be feared that all too often this means that the party had spent the past twenty-four, or even thirty-six, hours in a state of riotous indulgence. In fact, presumptive evidence of this exists. And that evidence is as follows. During their stay at Deptford the party were, by the King's orders, lodged in a house near the Royal Wharf which had been specially re-decorated in accordance with the standing of the eminent visitors; but when the three months' sojourn was ended, and the visitors had taken their departure, the owner of the house found himself faced with a bill for damages of such a nature that he could not but bring it to the attention of his Government. True, some of the items in this bill may have been set down to an exaggerated amount: yet even if they were, the bill makes appalling reading. For in the statement of claim it is said that the floors and the walls of the residence had been found smeared and bespattered all over with traces of the above-mentioned "merry-makings," and furniture smashed to pieces, and curtains torn down, and pictures riddled through being used for target practice, and the lawns of the garden trampled as though they had been used for drilling a whole regiment of iron-shod soldiers: wherefore, concluded the owner, he could not possibly assess the damages at less than £350 sterling, a sum which, if translated into then Russian currency, and set against the pound sterling exchange rate of the day, works out at a total not far short of five thousand roubles! The truth is that when our Muscovite pursuers of scientific culture decided to visit the West for educational purposes they forgot also to consider the question of how they should comport themselves in a Western setting—they kept their eyes so exclusively fixed upon Western handicrafts as to overlook the point of conforming with Western manners and customs, and failed to discern that this German Suburb had never given them examples of Western intercourse save as that intercourse was understood by Western Europe's off-scourings; with the result that, on coming into contact with the social refinements of Amsterdam and London they could only leave upon those cities' social circles an impression of Muscovite usage of a kind which led more than one Western observer to doubt whether the party really had been as influential and representative as it had professed to be. One who had this impression particularly forced upon him was the English Bishop Burnet; and after Peter's departure he felt driven to remark (none too piously) that, though he had been struck with Peter's conversational abilities, he had stood appalled at his confession of faults and vices, and, above all, at his boorishness, and that it was impossible to estimate the designs of a Providence which could dower so rude a fellow with a measure of rule so absolute over a realm so vast.

At last, in May 1698, and before he had had time to realise the extent to which he had electrified Western Europe (though not before he had had time to contract into the service of Russia upwards of 900 Dutch nautical men, from a vice-admiral to a ship's cook, and to spend over 2,500,000 roubles upon the expenses of his wanderings), Peter hurried away to Vienna, and thence, abandoning a contemplated *détour* into Italy, home. This was because he had received word of a new conspiracy on the part of his half-sister, and of a new rebellion on the part of the *Strieltzi*. Yet we can imagine the impressions left upon him by Western Europe, since, as all his investigations had been confined strictly to the workshops of Western culture, and he had looked no further, nor ever tried to pass the point of being merely a passive gaper at the many other aspects of European life, his whole impression of that quarter, as derived from his fifteen months' tour, must have been a noisy, vast, smoky vista of factories, foundries, shipyards, wharves, and machinery.

Arrived home to find himself faced with the new revolt, he spent whole days together in wreaking vengeance upon the foes whom his kinswoman had stirred to renewed activity. For the affair brought poignantly back to him his recollections of 1682; once more it set before his nervous imagination the hated images of Sophia and Shaklovit and the Miloslavskis; it re-filled him with apprehension of danger from that quarter. Hence he had reason for his almost frenzied energy in purging the rising, an energy which, according to some accounts, even led him to behead some of the rebellious *Strieltzi* with his own hand. Yet he had not been two years at home, he had not yet had time really to draw breath, before a still more onerous task fell to his lot in the shape of a war with Sweden. Consequently, until he was past the age of fifty, and approaching the close of his life, he had to maintain unabated the same restless, ever-fluctuating activity that had been his self-adopted rôle in early manhood. On the other hand, an outcome of the many anxieties, and initial defeats, and ultimate victories of the war was that his habit of life became definitely fixed, and his efforts in the direction of reform acquired a definite tendency and *tempo*. For during the war his mode of life was, from start to finish, a hand-to-mouth existence, through the fact that at one and the same time he had to strive to overtake the loosely-knit events of the day as they fled past him, and to strive to grapple with the State's perils and requirements. And all this without a moment in which to draw breath, or to think things out, or to decide upon a settled course. At the same time, all his self-assumed activity in the Northern War was in harmony both with his inborn tastes and habits and with the knowledge and impressions gained from travel abroad. For the rôle which he now adopted was not, like that of the ancient Tsars, the rôle of a Supreme War Lord who, seated in his palace, despatched thence *ukàzi* for his subordinates' guidance, but the rôle of a man who, like his antagonist, Charles XII., personally headed his troops, and personally led them into action. And of his military prowess on land and on sea Russia's military history will for ever preserve two glorious, pre-eminent memorials in the shape of Poltava and Hango. But he was not content with his achievements at the front: at times he would commission a subordinate to take his place there, and himself retire to a spot behind the lines whence he could superintend the less conspicuous and more technical sides of warfare—whence he could organise reserves, and muster recruits, and frame plans of operations, and build warships, and erect munition factories, and accumulate armaments and equipment and supplies, and overlook the commissariat, and encourage all, and spur all, and lose his temper with all, and hang defaulters, and dart to various points of the Empire, and, in short, act as at one and the same time a Master of Ordnance, a Director of Victualling, and a Controller-General of Shipping. Until at last this tireless activity, maintained for a space of thirty years, had for its general result such a confirmation of his ideas, tastes, sentiments, and habits, that, though the mould of his casting was a mould one-sided in its tendency, it eventually shot him forth as a man at once ponderous and mobile, at once cold and as liable to explode as one of his own Petrozavodsk-forged cannon.

CHAPTER II

Peter's physique, habits, mode of life, ideas, and character.

In his spiritual composition Peter the Great was one of those simple individuals who need only to be studied to be understood.

In person a giant nearly three *arshini*[1] in stature, he towered a full head above those amongst whom it was his lot to move, and not infrequently found, when performing the ceremony of according the Easter Greeting, that his back ached with the necessity of having to bend forward so frequently. Also his strength was proportionate to his height, for a regular course of the axe and hammer developed the vigour and the dexterity of his muscles until he could twist a silver plate into a scroll with his fingers as easily as he could cleave a flying shred of cloth with a sword. Earlier I have referred to the physical debility which clung to most of the male posterity of the Patriarch Philaret; but whereas Alexis' first wife only perpetuated that debility, Natalia Kirillovna opposed to it a bar—and it was principally after his mother that Peter took. The member of her family whom he most of all resembled was her brother Theodor, as one who had summed up in himself the whole nervous force, and the whole mental agility, of the Narishkin stock, a stock which already had produced many *beaux esprits*, and was later to gain further notoriety in the person of a wit at the Court of Catherine II. A foreign ambassador presented to the two young Tsars in 1683, tells us that Peter was then a lively, handsome lad, and formed a sharp contrast with his brother Ivan, who, seated on the great silver, *ikon*-surmounted throne with Cap of Monomakh pulled down over lowering brows, and eyes looking at no one, almost resembled a lifeless statue, whereas the little Peter, by his side, was sporting jauntily the duplicate Cap manufactured to meet the occasion of the joint Tsarship, glancing cheerfully and trustfully about him, and with difficulty being kept in his seat at all. Later, however, this picture of Peter changes for the worse, when either the shock sustained by his childish intelligence through the horrors of 1682, or an injudicious mode of treating an immature constitution, or (the most likely explanation of all) these two

---

[1] Approximately seven feet.

factors combined developed in him a nervous disorder which first showed itself
during his twelfth year, and took the form of tremblings of the head, and of the
circumstance that, on lapsing into profound thought, or into violent emotion,
his features would assume a scowl which wholly marred their comeliness.
And since there went with these a birthmark on his right cheek, and a habit of
tossing his arms about when walking, he came to be such a remarkable figure
that in 1697 the customers in a barber's shop at Saardam easily recognised
in the ostensible carpenter from Moscow who was passing the establishment
the Tsar of All the Russias—though perhaps they did so the more easily
in that there were present in the shop at the time some officious Dutch
ex-residents of the Muscovite capital, and that in moments of forget-
fulness Peter's large and restless eyes would be wearing a distraught stare,
and his mien in general bidding fair to terrify anyone not possessed of the
strongest of nerves. As regards portraits of him, we encounter two more
frequently than the rest. Of these the first was executed in 1698 by the English artist, Kneller, for William III., and depicts Peter with locks flowing
free, and large, rounded eyes, and altogether an animated expression, whilst,
despite a certain angularity in the artist's manner of delineation, he has
caught something of the vaguely bright, indefinably cheerful expression
which is to be noted also in a portrait of Peter's grandmother (a Strieshnev)
on his mother's side; whereas the other of the two portraits was
executed in 1717 by the Dutch painter Charles Moro, and dates from the
period when Peter was returning from Paris (with a view to speedily bringing the Northern War to a conclusion) after an unsuccessful attempt to
effect a match between his daughter, the eight-year-old Elizabeth, and the
seven-year-old King of France, Louis XV. On this occasion Parisian observers
said of him that, even in spite of his fierce and almost barbaric countenance, he fully looked the part of a Sovereign, and proved himself capable
of establishing good diplomatico-political relations with anyone whom he
deemed likely to prove useful; whilst that he too had had an idea of his own
importance is shown by the fact that once, on leaving his Parisian hotel,
he flouted all *les convenances* by nonchalantly springing into a carriage
which did not belong to him. The truth is that, as always and everywhere
he had become accustomed to play the master, he felt himself to be
as much master on the Seine as on the Neva. Yet this is not wholly how Moro's
artistic vision seems to have regarded him, for in the eyes, as well as in the
set of the lips, of the portrait by that artist (which, incidentally, shows a
heavier moustache than the portrait by Kneller, a moustache seeming
almost to have been secured in place with gum) we can see lurking
a sort of half-distressful, half-mournful weariness, so that a beholder might

say: "This is the portrait of a man who yearned for a little breathing-space, and, though conscious of his greatness, stood dissatisfied with the accomplishments of his maturity after the self-diffidence of youth." But let it be remembered, that at the time when this portrait was executed Peter was on his way to break his journey at Spa for treatment for the malady which, eight years later, was to bring him to the grave.

In his own home Peter was never anything but a guest, for alike during adolescence and during manhood he was forever either on a journey or engaged in some out-of-doors occupation. In fact, if at about the age of fifty he could have halted for a moment, and reviewed his past, he would have seen that his adult years had included few periods when he had not been bound for some destination, when he had not been journeying on one of the tours which took him from Archangel to Azov, and from Astrakhan to Derbent, and from the Neva to the Pruth. And an effect, amongst others, of these years of travelling was to develop, and to fix, in him a restlessness, an itch for changes of scene, a yearning for swift sequences of impressions, which converted haste into a habit, and rendered him a man always in a hurry. In this connection we know even the length of his stride, and can see that, to keep pace with him, the ordinary man must either have run or have progressed by a series of leaps. Besides, he never could remain seated for long: even when taking part in a Court festivity he would leave his chair at intervals, if the function proved protracted, dart into another room, and stretch his legs. And the same restlessness led him, during his earlier years, to cultivate the art of dancing, and to become a familiar and a welcome guest at the merrymakings equally of artisan, of aristocrat, and of tradesman. Nor was his tirelessness in the pursuit of the Terpsichorean art deterred by the fact that he was never able to take any regular course beyond what he picked up at the "eventide practisings of the Lefort establishment." Meanwhile, if not sleeping, travelling, feasting, or inspecting, he was constructing, for his hands were ever at work, and, owing to the fact that he never lost an opportunity of applying them to manual labour, they never lost their horniness. Especially during his younger and more inexperienced days did he never visit a factory or a workshop without engaging in the special process to which it was devoted; in such places he simply could not remain an onlooker, and least of all if he had not previously encountered the operation which he happened at the moment to be investigating. Instinctively his fingers itched for a tool, that he might fall to with the rest. It need hardly be added that this innate taste for the practice of handicrafts developed in him a manual dexterity which, added to his mental alertness, led to his needing merely to scrutinise an unfamiliar task for that task to become his own. In short, a taste originally only a precocious addiction to industrial pursuits and technical labour eventually became a permanent trait. Come what might, he felt that he must learn and master any new accomplishment encountered; and he would do so even before he had considered whether the accomplishment was likely ever to prove useful to him. All this, added to the truly marvellous stock of technical knowledge which he acquired, enabled him, as early in his career as his first foreign tour, to inform the Princes present at the banquet at Koppenburg that he was familiar with the working of fourteen trades. Nor was this an overstatement: never did he need to be present in a factory for long before he had made himself at home with its specialised appliances. One outcome of this was that when death had removed him every place in which he had ever resided was found to be heaped with articles of his own manufacture, such as boots, and chairs, and crockery, and snuff-boxes, and the rest, and heaped to a degree which renders it a marvel how he can have gained time for those articles' construction. Also, his mechanical prowess filled him with an immense belief in his own skill, and, amongst other things, he came to consider himself both a first-rate surgeon and a first-rate dentist. Yes, no matter what the horror which his prospective patients might display on realising that they were to be attended by the Tsar in person, he would present himself before them with his instruments, and officiate then and there. And to his dental prowess in particular, and to the magnitude of his dental practice, he left behind him a memorial in the shape of a whole sackful of teeth! But above all other things he loved shipbuilding, and no affair of State could detain him when, instead, there was an opportunity of plying an axe on a wharf. Even in his later years, in the years when he had come to live in his self-built capital of St. Petersburg, he never let a day pass without devoting at least two out of the twenty-four hours to the practice of some nautical pursuit. And, naturally, he attained a proficiency in marine technique which led contemporary opinion to regard him as the best shipwright in Russia, seeing that, besides being able to design and sketch-plan a seagoing craft, he could construct it with his own hands, from keel-laying to the last technical detail. The less wonder, therefore, that he took an immense pride in this manual dexterity, and stinted neither money nor efforts to extend and consolidate the country's shipbuilding industry. True, some may think it curious that a man who had been born in an inland city like Moscow should have come to be a sailor standing in as much need of the breath of the sea as a fish stands of water; but with that it must be remembered that it was to that breath, and to hard physical exercise, that he always attributed the ultimate recovery of his physical constitution, and the annulment of the damage wrought it through youthful excesses. And to the same cause, probably, was due his invincible, truly sailor-like appetite. At all events, we are told by contemporary writers that a meal never came amiss to him —that, on attending a reception, he could always, no matter whether he had dined or not, sit down again, and fall to with the best. Usually his routine was that he rose at five, and, after lunching from eleven until twelve, retired for a nap (never, even when guests were present, did he omit this item) before rejoining his table-mates for dinner, and with renewed vigour resuming the task of eating and drinking.

Hence there stand before us the factors (1) that early in his career certain untoward incidents of childhood and youth wrenched him clear of the finicking forms of the old Kremlin Court, (2) that the society surrounding him during his later youth was of a nondescript and non-exacting type, (3) that the tenor of his early pursuits early made him handy with the axe, with the lathe, with the saw, and with the correctional cudgel, and (4) that his essentially non-sedentary life converted him into a foe to all ceremony. Indeed, so little could he stomach formality or constraint that, though he was masterful as Tsar, and felt himself at all times and in all places to be overlord, he could not even take part in a State pageant without succumbing to awkwardness and confusion, and, when forced to don ceremonial robes, and stand before the Imperial throne, in order that some newly-accredited foreign ambassador might mouth to him a few high-sounding phrases, would soon be breathing hard, growing red in the face, and dripping with perspiration. Which led him more than ever to strive to be simple and frugal in his own private life; so that it was quite a frequent thing for the monarch whom Europe deemed to be the world's wealthiest and mightiest potentate to be seen stalking the streets of Moscow in slipshod boots, and in stockings which his wife or his daughters had darned. Even his morning receptions of State he would hold in the same rough serge dressing-gown as he had donned when first arising; and as soon as a reception was over he would exchange the dressing-gown for the *kaftan* which he hated to discard, and go for a walk or a drive—in either case, if the season was summer time, and the destination near, bareheaded, and, if driving, with his body thrust into a pair-horse gig or cabriolet shabby enough once to make a foreign observer declare that its use would have been scorned by the veriest huckster in the place. On solemn occasions alone (as when, for example, invited to attend a wedding) did he resort to his smart *Prokurator-General*, Yaguzhinski, for the loan of a coach. In other words, he never to the end abjured the domestic habits of the old-time Russian citizen. In particular he detested large and lofty rooms, and this was so much the case that, when travelling abroad, he always avoided the sumptuous palaces offered for his reception by his hosts. And if it be thought strange that a man reared on the boundless plains of Central Russia, a man deeming even the atmosphere of a German valley oppressive, a man dwelling all his life in the generous, spacious open air, could not bear to sojourn under a lofty ceiling (as a matter of fact, if he learnt that he was about to be lodged under a ceiling of the kind, he always had an under one of canvas constructed for the purpose), there may lie an explanation of the fact in the modest dimensions of the little wooden palace at Preobrazhensköe where he had spent his boyhood, a palace which a foreign writer of the day declares to have cost only a hundred thalers to build. However that may be, there can be no doubt that when he came to build his own palaces around St. Petersburg he had all of them made small, and their every room, whether for summer use or for winter, fashioned to a cribbed and cabined scale. Says the above-quoted foreign observer in conclusion: "Never can the Tsar stomach a large dwelling." Hence, when Peter forsook the Kremlin, he forsook with it all the pristine grandeurs of the Russian Court, and re-ordered things so plainly that in that respect no establishment of a European crowned head save that of King Friedrich Wilhelm I. could vie with his. In fact, he himself would frequently compare the personality of the Prussian Monarch with his own, and vow that the one cared as little for luxury and extravagance as the other did. For at Peter's Court there were no chamberlains, no seneschals, and no expensive plate, and whereas the upkeep of the pre-Petrine Imperial *ménage* had been accustomed yearly to swallow up hundreds of thousands of roubles, the new *régime* saw that sum fall to sixty thousand. Even Peter's personal staff was limited to ten or twelve *dvorianin* youths known as *dentschiki*—mostly youths of obscure origin, since he had no use for fine liveries and costly brocades. And though during his later years, after his marriage to the second Tsaritsa, he established a large and brilliant household which could vie even with the establishment of Germany, the probable reason why he did so was that, though he himself stood oppressed with any splendour as Tsar, he desired that his Consort should be surrounded with a measure of magnificence at least calculated to deter his *entourage* from remembering her obscure origin.

The same simplicity, and the same free-and-easy spirit, were imparted to his relations with his fellow men in general. His social attitude combined the ways of the Russian over-lord of olden days with the habits of the Russian artisan. For example, on entering a room to attend a social ceremony, he would, as likely as not, seat himself in the first chair which he found vacant; and if the room proved too hot for him he would straightway divest himself of his *kaftan*. And once, on being invited to act as "marshal" (toast-master) at a wedding banquet, he, after accurate and prompt fulfilment of his duties, hurled away his wand of office, stepped to a buffet, plunged all ten fingers into a dish of roast meat, and fell to with the same disregard for the usage of knives and forks as had filled the Princesses at Koppenburg with astonishment. Hence subtlety of deportment was by no means one of his characteristics. In other words, he was lacking in good manners. Again, when holding one of his winter receptions in the Palace at St. Petersburg, or attending a gathering of the *beau monde* at the house of a State dignitary, he never had any hesitation in sending unexpectedly for a party of his seamen, seating himself in their midst, and, however much ladies might be dancing in that or an adjoining room, starting to play chess with his cronies, and drink beer with them, and smoke tobacco in a long Dutch pipe. But most of all he loved to mark the close of the day's work by either visiting or receiving personal friends, when he would shine forth as a man altogether cheerful, and sociable, and full of talk, as a man who liked to see merry-hearted guests around him, and, over a glass of Hungarian wine, to talk with them on unceremonious terms, or, without forgetting his glass, to walk up and down and listen to their conversation. But in proportion as he loved this intercourse he hated its infringement—he hated any unnecessarily malicious word, or any sharp sally, any sarcastic *mot*, or any open brawl: and if such an interruption did occur, he at once punished the offender by making him "drink a mulct" —that is to say, swallow at a draught either three beakers or an "eagle" (large ladleful) of wine, "to the end that he lie not again to excess, nor provoke." Yet, though this procedure usually sufficed to keep ticklish topics at a distance, there were times when the freedom induced by Peter's society led some too careless, or some too outspoken, an individual to blurt out an inopportune thought. For example, Peter had a special regard for a naval lieutenant named Mishukov, and so high an opinion of his professional skill that he made him commander of the Imperial yacht. And one night it befell (this was before the lamentable affair of the Tsarevitch Alexis had occurred) that, as Mishukov and the Tsar were seated side by side at a banquet in the fortress of Kronstadt, Mishukov, who up to that moment had been drinking in the best of style, suddenly relapsed into thought, and then into tears. And when the Tsar exclaimed in astonishment: "Why, what aileth the man?" Mishukov frankly, but all too publicly, explained the cause of his sudden affliction. He said: "What though the fortress in which we are sitting, and the capital which thou hast raised up of late, and the fleet which now is sailing the waters of the Baltic Sea, and the new host of Russian mariners which is on that fleet, and I myself, Lieutenant Mishukov, the commander of thine Imperial Frigate, and one who ever am sensible of thy favour, have been wrought of thy hands, and of thine alone, thou mayest yet at any time fail in health: and unto whom then shall we be left?" And when the Tsar retorted: "What sayest thou? Have I not a Tsarevitch to follow me?" Mishukov replied: "Verily, yea; but only a Tsarevitch so foolish as to be wishful to undo all that thou hast done." For a moment the speech pleased the Tsar with its frankness—yes, even though the frankness in question voiced an unpleasant fact; but presently, realising that diction so gross, and choice of an occasion so inopportune and indiscreet, called for severe reproof, he boxed the Lieutenant's ears, and closed the incident with: "Let that serve for a mark upon thee that it is unseemly to prate of such matters."

In proportion, also, as Peter himself never was idle, but always pursuing some task with simple directness, so he demanded of others that they should do the same, and likewise cultivate honesty and non-secretiveness. Evasion of any sort he could not bear. An example of this is to be found in the memoirs of an official named Nepluev, who was sent to Venice for a course of study, and, on his return, examined by the Tsar in person and appointed to be Superintendent of the St. Petersburg Dockyard, a post which brought him into almost daily contact with the Sovereign. But Peter did more than bid him superintend; he bade him also never in any respect conceal. And at last there came a day when Nepluev celebrated his name festival, and overslept himself next morning, and failed to precede the Tsar in arriving at the Dockyard. At first the panic-stricken Superintendent was for turning tail and "reporting sick," but presently, changing his mind, decided that a candid expression of regret would be the wiser course. "My friend," Peter began, "thou seest that I am here." "That I do see," Nepluev responded. "Also I see that I am at fault. The truth is that yester night I did sit over long with guests." The Tsar took Nepluev by the shoulders (incidentally, making him tremble until he could scarcely stand); but all that he said was: "Thou art a good fellow. Aye, and I thank thee for having spoken unto me the truth. For the rest, God pardon thee. He who standeth without sin before God is other than the grandson of his grandmother. Now come with me unto a place of bearing." Upon that the pair proceeded to a hut where the wife of a poor carpenter was lying in childbed; and when the Tsar had given her five *grivni*, and kissed her, and bade Nepluev also give her five *grivni*, Nepluev complied. Yet in his manner of doing so there was something which made the Tsar smile and exclaim: "Truly, brother, thou dost not give altogether after the fashion of the seas!" And, despite himself, this led Nepluev to reply: "Sire, I give not even as thou dost in that I do lack the wherewithal for gifts like thine; I am but a poor *dvorianin* who hath a wife and children, and doth so stand that if ever thine Imperial bounty should fail, I and my household would have nought to eat." Upon that Peter hastened kindlily to enquire how many peasant souls he possessed, and precisely where his *pomiestie* lay; and when their host the carpenter approached them with glassfuls of *vodka* on a wooden salver Peter drank some of the liquor, and consumed a piece of carrot pie, and, when Nepluev refused the proffered refreshment, exclaimed: "Come, man! Do thou at least eat and drink what thou canst, lest our man be offended," and broke off a piece of the pie, and handed it to Nepluev with the words: "Now, verily, I bid thee eat. Good food of our own country this is. It is not the food of Italy." [1]

Yet, though Peter was kindly as a man, he was cruel as a Tsar, and, as such, took too little account of the human element, both in himself and in others. On the other hand, we have seen that the setting of his rearing was anything but favourable to a conception of the sort; and though in time his native wit, added to a growing sense of his Imperial position, contributed to the defect's obscuration, it nevertheless burst forth, at intervals, up to the very end, and more than once caused the features of "Alexashka" Menshikov, his principal *protégé*, to receive the full weight of the Imperial fist. Another instance occurred at a festival to which a foreign artillery officer who was also a tedious braggart had been invited. So long did this officer keep boasting of his knowledge that at length the Tsar, powerless either to get a word in edgeways or to bear the situation any more, spat full in the fellow's face—then silently withdrew. Naturally, such simplicity and levity of behaviour tended to render Peter a difficult person with whom to have dealings; and the same applies to the nervous attacks which usually culminated in convulsive spasms. The rule was that as soon as Peter's attendants perceived an attack of the sort to be impending they sent for Catherine, who made the Tsar lie down, took his head upon her lap, and smoothed his temples until sleep supervened. And from that sleep, some two hours later, he would awaken as fresh and vigorous as though nothing had happened. Yet not even the excuse of these seizures justified the ordinarily frank and outspoken monarch in his many grievous failures to appreciate other people's position. The fact of those failures went far to stultify the otherwise good effect of the unconstrained atmosphere

[1] A reference to Nepluev's late travels.

of his society. True, his milder quips and jests were cracked out of friendliness alone, but the unfortunate point was that those pleasantries sometimes went further, and degenerated into licence, or even into cruelty. For example, one of his customs was to celebrate the State holidays of the summer season by inviting the Metropolitan aristocracy to attend him in an oaken grove which he had planted in front of the Summer Palace with his own hands, and there to have the secular officials give him their opinions upon politics, and, as regards the Church's dignitaries, to take their views upon matters spiritual. But though, like all good hosts, he took care to have abundant refreshment provided for his guests, he sometimes rendered the hospitality embarrassing through the fact that, inasmuch as he himself always drank his *vodka* neat, he would take it into his head that his guests (including even the ladies) must do the same. And upon that horror would seize upon the visitors as officers of the Guards appeared with pailfuls of *sivukha*,[1] and the liquor sent its odour stealing along the avenues, and sentries could be heard being ordered to let no one depart without further instructions. The standing orders to the Guards officers customarily detailed for the duty were that everyone present should be served with a measure sufficient to drink "a health to the Tsar in full"; and lucky indeed was the wight who could get clear of the premises in time! Only the spiritual dignitaries turned not their faces from the fiery cup, but, reeking of *vodka* and condiments, maintained their ground unmoved. Indeed, a foreign visitor present at such a gathering subsequently wrote that, of all the guests present, he saw none so intoxicated as the members of the clerical profession. And in the same way we have it on record from a Protestant preacher, that if he had not witnessed what he did with his own eyes, he would never have believed such scandalous doings to be possible. Take also the occasion of the marriage of the elderly Prince U. U. Trubetskoi to the twenty-year-old Princess Golovin in 1721. At the wedding-feast on that day trayfuls of jelly in glasses were handed round to the guests: and as soon as the jelly arrived Peter bade the bride's father, a man whom he knew to have a particular love for the delicacy, open his mouth to the widest extent to which it would go, and then stuffed glassful after glassful into the gaping orifice, and, every time that the victim's jaws failed satisfactorily to remain parted, wrenched them into position again with his own fingers. And in the meantime, not to be outdone, the fabulously wealthy and superlatively fashionable Princess Trubetskoi, daughter to the host, left her place at table, stationed herself behind her brother's chair, and, at the moment when the smart young fellow ("best man" for the occasion) was swallowing the share of jelly that had been handed to

[1] Corn brandy.

him, so tickled him in the ribs as to leave him spluttering like a calf in process of having its throat cut, and the company, a company drawn from the most *recherché* society of the capital, roaring with appreciative merriment. Naturally, such tendencies to humour rendered Peter's court entertainments rather arduous functions. Yet their number was very large, and it became still larger towards the close of the Northern War, when a regular calendar of festive occasions was compiled, and, in 1721, crowned with an order for an annual celebration of the Peace of Nystadt. But most of all did Peter let himself go at the launching of a new ship. A ship delighted him as a toy delights a child; and since his period was a period of heavy drinking everywhere, and especially as regards Europe's court and aristocratic circles, and in this respect the Imperial establishment of Russia fully lived up to its foreign models, Peter, though a careful man in all else, stinted no expenditure in the convivial baptism of a freshly-rigged cleaver of the deep, but invited to that baptism the *élite* of the capital, and then poured forth libations equally worthy of the deep and of the ship—thereby illustrating, if not originating, the saying that the ocean gives rise to a bibulous stock. And the drinking was such as on one occasion to plunge our Grand-Admiral Apraxin into a flood of hot and senile tears, and lead him mournfully to reflect that in his old age he was an orphan without father or mother, and to send the brilliant Prince Menshikov, Minister of War, under the table, and leave him lying there until the terrified Princess Dasha came running in from the women's quarters to bathe and chafe her senseless husband. Sometimes, too, these banquets ended in less simple fashion, for if Peter happened to take offence at anything said at table he had a habit of then and there commanding his guests to remain where they were until he returned, and then posting a sentry over the exit, and going off for a sleep in the women's quarters; whereupon the company could do nothing save sit waiting until Catherine's usual resource of rest and slumber had conjured away the Tsar's *malaise,* and meanwhile pass the time with fresh potations and similar expedients. Peter's crowning achievement in this way was the first celebration of the Peace of Nystadt, which lasted for seven days, and during which, half-demented with joy at having brought the struggle to a successful issue, and forgetful alike of years and gout, he danced upon the tables, sang songs, and wound up the junketing (which was held in the Senatorial Building) by issuing his well-known command for his guests to await his return, and going off to take a nap on his yacht on the adjacent Neva. True, on this occasion a certain proportion of the participators in the unexpectedly prolonged feast did decline to remain indefinitely in the scene of enforced gaiety, even though they knew that a refusal to do so meant a fine of fifty

(400) roubles apiece; but the rest of the masqueraders, until the close of the week, could but spend their time in walking up and down, drinking, dancing, and quarrelling as they awaited the official proclamation for the festivities' closure.

Hence, to speak candidly, Peter's merrymakings of State were boorish, oppressive functions. But other official revelries there were that were worse still; they were so much worse as to be almost shameless in their cynicism and indecency. The cause of those revelries is obscure. Perhaps the cause was a need of rude relaxation after severe labour; perhaps it came of habitual looseness of personal conduct. At all events the system of State dissipation which I am about to describe, was one to which Peter sought to communicate a proper departmental form, and to convert, under the style variously of "Our Imperial College of Drunkards," and of "Our Imperial All-Foolish, and All-Jesting, and All-Drinking Council," into a permanent institution of State. This "Council" held periodical meetings under the presidency of a Chief Buffoon known variously as "Our Prince Priest," and as "Our All-Bawling and All-Jesting Patriarch of Moscow, Kokua, and the Yāuza Territory," and was made up of twelve "Cardinals" (professed tipplers and gluttons), a long list of "Bishops," "Archimandrites," and other "spiritual dignitaries" (who, in each case, bore nicknames which the conditions of our censorship will not allow me to set down in print), and, lastly, Peter himself, the "Archdeacon" of the Order. Moreover, with as much legislative skill as he devoted to his beloved *Reglamenti* Peter personally framed for the Order a "Charter" which minutely defined the Order's grades and ranks, mode of electing and installing a "Prince Priest," and suitable programme of ritual for "consecrating" other officials of the bibulous hierarchy. More. In the "Charter" there were embodied regulations charging every member of the Order to make a daily practice of consuming liquor until intoxicated, and never to go to bed sober; and since the prime purpose of the "Council" was to offer libations to the glory of Bacchus in an unstinted degree, and proper procedure in debauchery needed to be formulated "if our service unto Bacchus through honourable and strong drinking is to be done in due manner," the "Charter" went on to award the Order its own "vestments," "Psalter," and "Liturgy," and to create "All-Jesting Mothers Superior" and "Lady Abbots," and even to imitate the Church's formularies by ordaining that, just as a candidate for true Baptism was asked the question "Dost thou believe?", so a would-be member of the bibulous fraternity was to be asked, "Dost thou drink?" On the other hand, lapsers into sobriety after initiation were to be debarred for a while from all taverns throughout the Empire, and

"heretics," or indulgers in free thought on the subjects of drinking and
roystering, to be banned thence in perpetuity. In short, the institution
ended by constituting an indecent parody of the true Hierarchy and true
Liturgy, and a parody so indecent as to lead many pious folk to regard its
membership as a sheer death of the soul, and to believe that resistance to
such an apostasy from Christianity would infallibly ensure to the resister
a martyr's crown. At Christmastide, in both the old capital and the new,
the "Council" organised all-night processions of a whistling, shouting
throng which, crammed into overflowing sleighs, and headed by the mock
"Patriarch" in "robes" and "mitre," and bearing his wand, toured the
principal streets, and made any citizen deemed worthy of a visit entertain all at his own expense, regardless of the fact that, to quote a contemporary, "such fellows did drink terribly." Similarly was the first week
of Lent "celebrated" with "progresses of penitents," when, for the edifica-
tion of the genuinely faithful, "his All-Jestingness" and "the All-Jesting
Council" compelled those faithful to see their streets paraded by revellers
who, with coats turned outside in, sat mounted on the backs of asses or bul-
locks, or in sleighs drawn by bears or goats or swine. An occasion in particular when Bacchus had rites and Court banquets arranged in his honour was
the Shrovetide of 1699, when the "Patriarch," the "Prince Priest" (now
Nikita Zotov, the Imperial tutor of our earlier acquaintance), quaffed
a health to the assembled guests, and bade them go upon their knees
to receive his "blessing," then "crossed" them with tobacco pipes in
the same manner that the Church's ministers cross genuine congrega-
tions with double- and triple-branched candelabra, and, lastly, taking
"pastoral staff" in hand, executed a dance. At this point, a foreign ambassador who had been watching the scene of folly could endure it no more,
but precipitately left the company to continue its mocking derision of the
Orthodox Church without his assistance; but, as a rule, foreign observers
took the view that the aim of the "Council's" enormities was political, and,
possibly, popular-educational, rather than sheerly profane, and that the
movement was directed politically against the Church and the Church's
Hierarchy, and educationally against the vice of drunkenness—that the
Tsar had a mind at one and the same time to ridicule an institution which
he wished to see banned and discredited, and to afford his people periodical
occasions of diversion—that his object in devising his "College of Drinkers"
was at once to fill his subjects with a contempt for prejudice and to disgust
them with wrongdoing. However, the truth of the matter is hard to determine. It is the more so because the above view constituted only a justification of, not an explanation of, the phenomenon concerned. More likely is it

that if Peter had for his primary object mockery of the Church and her Hierarchy and Liturgy, his secondary object was a display of his own power. And I say this although we know that he appointed Prince T. U. Romodanovski "King" or "Emperor" of the Order, and dubbed him "Your Imperial and Illustrious Majesty," and himself only "thy bondsman and eternal slave, Peter," or, in more simple Russian style, "Petrushka Alexeiev." In other words, I conceive that the phase was a mental tendency rather than a mental attitude, and that it came of the fact that to an Imperial son already inclined to levity an Imperial father had bequeathed a further tendency in the same direction, in spite of its being coupled with an aversion to serving as levity's butt. Hence we may view Peter and his "Council" rather as a band of spirits addicted to playing the fool than as a band of spirits creative of folly, and believe that that band seized upon imbecility in its every form, and without regard to tradition, popular sentiment, or self-respect, much as mischievous children will parody the words, the deportment, and even the facial expression of their elders, without meaning to do more than parody them playfully, and without any intention of subjecting them to adverse criticism, and still less to insult. In short, I consider that the object of the "Council" was less to mock the Church and her Hierarchy as institutions than to vent the "Council's" resentment against an ecclesiastical caste which it knew to be numerous, and suspected to be harmful. And the "Council's" disregard for the impression which its antics were bound to produce upon the people is the less to be wondered at when we remember Peter's lament that he had not, like his father, merely *one* "Church longbeard" to deal with, but a thousand, and that frequently unpleasantness, if not actual danger, confronted him thence. Moreover, it was all too well known that the Church's Hierarchy deserved the reproach levelled at Patriarch Adrian, the last of the Patriarchal office, that he and his brethren lived solely for the purpose of eating and drinking and walking about white-cowled and black-cassocked, and never uttered a word in genuine denunciation of sin. No, the true danger inherent in the "Council's" doings came of the fact that in time they originated a popular fable that the Tsar was no less than Antichrist himself. Yet, even so, the people's own morals were of such a nature as to explain, if not wholly to justify, the fact that the country's then ruling circles turned to the *knut* and the torture-chamber to suppress the Antichrist legend rather than to consideration of the best way in which to remove the cause of the people's offence. For who does not know the Russian custom of deriding Church subjects on festive occasions, and garnishing buffoonery with a sacred apophthegm? And who does not know the relation of popular legend to the clergy and sacred ritual? The Petrine Hierarchy had only itself to blame for its popular abasement, since by continually insisting upon a strict external observance of the Church's system, yet neglecting to earn observance of respect for itself, it so degraded its status in the eyes of its countrymen as to infect even Peter himself, and render him, though a man of pious nature, and one who often lamented the priesthood's grossness and lack of discipline, and studied and memorised the Liturgy, and loved to honour holy days by joining his powerful voice to those of his choristers, a man, nevertheless, capable of including in his programme of festivities for a celebration of the Treaty of Nystadt a licentious travesty of the marriage rite, and, when old Buturlin, the "Prince Priest of the Council," was united to his predecessor's elderly widow, crowning the indecent ceremonial by personally gracing the bride and bridegroom with the "nuptial chaplet," and going straight thence to the Troitski Monastery, and offering up prayer. In short, the only possible explanation of all this is political: the only possible purpose of it was the purpose sought through the device of having the "Council's wooden *vodka*-holder shaped like a copy of the Sacred Testament, the purpose of, in spite of everything, keeping the drunken fraternity for ever reminded of the Most Holy Book. To sum up, therefore, the movement was less a cunning, subtle movement of politicians against the Church than a movement born of the grosser instincts of a band of well-born revellers who desired to show the extent to which the Church's authority had dwindled through the dual factor that the monastic tendency of the day had debased the quality of the White Clergy, and that the White Clergy had allowed their pastoral task of uplifting the popular morals to degenerate into a mere dragooning of the popular conscience.

At the same time, Peter had a nature which could create for itself also seemly diversions, for his sense of the healthily and genuinely refined was sufficient to lead him to spend vast sums and efforts upon procuring pictures and statues from Germany and Italy which eventually laid the foundation of our artistic collections in the Hermitage Museum. Especially was he a cultivator of architecture, as may be seen from the palaces of ease which he built around his new capital with the aid of, and from the designs of, Western experts, but more particularly of an expert named Leblanc whom he hired from the French Court for an immense fee, and dubbed "mine absolute marvel." And certainly Leblanc's "Mon Plaisir" pavilion at Peterhof inspires every visitor who beholds it to eulogies of the magnificence of its carvings, of the beauty of its marine views, and of the shadiness of its garden avenues. Yet Peter had no love for the classic style for its own sake, since in art he aimed most at the bright and the cheerful, and so, as regards pictures, had his palace at Peterhof adorned principally with Flemish seascapes and landscapes in which there was a touch of the whimsical. For not even the fact that he devoted most of his days to manual labour could blur his appreciation of scenic effects, especially if those effects happened to include the ocean in any one of its aspects; and for the same reason he spent whole fortunes in embellishing his suburban residences with terraces, and cunningly contrived cascades, and fountains, and flower-beds, and the like. Unfortunately, though his artistic sense was thus strongly developed, its development was as one-sided as that of his character and mode of life, in that whilst his habit of delving to the root of things, and poring over technicalities, had given him an almost geometrical exactitude of eye, a faultless faculty of perspective, and a sure instinct for form and symmetry, so that the plastic arts came readily to his hand, and he delighted in drafting complicated building-plans, his appreciation of art stopped short (he himself always confessed as much) on the threshold of music, and he could not bear even the playing of an orchestra in a ballroom.

Moreover, there were moments when even the uproarious din of the "Council's" gatherings could not deaden to extinction the accents of serious political discussion. For in proportion as the Northern War, and, with it, Peter's reforms, developed, he and his coadjutors found themselves increasingly obliged to concentrate their thoughts upon the trend of Peter's policy; and though the colloquies of these men are not invariably interesting to us for the opinions which they expressed, they at least give us "close up" views of the disputants themselves, and enable us to gain an idea both of their mental standpoint and of their mutual relations. Moreover, in some cases these "close up" views enable us to mitigate our first impression even of the "Council's" bibulous and disorderly surroundings, since we catch through the reek of tobacco smoke and the clatter of tankards stray echoes of lines of political thought which throw the statesmen of the day into a less lurid light. For example, in 1722 we see Peter, during an hour of exhilaration induced by copious draughts of Hungarian wine, unbosoming himself to a party of foreign guests on the subject of his early and more difficult years, the years when at one and the same time he had had to create a regular army and fleet, and to instil into a gross and idle people a taste for culture, and the virtues of honour, valour, and veracity. But, said Peter, though the task had cost him an indescribable amount of labour, it was now over, thank God, and he himself at rest in every respect save that, like all rulers, he must still strive for a yet fuller knowledge of his subjects. Whence the words clearly embodied an old-established idea of his which had come to be a habit, although it is improbable that he himself first started the legend of his posthumous creative activity which an artist subsequently crystallised into a cartoon representative of a sculptor arrested in his task when half-way through carving a human figure from a block of marble. Even when the Swedish War had come to an end, we find him and his helpers acknowledging the fact that, for all the war's military successes and civil ameliorations, their labours must still be continued, and the question of what more needed to be done must still be faced. Thus Tatistchev relates a dinner-table conversation which he appears to have had reported to him by one who had himself been present at it, and of which he gives the following particulars. In 1717, when the conflict with Sweden was bidding fair to be brought to a successful conclusion, Peter and some of his chief workers of State were taking part in a banquet when the conversation turned upon the achievements of Tsar Alexis, and, in particular, upon the difficulties caused him by the Patriarch Nikon. And when Peter had had his say, Mussin-Pushkin took up the tale, and, after lauding Peter as the son, uttered words of disparagement of Alexis as the father on the ground that, after all, he, Alexis, had not accomplished so very much, and had accomplished even that little with the help of Morozov and other ministers of his, rather than unaided, whilst at all times matters depended more upon a Sovereign's ministers than upon the Sovereign himself, whose work issued only as did the work of his statesmen. The speech, however, irritated the Tsar. Rising in his place, he cried: "Alike in thy denial of my father's work, and in thy praise of mine own, is there more of blame than I do choose to abide," and then, turning to Prince Y. T. Dolgoruki, a senator who had never hesitated conscientiously to oppose him, and stationing himself beside the Prince's chair, added: "More than all others art thou one who doth chide me, and vex me with thy many disputings until my forbearance faileth: yet also art thou one whom I do adjudge and perceive to love the State and mine own person more than doth any other man, and to speak unto me nought save the truth. For that do thou receive my thankfulness, and tell me, in requital, what thine own judgment of my father's deeds may be, and what thy judgment of mine own. That thou wilt reply without guile and without deceit I know full well." And though, for the moment, Dolgoruki replied merely: "O Tsar, do thou be seated during such time as I consider the matter," and the Tsar duly seated himself, and for a while the eyes of all remained turned upon the Prince without his saying anything further, Dolgoruki at length went on, with the smoothing of his long moustache that was his constant habit: "O Tsar, it is not possible to return but a brief answer unto thy question, in that a difference lieth between the deeds of thy father and the deeds of thyself, and that whilst thou hast merited the more praise

IV—D

and gratitude in certain things, he hath merited the more in others. Now, there do stand always before a Tsar three chief works of State. The first of those three works is the work of inward governance of the State, and of dispensation of justice in the same. This work is a Tsar's chief work of all. And for it thy father had more leisure than thou hast been vouchsafed, in that never from the first hast thou been given due occasions for pondering upon the same. Yet though thy father did accomplish more in this than thou hast done, yet wilt thou, when thou shalt be able properly to set thyself unto its consideration, accomplish more therein even than did thy father. Unto that end time still remaineth for thee in abundance. And as regardeth the second chief work of a Tsar, that work is the work of war: and herein thy father certainly did merit much praise, and greatly advantage the State, through showing unto thee in advance how it is meet to fashion a regular army. Yet though certain foolish men have since that time undone thy father's beginnings, and so constrained thee to enter upon things anew, already thou hast not only brought those things to a pass well enough in itself, but brought them to a pass even better than was theirs under thy father's governance, and thereby placed me in doubt, for all my ponderings upon this second chief work of a Tsar, as to whether rightly I should award the preference therein unto thee, or whether I should award it unto thy father. Haply it will not be until this present war shall have come to an end that there will stand revealed unto us the which of you twain ought to receive the preference. Lastly, the third chief work of a Tsar is the building of a fleet, with all makings of alliances with foreign States, and treatings with the same. And in this thou hast advantaged the State more even than did thy father, and merited more of honour, as all do now acknowledge. For the rest, and as toucheth that which a certain man hath said this night when he did declare that the deeds of a ruler do issue as doth the work of a ruler's ministers, I, for my part, do maintain the contrary, in that it is only the wisdom of a wise Tsar that enableth the faithfulness of his ministers to be discerned at all, and only an imprudent Tsar that possesseth imprudent ministers, since the prudent Tsar can judge beforehand of the worthiness of each, and distinguish between counsel that is true and counsel that is false." Upon that Peter (who had listened all this while with absolute patience) embraced Dolgoruki with a cry of: "O good and trusty servant, faithful hast thou been in a little, and now I will set thee over much," and by doing so, adds Tatistchev, so offended Menshikov and others that "they did seek in every manner to render the Tsar angered with the man—albeit they prevailed not."

Thus, twisting and twirling in the current of his external impressions,

Peter spent his whole life in tense physical labour, and, so, developed a marked capacity for internal assimilation, a marvellously observant bent, and a faultless instinct for practical neatness. At no time was he one for general or leisurely-thought-out schemes: always he found it easier to grasp the details of a scheme than to view the scheme as a whole, to devise ways and means than to divine those ways' and means' outcome. And, in combination, these factors evolved a bent of mind further illustrated by his moral and political character. Though reared in circles anything but conducive to political growth, and limited to the family and Court entourage of Tsar Alexis (both of which teemed with enmities and petty interests and insignificant personalities), so that he had for his early political school only that Court's intrigues and revolutions, he nevertheless acquired political benefit through the fact that quite early in his career his half-sister's malice banished him from the old Imperial *milieu*, and therefore from the political environment of which that *milieu* had come—both from the medley of ceremonial observances and seignioral customs bequeathed to the younger dynasty by the older, and from the jumble of political ideas and political ambiguities tending to hinder, rather than to help, the new order of Tsars in the matter of a proper appreciation of their State position. On the other hand, Peter suffered through the fact that the same factors gave him, for a political sense, only a sort of dim and unsubstantial consciousness that he had at his disposal a power both unlimited and fraught with peril; and this profound politico-moral void in him long failed to become filled up, since the self-adopted artisan pursuits of his youth combined with his addiction to hard manual labour largely to hamper his reasoning faculty, to deflect it from the subjects which really constitute the political education of a State ruler, and to make of him a ruler as destitute of precepts for spiritualisation and correction of his methods of rule as of the usual civic stock of elementary political ideas and social checks. The result was that as late even as when he had come to be twenty-five years old foreign observers stood amazed at the manner in which he contrived to combine in himself lack of judgment, moral faultiness, traits of genius, and wide technical skill. And as a rule those observers' eventual verdict was that the rôle cut out for him by nature was the rôle of a good carpenter rather than the rôle of a great Sovereign. Yet though Peter had, from childhood onwards, only sorry moral guidance, and though he was marred by physical disabilities, and though he was left to become incredibly rude of bearing and manners, and though he might well have become dehumanised by the terrible experiences which early befell him in the Kremlin, he yet possessed such an abundance of energy, and such a keenness of instinct, and such wonderful powers of observation that these qualities in sum came gradually to brake the faults and vices born inevitably of his avocations and environment, until by 1698 Bishop Burnet could remark that Peter at least seemed to be putting up a good fight against a weakness for liquor. Also, although, during his first foreign tour, he took little note of the political systems and social observances of the West, he had acumen enough to realise that not upon the *knut* and the torture-chamber had the populousness and the strength of the Western nations grown up and become based. And to those early lessons learnt from Europe the first expedition against Azov, and the struggles around Narva and on the Pruth, added a training of a sterner nature, until Peter came really to be aware of his political unpreparedness, and set himself to develop and encourage his consciousness to a habit of political self-education which eventually revealed to him in their entirety the vast blanks in his mental equipment, and turned his mind to such hitherto undreamt-of conceptions as a State, and the people of a State, and justice, and duty, and the functions and obligations of a Sovereign. Yet whilst this augmented Peter's moral sense as Tsar, until self-sacrifice became a permanent rule of his life, it never befell that that augmentation included a rule of suppression of personal addictions, nor did an early riddance of political affectation through early personal misfortunes ever enable Peter's blood wholly to slough the instinct of freewill which from the first had been the dominant element in Muscovite policy, and permit of his mentality grasping the logic of history, and the psychology of his people's life. Yet even for this we can scarcely blame him when we remember that the same factor nearly brought Leibnitz, one of Peter's best counsellors and politicians, face to face with failure, in that for long he held the theory, and caused Peter also to hold it, that culture can be instilled into a country the more that the country stands culturally unprepared! This was why Peter directed his activity as a reformer exclusively to measures needing to be imposed by force, and relied exclusively upon that agency for conferment of popular benefits. Which belief that the impossible was not the impossible, and that the life of a nation could at any time be diverted from its historical channel into an entirely different one, brought it about that Peter's policy, a policy designed to improve the popular labour, only overstrained that labour, and led to reckless and prodigal wastage of human lives and human resources. True, Peter in himself was honourable and sincere; towards his own personality he was as censorious and exacting as he was just and benevolent towards the personalities of others; but the unfortunate point was that the whole bent of his activity insensibly made him a better manipulator of inanimate objects and tools than a manager of living and breathing human beings. He looked upon the latter as so many mechanical instruments, and knew how to use those instruments to the best possible advantage, and had an instinctive sense for the task most suitable for each: yet all the time either inability or disinclination rendered him powerless to put himself in the human instrument's position, or to understand the instrument's nature as that nature really was. The sphere in which these psychological peculiarities found their supremely lamentable expression was the sphere of his own domestic relations. And so much was this the case that even his vast knowledge of his vast dominions never brought him enlightenment as to the one small corner represented by his home and family. Thus to the end of his life he remained a guest on his own hearth. With his first wife he never really lived. His second wife gave him only too much cause to complain. And so far did he fail ever to conciliate the Tsarevitch, his son, that when the time came he could not save that son from baleful influences, and for a while the very existence of his dynasty stood in danger.

To sum up: Peter became, eventually, a ruler wholly different from his predecessors, despite that a certain genetical connection, a certain historical sequence of type and career, is traceable between them all. For first and foremost Peter was a Steward of State, and none of his forerunners had been able to excel him in grasp of, and in discernment of, the prime sources of a nation's wealth. True, the earlier Tsars, of the old dynasty as of the new, also had been Stewards of State; but they had been Stewards of sedentary habit only, soft-handed men, rulers who administered only through the agency of others; whereas Peter issued as a Steward-Labourer-Governor, as a Self-taught State Dispenser, as an Emperor-Artisan.

CHAPTER III

Peter the Great's reforms and foreign policy—The problems of that policy—European international relations—The beginning of the Northern War—The course of the struggle—The struggle's influence upon the Petrine reforms—The progress and inter-connection of those reforms—Peter's system of military training—His military reforms—His organisation of a regular army—His Baltic fleet—A military budget.

THE question of how far the Petrine reforms were planned and thought out before Peter's day, and of how far they were executed according to a plan at all—in these two problems we see the task which next confronts us as we follow, step by step, the Reformer's career. There exists a tendency to assume, at all events to accept, a theory that Peter was born to, and grew up to manhood possessed of, a set programme of reforms which owed its origin exclusively to his own intellect, and was created exclusively of his own genius, and that all the statesmanship of his predecessors was but a preparatory stage towards the same, and did not furnish him with incentives in that direction, but only with ideas and resources for practical execution. But the case is otherwise. In closing my review of his predecessor's career, I pointed out that certain seventeenth century statesmen had outlined Peter's programme already. The truth is that we must take care to distinguish between his fate-alloted tasks and his manner of accepting and fulfilling those tasks. The tasks in question lay in satisfying certain State and popular demands the existence of which more than one statesman of the seventeenth century had divined, but which, when eventually fulfilled in the shape of Peter's reforms, were so fulfilled under conditions which had not yet come into operation during that century, but owed their creation partly to Peter's own agency, and partly to the fact that he had them projected into his work from outside. In other words, Peter owed his programme neither to covenants nor to tradition, but to needs of State which could not be set aside when once they had made themselves manifest to all.

Of those conditions the most important was the condition of war. Seldom did Peter know peace: almost always, during his career, he was fighting either his half-sister, or Turkey, or Sweden, or Persia. And, indeed, if we make a computation of his war-makings from the autumn of 1689, from the close of the Regency of the Tsarevna Sophia, we shall see that the only

46

quiescent year during his reign was the year 1724, and that in the period of the remaining years there were comprised only thirteen months of peace. Nor were the wars which he waged with his two principal enemies, Turkey and Sweden, wars such as ever had fallen to the lot of his predecessors, for they were coalition or alliance wars. Fully to understand their significance we must take a glance backward at the Muscovite Empire's foreign policy, and observe the working of that policy during a portion of the seventeenth century.

From his predecessors Peter inherited two tasks whose eventual decision was absolutely vital to a consolidation of the State's security. Of them, the first was a political unification of the Russian people, nearly one-half of whom still were dwelling outside the confines of the Empire proper; whilst the second lay in a necessity for correction of the Empire's frontiers, which still lay open to attack in more than one direction, but especially southward and westward. True, both of these tasks had been tackled before Peter's day, and in the case of the territorial task, it had brought the State into collision with the two external foes represented by Sweden (from whom it had been necessary to wrest the Baltic's eastern shores) and the Tartars of the Crimea, or Turkey, whilst the national political task of a State unification had evoked a stubborn contest with the *Rietch Pospolita*,[1] who was Moscow's nearest neighbour; but it was only when Peter appeared on the scene that the Muscovite Government went beyond the stage of believing that the two tasks could not be carried through at one and the same time. From the fact that at an earlier stage Alexis' Government had found itself unable simultaneously to wage war on the three fronts of Poland, Sweden, and Turkey there had resulted a Governmental policy of discrimination between foes, of conclusion of peace, or a *rapprochement*, with two foes at once in order the better to grapple with the third; but this policy had brought about a sharp break in Moscow's conduct of foreign affairs. Up to that break the main objective of Moscow's foreign policy had been Poland, Moscow's nearest neighbour westward, and for centuries past Russia had devoted to that neighbour the whole of her military energies; but in 1667 the truce of Andrusovo cried a halt to the contest, for Poland was now so weak as to seem innocuous and negligible, and capable safely of being received as a friend again (as, for that matter, Ordin-Nastchokin had fore-told,[1]) whilst in 1686 the Treaty of Moscow converted that armistice, if not into a permanent stay, at all events into a temporary offensive alliance, of arms, and enabled Russia definitely to join hands with her late enemy, and, with the latter, to become a member of an Austrian-Venetian "Holy

[1] See vol. iii. p. 93.   [2] See vol. iii. p. 125, and chap. xvii. of the same volume.

League" against Turkey. Unfortunately, a necessary outcome of this was that once more Russia's national-political unification had to be set aside, since Moscow could not well maintain good relations with Poland, now that that neighbour of hers had also become her ally, and at the same time go on talking about adding Western Russia to her dominions.

Thus from the very start Peter inherited a combination of international relations which had been formed before his time, but now compelled him, as his first step, to devote his own and his people's energies exclusively to a resolution of the southern question, and particularly to the task of correcting and enclosing the Empire's southern frontiers. Peter's scheme to this end was a scheme of, first of all, putting the littorals of the Black Sea and the Sea of Azov into a state of security and defence, and then building there harbours, wharves, and a fleet; but before he could do so yet another phase came about in Western Europe's international relations. Ever since the close of the Thirty Years' War those relations had had for their arbiter-in-chief the diminutive Sweden, and this predominance of hers had proved particularly oppressive to Denmark, Poland, and Russia, as the three States immediately bordering upon the rest of the Baltic—the predominance in question placing upon Denmark's flank her implacable enemy, and Sweden's pet *protégé*, the *Hertzog* of Schleswig-Holstein, and enabling Sweden to filch from Poland the two considerable territorial slices represented by Esthland and Livland, and, finally, through the Peace of Cardis, disappointing Russia of her hopes of regaining Ingria and Karelia. Hence now, just when Peter had proceeded southward, the fact that this trio felt themselves to have been robbed and browbeaten by Sweden led to a determination that hands should be joined against the common foe, and therefore to a necessity that Peter, as one of the trio, should set about transferring his new foreign-service forces from the shores of Azov and the Black Sea to those of the Baltic, and selecting the site of St. Petersburg for the site of his intended new capital, instead of Azov or Taganrog, and making correction of his southern frontiers give place to enclosure of his north-western. In all of this, of course, he only stepped into the shoes of his predecessors, though he in no way sought to extend their scheme of foreign policy and its derived problems, but, rather, to curtail things in that respect.

We see, then, that the factor through which the Muscovite Empire first began to be converted into an active, organic member of the family of European Powers, and to be brought into the circle of Western Europe international relations, was coalition wars against Turkey and Sweden. At that period three States in particular had aggressive tendencies which periodically welded other States into coalitions against them. The three

States in question were France, Sweden, and Turkey. At one time France brought about an alliance between England, Holland, Spain, Austria, and the German Empire; at another Turkey led to Austria allying herself with the Venetian Republic and Poland; and at a third Sweden threw Poland into the arms of Denmark and Prussia (the Electorate of Brandenburg). Yet, though partners in these coalitions, no one of the three states ever so influenced a coalition as to fuse it into a durable form: all that resulted thence was an added complication of Europe's international relations. For example, when, in 1686, Moscow allied herself with Poland and Austria against Turkey, each of the allies still had in view an interest supplementary to the interest immediately in hand; so that in 1699, when the advantageous Peace of Karlowitz freed Austria's hands in the direction of Turkey, she, Austria, lost no time in turning her attention to quarters whence a turmoil over the question of the Spanish Succession might be expected, and left Peter face to face with a task calling for the resources of a whole coalition rather than of a solitary combatant, seeing that that task meant guarding the Austrians' rear against a possible renewal of Turkish-Tartar hostilities. Also, there was the factor that Peter's friend August, the new King of the *Rietch Pospolita*, had for some time past been finding his throne as comfortless as a hot brick. We can judge of this from the circumstance that during the peace negotiations of 1700 in Constantinople Ukrainetz, the then Polish Ambassador to Turkey, actually put in a covert plea with Turkey that, instead of making peace with the Russian Tsar, she should oust from his position Russia's Polish *protégé*! And even when the Treaty of Karlowitz brought peace, and Turkey had to cede the Morea to Venice, and Transylvania and Turkish Hungary and Slavonia to Austria, and to do what Voznitsin, Moscow's Ambassador to Turkey, expressed as "a last choking up of herself"—that is to say, to surrender the devastated regions of Podolia to Poland, and Azov and other of the newly-built southern seaboard towns to Moscow, Peter was no better off than before, since at a swoop the Treaty stultified the whole of the shipbuilding work which he had done at Voronezh, and there must be left to rot in harbour the fleet for navigation of the Black Sea, upon which he had spent such endless money and time and labour and there could be no further question of acquiring Kertch and, thereby, a footing in the Crimea, and he must even abandon the Volga-Don canal scheme, the scheme for which many thousands of labourers had been provisionally commandeered. Also, the Eastern question still remained, and that of allaying the anxieties of the Balkan Christians, and effecting a consolidation of the frontiers of Southern Russia against the Tartars.

Nevertheless, all had to be set aside whilst Peter changed front from south to north, in order that he might bear his part in the new Baltic coalition against Sweden. And when, hurled from the Don country, like a ball, by this new conjunction of European relations, he landed at Narva, he did so to find no preparations made for his coming, and to realise that, with all his grandiose plans for employing sailors on the Black Sea indefinitely postponed, he and those same sailors, men recruited from Periaslavl and the White Sea, added to mercenaries from England and Holland, must embark upon a dry-land and, possibly, long-extended war before Russia's sailors could break through their way even to the waters of the Baltic.

Hence it has seldom occurred that a country has been caught at such a disadvantage for war as was the case with Russia with regard to the Northern struggle. To begin with, she lacked plans and material alike. And whom had she for allies—at all events at first? Why, only Poland—rather, the King of that country, August II., an unscrupulous Saxon adventurer and German Elector who had no sooner grabbed the Polish throne than half his subjects would gladly have seen him out of it again—and the State of Denmark, a State which, when 15,000 Swedes cast anchor before her capital, could not muster sufficient men to defend it, and thereupon left the Coalition, entered into separate negotiations, and concluded with Sweden the Peace of Travershaal. And at first the Coalition had for leading spirit in this comic-opera alliance of Russia with Poland and Denmark only a Livonian named Patkul, a rascal whose design was to cast Peter, as the one really effective partner in the alliance, for the part of a property simpleton, and induce him to swop possible victories in the coming struggle for hopes of possessing the swamps of Ingria and Karelia in the future. And so, the ring pitched, the belligerents turned up their shirt sleeves, and fell to with "trade" cannon which Peter had been purchasing, for five months past, from the very Swedes whom he was now to fight with a thirty-five-thousand-strong army hastily transferred from Southern Russia to the Narva, made up, for the most part, of raw recruits, and commanded jointly by incompetent Russians and distrusted foreigners. Nor were strategic railways then in existence, and the autumn rains soon rendered the roads so sodden as to make adequate transport of supplies and equipment impossible. The first step was the storming of a small fortress; and that storming continued until every heavy gun had either given out or had found itself forced to cease firing for want of powder: after which, an eye-witness says, "the besiegers did march ever around the fortress even as cats might march around a basin of hot soup," whilst the idea of a surprise attack was so little dreamt of that at last, during the height of a November snowstorm, Charles XII. crept up to the place with a brigade of 8000 Swedes, and routed a whole Russian army corps. Yet this Swedish victory might still have been turned into a Swedish rout if the Russians had utilised the fact, a fact both known to and feared by the Swedish king, that at any moment a still free force of Cossacks and mounted *dvoriané* under Sheremetev could have taken the Swedes in the rear. But, as it was, that force of reserves itself retreated across the Narva with such precipitate haste that it lost over a thousand horses, through drowning, during the process, whilst, as regards even the victor, his dread of his vanquished foe was such that the same night he threw a make-shift bridge across the river in place of the old one which the shock of the Russian fugitives' passage had destroyed, and hastened to re-station himself on his own bank. Also, although, to avoid any chance of hampering his commander-in-chief, a foreigner, Peter had left the Russian camp the evening before, that commander-in-chief proved to be so little hampered that he was the first to offer his submission to the foe, and with him went the whole of his foreign colleagues—the more so as from the first their men's evident resentment against them had rendered them nervous. Accordingly, it is not to be wondered at that shortly afterwards Europe began to pass from hand to hand a memorial of the battle in the shape of a medal which, whilst depicting Peter in the act of fleeing headlong from the Narva with sword and headgear thrown away, and handkerchief clearing his face of streams of tears, had inscribed over this presentment the Biblical passage, "Peter went forth, and wept bitterly." True, there was a portion of the Russian army which did contrive to escape both battle and frost and famine, and to dribble back to Novgorod; but a contemporary says that "even when it did reach that town it reached it so worsted of the Swedes as to be without remnant left," since it had been stripped of its last shred, stripped of guns and baggage and tents and everything else. However, Peter was honest enough when, some twenty-four years later, he had become a famous sovereign, and was drawing up his programme for his third annual celebration of the Peace of Nystadt, to annotate that programme with a confession that at the beginning of the Swedish War his ignorance alike of his opponent's strength and of his own resources had been such that he had entered upon the struggle as a blind man might have done.

Peter's total losses at Narva amounted to a third of his siege train, the whole of his artillery, and the fact that an eighteen-year-old young Swede now could boast that he had easily recovered Narva, shattered an army, and taken prisoner a whole general staff. And eight months later an onslaught delivered in the same way recovered for that young Swede Riga as well, after shattering a Russo-Saxon force which had been posted on the Western Dvina in readiness to besiege the town. But, whether supported by mental hardihood, or whether suffering from a lack of a sense of responsibility, Peter still remained undismayed, and, swiftly recovering himself, hastened to stop the gaps in his forces through the expedient of fresh recruit-enrolments, and the gaps in his guns through that of confiscation of a fourth portion of all church and monastery bells. And these endeavours of his Charles did his best to assist by pursuing August from town to town in Russia, and thence through the forests of Poland, and leaving, meanwhile, only a few weak Swedish detachments to guard the Swedo-Russian frontier. Then there began a further seven years of blood-letting. The first thing that Peter did, as soon as he and his demoralised army had been restored by their breathing-space, was to initiate such a series of petty pin-prickings, of storming of minor frontier fortresses, and of small sieges and raids, as should gradually render his men competent to take part in military operations of a larger nature. And, meanwhile, he spared his civilian population no sacrifice, he gave the condition of the people never a thought, for the game had to be played to a finish, and he had staked his last upon the cards, and even gone so far as to promise August a subsidy without knowing in the least whence that subsidy was to come. Unfortunately, during the summer of 1705 the difficulties of the external struggle became increased through an internal upheaval with which that struggle had a close connection. This was a revolt which covered the whole of the Province of Astrakhan, and was an echo of the *Strieltzi* risings of earlier days, and compelled the Tsar to detach a whole division from the seat of war. And scarcely had the rising been quelled when, in the following January, Charles XII., who had now rested his 24,000 men at Warsaw, and, incidentally, lost an eighth of them through frostbite, reappeared at Grodno, and cut off Peter's main body of 35,000 which he had had concentrated in that region. This move of Charles's exceeded in dash even the move at Narva, for when he made it a strong force of Cossacks was lying in the south-eastward towns of Nesvizh, Slonim, and Mir, and Peter had with him also a force of 12,000 regulars which might have joined up with an additional force of Cossacks at Minsk. Unfortunately, the Russians had not yet sloughed their Narvan paralysis, and "for a while Peter could but stand dumbfounded, and in bitterness as of Hell." But soon he recovered himself, hurriedly ordered the Pskov-Smolensk portion of the frontier to be fortified with *abattis*, summoned from Volhynia the *Hetman* Mazeppa and his Cossack command, and, having thus mustered a force twice as large as Charles's, set to work to elaborate a circumstantial, detailed scheme for rescuing his force marooned at Grodno. Lastly, with instructions including an order of the day that "the troops shall take with them no more than a little, whilst even that little shall, if need be, be cast aside," he, on a day in March, when a thaw had broken the ice on the Niemen, and the Swedes could not well pass the river in pursuit, jettisoned upwards of a hundred guns and caissons into the river's waters, crossed the latter, and then, skirting Brest, and traversing Volhynia, brought his army, "albeit with exceeding great need and difficulty," to the neighbourhood of Kiev, where he took up a position at the south-western corner of the almost impenetrable *Poliess*.[1] Unfortunately, it befell that just when Charles, after settling August's account, was turning Moscow-wards with his splendidly-equipped force of 44,000 plus a reserve of 30,000 quartered in Livland and Finland, Peter's rear became threatened through the fact of a Bashkir revolt which gradually came to embrace Kazan, Ufa, and the whole of the region beyond the Volga, whilst upon it followed a rising in the Don basin, as a result, first and foremost, of Government prosecutions of military deserters. And, on these upheavals extending yet further, to Tambov and to Azov, they, in any case formidable, grew more so than ever, since, in addition to forcing Peter to divide his forces, they forced him to keep turning his head, and glancing backward, as he pursued his western foes. However, even bodily indisposition (he says of himself at the time, "I was as weak as a babe with physic"), did not prevent him from straining every nerve to quell the popular disturbances as, leaving his western army to look after itself for a while, he marched to the Don with open offers of pardon, and secret orders for wheels and stakes, "that thereafter there be safeguardings to leave me free in the war." Fortunately he received help in this, for, true to his usual rule of extricating Peter in the nick of time, the Swedish King, who had thrown a whole year to waste, passed the Lithuanian marshes in order to occupy Mogilev, and so enabled the Tsar to prevent him from effecting a junction with General Lebenhaupt, who was on his way from Livonia with a convoy for the re-equipment and revictualment of Charles's now almost foodless and munitionless army. If, on the other hand, the junction had been effected during that month of July, 1708, Charles would have stood for ever invincible, but, as it was, he made his objective Smolensk, and thence wheeled southward into Little Russia (where he expected to receive assistance from Peter's betrayer, the futile *Hetman* Mazeppa), and thereby delivered Lebenhaupt so completely into Peter's hands that the battle at Liesna-on-the-Sozh on 28 September saw two-thirds of 16,000 Swedes destroyed by 14,000 Russians, and the whole of the stores intended for Charles's use captured, and the Swedish self-confidence based upon Swedish invincibility permanently broken in two. Whence it may be said that the victory at Liesna-on-the-Sozh rendered possible the victory at Poltava-on-the-Vorskla. And that this was

[1] Great forest region north-eastward of that city.

the case was Peter's own belief. In any case, Sweden had only herself to blame, since manifestly it was a strategical error for Charles to have selected the moment that he did for marching southward and eastward, and taking the Mogilev-Poltava line. True, certain writers explain the step by saying that what attracted him to the Ukraine was the abundance of its supplies, its absence of fortifications, its proximity alike to Poland and to the Crimea, and a hope that in it he would find Cossack reinforcements both able and willing to help him to reach Moscow by way of Smolensk rather than *via* the midst of Peter's forces; but though these events occurred a whole century before Napoleon, it would almost seem as though Charles had had a presentiment of that commander's retreat in 1812. However that may be, the victory at Poltava relieved Peter of a burden of anxiety which had been his for nine years past, since at Poltava the Russians annihilated the last 30,000 of Charles's hunger-weakened, demoralised, and brought-to-bay soldiers, men dragged to Russia against their will by a headstrong young fellow of twenty-seven. Nevertheless, Peter celebrated Poltava as a magnanimous victor, and, meagre though his table necessarily was, invited the captured Swedish generals to share it, and drank their healths at it, and, whilst doing so, dubbed them his military tutors, even though he allowed his transports of joy to cause him to overlook the question of following up the remnants of Charles's shattered host, and instead, to do himself the pleasure of attending the local Cathedral of St. Sophia, in order that he might listen to a resounding, panegyrical sermon preached in his honour by Theofan Prokopovitch, Prefect of the local College of Theology. At the same time the result showed that the victory of 27 June did nothing to hasten the coming of peace, but merely complicated Peter's position, and so indirectly prolonged the war. This was because, although the victories at Liesna and Poltava ought once and for all to have taught Peter that he was stronger alone than with allies, he had no sooner fought and won those two battles than he proceeded to help in reconstructing the Coalition long ago broken up by Charles. Nay, more: he also let his views of himself expand. Earlier, on the morrow of Narva, he and August had carried out an anticipatory division of the pelt of the as yet unslaughtered bear by concluding with one another an agreement of 1701 which awarded Peter Ingria and Karelia for his future share, and resigned in August's favour Peter's claim to Livland and Esthland; whilst in 1707, when Charles had settled August's hash, and decided to march upon Moscow, Peter had told August that eventually he did not intend to rest satisfied only with one harbour on the Baltic. Wherefore, now that Poltava had been won, the Lord of Moscow sent Menshikov to re-establish "my faithful ally" upon the throne of Poland, and also dispatched

Sheremetev to besiege Riga: with the result that though by 1710 Peter had made himself master of the Baltic littoral between Viborg and the Western Dvina, earlier, in 1709, the Treaty of Tornea had allowed August also to assume hereditary rights over Livland in virtue of his Saxon Electorship! Naturally, such a combination of factors served still further to disintegrate Peter's energies, and to cause his attention constantly to vacillate. Moreover, another effect of Russia's military successes was once more to bring French diplomacy into the field, and to inspire it, during the summer of 1711, to use Charles towards involving Peter in a new struggle with Turkey, towards sending him forth into the desolate heart of the steppes with no more spiritual equipment than an excessive reliance upon the Turkish Christians, upon a few empty promises from the rulers of Moldavia and Wallachia, and upon himself because of Poltava. All of which means that though Peter had an insufficiency of material supplies, and was not sufficiently posted as to the military conditions of the contemplated campaign, he was not merely for rendering Little Russia finally proof against Turkish assault, as on the occasion of the previous southern campaign, but also for overthrowing the very Turkish Empire itself. Only on reaching the Pruth did he learn the much-needed lesson, for there he found himself confronted with a force five times outnumbering his own, and, after narrowly escaping personal capture, had to arrange a meeting with the Grand Vizier, and conclude with him a treaty whereby he surrendered all his strongholds on the Sea of Azov, and so to lose at a stroke the fruits of sixteen years' output of labour and sacrifice. True, his Government and himself had consolation still left them in a hope that this failure in the south would strengthen them in the north, where vastly more was hanging in the balance; and as he was at no time a man sparing of human lives and material resources, he redoubled his expenditure of both; but the real result of the affair on the Pruth was to call a full half-century's halt to Russia's naval progress on the Black Sea, in spite of Anna's subsequent senseless and futile campaign.

Next, turning once more his efforts, and those of his allies, to the Baltic, Peter cleared the Swedes out of German territory, and in 1714, at Hango, saw his Baltic flotilla put to flight the Swedish fleet which hitherto had dominated that sea, and by 1715 bring Finland into his possession. Unfortunately, he then committed the blunder of allowing Brandenburg and Hanover to join the alliance (Hanover had just sent its Elector to become King of England), and so of allowing himself to acquire such a taste for interference in German affairs as led him to wed his nieces to an obscure *Hertzog* of Courland and an equally obscure *Hertzog* of Mecklenburg, and so to become caught in the huge feudal network of Court and petty dynastic quarrels and differences which in those days distinguished the German nation much as *Kultur* does to-day. And, of course, this Muscovite inter-meddling aroused German resentment and alarm in general, and had the particular effect of involving Peter in a dispute that was in progress between his nephew-at-law of Mecklenburg and the nobles of that nephew. And in-asmuch as some of the nobles concerned had friends at the Hanoverian and Danish Courts, the affair also, in the end, embroiled Peter with his own allies to the extent that they flouted him in public. Also, these new relations with Germany radically altered Russia's foreign policy, since it converted old friends into new enemies, whilst converting not a single old enemy into a new friend: until, after more vacillation, and a narrow escape from being drawn into a fantastic scheme which the professed "Holsteiner" Patkul (his real name was Hertz, and his real office the office of a secret agent for Sweden) evolved for reconciling Russia with Sweden, and then ejecting the Hanoverian Elector from the English throne, and then re-establishing upon that throne the Stuart dynasty, Peter set forth for France in the hope of effecting a match between his daughter Elizabeth and the young Louis XV., and so making of France, Russia's hitherto antagonist, one of Russia's allies.

From all this we see that even the victory of Poltava did not prevent Peter from allowing the pressing task of dealing Sweden such a blow on the Baltic as should finally compel her to desist from the struggle to become sub-ordinate to triflings with Saxony, Mecklenburg, and Denmark which pro-longed a ruinous nine-years conflict for twelve years more, and in the end compelled Peter to jettison much of his own work, and to consent to help his antagonist not only to recover the German provinces which he himself had been the prime cause of that antagonist losing, but also to drive from the Polish throne the friend whom he had so long and so platonically supported. And on Charles's death in 1718 (he died of a wound received whilst besieging the Norwegian fortress of Friedrichstal), fortune still further mocked Peter, for upon that the Swedes concluded peace with his allies, but not with himself, and thenceforward he had to confront his adversary alone. Yet even as he had struck a single-handed blow at Poltava, so in 1719 and in 1720 he dealt his antagonist two single-handed "staggerers" by twice invading and ravaging that antagonist's country, until eventually, in 1721, the Treaty of Nystadt put a long-deferred end to the struggle which in his after years he dubbed his "threefold school of war," for the reason that, whereas it was customary for pupils to attend a school of war for seven years at the most, he himself had been so slow to learn that he had had to attend thrice as long before, after a protracted and painful process of feeling about him for allies, the Swedes had taught him that unaided Russian prowess, not ally-aided Russian prowess, alone could bring the contest to a successful termination.

The sphere, however, where Poltava did show its supremely far-reaching effect was, not Peter's sorry foreign policy, but his internal administration. When, after the conclusion of peace, Peter's "Inspector-General of Town Commissions" (a sort of overseer of urban finances and administration) sent the Tsar a letter of congratulation couched in the form of a Church canticle, and having for its refrain the word "Rejoice!" the writer took care to remind his Sovereign that "although thine army hath been purged as in a furnace, there remaineth unto thee the matter of civil administration," and that though the war had proved successful, that success had been attained at the cost almost of ruin of the people, and that therefore it would be well to, for one thing, abate suits for recovery of taxatory arrears, if the country was not to "have called forth in it an exceeding great outcry of all." Poltava, therefore, had the effect of causing Peter's internal policy to undergo as great a revolution as his foreign. Hitherto all State business had been transacted on the from-hand-to-mouth system, with, for its driving-force, Peter's pen addressing torrents of documents to such officials as he chose to commission for temporary or current requirements; and from the very fact that hitherto Peter's letters had represented the whole machinery of government those letters had tended to become substituted for laws, and their recipients to become converted, for all intents and purposes, into State Departments. Moreover, the system had always been directed exclusively to military ends, and identified exclusively with a war-chest and a General Staff, and made to concern no matters of reform beyond such a matter as we find outlined in a letter of 22 January, 1702, written by Peter to Bruss, his then Major-General of Artillery, on the subject, firstly, of discovering a master-artificer who should be able to construct gun-carriages of oak, and, secondly, of effecting a saving in timber by ceasing to make use of large logs, and in future, sawing up smaller ones lengthwise instead of transversely, "to the end that further squandering of our timber do not take place." To this letter Bruss replies that guns differ, and in any case oaken timber need not be wasted upon gun-carriages, since fir is equally serviceable for the purpose, and especially if it be given a thick coating of paint. In fact, in the legislation of Peter's day anterior to Poltava we find only two Acts of a constructive tendency, in the shape of an *ukaz* on local government of 30 January, 1699, and of an *ukaz* on the question of a re-division of the Empire into provinces of 18 December, 1708; and we see in the fact yet another outcome of the circumstance that Peter, in his youthful days, never received the political education which would make the prospect of "an exceeding great outcry of all" inevitably give him food for thought. But there were other, wholly unsentimental, considerations which did at last call his attention to the point—though even then he remained as obdurately unable as ever really to understand the people's needs, and took action only because he was beginning to have a more thorough consciousness of his international position, and had been made to realise, through Liesna and Poltava, that, though his first and principal task was the task of creating a regular army and a Baltic fleet, and it yet stood unfulfilled, he also must provide for the upkeep of those two forces, and maintain, or even increase, their numbers, and that, owing to the fact that Poltava had brought Russia a more commanding position in Europe, there must be added expenditure, and that, owing to the further fact that the West was beginning to fear Moscow, and to look upon her as a new international power, and, in some cases, to think that an old enemy of Russia had better become one of Russia's friends, the cost of military upkeep would have added to it costs of upkeep of military and diplomatic prestige, and that the sources of the State's income were fast drying up, and taxatory arrears as fast accumulating. Hence Kurbatov's meaning is intelligible when he tells Peter that the only result of continued stringency in taxatory prosecution would be wholesale taxatory exhaustion, and the same reason accounts for the fact that five months after the battle of Poltava Peter gave orders that no further suits in that connection should be instituted save where the owing arrears dated from the years 1707–8. Yet it was not until 1710, when the framing of a retrospective estimate of revenue and expenditure for the years 1705–1707 brought to light the fact that during that period the Treasury's income had been a fifth less than the Treasury's disbursements, and two-thirds of the remainder had gone solely upon the army and the fleet, and, owing to Government agents' inability to recover defalcations through what we should now call "credit operations," the resultant deficits had been reimposed upon the taxpayers as "supplementary imposts," that the game was seen really to have outstripped the pocket, and the fact absolutely made clear that attention must be turned from war affairs to home, must be diverted from military operations to the question of furnishing the State with new sources of revenue. Unfortunately, although those sources lay specifically in improved organisation of the people's labour, and in improved State husbandry, they were just the sources which Peter's hitherto lack of leisure for anything beyond diplomacy and the conduct of war had led him to disregard. We find a reflection of the consequent administrative revolution in a compendium of materials for an account of the progress of the military struggle which Peter compiled long before the struggle's conclusion, for the compendium, headed "A History of the Swedish War," begins by remarking that upon the celebration of the victory of Poltava there must follow amendments of the State in respect of its civil affairs; whilst further evidence of Peter's post-Poltavan legislative activity may be gleaned from the highly incomplete digest of Russian legislative memorials which we know as *A Complete Collection of the Laws of the Russian Empire* (1830). Even in this "Complete Collection" there are included between the year 1700 (which for some reason or another Peter chose to regard as the opening year of the century) and the year 1709 as many as 500 legislative Acts, and during the next decade (to the close of 1719) 1238 more, and, during the next *half*-decade (for Peter died on 28 January, 1725) nearly as many again. And with that we see that the whole of this mass of Ordinances and Regulations and Statutes and Instructions and International Treaties marched strictly hand in hand with war; and that right up to the time of Poltava Peter used no other method of coping either with military demands or with administrative shortcomings and abuses than the method of issuing *ad hoc* letters and *ukazi* for such corrective measures as he deemed immediately necessary, and that in every province of his administrative activity until he attained both sufficient leisure and sufficient familiarity with State management to develop his temporary measures and amendments into regular laws and ordinances and institutions (though, even then, most of these regular laws and ordinances and new institutions were made to refer to one or two departments only, as well as were initiated on no definite system), the foregoing remained his only way of doing State business. At all events, his capital legislative Acts belong exclusively to the post-Poltavan period, and therefore war must have been the factor that converted his administrative legislation into institutional, and himself, originally only a builder of ships and a military organiser, into an all-round purveyor of reforms.

Hence there now lies clear to our view the connection between the reforms and Peter's conduct of military affairs. At first sight his reforming activity seems to have had no definite plan, no system of consecutiveness, and, though eventually covering the structure of State throughout, and affecting many sides of the national life, to have revised no sphere of government homogeneously, or integrally, or at a stroke, but always to have progressed by fits and starts, to have modified departments piecemeal, or intermittently, or merely as necessity and current requirements demanded. Yet also we see from study of Peter's measures of reform that at least they had before them a general object of a sort, though no regular order of sequence, and no fixed plan or programme. We shall best understand their ordering if first we take them in connection with their warlike setting, and with the consequences of that setting. For just as war dictated their order, so war gave them their *tempo* and scope, and military necessities determined the system under which they developed into, and became established as, legislative enactments. First of all, requirements of campaigning gave rise to reforms of the country's military forces; and from those reforms sprang a double series of legislative measures for maintenance of naval and military establishments on a regular footing, and for consolidation of the necessary pertinent means. Next, those measures gave rise to changes in relative positions and mutual relations of social classes, and at the same time augmented, yet strained unduly, the State's main source of revenue as represented by the people's labour. And finally, all this being so, and Peter's military, social, and economic innovations being what they were, his administrative staff had to follow suit with a corresponding augmentation and acceleration of its performance of State business, and to grapple with new and complex problems which would altogether have baffled it on the basis of its old organisation and composition. And just as an indispensable condition to further reforms was a process of preceding and accompanying current innovations with a step-by-step overhauling, so Peter's workers of State and the popular mentality alike had to be given a certain course of preparation for those reforms' acceptance—success in present accomplishment of and future conduct of administrative changes could come only of anticipatory provision of trained, efficient executive officials, and of such a preliminary education of the people as should lead the people to support reform because the masses had become aware of reform's nature and significance. Wherefore, taking these factors together, we can understand why Peter began to display an ever-increasing solicitude for popular education, and to establish an ever-increasing number of popular training-schools based alike upon general-reformative and upon purely professional-technical principles.

Hence the general plan, rather, the general sequence, of the Petrine reforms was not one born of any thought-out programme, but one due to the fact that the goad of circumstances played upon the course of affairs. And since the driving-power of Peter's activity was always war, and the initial field of operations of that activity was military reform, and its ultimate goal was financial re-organisation, Peter began his work by reforming the State's defensive resources, and only when that had been done went on to reforms of the State's internal system. All of which, and other such, measures flowed inevitably from the main task, or were steps inevitable before that main task could be finally achieved. Peter himself traces this link between war and his reforming efforts, for in 1722, when, getting on in years, he was engaged in collecting further materials for the already-mentioned treatise on the Swedish struggle, and jotting down still surviving annotations, he adds items "for a record of all deeds which have been done in this war, with dispositions of territories and armies, and my makings of regulations and spiritual ordinances, and my buildings of forts and harbours and fleets and ships and galleys, and all matters concerning manufactures and establishments at Petersburg, Kotlua, and elsewhere"; whilst a month and a half before his death he adds further notes, "for a history of such things as in my lifetime I have begun upon, both for warfare and for the other arts, and those things' causes and necessity, so that this my record may serve as an example unto men, and as a warning, and be not speedily forgotten as in times past." That is to say, it was Peter's idea that his *History of the Swedish War*, his account of all matters connected with the conflict, should cite not only measures accomplished for Russia's military re-organisation, but also measures accomplished for her territorial and ecclesiastical revision. We too, therefore, as we study his reforms, might do worse than follow a plan comprising (1) Peter's military reforms, (2) his measures for maintaining his naval and military establishments—in particular, his measures for so altering the State position of the *dvorianstvo* as to increase that class's service efficiency, (3) his measures for augmenting the State's revenue, for enlarging the aggregate of taxpaying labour, and for improving the quality of that labour, (4) his financial innovations, and (5) his measures for assuring successful execution of his military and popular-industrial reforms, and especially of his administrative reforms, through the establishment of schools and colleges. Yet let us not, because we adopt this plan, suppose that Peter's reforms followed one another so precisely that always a reform was taken in hand only when its predecessor had been brought to a completion. No, Peter's re-organisation of his various spheres of State progressed, rather, integrally, or fragmentarily, or simultaneously, or by fits and starts, as the case might be, and only towards the close of his reign so coalesced as to enable ourselves to feel that, when we too shall reach that point in history, it may become possible for us to set them forth according to a regular scheme.

The first reforms to which Peter laid his hand were military reforms; and they constituted at once the heaviest and the most protracted task that fell to his and the nation's lot. And they are the more important in the story of Russia in that they involved not only State defence, but also something profoundly affecting, in equal measure, the adjustment of the Petrine community and the course of subsequent events.

From a roster of 1681 [1] we see that by that year a sufficiently large portion

---

[1] See vol. iii. p. 245.

of the Muscovite, or Home Service, Section of the military forces had been transferred to the Foreign Service Contingent to raise the total of the latter from 89,000 to 164,000, exclusive of the Cossacks of Little Russia. Yet that re-formation of the Foreign Service Contingent does not seem to have been continued further, seeing that, whilst the force of 112,000 which Prince V. V. Golitzin led upon the second Crimean expedition in 1689 included exactly the same sixty-three regiments of the Contingent which figure also on the roster of 1681, those regiments are shown on the expedition's "state" only to a total of 80,000, and with reduced complements per regiment, and with a mere 8000 of the Home Service Section's *dvorianin* mounted militia —a number equal to no more than a tenth of the Foreign Service Contingent as a whole, whereas in the roster of 1681 that militia is given at a total equal to a fifth, or to a sixth, of the Foreign Service Contingent. And a similarly unexpected composition is encountered in 1695, when we scrutinise the military forces dispatched by Peter upon the first expedition against Azov, since we can count amongst the 30,000 men who marched with Peter himself (at the time, a "bombardier" of the Preobrazhensköe "Company") only 14,000 members of the Foreign Service Contingent, whilst the huge force of 120,000 which he at the same time detached for the purpose of creating a diversion in the Crimea consisted exclusively of men of the Muscovite establishment, and, at that, chiefly of non-regulars, of men dubbed by Kotoshikhin "fellows altogether ignorant of array." So whence came this mass of Muscovite non-regulars, and what now had become of the Foreign Service Contingent which had marched on the Crimean expedition of 1689 to the number of 80,000, but is seen to have marched to Azov with Peter only to the number of 14,000? The answer lies in the reply given to Peter by Prince Y. T. Dolgoruki when at the already-related banquet in 1717 the Prince, a man familiar with the composition of Moscow's armies during the times both of Theodor and of Sophia, and Prince V. V. Golitzin's ex-colleague in the leadership of the second expedition to the Crimea, he told his Sovereign that, though Tsar Alexis had shown him, Peter, the way in which to organise a regular military establishment, "foolish men have since undone Alexis' beginnings, and compelled thee to begin things anew—not but that thou hast not by now brought them to a better pass even than he." For that the reply cannot have referred to either Theodor's or Sophia's period of rule is shown by the fact that already we have perceived the regiments dispatched upon the second Crimean expedition shortly before Sophia's fall to have been in perfectly good order. No, clearly what the reply referred to was the fact that, whilst the *dvorianstvo* had ranged itself on the side of Peter's mother during the struggle against Sophia and her *Strieltzi*, the swarm of Narishkins and Strieshnevs and Lopukhins which had risen to the surface after the Tsarevna's defeat, and attached itself to the imperious Tsaritsa's train, had been a mob of hangers-on who had cared nothing at all about State defence, but calmly transferred all *dvoriané* who deemed service in the ranks of the Foreign Service Contingent too heavy for their taste to the more lightly worked Muscovite, Home Service, Section, and thereby given rise to the situation that, on Peter later being forced to supplement his army, the *dvorianstvo* were found to be in such a state of disorganisation that, whereas hitherto, at the close of a campaign, both mounted and dismounted *dvorianin* troops had been accustomed to be dismissed to their homes, and not again summoned to the colours unless a special need arose (so that mobilisation had meant merely a re-mustering of discharged, reserve, and time-expired men, men already inured to active service), Peter had to muster his armies for the Swedish War in face of the circumstance that he would have no reserves to fall back upon if ever such reserves should become necessary, and that the existing regiments of the Foreign Service Contingent must be supplemented through the expedients alternatively (1) of "calling unto willing men to be soldiers" (that is to say, appealing for volunteers), (2) of collecting *datochnie*, or "ceded men," from seignioral estates in proportion to local numbers of peasant homesteads, and (3) of enrolling service-fit freed *kholopi* and *krestiané*, and allowing bonded *kholopi* to enter infantry corps without losing their right to return, after service, to their old employ. Yet whilst the system resulted in a raising only of hastily formed and German-trained conscript forces, and in their dispatch merely as what Korb, Secretary to the Austrian Embassy, a man resident in Moscow between 1689 and 1699, calls "a concourse of unworthy soldiers, mostly from the lower people," and as what another foreigner, Weber, Russian Resident for Brunswick between 1714 and 1719, dubs "an exceeding sorry multitude," Peter at least formed an army of twenty-nine regiments of freedmen and *datochnie* 29,000 strong, added to the four veteran corps represented by the two corps of Guards and the two cadral formations, and dispatched the whole to Narva. Moreover, lamentable as was this army's display of military incapacity at Narva, it yet befell that in time the very course which the war assumed converted Peter's original rabble of freedmen and "ceded men" into a regular army in the true sense of the term, since, owing to the number and the length of the spells of campaigning, a new corps frequently was retained on service for several years at a time, until it had changed practically into a permanent unit. On the other hand, there set in, from Narva onwards, an enormous wastage of man power, an enormous melting away of Peter's improvised regiments under the stress of battle, of famine, of disease, of wholesale desertion, and of forced marches from the Neva to Poltava and Azov and Astrakhan and Riga and Kalisch and Vismar, whilst ever the theatre of operations kept extending, and, calling for an increased army strength. And the method by which this shrinkage was made good, and the military complement reinforced, was a method of percentage enrolments of volunteers and "ceded men" from every class without exception —even to sons of *boyaré*, and to *posadskie*, *dvorovie*, sons of *Strieltzi*, and unbeneficed clergy: the year 1703 alone seeing 30,000 men thus recruited. On the other hand, the very fact that the army became an army drawn from the people as a whole infused into the forces an alloy of raw material which, if not absolutely non-military, was at all events inferior: and this gave rise to a need for such a system of filling up gaps as should serve not only to furnish a really trained reserve, but also to send that reserve to the front more regularly and quickly than had hitherto been the case. Hence to Peter's first fortuitous and ill-organised enrolments of volunteers and "ceded men" there succeeded a system of regular and periodical and all-round conscriptions in which we see his heretofore conditions of recruitment only partially repeated. For under the new system all single men between the ages of fifteen and twenty (and, later, all married men between the ages of twenty and thirty) were sent to *stantzii* or muster-points (mostly these coincided with the towns nearest to the recruits' places of origin), and there divided into detachments of from 500 to 1000, billeted in cantonments, and entrusted, for their daily inspection and supervision, to corporals and *efreitori* (squad commanders) from among their own number, and, for their purely military instruction, to officers and men who had been retired for wounds or sickness, "so that all our warlike companies may be taught regularly, and according unto due ordinance." Later, when trained, and as the need might arise, these recruits were dispatched to "places of default," and used either for supplementing existing corps or for forming new ones. Wherefore, Peter's new military training-schools, as a whole, had for their purpose the purpose "that whensoever requests shall be made for a fresh filling of the army there shall be in readiness a sufficiency of men for all places of default." Also, these conscripts gradually came to be known as *bezsmertnie*,[1] since an *ukaz* ordained that, in the event of a conscript dying at a training-centre, or on ordinary service, or in action, or deserting, his place was at once to be taken by a conscript from the same district, "to the end that always there be soldiers in full, and ready to serve the State." The first general conscription Peter carried out in 1705; and thenceforth the process was re-

---

[1] Literally, "deathless men," but used in the sense of men in reserve against vacancies caused by casualties.

peated every year up to the close of 1709. As a rule the prescribed ratio was one recruit per twenty taxpaying homesteads; but though, at this rate, each of the first five conscriptions should have provided a total of a little over 30,000 men, and the warrants for them called for, provisionally, and in all, 168,000, we do not know what total actually was obtained, since with enrolments went defaultings — we know merely that between the opening of the Swedish War and the first general conscription the number of freedmen and "ceded men" commanded to be enrolled was 150,000, and that on the basis of that figure there were absorbed into the army, during the first ten years of the contest, 300,000 males out of an approximate population of both sexes of 14,000,000.

Thus, then, did Peter create his second, or Poltavan army: and, by the close of the year 1708, a series of three conscriptions had raised the complement of that army to 113,000. And during the next few years the army was filled up and augmented in the same way, whilst incidentally we find Weber, a foreign observer who made a careful study of Russia's then military establishment, writing in his curious *Notes on Reformed Russia (Das veränderte Russland)* that, though, ordinarily, 20,000 State recruits were enrolled per year, the number taken into service nevertheless varied according to whether the ratio of collection was one recruit per fifty homesteads, or one per seventy-five, or one per eighty-nine, so that the total might be variously, 10,000, 14,000, or 23,000, apart from naval service recruits: to which he adds that especially during the year 1724, although warfare on every front had then come to an end, the forces had impressed into them for completion of establishment of field and garrison regiments, artillery, and fleet, 35,000 fresh recruits. Such a swollen enrolment can be explained only by the fact that, in addition to the usual necessity of reinforcing units, heavy shrinkages had taken place, through desertion, sickness, and death, in the regiments specially assigned to fatigue duties by Peter's new military scheme, and that grave deficits of man-power had accumulated from past recruit-musters. At all events, we know that in 1712 the number of defaulters, of men who had failed to "join up" when called upon during their respective years, had reached the huge total of 45,000, and, of deserters, a total of 30,000. In which connection Weber remarks that, owing to bad organisation of maintenance, far more recruits died of hunger and cold before their training had come to an end than ever fell in subsequent battle. In sum, Peter's regular cavalry and infantry (exclusive of aliens) were estimated to be standing, towards the close of his reign, at a total of between 196,000 and 212,000, apart from his force of 110,000 Cossacks and other irregular details.

At the same period there came into being an altogether new armed force, an armed force never before known to Russia: which force was a Russian fleet. We have seen that when the Northern War began, Peter had to lay up his Azov squadron, and that, later, the battle on the Pruth lost him the whole of that marine region; and it was these circumstances that first led to his so thinking of creating a fleet on the Baltic that in 1701 he could dream of coming to have eighty large vessels afloat there, and by 1702 was at least engaging crews for those warships, and giving Kurakin cause to write that "now are youths of every age being called upon to be mariners, and having three thousand of their number chosen," and by 1703 launching six frigates from the Lodeinopolsk Wharf, the first Russian squadron to take the Baltic's waters, and by the close of his reign beholding Russia in possession of forty-eight ships of the line, of 800 galleys and minor vessels, and of a man-power afloat of 28,000. Also, since the controlling, reinforcing, training, feeding, and clothing of the men of the fleet and the army called for a corresponding amount of military-administrative machinery, there came into being a War Office and an Admiralty, with, later, an Artillery Office under a Field-Marshal-in-Chief, an Office of Commissariat under a Director-General of Victualling, and a Chief Office of Supply under a *General-Kriegs-Kommissar*, an official so varied in his functions as to have under his charge the distribution of pay to the forces, their provision with uniforms, weapons, and horses, the reception of recruits at training-centres, and those recruits' corps-allotment. Also there materialised a General Staff consisting of, according to a roster of 1712, two field-marshals (Menshikov and Sheremetev) and thirty-one generals, with fourteen of the latter foreigners. And, lastly, there was issued to the land forces a standard dress, and if we look at illustrated works bearing upon our military history we shall see Peter's Guardsmen manipulating their muskets, and locking their "baginets," in a costume consisting of (in addition to other things) a *kaftan* of German cut and a three-cornered hat.

Thus Peter based his system of establishment of regular warlike forces upon the technical changes (1) that to enrolments of volunteers for the filling up of gaps there succeeded general recruit-enrolments, (2) that the old peace cadres of "chosen men" were developed until they became permanent corps, (3) that by degrees infantry were given a considerable predominance over cavalry in the correlation of military arms, and (4) that the State's armed forces all became transferred, for costs of maintenance, to the Treasury. Of which changes, and especially of the last, the net result was that the cost of military upkeep grew until in 1712 the General Staff alone was found to be absorbing 111,000 (900,000) roubles per year, as against a sum of 10,000,000 for the cost of the whole of the army put together about thirty years earlier, and that the land forces increased both in numbers and in costliness until by 1725 the military budget stood multiplied by five, if not more, and had reached 5,000,000 (Petrine) roubles for the army, and 1,500,000 roubles for the fleet, or a total which, if reckoned in modern currency, means, in all, a sum of from 52,000,000 to 58,000,000 roubles, or two-thirds of the General Budget designed for the State's every purpose!

CHAPTER IV

NEXT let us review Peter's measures for the attempted upkeep of his army and his fleet. In the last chapter we studied his methods for bringing his armed forces up to strength, and saw that by extending liability to service to hitherto non-service classes like the *kholopstvo*, the urban and the rural cess-paying populations, the free *krestianstvo*, and the Church *krestianstvo*, he converted his new army into an army composed of recruits from all sections of the community without exception. Now let us study his measures for organisation of regimental commands, and those measures' effect upon the *dvorianstvo* as the ruling class, and their success or otherwise in maintaining the ruling class's service efficiency.

Even if Peter's military reforms had not made the deep and lasting impression upon the social and moral adjustment of the community which they did, and also upon the course of political events, they would still have remained an outstanding feature in Russia's military history. For one thing, they inevitably gave rise to a need for some method of providing for the upkeep of Peter's reformed, but exceedingly costly, armed forces, and therefore to a series of measures for placing those forces' establishment upon a regular and permanent basis. And in proportion as Peter extended the obligation to perform military service to classes which had hitherto stood exempt from that liability, until the army had become an army drawn from the nation at large, there resulted an alteration also in social correlations, and, above all, an alteration in the service position of the *dvorianstvo*. Hitherto the *dvorianstvo*, as a class, had constituted the bulk of the army, but when conscriptions began to sweep even the *dvorianstvo's*, *kholopi* and bonded *krestiané* into Peter's reformed military corps, and to hold them there in the capacity, not merely of their masters' menials and henchmen whilst on

service, but in that of full men-at-arms serving on an identical service footing with that held by their masters at the beginning of those masters' service,
the *dvorianstvo* ceased to be the principal constituent in the country's
armed forces.

At the same time, the *dvorianstvo's* new service position was not an outcome of Peter's reforms alone, but had been led up to by certain events of
the sixteenth century. During the century in question, as we have seen, the
dvorianstvo first entered into politics as Ivan IV.'s *Oprichnina*,[1] as a police
force directed against the *Zemstchina* in general, and against the *boyarstvo*
in particular, and, after supporting Boris Godunov throughout the Period
of Troubles, and deposing the *boyar* Tsar Vasilii Shuiski, figured in the pan-
territorial treaty of 30 June, 1611 (the camp-framed document executed
before the walls of Moscow [2]) as a body not so much representative of "all
the land" as itself constituting "all the land"—thus ignoring its fellow-
classes, seeking its own interests alone, and excusing its self-proclaimed
autocracy with a plea that the Orthodox Faith and "the House of the Divine
Mother" were in danger, and needed to be protected. Also, we have seen
that establishment of serf-right still further increased the estrangement
between the *dvorianstvo* and the rest of the community, and lessened the
class's territorial sense, yet at the same time joined with the camp conspiracy
in providing the class with a common interest, and compounding its many
heterogeneous strata into a single social element. Finally, we have seen that,
through abolition of the *Miestnichestvo*,[3] there became added to that element
the last remnants of the *boyarstvo*, and that the latter joined the element the
more readily because Peter and his plebeian statesmen only mocked at the
aristocracy of birth, and sought to degrade it in the popular eye. Indeed,
more than one observer then expressed the opinion that, as a ruling class,
the *boyarstvo* was on its deathbed, and we read that in 1687 Sophia's favourite,
the plebeian *dumni diak* Shaklovit, informed some of the *Strieltzi* that
"the *boyarstvo* hath become but a withered and a falling tree," and that,
later, Prince Kurakin himself came to the conclusion that the Regency of
Natalia (1689–94) was the period when "such an abasement of the chief
families did come about that the very name of prince began to stand abhorred,
and to be set at nought, whilst even fellows of the lower and the richer
shliachetstvo did raise themselves up, and become masters" (by which
Kurakin evidently meant certain members of the Narishkin-Strieshnev
faction). Hence the *boyarstvo's* later venture of 1730 [4] was only a cry from the
tomb, for the class had long ago become absorbed into the *dvorianstvo*, and

---

[1] See vol. ii. chap. v.   [2] See vol. iii. chap. ii.
[3] See vol. ii. chap. iii.   [4] Described in chap. xiii. of this volume.

the *dvorianstvo* had so consolidated its ranks as to cause all members of its two sections who were liable *po otechestvu* ("through heritable property,") to State service to figure in Peter's legislative Acts either under the Russian term of *dvoriané* or under the Polish term of *shilachtichi*. But, unfortunately, the class had developed also into a social body possessed of few or no qualifications for culturally influencing the nation, or even for educating the classes standing beneath its own, or for evolving for itself any practical interests or useful ideas, or for, least of all, introducing any such interests and ideas into its fellow social sections. No, the *dvorianstvo* came merely to be a class corporation with a conception of duty bounded by defence of the country from external foes. There remains, however, the curious fact that, owing to the very course of history, the class did come to help Peter in introducing reforms, even though he used other classes as well for the purpose, down to the *kholopstvo* or slave class itself, and even though the new *dvorianstvo* in no way surpassed the rest of the people in point of moral and intellectual development, nor differed a whit from the rest of the people in a lack of sympathy with Western nations which led it to dub them "heretical." And even with regard to its own particular trade, the trade of war, the new *dvorianstvo* developed no especial degree of martial skill or martial spirit. Rather, it led both Russian and foreign observers to describe its warlike qualities in pessimistic terms, and Pososhkin, in particular, to remark in a "Report on the Bearing of Our Men-at-Arms" which he presented to a *boyarin* named Golovin in 1701 that he could not but bewail the cowardice, and the want of spirit, and the lack of enterprise, and the absolute inefficiency of the new military class of Russia, and to add that "now is there being driven into service a multitude of men whom, should one behold them with a discerning eye, one will perceive to contain nought save dishonour. For, of them, the footmen have but sorry arms, nor know the usage of those arms, but, when fighting hand to hand, do fend themselves with axes and pikes blunt of edge, and yield of their own heads, for the head of each foeman, in threefold, or fourfold, or even greater measure. And if, again, one beholdeth the horsemen, they do appear both unto us and unto strangers a shameful spectacle, for they have for steeds but sorry jades, and their swords are dulled, and they bear themselves indifferently, and lack apparel, and are skilled in no sort of weapon. And there are *dvoriané* who know not even how to charge their arquebuses for shooting at a mark, nor care at all for slaying the foe, but only for seeking how they may rest alway in their homes. And when they make prayer unto God often they do pray that he may suffer them to receive a light wound, and not a grievous hurt, so that they may acquire recompense of the Tsar thereafter. Nay, some even do spend the times of battle in withdrawing themselves into a thicket, and live but to flee into fastnesses and forests, so that ofttimes I have heard such say, 'May God send that I have but to serve the great Tsar without ever drawing my sword from its sheath.'"

At the same time, it was not long before the *dvorianstvo's* new social and State position led to at least the upper stratum of the class imbibing manners and ideas more in consonance with its new tasks. Originally confined to service families which had settled at the Muscovite Court in appanage days, at the time when the first Suzerain Prince had selected Moscow as the site of his future palace, the class had subsequently had its families infiltrated with State service men from other principalities, and also from such foreign points as the country of the Tartar Horde, Germany, and, above all, Lithuania; whilst later still, when Muscovite Rus had become consolidated, yet other newcomers had arrived in the shape of provincial *dvoriané* promoted to be *dvoriané* of the metropolis for military prowess, or for good service in some civilian capacity, or for industrial self-enrichment: and this compound mass of officials had then, through its very functions at Court, become knitted into a tangled and highly complex scale of *stolniki*,[1] or attendants who handed the Tsar his cup and platter during State banquets, of *striaptchie*, or persons who escorted him during the progress of processions, and also looked after his *striapnia* (sceptre), head-dress, and mantle whilst he was in church, and carried his sword and cuirass on military campaigns, of *zhiltsi*, or chamberlains who did night duty in the Imperial palaces by turns, and of certain functionaries who, inferior to *stolniki* and *striaptchie* on the many-runged ladder of social-official grades, stood, nevertheless, superior to *zhiltsi*, and were known as *dvoriane moskovskie*, and represented at once the highest grade to which a *zhilets* could rise through good service, and the class status which ordinarily could be attained by a *stolnik* or a *striaptchi* not hailing from the aristocracy when, after twenty or thirty years' service in that functionary's particular grade, he had to retire as unfit for further Court duties, yet still remained eligible for service posts of the kind which Kotoshikhin calls "sundry affairs," for a post as *voevoda*, or as ambassador, or as a troop- or company-commander in a contingent of provincial *dvoriané*, and so forth. And, naturally, the reign of Alexis saw this inflation of the metropolitan *dvorianstvo* with an influx of provincial *dvoriané* attain exceptional dimensions, since during that reign there began the custom of awarding membership of the metropolitan *dvorianstvo* also for wounds, and for battle prowess, and for hardships whilst in captivity, and even for the death of a kinsman through any one of those causes, whilst the mere fact that the

---

[1] From *stol*, a table.

period of Alexis' dispensation was the most bellicose period in all our history caused these several sources of creation of metropolitan *dvoriané* to sprout so vehemently that, to take only two instances, the *débâcle* at Konotop in 1659, when the Tsar had his best cavalry cut to pieces, and Sheremetev's capitulation at Chudnovo, these two occasions alone added hundreds of new *stolniki* and *striaptchie* and *dvoriané moskovskie* to the register of metropolitan *dvoriané*. The net result of these influences was that the metropolitan *dvorianstvo* developed into a corps of, according to a list for the year 1681, 6385 members, and one which, nineteen years later, could furnish 11,533 men-at-arms as its contribution towards the Narva campaign. Also, up to the period of general conscriptions the fact that that *dvorianstvo* possessed large *otchini* and *pomiestia* enabled them to take with them on campaigns, or to send in their stead, no small numbers, frequently thousands, of "ceded men" or armed slaves, whilst in any case the very nature of their duties at Court obliged them, in addition, to own establishments in or near the capital itself—an instance of this being that between the year 1679 and the year 1701 no fewer than 3000 out of Moscow's 16,000 premises had for owners members of the metropolitan *dvorianstvo*. In short, the latter stood charged with multifarious duties of a Court nature, and therefore came to be, for all intents and purposes, the Emperor's *Dvor* or Household, so that documents of Peter's time actually term members of the class "*tsaredvortsie*," or "Tsar's Court men," in distinction from the plain "*shliachetsvo* of all callings" which the provincial-urban and rural *dvoriané* and "sons of *boyaré*" represented. Further, the metropolitan *dvorianstvo* acted as the Tsar's personal suite, or corps of officiants, for purposes of Court functions, and provided the principal *personnel* of both the central and the provincial administrations, and became the Tsar's own or crack regiment in times of war, and furnished staffs for regiments of the line quartered in the metropolis, and commanders for provincial *dvorianin* battalions. All of which enables us to say that the *dvorianstvo* of the metropolis constituted at once the country's chief administrative class, a General Staff, and a Guards Brigade. And, of course, these many weighty and valuable services qualified that *dvorianstvo* to receive higher rates of pay than its provincial colleague, and to be allotted larger *pomiestia*, whilst also its dominant rôle and greater security of material tenure developed in it an usedness to exercise of authority, a familiarity with public affairs, and an *aplomb* in the management of social matters which gradually brought it to look upon State service as its peculiar calling and peculiar social function. Similarly, the fact that the section resided permanently in the capital, and paid only brief, occasional visits to its rural *pomiestia* and *otchini*, ended by communicating to its members a consciousness of standing at the head of the community, of having an inner knowledge of the State's domestic policy, of being able to view the Government's foreign relations from a closer distance than was possible for the other classes, and of surpassing the latter in acquaintance-ship with the localities of the outer world with which their own held dealings. With the result, in sum, that these qualifications rendered the metropolitan *dvorianstvo*, next after Peter, the prime introducer into Russia of Western influence. This followed the more inevitably in that introduction of that influence was called for by the State's very requirements, whilst also there was the fact that such an introduction could be effected only by men accustomed to exercise control. Hence, aware already that Western innova-tions were entering the realm, and realising, therefore, that the State needed competent workers if those innovations were to operate in the desired manner, the Government instinctively turned to the metropolitan *dvorianstvo* as its nearest and most suitable instrument, and selected from it the officers necessary for co-operation with the foreign military staff in commanding the Foreign Service Contingent, and in providing instructors for Peter's new military training-schools. The task proved the easier because the class concerned was inclined already to be comparatively pliable and subservient, and already had produced such champions of "Westernism" as Khvorostinin, Ordin-Nastchokin, and Rtistchev. And as soon as Peter finally selected it for his chief agency of domestic reform, and set about organising a regular army, it converted itself also into a Corps of Guards, and so led to the Preobrazhenski, or the Semenovski, Guards officer figuring simultaneously as an executant of reform functions and of warlike, and to the ex-*stolnik* being despatched to Holland for nautical study, or to Astrakhan for initia-tion into the salt-boiler's art, or to the headquarters of the Holy Synod for entry in its offices as an *Oberprokuror*.

Next let us turn to the provincial-urban service class *po otechestvu*, or the class termed by the *Ulozhenie* "sons of ancient *boyaré* through birth." This class, in the old Muscovite Empire, held a status akin to that of the metropolitan *dvorianstvo* at least in so far as that it performed functions at once military, industrial, and administrative, since, besides constituting the country's armed forces as a whole, it served as the Government's main in-strument in dispensing justice and managing local affairs (it provided the *personnel* for the provinces' legal and subordinate-administrative posts), and held in its hands most of the country's fundamental capital, the capital represented by land and (after the sixteenth century) agricultural serfs. But the result of this triple status, in the case of the provincial *dvoriané*, was to render those *dvoriané's* performance of State service irregular, since

IV—F

each of their three divisions of functions tended to clash with the other two. That is to say, if an interval occurred between two "servings" or campaigns, and the service men of the capital and the provinces were, as usual, disbanded to their homes, those metropolitan and provincial *dvoriané* who did not depart upon a visit to their country estates very likely secured for themselves temporary posts as members of provincial-urban administrations, or else the type of administrative or diplomatic commission currently known as "dwelling in affairs," or "dwelling in charges"; and this, in its turn, led to a mergement of civilian service with military, since, however temporary the former might be, it was, in such instances, performed by military men. Besides, there followed the result that certain such civilian posts and commissions came to carry with them a privilege of exemption from military service to which the only limit was an obligation, in case of war, to furnish, per estate, a given number of "ceded men" according to number of peasant homesteads: and in time this limited obligation became extended even to such officials as clerical *diaki* and *podiachie*, on the ground that, being permanently employed in Government offices, they might reckon themselves either as enjoying permanent leave from military service or as holding permanent staff appointments—though this was to hold good only if the official seeking exemption was also an owner of serf-tenanted lands. Naturally, the system led to abuses, for it facilitated wholesale evasion of the military function, and also tempted owners with connections in the right quarter to use the perils and hardships incidental to campaigning, not to speak of the industrial losses occasioned by permanent or periodical absence from their estates, as excuses for procuring posts *automatically* exempting them from service, or for "laying themselves aside" in rural retreats whither a service summons could not penetrate. Which consummation was the easier to effect through the fact that rural manors often were situated in localities where the bear alone had its habitation, and where a *Strieletz* or a *podiachi* armed with a mobilisation notice could easily be made to believe that the dwelling was deserted, and that the wanted man's whereabouts were neither known nor ascertainable.

Not that Peter himself did anything to relieve the provincial *dvorianin* of the established obligation to render the State personal and indefinite service, for, on the contrary, he increased that liability both with additional restrictions upon exemption and with a process of "drawing" every possible member of the class concerned. The method by which he sought to effect this last, and to abolish "harbourage," was the method, firstly, of having an exact and complete return of the class's eligible members compiled, and, secondly, of ordering that both the *Razriad* (War Office) and the Senate should have furnished to them full lists of minor sons of the *dvorianstvo*, and of any such kinsmen over the age of ten who might be residing in *dvoriané's* households, so that, the returns compiled, the body of youth named in them might, with adult orphans added, present themselves in Moscow for periodical registration and inspection. And from the returns we see that those periodical registrations and inspections were carried out in very large numbers—Peter himself reviewing, in 1704, 8000 minors who had been summoned to the capital for the purpose; whilst after each such review the newcomers had training-schools or regiments allotted them, as when, in 1712, a party of minors who had either been living at home or studying at school had to present itself at the Senate's Chancellory in Moscow, and then be dispatched by waggon to St. Petersburg, and, after a fresh inspection there, and division into categories according to age, proceed, the youngest category to Revel for study of navigation, the medium category to Holland for the same purpose, and the eldest category to immediate military enrolment. Mournfully indeed remarks a V. Golovin, one of the youngsters allotted to the second category: "Now have I, for my sins, and as my prime calamity, been apportioned unto them who are for the sea!" No status of birth, however eminent, absolved from this liability to inspection. We see this from the fact that in 1704, after reviewing from 500 to 600 sons of "persons the most illustrious," the Tsar ascribed the whole—yes, even such youngsters as the Princes Golitzin, Cherkasski, Khovanski, and Lobenov-Rostovski—to the Guards, "where still," adds Prince Kurakin, our informant, "they are in service." And Peter went further yet, for he tackled Government clerks, a class which by this time, owing to the lucrative nature of their functions, had increased out of knowledge, and in 1712 issued orders for an overhauling of the staffs of all provincial chancellories, and even of the staff of the Senate's own secretariat, so that any redundant *podiachie* that were young and service-fit might at once be transferred thence to the army. To which orders the accompanying *ukaz* added also, in the form of a postscript, the names of certain *dvoriané* whom Peter specially desired to see submitted to inspection, owing to a ground for believing that they meant, otherwise, to go into hiding at home, and render themselves non-service-efficient. Equally severe did he show himself towards *nietstvo*, towards wilful absence from inspections or "listings": so much so that when, during the autumn of 1714, he issued a customary proclamation for Senatorial registration of all *dvoriané* between the ages of ten and thirty during the ensuing winter, he, this time, appended to the document a threat that if an informant should report any *dvorianin* for having designedly absented himself, that *dvorianin* should forfeit his estate and chattels to the informant in question—yes, even if the informant happened to be the *dvorianin's* own servant; whilst by a still more ruthless *ukaz* of 11 January, 1722, he ordained that any wilful defaulter from an inspection should undergo *shelmovanie* (political death)—be driven forth from his fellows, declared outside the law, and, after having had his name affixed to the gallows of the local square by the common hangman, publicly, and to beat of drum, recognised as a traitor and contemner of the Tsar's *ukazi*. Contrariwise, such a defaulter's apprehender and bringer-in was to receive for himself one-half of the defaulter's movable and immovable property, even though he might happen to be merely a serf in the defaulter's own employ.

However, these harsh measures succeeded to a partial extent only, and in his work *Poverty and Wealth* (indited towards the close of Peter's reign) Pososhkov gives us a graphic description of the tricks and stratagems for evasion of service to which *dvoriané* resorted. Frequently, according to him, a *dvorianin* who had been ordered to march upon a campaign would contrive to procure for himself "a commission unto vain affairs," to some such sinecure post as the office of a police official, and then, under cover of it, retire to his *otchina,* and there lie *perdu* until the campaign was over. Nor scarcely need it be pointed out that tricks of the sort were rendered the easier by the steady growth in the number of commissaries and other high officials. Writes Pososhkov: "For our governing, at the present time, is there being attached unto us a veritable plenitude of idle youths, of whom any single one might well repel five foemen. Such a youth, however, doth obtain a work of profit, and then live unto himself alone, and make his advantage, and shun calls unto service either with gifts, or with feigned sickness, or by imputing unto himself *urodstvo*.[1] Or, rather than be taken for service, he will leap into a lake, and there remain to the very chin! Yea, only the rich man escapeth, whilst the poor and the aged all are seized, and sluggards so suffered to mock at the Tsar's *ukazi* and strictness that, though Zolotarev may seem as a lion unto his neighbours when he is abiding at home, afield he marcheth looking worse than a she-goat, or will avoid an expedition altogether by sending thither a needy *dvorianin* in his stead, and yielding unto him man and horse, and then himself riding through, it may be, six villages, and despoiling the dwellers therein. For these things the blame should rest chiefly upon the ministers who do stand nearest unto the Tsar, in that they use false reports to draw sayings [2] from the Tsar's mouth, and then act as they think good alone, and cozen folk." To which the writer adds: "Yea, nowhere can one behold virtuous upholders for the Tsar, but only administrators who walk crookedly, and set apart the man

---

[1] Holy imbecility. See vol. ii. p. 156, n. 2.　　　　　[2] That is to say, *ukazi*.

fit for service, and compel unto service the man not proper for the same. Wherefore, for all that our great Monarch toileth, his toil profiteth him nought, in that his helpers are few, and if he addeth ten of aught unto an heap, others do drag thence millions. How, then, can his work prevail? In no wise hath the old order changed, and at best the Tsar will, for all his strivings, be forced to forgo his tasks."

Yet whilst the utterance shows that even Pososhkov's pious reverence for the Reformer could not prevent the self-taught publicist from drawing a picture of current circumstances that is pitiful almost to the point of bathos, the chief value of his remarks lies in the fact that they warn us to avoid adopting an idealistic view when criticising the military system created by Peter's legislation. Wherefore, that warning received, let us proceed to consider the precise manner in which the *dvorianin* performed his ordained service. The age for entry upon service Peter retained at the hitherto age of fifteen; but on the other hand, he complicated the obligation by ordaining a preliminary course of elementary study, and through *ukazi* of 20 January and 28 February, 1714, commanded all sons of *dvoriané, diaki*, and *podiachie* to be set to a pre-service course of "ciphers" and geometry, and, if found faulty in the same, to be subjected to "such mulcts as shall leave them not free to wed until those bidden things be learnt"—in other words, be disqualified from even applying for a marriage licence until they could produce a tutorial certificate of scholastic efficiency. To the same end also, to the end of those youths' pre-service education, it was that Peter commanded every episcopal palace and every principal monastery to have erected on its premises a school with a curriculum worked by student-preceptors from the mathematical colleges (equivalent to the gymnasia, or polytechnics, of to-day) which he had founded in or about the year 1703, and the student-preceptors in question to be given an annual salary of what would amount, in modern currency, to 300 roubles. By these *ukazi* of 1714, therefore, there became introduced into the history of Russian education, for the first time, compulsory secular instruction. Not but that the scheme was conceived modestly enough, for, as regards numbers of instructors, it provided merely that from the above-mentioned mathematical colleges there should be posted to each province a couple of graduates in geometry and geography, whilst all that these preceptors had to teach their service pupils was elementary geometry, "ciphers," and a smattering of hornbook Holy Writ. The education, therefore, was rudimentary, and no more. Nevertheless Peter considered it at least adequate for the military profession, and believed any extension of its scope likely to work the service harm. And through it every young *dvorianin* had to pass—beginning it at the age of ten, and compulsorily breaking it off at the age of fifteen, the age for entry into military service proper. So insistent upon this last was Peter that by an *ukaz* of 17 October, 1723, he specially forbade the later retention of any *dvorianin*, no matter how brilliant, "or howsoever much he himself may desire it, lest, in the name of learning, he be able meanwhile to hide himself away from inspections, and from apportionment unto service." Yet Peter's anxiety was misplaced. In this connection let us turn to our friend Pososhkov again. According to him, Peter's own *ukaz* found itself forced to admit that up to the time of its promulgation only one episcopal school, a school in the Diocese of Novgorod, had attained actual establishment, and that the mathematical colleges which Peter had instituted for public and general instruction apart from Church schools were existing only with difficulty, and that in 1719 an official sent to inspect colleges of the sort at Pskov and Novgorod and Yaroslav and Vologda and Moscow had had to report that the college at Yaroslav had booked only twenty-six pupils (exclusively sons of ecclesiastical persons, at that), and that the other colleges had booked no pupils at all, and their instructors were "sitting without tasks, and therefore accepting payment for nought." In fact, everywhere it became only too much the rule that sons of the *dvorianstvo* developed such a distaste for "ciphering" that, deciding that the obligation was a useless burden, they did their best, in future, to avoid it, whilst one young band of *dvoriané* in particular went so far in the effort to play truant from a certain mathematical college that it had itself enrolled in the Zaikonospassk Ecclesiastical Seminary, and put Peter to the necessity of having these youthful devotees to the study of theology dispatched from Moscow to the Naval College at St. Petersburg, and there punished with a course of pile-driving in the Moika Canal. Incidentally, this action on Peter's part offended Grand-Admiral Apraxin, since one of the culprits was a younger brother of his, and he retained all the old-fashioned notions about family honour. Hence, to voice his protest, he proceeded to the Canal, and, as soon as the Tsar drew near, divested himself of his admiral's coat and riband of St. Andrew, hung the lot upon a pole, and fell to pile-driving with the young *dvoriané*. "How now, Thedor Matveitch?" said Peter in surprise. "How cometh it that thou, who art a Grand-Admiral and a Knight, art thrusting piles with the rest?" And to this Apraxin retorted as though jesting: "Sire, thou dost see nephews and grandchildren [1] of ours thrusting piles; and who am I that I should avail myself of my birth?"

Next, on attaining the age of fifteen, and actually entering military service, the young *dvorianin* had to serve for a while as a private, and was

---

[1] The Miestnichestvo term for the younger brethren of a family.

allotted to some specified regiment—youths from the wealthier and more ancient families to the Guards, and youths from the poorer and more modestly born to corps of the line, since it was Peter's theory that, though a *dvorianin* was an army officer in essence, he had better become one through preliminary service in the ranks. For the same reason it was that a Law of 26 February, 1714, proclaimed that promotion to be officer was "never to be granted to men of the *dvorianstvo* save that they shall first have served as common soldiers in Our Guards, and learned the labours of a soldier from the foundation of the same"; whilst by a *Voinski Ustav* [1] of 1716 it was enjoined that "for the *shliachetstvo* of Russia there must be no means of advancement to officer save that first every *shliachtich* shall have served for a season in Our Guards Corps." All of which regulations make clear to us why Peter's Guards were preponderantly *dvorianin* in composition. By the close of his reign the Regiments of Guards had come to be three in number, since in the year 1719 the two older-established regiments had had added to them a third in the shape of a "*Leib-Regiment*" (later known as the Russian Horse Guards); and these corps served practically as three schools-of-arms for the upper and the middle *dvorianstvo*, and as nurseries for officers of the line, since always a *dvorianin*, after serving a term in the ranks of the Guards, went on to become an officer in a working regiment, whether of infantry or of dragoons. Thus, frequently the *Leib-Regiment*, a corps basically confined to "sons of the *shliachetstvo*," had as many as three hundred princely scions in its ranks, and so afforded St. Petersburg the quite common spectacle of a Prince Golitzin or a Prince Gargarin doing sentry-duty, musket on shoulder. And during his term as a Guardsman private the *dvorianin* lived in barracks, drew rations as a "ranker," and was spared none of the usual fatigue tasks, so that Derzhavin [2] relates in his memoirs that though he himself was the son of a colonel and a *dvorianin*, he, whilst first serving with the Preobrazhenskis, lodged with comrades drawn from the masses, and took part in every duty of latrine-scouring, guard-mounting, stores-carrying, and dispatch-running. Of which expedients of the Petrine military system in combination the general result was to make of the *dvorianstvo* a preparatory cadral reserve which could furnish commanding and regimental officers to regiments of the line *via* service in the ranks of the Guards, and officers to the Fleet *via* residence in the Naval Academy. In each case, owing to the interminable length of the Swedish War, this service became practically permanent, for only when peace arrived did the average *dvorianin* ever obtain even rotation leave to visit his estate, and then but for six months at intervals of two years; whilst permission permanently to retire was granted

---

[1] Army Act.   [2] The leading poet of the times of Catherine II.

only for old age or disablement, and on such terms, designedly, as should secure that the *dvorianin* did not drop altogether out of the service roster, but still remained available for garrison duty or such civilian work as a post under a local government body. Only hopelessly incurable or disabled men were awarded pensions from the "hospital moneys" levied for military sanatoria, or else were dispatched to monasteries, and there placed upon the private funds of those institutions.

Such, therefore, the normal military career of a *dvorianin*, as Peter designed it. But the *dvorianin* was required for other purposes as well, since the tendency of civilian service to become more and more stringent in its conditions caused the work of the new judicial and administrative departments to become more and more responsible, and to call for special courses of preparation, and special standards of technical knowledge, until combination of the two branches of State service in the same individual was found impossible, and any plurality of posts in that way became a privilege confined to Guards officers and senior generals, to the section of Russian society which ever has deemed itself fit to hold any and every position, no matter what its nature. Which circumstance, in its turn, brought about a differentiation between the *personnel* of the civil branch of the service and the *personnel* of the military, and led to the *dvorianin* class being allowed no choice as to the branch which it should select, since, had it been allowed that choice, it would have used it almost exclusively for obtaining posts in the civil departments as the lighter and the more lucrative of the two. Indeed, the numbers of *dvoriané* appointed to each came to be fixed in an exact proportion: an "Instruction" of 1722 charged the King-at-Arms, as the official supervisor of the *dvorianstvo*, to see to it "that never do more than one-third of a family be put to service in Our civil ranks alone, lest thereby Our forces both of the land and of the sea be weakened"—lest the Army and the Fleet should suffer in point of maintained strength. The "Instruction," therefore, clearly shows what was the principal motive inspiring Peter's system of dividing *dvorianin* service into two—that that motive was realisation of the fact that proper fulfilment of State civilian duties called for something more than mere ignorance and conceit. Sternly the "Instruction" bade the King-at-Arms see to it that, in view of the existing paucity, the existing practical absence, of civilian scientific attainment, and especially of civilian economic attainment, there should be instituted such a system of "short schooling" as would speedily render the statutory third of principal and secondary *dvorianin* families allotted to civilian service of State "learned both in citizenship and in economy."

Hence the effect of dividing *dvorianin* service between the military branch and the civilian of that service was to improve both branches from the technical standpoint, and, through abolition of the heretofore conditions of promotion, to communicate to the *dvorianstvo's* genealogical composition an element which had never before been one of its constituents. Hitherto members of the State service class had held their posts strictly "according unto heritage," strictly according to degree of family status, so that before each family of the class there had stood a definite ladder of service grades and ranks which each male member of the family had had to climb in a definite and pre-ordained manner, and of which usually, in climbing it, he had reached the highest rung to which his birth entitled him strictly in proportion as he had possessed personal fitness for, and showed personal capacity in, the performance of duty. But, of course, the fact that his service promotion had depended upon family position, as well as upon personal deserts, had ended by causing the former factor greatly to outweigh the latter, and to make deserts go to reinforce family rather than to act as the more effective producer of promotion. This was an antiquated basis, a basis designed primarily to support the genealogical composition of the State service class: and to it Peter dealt a first blow through abolition of the *Miestnichestvo*. Yet morally, if not actually, the system held good for a while; until, radically to oust it, Peter made service merits outweigh claims of birth, and, beginning with an assurance to the *dvorianstvo* that State service was that class's only proper obligation, the one obligation "wherein the *dvorianstvo* hath any sort of nobility, and doth stand apart from baseness," [1] went on to inform the class that thenceforth, no matter who or what a *dvorianin's* superior officer might be, he, the *dvorianin*, was to pay that officer respect. Clearly, in this regulation, as in all other regulations of the sort, Peter had for his purpose the facilitation of a process of permeating the *dvorianstvo* with a proportion of men of non-*dvorianstvo* origin. Hitherto the *dvorianin* had begun service as a private, but had nevertheless been a prospective officer; whereas an *ukaz* of 16 January, 1721, commanded that non-*dvorianin* privates should thenceforth be eligible for officer's rank, and even, on rising also to be "over-officer," for membership of the *dvorianstvo* in virtue of birth, since it was Peter's theory that, though every member of the class was vocationally an officer, every officer, no matter who he was, should have good service on his part rewarded with a chance of qualifying for *dvorianin* status. And the fact that he placed this maxim at the root of his service system led to the old graded hierarchy of *boyaré* and *okolnichi*, of *stolniki* and *striaptchie*, the old graded hierarchy that had stood based upon birth and Court position and membership of the old

Lowliness of origin.

Boyarskaia Duma, losing its original importance in the same way that transference of the Imperial Seat from the banks of the Moskva to those of the Neva had led to the old Kremlin *régime* being abolished, and as the demise of the *Duma* had led to the Senate becoming extinguished as an institution. Next, Peter's well-known register of *chini* or grades, his well-known "Table of Ranks," promulgated on 24 January, 1722, introduced into the main body of the State service *personnel* a new classification, and, whilst allotting most of the newly constituted posts to persons of German or Latin name, instituted three parallel series of ranks (military, civilian, and Court), and subdivided each, again, into fourteen grades or classes. Which reform substituted for the old aristocracy, the old hierarchy based upon birth and the genealogical tree, a new bureaucracy, a new hierarchy, based upon service and general merit. With especial emphasis did the "Table's" Appendix state that no significance could lie in eminence of birth if service itself was faulty, or qualify even the highest birth for office or position if the individual concerned did not first advantage the Tsar and his country, "and acquire note through the same": wherefore it, the "Table," now proceeded to enact that "membership of the best and most ancient *dvorianstvo*" should, "in respect of all dignitaries and advantages," descend solely in the line of such Russian and alien servants of the State as the Table had assigned to its first eight ranks, with the rank of major ending the military branch, and that of "Collegiate Assessor" the civilian, no matter whether or no the given individual's line had originally been well-born. The result of this general concession to meritorious service was a radical change in the genealogical composition of the *dvorianstvo.* True, no exact estimate of the *parvenu,* or non-*dvorianin,* element which then became introduced into that genealogical composition is possible, but at least we know that whereas, at the close of the seventeenth century, the *dvorianstvo* had contained only 2985 registered family stocks, and, exclusive of sons, no more than some 15,000 landowners, Fokkerodt, Secretary to the Prussian Embassy in St. Petersburg shortly before the close of Peter's reign, records, under date of 1737, that at the time of the first revision of *dvorianin* families the class was found to comprise upwards of 500,000 male members. And though these data afford an inadequate answer to the question of how far Peter's new system of *chini,* or ranks, adulterated his *dvorianstvo* with a non-*dvorianin* alloy, it may at least be assumed that at the period mentioned by Fokkerodt Peter's newly-created *dvorianin* families stood at a total of about 100,000.

Hence the changes wrought by conversion of the old *pomiestie,* or manorial-tenant, contingents of retainers into a regular army drawn from every class of society numbered three. For in the first place, that conversion formed into two branches of *dvorianin* service what formerly had been one, by constituting a military service branch, and a civilian. And in the second place it imposed equally upon the two forms a liability to a preliminary course of education. And in the third place (and possibly this change influenced Russia's subsequent fortunes as an Empire more than did either of the other two), the conversion in question caused Peter's regular army to lose its territorial composition, and become modified in its constituent portions. Of this last result the principal cause was that, whereas, hitherto, "execution of regimental service" had been carried out by garrison corps and field service contingents made up exclusively of *dvoriané* drawn from one and the same district, this territorial system now sustained a blow through the fact that Peter initiated a system of forming regiments for the Foreign Service Contingent from recruits drawn from several. And to the same result contributed enrolments of volunteers and compulsory conscription, since those expedients in either case evolved corps of a heterogeneous class composition, and deprived them of their old local *personnel* to the extent that the recruit from Riazan who had not for long past seen his home, and had no expectation of ever seeing it again, gradually forgot that Riazan was his home at all, but merely remembered that he was a member of a dragoon regiment commanded by a colonel. In other words, the new barrack life tended to extinguish the recruit's sense of territorial origin; and the same occurred in the case of the Guards. Always the provincial *dvorianin* promoted to membership of the metropolitan *dvorianstvo* had not long stood divorced from his home associations before he had completely identified himself with his new comrades and *milieu*, and he and all of them had been helped by their constant residence in Moscow, and by their daily intercourse with colleagues in the Kremlin and on their suburban *otchini* and *pomiestia*, to convert the city into just such a metropolitan-*dvorianin* stronghold as, say, Kozelsk represented for the Kozelskan *dvoriané* and "sons of *boyaré*"; and now the metropolitan *dvorianin* who became a private in the Preobrazhenski or the Semenovski Regiment, and was transferred to the capital on the Neva, and marooned amongst the swamps of Finland, quickly forgot his original status, and came to figure to himself solely as a Guardsman. And ever afterwards, this abrogation of home ties in favour of barrack-regimental connections inevitably helped a strong hand to convert the Corps into an instrument of blind force, and a weaker one to convert it into a cohort of Janissaries or Prætorians. In 1611, as we have seen, when the Period of Troubles was in being, the Princes Trubetskoi, Zarutski, and Liapunov mustered an army to deliver Moscow from the Polish conquerors, but, whilst holding that army before the walls of the city, went on to evolve an idea springing from a lust for added military prowess which suggested to them that the defence of the country from external foes would make a good pretext for getting hold of the rest of the Empire as well—an idea originally hailing, in all probability, from the new dynasty's recent consolidation of serf-right: and Peter's creation of a regular army, and especially of the Corps of Guards, now revived this idea, though he cannot have foreseen either the use which his male and female posterity would one day make of his support of it, or the use which the idea would one day make of that posterity.

Another result of the process of complicating the *dvorianin's* service obligation which I have described was to evoke a need for improved material guarantees of the *dvorianin's* service efficiency, and to bring about an important change in his industrial-agrarian position. Earlier we have noted that originally there existed between the two forms of service land-tenure, between hereditary proprietorship of an *otchina* and conditional, temporary (usually only for life) occupation of a *pomiestie*, certain juridical differences. But long before Peter's day the two forms began to approximate to one another, and features of *pomiestie* occupation to creep into *otchina* proprietorship, and *pomiestie* occupation increasingly to assume juridical peculiarities formerly peculiar to the *otchinal* or proprietorial form. The cause of this was the conditions of tenure of a *pomiestie* as a landed estate, since the nature of those conditions themselves conduced to that approximation. Originally, in the days when the *krestiané* were free, the essential design of *pomiestie* tenure was to dower the service beneficiary with an agrarian emolument in the form either of tithes paid by the *pomiestie's* taxpaying inhabitants or of labour (*barstchina*) performed by those inhabitants: whence the *pomiestie* represented a reward for military service closely akin to the older *kormlenie*,[1] and no difficulty was involved in its passage from one to another occupier. But of course it also came about that frequently a *pomiestchik* would conceive a definite mental interest in his estate, and fit it out with a farm, and equip that farm with agricultural *kholopi* and implements, and have its arable land cultivated on the *barstchina* system, and its timbered portions cleared, and the whole settled with *krestiané* holding plots on a *ssuda* basis.[2] Hence, State lands originally granted to service men merely for temporary possession tended to develop into industrial assets having about them something of the nature of absolute, hereditary properties. Or, in other words, the mutually contradictory pressure of right and of practice, aided by subsequent legal establishment of peasant serfdom,

[1] See vol. ii. p. 248.   [2] See vol. ii. p. 201.

enabled usage gradually to triumph over legality. For how could a *pomiestie* remain a temporary holding when once the *krestiané* on it stood bound to its occupier on a *ssuda* or a *podmoga*[1] basis? Hence, to meet the difficulty without infringing *pomiestie* tenure-right, legality so far yielded to practice as to grant *pomiestchiki* an extended right of *pomiestie* disposal which permitted the *pomiestie* to be bought in, and held as an *otchina*, and therefore made exempt from distraint, and exchangeable with, or cessible to, either (1) a direct relative, (2) the accepted suitor of a daughter or niece (by way of dowry), or (3) a collateral relative—though, in the latter case, only on condition that the collateral relative concerned should undertake to make the estate support its late owner for the latter's lifetime (or, if that late owner were a female, until she entered wedlock). Next, the law awarded the *pomiestchik* right of disposal in return for a monetary sum—though expressly it withheld right of complete sale. And, lastly, through rangement of the *pomiestie* for *otvod* or *pripusk*[2] there became established a rule practically legalising not only hereditary succession, but also sole succession, non-divisibility of the *pomiestie*—a rule to be found expressed in contemporary registers by the formula, "When two sons shall accede to service, the elder of the twain shall be inscribed for *otvod* forthwith, and the younger continue to serve from his father's *pomiestie*"[3]; whilst as a finishing touch the law added a regulation that, on the death of the father, the *pomiestie* concerned was to pass undividedly to the son thus "serving with his father"; which enables us to understand why *ukazi* of Tsar Michael's day sometimes display juxtaposition of the seemingly irreconcilable ideas expressed by "*rodovia pomiestia*" and "*pomiestia* in virtue of birth" (or "of family")—the latter a term springing from the ordinance that "*pomiestia* never shall be set apart from birth," that is to say, conveyed out of the family. But the actual result of *pomiestia* being made heritable was to give rise to the difficulty that, since *okladi* ("apportionments" or "lots" of *pomiestia*) marched strictly with the rank and the service merits of a *pomiestchik*, it became a question whether a father's *pomiestie* (especially if that *pomiestie* were a large one) ought properly to be conveyed to a son who had not yet earned, through the amount of his service, an amount of *pomiestie* equal to the paternal *oklad*; and, to solve the problem, Moscow's departmental intellects framed an *ukaz* which, on 20 March, 1684, ordained that, on the demise of any large *pomiestie's* occupant, the estate was to devolve in the descending line direct, and "whole"—that is to say, to descend to the late holder's sons and

---

[1] See vol. ii. p. 201.
[2] "Assignment" or "surrender" to a son of a portion of his father's *pomiestie* during the father's lifetime.
[3] See vol. ii. p. 131.

grandsons irrespective of whether or not those sons and grandsons yet stood registered for service; whilst, in addition, the heirs were to enter into possession altogether "apart from" (independently of) *okladi*, and under bond not to subtract, or to cut off, any portion of the estate for conveyance to another direct or collateral relative. Only in a case where no direct heir or heirs were present might the *pomiestie*, under certain further conditions, pass to a kinsman. Which *ukaz* effected a complete revolution in *pomiestie* tenure, in that, without wholly establishing hereditary succession, legal or by testament, it so made use of the process which I might term "familisation of *pomiestia*" as practically to establish family entailment, and so convert assignment of a *pomiestie* at death into, for all intents and purposes, equal distribution amongst the whole body of extant and competent heirs, descending and collateral. Or, in other words, the *ukaz*, by displacing sole succession, led up to disintegration of *pomiestia*, and so to disruption of the essential bases of *pomiestie* tenure. And to this disruption Peter's formation of a regular army added the final touch, since as soon as *dvorianin* service became permanent and hereditary, *pomiestie* tenure had to follow suit, and, thereby, finally to identify itself with *otchina* tenure. Which fact, again, caused allotment of *pomiestia* gradually to yield altogether to *otchinal* conferment of populated lands, and in a surviving list of Court *sela* and *derevni* assigned to monasteries and individuals during the years 1682–1710 we find few instances (and, even so, only up to the year 1679) of estates being conferred "for usage as a *pomiestie*," but instances in large numbers of *otchinal* bestowal—the twenty-eight years in question seeing no fewer than 44,000 peasant *dvori* allotted on the latter basis, with 500,000 *desiatini* [1] of tillage, and attached rights of wood and water. All this means that by the opening of the eighteenth century the *pomiestie* had come so closely to approximate to the *otchina* as almost to be indistinguishable from it, and to be fast disappearing as a distinct form of tenure. Wherefore the three main features of *pomiestie-otchina* mergement were (1) equalisation, in point of heritableness, of the two kinds of estate, (2) disintegration of the *pomiestie* through equal distribution of the same amongst the whole body of descending and collateral heirs, as the heritable *otchina* had from the first been distributed, and (3) gradual replacement of provisional allotment of land for *pomiestia*, with absolute conferment of the same for *otchini*.

The result of this position of affairs was that by 1714 Peter had to issue the well-known *ukaz* of 23 March. The fundamental conditions of this Act, or set of "*punkti*" (clauses), were (1) that "immovable chattels" (*otchini*, *pomiestia*, *dvori*, and agricultural buildings) were in no case to be alienated,

---

[1] Approximately 1,350,000 acres.

but "returned into the stock" [1]; (2) that such "immovable chattels" should always pass strictly to the son specifically selected by the testator, but the latter's movable property to such of his other children as parental desires had designated before death (or, alternatively, and if a testament was absent, with the "immovable chattels" passing to the eldest son, and, if there was no eldest son, to the eldest daughter, and the movable property in equal shares to the remaining children); (3) that a testator having no issue should bequeath his immovable property to "whomsoever in the family he will," and his movable either to kinsmen or to extraneous individuals as he might please (or, alternatively, and if a testament was absent, with the immovable property passing to the deceased's nearest kinsman in lineage, and the remainder "in equal portions unto whomsoever may be thought proper"); (4) that a testator who came last in his family should bequeath his immovable property to a married woman, or an engaged woman, of the family, on condition that her husband, or her betrothed, undertook in writing to assume for himself and his heirs, and to add to his and their family name, the family name of the stock become extinct; and (5) that the fact of a "cadet," a portionless *dvorianin*, who was forty years old or more, entering into either the mercantile profession, the pursuit of any recognised handicraft, or the White Clergy should not involve either him or his relatives in any sort of odium. The Law, besides, was circumstantially motived. Thus the sole heir to a non-divisible property was on no account to set to work to ruin his *krestiané* (his "poor underlings") with new imposts, as was done only too often by co-sharing brethren who aspired to live on the same scale as their father, but, rather, to relieve his *krestiané* by lightening their tithes-renderings. Similarly, *dvorianin* families were to take care not to let themselves decline, but to "abide in eminence, and be houses un-shakable, and exceedingly great and glorious," since the splitting up of a landed property amongst a plurality of heirs always tended to impoverish an illustrious family stock, and to convert that stock into plain yeomen "such as already we can see abiding in over-many examples amongst Our Russian people." Also, said the *ukaz*, a *dvorianin* who accepted *gratis* even a crumb of bread came to lack a spur in life, and rendered the State the more indifferent service, and relapsed into idleness outright: wherefore it was the desire of "this Our now enacted Law" that every cadet should "seek his own bread for himself" through, variously, service of the State, tutorial labour, a trade, or, in any case, something. Whilst, as a last touch, the *ukaz* added that, though Peter, the *ukaz*' enactor, was the realm's Supreme Tsar and Legislator, even he, as he well realised, could not wholly afford his

---

[1] That is to say, into the family.

subjects protection against rascally and impoverished *pomiestchiki*, against a *dvorianstvo* the majority of whose members were ne'er-do-weels, and hated every useful form of activity. By these dispositions the *ukaz* introduced into tenure of land for service several important changes. Though in no way was the document what commentators have frequently alleged it to be, namely, an instrument designed definitely to regularise a system of majority or primogeniture, an instrument inspired by the feudal systems of Western Europe (not but that it is practically certain that Peter had first made enquiry into the successional rules of France, England, and the Venetian Republic, and also questioned foreign visitors on the subject); and though in no way did the document award exclusive rights to eldest sons—rather, it treated the question of majority as one scarcely likely to be encountered unless a testament was absent, and left a father free to leave even the eldest son passed over as regards disposition of the paternal immovable property; what the *ukaz* did establish was sole succession to, and indivisibility of, immovable property, as a procedure designed to remove the prevailing evil of disintegration of *pomiestia*, and to obviate the effects of the *ukaz* of 1684, all of which had steadily been lessening the *pomiestchik's* service efficiency. Another feature is that the *ukaz* displays no little originality of juridical structure. For one thing, inasmuch as it simultaneously consummates the process of approximation of the *pomiestie* to the *otchina* and establishes an identical system of inheritance for both, it raises the question of whether it converts the *otchina* into a *pomiestie*, or whether it converts the *pomiestie* into an *otchina*. Well, that certain thinkers of the eighteenth century took the latter view is shown by the fact that they termed the *punkti* of 23 March "an abounding grace," and said that by it Peter intended to make *pomiestia* bestowable and tenable on absolute manorial right. But, as a matter of fact, the *ukaz* did neither of these two things: what it did was so to combine the juridical features of the *pomiestie* with the juridical features of the *otchina* as to evolve thence a wholly new, and altogether unprecedented, form of agrarian tenure which we might term "landownership hereditary, indivisible, and perpetually obligatory," as rendering service of State by the landowner at once heritable, constantly descending, and permanent. And though each of these features is to be found also in earlier forms of Russian land-tenure, no two of them are then found occurring side by side, since heritableness had always been a feature peculiar to *otchina* proprietorship, and indivisibility a feature peculiar to *pomiestie* occupation, whilst never before had the *otchina* been indivisible, or the *pomiestie* hereditary, and service always had fallen equally upon both. But Peter took and combined these various features, and then, by extending them to every sort of *dvorianin* property, rendered service landownership, if less free, at all events more uniform.

From the changes introduced by the *ukaz* we gain also a good idea of Peter's mode of procedure in general as he reorganised the community, and proceeded to administer it. For, whilst accepting the existent stock of relations and systems, and importing into them no actually new principle, the *ukaz* yet adjusted those relations and systems into new combinations, and adapted those combinations to new conditions, without abolishing a single feature of the relations and systems concerned. Rather, it merely so altered existing rights as to make them conform with the State's new requirements. True, at first sight the new combinations may seem to give the reformed order a novel and unwonted aspect, but, for all that, the order was the pre-existent order reconstructed on the old basis of solid, long-standing relations.

Again, though the Law of 23 March assigned landed property exclusively to a single heir, it, with that, relieved cadets, and, in some cases, nephews of the heir, of the liability to service obligations, and left them free to choose some other rôle or occupation. This was because, though the *dvorianstvo* had hitherto constituted the bulk of the military arm, Peter no longer had need of the entire service *personnel* of the *dvorianstvo's* families —his quest had become, rather, sole-heir officers who would render their service the better for having means enabling them to prepare for service without at the same time overburdening their *krestiané* with an excess of exactions. Wherein the rôle assigned to the State service individual by Peter was consonant with the rôle which he assigned to the *dvorianstvo* as a whole —the rôle of a corps of commanding and company officers for the new all-class contingents of regular troops. At the same time, the Law of 23 March, like other social innovations of Peter's, took too little account of workaday manners, customs, and ideas; it thrust itself in upon workaday life so roughly as to divide the *dvorianstvo* into two strata—into a stratum of comfortable owners of inherited domiciles, and into a stratum of dispossessed, landless, homeless proletarian younger brothers and sisters who found themselves confronted with the alternative either of an existence as pensioners upon the sole heir, or of an existence of "turning to and fro amongst diverse dwellings." So that it is not difficult to imagine the complaints and the dissensions that must have come of this law, and how poorly the law must have facilitated its own execution! Moreover, in places the law was so faultily elaborated that it failed altogether to provide for given *casus*, or else furnished definitions capable of contradictory interpretation. Thus, whereas its first section forbade alienation of immovable property, its twelfth section normalised and provided for such property's conditional sale, and, whilst drawing a sharp distinction between "order of inheritance of movable chattels" and "order of inheritance of immovable property," failed to specify what either of those terms meant, and facilitated such abuses and misunderstandings as to call for subsequent *ukazi* to explain the first one's shortcomings, and lead to new *punkti* of 28 May, 1725 for a detailed revision of arisen *casus*; *punkti* which in many respects departed from the original instrument, and thereby hindered still further the instrument's execution. On the other hand, even Peter seems to have looked upon the original Act as temporary only and not final, for he permitted important deviations from it, and, when publishing a supplementary one of 15 April, 1716 for testamentary allotment of the whole of a married *dvorianin's* immovable (and, therefore, indivisible) property into the perpetual possession of the surviving issue, annotated the *ukaz'* margin with the words, "Let things be done thus only for a season." Also "cadets'" liability to service never became abrogated in whole, and they continued, as before, to have to join first-born sons in attendance at inspections. Again, to the very close of the reign parents are seen devising their property to children equally, if those parents had acquired the property previously to amendment of the Law of 1684; and probably it was this system which Pososhkov had in his mind when, in his work *On Poverty and Wealth,* he cited cases in which *dvoriané* had taken advantage of their parents' death to break up vacant plots or villages, and subdivide their lands, populated and non-populated alike, into a number of minute portions, and so quarrel over them as sometimes "to commit the capital sin"—all of which proceedings, Pososhkov said, had done the Treasury much harm. Indeed, we might even say that, for any real effect that it brought about, the Law of Sole Succession might as well never have been made, since though the *punkti* of 1725 re-accorded formal recognition to the system of equal shares to all a deceased's issue, the Ordinance of 1714, so far failed of its purpose as still further to complicate agrarian relations, and still further to disturb agrarian industry.

To sum up: Peter's theory or rule with regard to his *dvorianstvo* was that every *dvorianin* must serve the State either as a military officer or as a civil servant, and be given, as a guarantee of that service's efficient performance, a modicum of indivisible real estate.

CHAPTER V

The *krestianstvo* and the First Revision—The composition of the community under the *Ulozhenie*—Recruitment and recruit musterings—Registration of peasant souls—Billeting of troops—Simplification of the community's social composition—Souls-registration and serf-right—The popular-industrial effect of souls-registration.

WE have seen that the *dvorianstvo* gradually became linked, juridically and economically, with the *krestianstvo*. At the same time, Peter's measures of reform with regard to the latter were devoted also to fundamental and general ends, since his main design was to consolidate his military reforms, and therefore to reinforce the Treasury's resources. And as soon as he had completed his military reorganisation he set about the latter portion of this plan, as his next most pressing task.

In defining the community's rights and obligations, Alexis' *Ulozhenie* divided the community into three fundamental classes. Those three classes were (1) State service men, (2) members of the urban-industrial-commercial communities, and (3) the *krestianstvo*, or rural population. Which latter class was subdivided into bonded *krestiane*, *chernosochnie*,[1] State peasants, and *dvortsovie*, or Court peasants, whilst in between the above three fundamental classes stood the clergy and four categories of intermediate or indeterminate strata, strata which, whilst contiguous to the fundamental classes, did not form any integral part of them, or possess any class solidarity, but stood exempt from direct State imposts, and were free to consult their own interests alone. These four free categories were (*a*) full *kholopi* (permanent bondsmen), *kabalnie kholopi* (temporary bondsmen), and *zhilie kholopi* (bondsmen during their master's lifetime), (*b*) a body of free and vagrant persons who, known collectively as the *volnitza*[2] or unattached class, consisted, firstly, of dismissed *kholopi*, secondly of *posadskïe* and *krestiané* who had surrendered their tax-paying lands and pursuits, and, thirdly, of State service men who had squandered all their substance, or had never been awarded a *pomiestïe*, or had abandoned their *pomiestia*—the category thus forming a stratum of homeless and unemployed individuals which floated as a residuum between

---

[1] Literally, "black-ploughing" peasantry, though the category was not exclusively confined to the "black" or fertile regions of Central Russia.
[2] From the adjective *volni*, free.

the bonded peasantry and the taxpaying, free peasantry, and was, in the main, an aggregate of the professional idlers and mendicants who materialise wherever there operates ill-directed clerical or lay charity (though of course I am not including amongst this category the Church's genuine pensioners, the pious ancients sheltered in ecclesiastical or private institutions); (c) episcopal and monasterial servants and attendants, many of whom, as regards the former, acted as stewards of Church lands, and were akin to Civil Servants, and received lands on quasi-*pomiestie* conditions from ecclesiastical bodies, and at last became full Civil Servants, and stood altogether apart from the ecclesiastical attendants who remained Church serfs to the end, even if they did not function under an actual bond of enserfment; and (d) the great body of sons of clergy and *tserkovniki* [1] who either expected or had been ousted from posts in the Church's ministration, and, if not hanging about their fathers' parish churches, pursued some urban trade or industry, or acted in the service of private persons. And all these four categories are distinguishable from one another also by their respective positions in the State. *Kholopi* and *tserkovniki* were serfs in person, and exempt from State taxes; unattached vagrants and sons of clergy were freemen, but similarly exempt; "black-ploughing" *krestiané* were freemen, but taxable; and bonded *krestiané* and *zadvornie liudi* [2] come of the *kholopstvo* were taxable, but not free. Hence the multiplicity and variety of the community's intermediate aggregates of population not only communicated to the social composition of their day an extremely heterogeneous aspect, but on more than one occasion led foreign observers to express unbounded astonishment that the Muscovite Empire should harbour so many functionless individuals. And just because that mass was functionless, or at all events one of non-productive functions, and dependent for support upon the very workers, the very tax-paying classes, to whom the Treasury looked for its fiscal revenue, the mass in question constituted the State's rival, and helped to rob the Exchequer of the resources which the Exchequer most needed for the replenishment of its coffers. Naturally, Peter's instinct for economy led him to seize the first possible opportunity of finding work for such a large unemployed element, and converting it into an element useful alike for tax-payment and for military service, as a reform which, added to military conscription, and to registration of peasant souls, he considered the reform best calculated to purge the community from top to bottom, and simplify its composition.

So long as Peter was in the initial stages of his formation of a regular army the *volnitza* and the *kholopstvo* constituted his main sources of recruits, and, in particular, supplied the bulk of the rank and file of the Guards—

---

[1] Literally, church-folk, i.e. church hangers-on.   [2] See vol. iii. p. 175.

thus replacing, in that respect, the hitherto preponderant *shliachtich* element. Nor, during the process, did Peter scruple to infringe serf-right [1]—he even commanded that *kholopi* the property of *boyaré* should cease to need their master's consent before joining the corps in question: and, when utilising mostly these two classes, the slaves and the unemployed, for raising his regiments for Narva, ordered the enrolment of all *kholopi* freed by their masters, and of all bonded *krestiané* found service-fit, whilst the manuscript of Prince Kurakin's autobiography records the fact that "when there was declared unto the *chini* a will that he who would go for a soldier might do so forthwith, many, an exceeding great number, did leave their homes," and that when the Baltic fleet had to be manned, "and there did come a call for youths as mariners, three thousand of the same were chosen." And so thoroughly did this wholesale "combing-out" of superfluous individuals before ossification of the social framework should set in get to the root of the matter that, of the many tens of thousands who volunteered for Narva, few of those who lived to return home returned to their non-domiciled status, and the rest, except for the section which saved itself by deserting, either fell at Narva, or at Riga, or at Erestfer, or at Schlüsselburg, or (and this was the case with the majority) died of hunger, cold, or infectious disease. Hence the effect of establishment of periodical conscriptions was to sweep into military service such a haul of taxpaying *krestiané* (urban and rural), Court *krestiané*, vagrants, *tserkovniki*, monasterial attendants, and *podiachie* as brought about a new fusion of statuses, and imported into the State the wholly new constructive principle of liability of all classes to the military service obligation.

Another, and a still more potent, factor in Peter's simplification of the community's composition was his expedient of souls-registration. This expedient he carried out so characteristically that it alone will show us what were his customary administrative resources and methods. After the subjugation of Livland, Esthland, and Finland, and when the Northern War was beginning to slacken, he realised that the next question which needed to be settled was the question of placing his regular army upon a peace establishment, in that, even when hostilities should have come to an end, he would have to retain some of his forces under arms, and that they were better lodged in permanent Treasury cantonments than, as usual, sent back to their homes. And though the problem of means was not an easy one, he tackled it, and evolved the following ingenious scheme. On 26 November, 1718, before the peace negotiations with Sweden on the Aland Islands had come to an end, he issued an *ukaz* framed in his usual

[1] This term, throughout, means the right of a master over his serfs.

style, couched in the first chance words that entered his head at the moment, and phrased in the customarily hasty, careless, laconic manner of his legislative tongue. In its opening section it said: "Let there be taken of Our *dvoriané* reports, and, unto that end, the same be granted a term of one year, that they may render unto Us just lists of all male souls who do pertain unto each, and of the villages where such souls be dwelling. Be it likewise declared unto Our *dvoriané* that if any man shall conceal aught, that which he concealeth shall be given unto him who doth inform. Wherefore be there listed how many of a company, or of a regiment, or of the one, or of the other, each *dvorianin* shall be able to receive at a middling rate." After which, in phraseology equally cryptic, the *ukaz* added directions for its own fulfilment, and, with them, a threat that, should the fulfillers of the *ukaz* prove lax, they should have their property confiscated, and be made to experience "the Tsar's most cruel wrath," "ruin absolute," and possibly the penalty of death itself—though let me hasten to say that in these fulminations we see no more than the flourishes with which the Reformer habitually embellished his legislative drafts. Naturally, the *ukaz* put provincial and rural administrations and landowners to a vast amount of labour and trouble. So much was this the case that though, in the first instance, a year's grace was granted for making out the souls-lists, few lists materialised before the end of the year 1719, and fewer still then turned out to be correct. Accordingly, the Senate next "swept" the provinces with Guardsmen, and charged these emissaries to clap into fetters any dilatory listcollector or provincial governor, and to keep him there until the central bureau in St. Petersburg had safely received every single return, duly itemed and totalled: but even this severity had little effect, and the matter dragged over also into the following year. The two chief causes of delay were the obscure wording of the *ukaz* itself, and the crop of cases requiring explanation and addition to which that wording gave rise, since many officials, in the first instance, believed the *ukaz* to be applicable, only to peasants in private ownership, and, on later receiving orders also to enter upon the lists Court peasantry on private estates, could not do so until they had compiled supplementary lists. Which, again, gave rise to the difficulty that, taking it for granted that additional and most grievous taxation would result from the business, even if nothing else did, both landowners and their stewards set themselves to include only a proportion of their peasant souls in the lists—to "set them down only with great concealings": with the result that when the lists received a first overhauling, early in 1721, over 20,000 souls were found to have been suppressed, and the Senate had to instruct governors and *voevodi* to make tours of their districts with the local clergy, and, on discovering any cases of "*couverture*" or concealment, to deprive the escorting clergy of benefices, spiritual rank, and material property, and, "even though a priest be stricken in years, to administer pitiless chastisement unto the body of the same." Yes, even to get the wheels of the rusty administrative machine greased, Peter had to resort to stringent injunctions of this kind, and to torture and confiscation right and left: yet at least the wheels, when greased, brought him to the point that by the early portion of the year 1722 he had the required estimates lying before him, and found them to return the country's peasant souls at 5,000,000. Which done, the Government set about implementing also the command contained in the second section of the *ukaz*, the command that "Our army be apportioned unto the land": and it did this by billeting each regiment in a given locality, and providing for that regiment's upkeep, meanwhile, with ascription to its service of a varying proportion of local souls. Previously, however, the authorities detailed to each of the ten provinces a certain number of *raskladchiki*, or billeting officers—ten generals in all, ten colonels, and a "brigadier," so that the regiments should have "constant lodgement" assigned to them by companies, and be housed in cantonments especially built for the purpose, under the idea that that would be a better system than a system of spreading them about amongst the cots of the peasantry, and so, very likely, breeding ill-feeling between guests and hosts. But though the orders given to *raskladchiki* were that they should first consult the local *dvoriané*, and endeavour to persuade them to volunteer to undertake the building of the necessary cantonments, and to fit them out for the reception of officers, companies, and regimental staffs, this only caused universal trouble, since an additional order to the *raskladchiki* was that they should likewise examine all the local souls-lists, and this second revision brought to light cases of "harbourage" frequently amounting to as much as fifty per cent. of what should have been the total entries! (For the same reason, incidentally, we had better not place too much reliance upon the above total of 5,000,000 when later we come to enquire in what proportion, in general, souls stood to regiments). And though, upon that, Peter and the Senate proceeded to ply *pomiestchiki* and *rashladchiki* and *starosti* with threats and blandishments and concessions of fresh time-limits for the compilation of new lists, either the vagueness of the instructions given to the revising officials or those officials' innate lack of intelligence led to further confusion in the souls-sortings, and to few of the functionaries concerned ever getting it into their heads what souls ought to be entered, and what not, so that constantly officials had to approach the Government with queries, and the more so because they were denied definite information even as to the strength of the army itself. Whence it was not until the year 1723 that the *raskladchiki* had locally collated the corrected lists. True, as soon as that was found to be the case they were given until the opening of the next year before they need return to the capital, but not a functionary put in a punctual appearance (though it is only fair to say that they had already given the Senate warning of the impossibility of completing the work within the time stated), and, though the time-limit was extended to the following March, it was not until nine months after the expiry of that time-limit that the whole body of revisers actually made its way back to St. Petersburg, and so enabled a general mustering of lists to be arranged for, and a final conclusion to be put to a business which had dragged its slow length over a space of six years. By the time that that consummation was reached death had closed the eyes of the scheme's originator for ever.

From the first the regiments found themselves awkwardly placed in their localities, since in most cases the local *pomiestchiki* refused to construct cantonments, on the ground that they preferred the army to be billeted amongst their *krestiané*. And in the end fresh official commands had to be issued on the subject, and, of course, these commands transferred the cost of construction to the peasantry, "upon whom it did fall as a new and a very great burden." Besides, there was haste and carelessness shown in the drafting of building plans, and local populations were wrested from their rightful avocations, and peasantry were further mulcted for the purchase price of the necessary lands. Originally the year 1726 was fixed upon by Peter as the time-limit for completion of erection; but, even when he was dead, four years further had to be conceded before any building work in any locality had been brought to a finish. The trouble was not that building work was not begun upon; the trouble was that almost nowhere was it carried out thoroughly, or as a whole, and that, consequently, immense stores of material compulsorily provided by the peasantry ran to waste. In the end the total of cantonment erection absolutely carried to completion had to stop at a few blocks of regimental staff quarters. The truth is that Peter entered upon this project with no definite, ready-formed method and no proper thought given to ways and means: merely at haphazard he pitchforked officers and men into peasant households, and made them the guests of, or the dependants upon, the souls who stood "listed" for their support. And still graver trouble came of the fact that some curious whim of his failing intellect also led him to suppose that these military men were the best possible instruments for purposes of local administration, and, instead of putting them to their proper work of replacing the peasants in the task of building the cantonments, to appoint them local overseers and police agents

charged with exceedingly complicated duties. Those duties let me describe.
First of all, to arrange for the regiments' upkeep, the local *dvoriané* were
requested to form of themselves cantonal associations, and, that done, to
provide for the work of souls-tax collection by co-opting *dvorianin* commissaries empowered to assist the commander of the local regiment in
adjudicating upon, and fining for, ordinary breaches of the law; whilst,
over and above this arrangement, the commander and his officers were
given an independent measure of authority to prosecute thieves and felons,
to prevent *krestiané* from absconding, to arrest runaways, to root out contraband stores and illicit stills, to restrain provincial-administrative *chinovniki*
from exploiting their publics, and, in general, to afford all and sundry protection from imposition and wrong. More: this measure of independent
authority was so conferred upon regimental officers that they could at
the same time join with governors of provinces and *voevodi* of districts in
prosecuting the *dvoriané's* own commissaries! Nay, they could make those
governors and *voevodi* themselves show cause for any failure to obey
an Imperial command, and report the same to the capital. What ought
to have been done was that Peter's new regiments ought to have retained
the territorial composition of the older forces, and to have been distributed
strictly to localities of origin, and so afforded a chance of living amicably
with the local inhabitants. But no: everywhere the regiments had to live as
strangers, as immigrants, as extraneous bodies thrust into local administrations and local communities, and so failing to hit it off both with the
local *krestiané* and with the local *pomiestchiki*, came to be looked upon by
each as an intolerable and an obnoxious burden, and the more so in that,
after their arrival, a *krestianin* could not even go to work in a strange
canton without first having to obtain a permit from his *pomiestchik* or
his parish priest, and then to report himself at the local regimental headquarters and have the permit *visaed* and registered by the local commissary,
and signed and sealed by the regimental colonel—who usually closed the
transaction by demanding a toll. Finally, it became borne in upon the
Government of Catherine I. that the "flights" of the poorer peasantry were
not so much due to scarcity of means, or to the souls-tax, as to "lack of
concord between the *muzhik*, the officer, the administrator, and the common
soldier," and that the grievance supremely militating against concord was
the fact that the military helped to collect the soul-tax, and so contravened
the *ukaz* of ordination of the census of 1718, which had imposed the task
of souls-tax collection exclusively upon the local *dvoriané's* co-opted commissaries, and in no way linked with it military participation. As a matter
of fact, it was only up to the year 1724 that local *dvoriané* took the trouble

to co-opt commissaries, since in the preceding year Peter's invincible faith in the efficacy of military folk for any and every purpose had led to a brief *ukaz* that, since *dvorianin* incompetence was "causing confusion," the *dvoriané* must, with the coming year, associate themselves, in the task of local tax-collection, with local regimental staffs and "over-officers," "and so cause a good beginning to be made." Which military-*dvorianin* partnership thenceforth was continued, and did indeed give the taxpayer reason to remember the "good beginning," seeing that the system, as operated by the regiments, outdid even the tax as a spreader of universal devastation. Under it, the collectors visited each district thrice annually, and spent two months in the district each time, and so caused every rural *selo* and *derevnia* in the land to spend the remaining six months in a state of panic-stricken expectation of the armed party's next visit. And, when carrying out these inquisitions, or when executing a distress for arrears, parties of the sort never neglected to secure maintenance for themselves at the local inhabitants' expense. In fact, even the Tartar Bashkirs under Batu[1] cannot have hectored it over the Russia of their day more savagely than did Peter's soul-tax bailiffs during the Petrine era. And after Peter's death matters reached the pitch that the Senate and some of Catherine's statesmen felt bound at least to protest against the military's doings, and to point out that such comings and goings of officers, commissaries, and other functionaries were certain eventually to harass the wretched peasant to extinction, seeing that every official was bent upon, on the one hand, despoiling the *krestianin* of his last mite, and, on the other hand, procuring his own promotion, regardless of the fact that inevitably, as the result, the *krestianin* would, when finally stripped of his goods and cattle, and even of his sown crops, "hasten him away unto strange borders." But in reality these official protests represented no more than a shamefaced washing of official hands, since why were the protests not voiced during Peter's lifetime? At all events, no sooner had Peter's regiments been allotted local quarters than there set in a vast shrinkage in returns of revisional souls—partly as the result of wholesale "flights," and partly as the result of increased mortality—an instance being that shortly after Peter's death a certain foot regiment quartered in Kazan found itself left with only half the 13,000 peasant taxpayers allotted it for its upkeep at its disposal! Wherefore it may be said that it is difficult to recognise the Reformer's hand in an army which could first win the battle of Poltava, and then, converted into 126 uncontrolled police commands, set itself to terrorise the ten populations of ten provinces.

But let us defer further study of the financial importance of the souls-

[1] A khan who ravaged Chernigov and the neighbouring district in 1238.

tax until we come to study Peter's fiscal reforms as a whole, and meanwhile pass to the social and popular-industrial effects of the exaction. It is clear that when Peter first thrust his *ukaz* for legalising souls-registration upon the country he failed to foresee the magnitude of the task which he was undertaking. For constantly during that task's performance the souls-tax kept swelling through its own internal logic. At first the Reformer seems to have confined his attentions solely to bondsmen the property of private owners —that is to say, to indentured *krestiané*, and to household serfs; but when he introduced into the taxation of those two classes the novel taxatory element of the revisional soul he appears to have felt that the other taxable classes could not be left on the different basis of the old homestead assessment, and that, to place them on the same basis as the first two, souls-registration must be expanded to cover also Court peasantry, State peasantry, *odnovortsi*,[1] and urban payers of *tiaglo*.[2] But, most important of all, Peter (since the highhandedness of his legislative disposal consistently surpassed that even of his predecessors) extended souls-registration to cover also the various intermediate classes, and in 1722 ordered registration to be made of all sons, grandsons, nephews, or other relatives, of "those who in the past have been, but no longer are, either church-serving priests, or deacons, or cantors, or sextons, or persons living in or around churches," and added to that a proviso that such individuals should invariably be attached to the owners of the lands bearing their parish churches, save that if a given church "stood apart," that is to say, on land not in private ownership at all, the individuals in question should be allowed, under conditions not specified in the *ukaz*, to choose their own landowners. Nor did the law mete out any milder treatment to freemen, since, whereas the *ukaz* of 31 March, 1700, had swept into the army no freemen at all except *kholopi* who had absconded from their masters, and then volunteered for military service, and whereas the earlier *ukaz* of 1 February had done the same only with unemployed *kholopi* and *kabalnie kholopi*[3] who had attained legal freedom on their masters' death (provided that they were physically fit), Peter, by an *ukaz* of 7 March, 1721, proclaimed that every *kholop* who had not been physically examined since the year 1700 should forthwith be inspected by the revisors, and, if found suitable, added to the military forces, and if found not suitable, assigned, under threat of labour in the galleys in case of a refusal, "unto other services," or else "unto some one man, to tend his household." And

[1] "Single homesteaders," or freeholders bound to the land (though not to the person) of their master.
[2] An inclusive term for direct State imposts levied upon individuals and communities, principally on the basis of lands and domestic premises.
[3] See vol. iii. p. 169.

as a further preventive against a single individual in the realm continuing to be either vagrant or undomiciled or workless, the *ukaz* enacted that, should any such individual prove inefficient after adjudgment to be fit for military service, and elect, instead, to be received into bondage, his receiver should furnish a service-fit substitute for him, and see to it that that substitute was enrolled. Of which the net result was to bring about situations of the kind that a *kabala* serf who was in the employ of an aged master, and was past the recruiting age, and reasonably expecting soon to receive his freedom,[1] might any day find that suddenly his master had been given permission to engage a *kabala* serf declared unfit for military life, and that therefore he, the original *kabala* serf, must now forgo his long-cherished wish for freedom, and also his rights under *kabala* law, and depart indefinitely into a military servitude which in no way differed from actual serfdom. Similarly drastic were Peter's dealings with members of the last-mentioned class, of the serf class. Long before his institution of souls-registration he assessed two categories of that class, the category of *zadvornie liudi* and the category of *dielovie liudi* [2] (categories based, in each case, upon agriculture, upon a *pozemelni nadiel*, or a plot for which a ground rent was paid), to rendition of *tiaglo* on the same footing as was held by bonded *krestiané*; but now he also brought it about that the two remaining forms of *kholopstvo*, in the shape of (*a*) the body servants of spiritual and lay masters, and (*b*) household serfs, agricultural and non-agricultural, rural and urban, became juridically and economically fused into a single, uniform mass, and, by Resolution of 19 January, 1723, placed on the souls-register along with bonded *krestiané*, and permanently made serfs to their masters. The result was complete disappearance of *kholopstvo*, of the one juridical status which hitherto had stood exempt from State obligations, and such a complete identification of that status with bonded *krestianstvo* as to weld from the two categories a single class of "*kriepostnie liudi*," or serfs wholly and absolutely controllable and exploitable by their masters.

Hence, the general effect of Peter's registration of souls was to complete the arbitrary simplification of the social composition for which his dispositions had always striven. For souls-registration took no account of existing rights: it compressed all the intermediate popular strata into two compact, fundamental statuses: into a status of State *krestiané*, and into a status of privately-owned serfs, *odnovortsi*, *chernososhnie*, Tartar persons, the "service husbandmen" of Yasazh and Siberia, and a category including pikemen, cavalrymen, dragoons, and the rest.[3] And the same

---

[1] Due to all *kabala* slaves, under *kabala* law, on the master's death.
[2] See vol. iii. p. 176.　　　　　　　　　　[3] See vol. iii. p. 223.

operation caused the area of serf-right to undergo a correspondingly great expansion. Yet did that right also undergo a change in juridical composition? Yes, it did, for a complete revolution occurred in this regard, even though a revolution more negative than positive, in that though abolition of *kholopstvo* as a non-taxpaying status did not carry with it abolition of *kholopstvo* bondage, but, rather, rendered that bondage specifically liable to payment of State imposts, it extinguished the limitations upon *kholopstvo* bondage which hitherto had stood uniform with the conditions ruling *kabala* and *zhiloe* (life) bondage, seeing that entry of a soul upon the souls-list of the landowner automatically entailed enserfment, and abrogated any existent contract, either of service *kabala* or of *zhilaia zapiss* (life contract). The revolution was one which had been maturing for seventy years before the first revision. We have seen how faultily the *Ulozhenie* expounded the nature of *krestianin* serfdom, and how loosely it distinguished between the serfdom of a *krestianin* and the servitude of a *kholop*[1] : and it was that code's laxity of definition when it instituted serf-right in 1649 that now rendered it possible for serf-right to come to such a pass. The *Ulozhenie* had bound the bonded *krestianin* to the person of the landowner in return for a plot of land—but not the *krestianin* to the land, nor yet to the proprietor of the land, save where agrarian relations happened to be concerned; whereas what the legislation of Peter's later days sought to develop in this connection was, not so much the limitations and the conditions of serf-right *qua* serf-right, as means for exploiting to the utmost serf labour in two particular aspects of that labour—in that labour's physical aspect, as concerned the Treasury, and in that labour's industrial aspect, as concerned the landowner. Hence, on the close of the *Ulozhenie* epoch we cease altogether to see before us the master and the agricultural hand as the two parties necessary to constitution of serf proprietorships, since then they become merely enserfer and enserfed, with the latter paying his owner (or that owner's steward), as representing the Government, a series of arbitrarily imposed dues, and the Government conferring upon the owner (or permitting him to assume) such powers of a police nature as eventually converted that owner into the Government's financial agent on his estate, and the fiscal assessor of his serf's labour, and a commissary (at least so far as his estate was concerned) for local preservation of law and order, and the prevention of "flights." Next we see *pomiestchiki* beginning humbly to represent to their districts' *dvorianin*-staffed local government bodies that they have been obliged to resort increasingly to stringent measures for recovery of runaway serfs, and legal looseness becoming so

---

[1] See vol. iii. p. 185.

prevalent in this respect as to open wide the door to arbitrary methods on the part of the stronger side, and, after the close of the *Ulozhenie* period, to the occurrence of a dual change in the serf status in proportion as the later industrial forms of that status became increasingly fused with the earlier juridical forms of *kholopstvo*, until the features hitherto distinguishing peasantdom from serfdom stood wholly obliterated. For example, landowners now contravened the *Ulozhenie* by taking *krestiané* into their household service, and also transferred sons of *krestiané* in the same way, on an undertaking that those sons should receive their freedom on the master's death, as obtained in the case of *kabalnie kholopi*, and removed *zadvornie liudi* from the *krestianstvo*, and converted them either into full *kholopi* or into *kabalnie kholopi*, and re-settled them on the land as was done with *kabala* serfs and "old service men," [1] but kept them liable, in the event of the estate changing hands, to depart thence, bag and baggage, with their master. Hence by the close of the seventeenth century the hitherto ring of agrarian relations had become permanently modified through a process of interfusion of the various forms of *kholopstvo*, and their conversion into a single serf status. The origin of the idea was the *de facto* position which practice had created through the lack of any authority to control that practice. And Peter's scheme of souls-registration conferred ultimate confirmation upon the idea. Another point in which the *Ulozhenie* was contravened was that *pomiestchiki* gradually assumed criminal (as well as civil) jurisdiction over their serfs, down to rights of discretionary punishment. Of this we gain an instance from some private documents dating from the close of the seventeenth century: which documents set forth how, for the treble offence, firstly, of stealing two *vedra* [2] of wine from a *prikastchik* [3] and secondly, of framing for some fellow serfs a petition to their master that, since their lack of land and general poverty had failed to protect them from being assessed to an *obrok* (tithe) "over and above our strength," they might forthwith be assigned to another *pomiestchik*, and thirdly, of adding to that petition a statement on the framer's own part that he considered himself bound to no master or set of masters in the world at all, the owner of the offender adjudged "him, thus guilty, to be beaten with the *knut* so mercilessly as scarce to leave aught of breath in his body." True, the *krestianin* commune, or *obstchina*, continued to remain in existence, but only for the purpose of reinforcing the *pomiestchik's* authority in carrying out his inquisitions,[4] since thereby he could with the more assurance issue the

[1] Freeholders akin to *odnodvortsi*, but charged principally with duties of a military character.

[2] Approximately, two gallons.   [3] Estate steward.

[4] That is to say, informal trials of his serfs.

stereotyped command, "Let all the *krestiané* be questioned," and proceed to pronounce sentence as the enquiry might result. Naturally, as Peter's reign approached its close such an unchecked growth of seigniorial authority led more than one thinker to conceive that that growth called for legislative control, and Pososhkov's was not the only brain in which an aroused recognition of the fact ripened to a clear and assured conviction. Yet it is interesting to note that though Pososhkov himself hailed from the peasantry, he believed peasant enserfment to be only a passing and temporary evil. "Not for ever will the *pomiestchik* possess the *krestianin*," he wrote. "He will not possess him for ever in that the true lord of the *krestianin* is the Autocrat of All Russia. Verily will these our other lords who now have him in their keeping hold him for a season only." So by then the more thinking portion of the peasant community, the portion whose literary spokesman Pososhkov was, evidently had awakened to a glimmering, if not to an actually flaming, apprehension of the fact that the *pomiestchik's* authority was not the chattel right of a proprietor over his beast of burden, but a trust from the State of which the State could at any time deprive him as much as it could retire a superannuated or a redundant *chinovnik*. Much else had Pososhkov to say about the highhandedness of masters in their disposal of their peasants' labour and property, and frequently did he call for legislation "for disposition of the rates at which the *pomiestchik* shall take of his peasantry either an *obrok* or aught else, and of the number of days in the week on which the *krestianin* need work for his master." In the same connection he suggested the holding of a general convention "both of our eminent lords and of the smaller *dvoriané*," in order that the two parties might consult together on the subjects of masters' inquisitions and the *krestianin's* amount of *sdielie* or *barstchina*, and that the *krestianin* might be enabled to feel that his rate of assessment emanated "from a common council, or from a proclamation from his Majesty," instead of from the *pomiestchik* alone. Wherefore what we see in this peasant writer's scheme is, in reality, a sort of prevision of the provincial *dvorianin* committees which did indeed come to be convoked for amelioration of the peasant's lot, but only 130 years after Pososhkov had laid aside his pen. But this scribe of the people carried his scheme further yet: he proposed to effect a complete separation of the *krestianin's* plot of land from the *pomiestchik's* estate, and to cease to regard that plot as belonging to the *pomiestchik* at all, and then, "through dispositions of *ukazi*," to compound a system of *pomiestchik-krestianin* relations which remind us to a certain extent of the *Polozhenie's* [1] clauses on temporarily bonded *krestiané*. And additional evidence that the

---

[1] The Act of Emancipation of 1861. See vol. ii. p. 140.

idea of untying the knot of serfdom was now really fermenting amongst the people has come down to us in the shape of a late-Petrine foreign item to the effect that, though frequently the Tsar was urged to abolish serfdom, and to stimulate and encourage his subjects with a grant of a moderate measure of freedom all round, he knew too well the rude nature of his people, and their invincible reluctance to work save under compulsion, to do so. Yet whilst he continued to support a system that was unsound, this does not mean that he failed to realise its unsoundness. The *Ulozhenie* of 1649 had left bonded *krestiané* and *kholopi* at their masters' disposal apart from those masters' land, and, of course, such a process had led also to a process of disintegration of peasant families—at first only in exceptional cases, but, later, as a general rule, or, at all events, as a general custom; and at last even Peter took alarm at the fact of serfs being bought and sold like cattle ("Nowhere else in all the world may there be seen such a trafficking in men, and it doth stir up much outcry,") and in 1721 instructed the Senate to see "that these sellings of men be estopped, or, if such estoppage be not possible in whole, then that they be made but by whole families or whole households rather than singly." Nevertheless this *ukaz* was not put forward as an absolute, peremptory ordinance: merely it was meant to be a hint to the Commission that was then sitting to compose "such a new *Ulozhenie* as in the end may seem good unto my Lords Senators." The truth is that even the Autocrat was not precisely certain as to the extent of his powers, and, in particular, was doubtful how much he could do, in this connection, in the face of the opposition manifested by the class which, more than any other section of the landowning corporation, engaged in the retail serf trade —namely, the class of petty *shliachtichi*. And as he had, rather earlier, and for the same reason, confirmed a Senatorial decree permitting *kholopi* who might volunteer for military service to take with them thither their wives, and also any of their children below the age of twelve, but prescribing that any children of an older age should be left behind in serfdom, it is clear that, in his view, the serf status called for consideration solely from the physical standpoint, and not at all from the equitable, and that his first and foremost preoccupation, throughout, was the Treasury's interest. Up to his time the Government and the *pomiestchik* owned the serf village and its denizens between them—owned it, as it were, *cherezpolosno,* or "in strips," [1] with the Government recognising the utility of the bonded *krestianin* and the agricultural *kholop* merely as individuals liable to payment of taxes through their *pomiestchik,* through the individual whom the Government at the same time authorised to act as its local police agent, and similarly leaving the

---

[1] A term derived from the old Russian system of rotation in husbandry.

non-taxpaying *dvorovie*, or household serfs, to the *pomiestchik's* care so long
as he retained them in that form of bondage: but when Peter arrived he
substituted for this "in strips" possession of the serf village a system of
joint tenure by the two parties, and thereby initiated a process of gradual
disappearance both of the more ancient forms of serf bondage and of the
conditions by which those forms had hitherto stood differentiated, until
there remained, as the residue, only an assortment of industrial categories
to which the landowner could assign a serf at pleasure so long only as the
landowner acknowledged this vast extension of his seigniorial powers by
allowing the Government to retain a partial lien upon the labour of his non-
taxpaying serfs. And the eventual outcome was what? Did the *kholop*
become a bonded *krestianin*, or did the bonded *krestianin* become a *kholop*?
Well, neither happened. What happened was what such circumstances have
always brought about in the history of the Russian *otchina* and the Russian
pomiestie: namely, that Peter's new combination of bondage relations, added
to fusion of the seignioral *krestianin* with the *kholop* and the member of the
volnitza, gave rise to an entirely new form of bondage status to the collective
form which subsequently became known as "*kriepostnie liudi*," or "bonded
men," a form in which the serf was both permanently and hereditarily bound
to his master as the earlier full *kholop* had been, through the same liability
to pay State taxes as formerly had belonged to the bonded *krestianin*.

In this regard, therefore, Peter's reforms not only re-converted Russia
into a land of servitude, but made of her more than ever a slave State.
The point whence his reforms really derived their development was the old
Russian right of *obilnoe kholopstvo* (the full slavery of the *Russkaia Pravda*),
a right closely akin to the ancient Greco-Roman bondage, but worked out
into less harsh, as well as more regularly circumstanced, forms: and, with
the seigniorial licence accorded to landowners during the seventeenth century,
and born of the weakness, or the class-selfishness, of the new dynasty, that
right tended ever more and more to aggravate the people's impoverishment,
and so to utilise industrial contracts as to obliterate any existent conditions
of bondage forms which masters found irksome, and, lastly, to enserf the
hitherto free *krestiané* almost wholesale. All of which tendencies were harmful
to the State. Yet to attack those tendencies, or, at all events, to attack them
directly, Peter's legislation did nothing at all. Rather, it forced further
categories of free persons into bondage, and, by approximating every form
of bondage to the full "slavery" of earlier times, threw back the community
to the Greco-Roman-Medieval-Russian norm: "Slavery ever is whole, and
indivisible. Never does the condition of a slave admit of a difference, and
never can he be said to be either more of a slave or less." True, Peter made

the amends of partially braking serf-right with a tax-liability laid upon the master—with a condition that, whilst the master's every male *kholop* was to render a State due, it was the master that was to be responsible for the due's forthcoming; but all the time Peter had in his mind, not popular freedom, but Treasury advantage, and was directing his endeavours, not to creation of citizens, but to acquisition of taxpayers. Perhaps the best that can be said of him is that, though his process of souls-registration militated against both equity and law, it brought in to its originator over 100,000 new furnishers of State revenue, and that, for all the non-rationality of the process, it worked considerable benefit to the rural industry of its day. For up to that day direct taxes like the *socha* tax [1] and its successor, the *dvor*, or homestead, tax (both of which had, fundamentally, been taxes upon land) had forced *krestiané* and landowners alike to curtail their taxable tillage, and to recoup themselves for the loss by practising tricks upon the Treasury, and doing so to such an extent that, as we have seen, an enormous sixteenth- and seventeenth-century shrinkage of *krestianin* plots took place; and though the Governments of the new dynasty sought to arrest the curtailment by altogether abolishing per *socha* taxation, and substituting for it taxation per *dvor*, landowners and *krestiané* still declined to increase their tillage areas, or, rather, took to curtailing their homesteads as well, and then cramming into them the greatest possible number of inmates, or else to burning them down until only the gateposts and the partition walls were left—the proportion of local burnings-down varying from three-fourths to ten-elevenths —and so injuring in equal degrees rural industry and the Treasury's revenue sources. But when the Government's taxation became transferred to souls, that is to say, to labour, and to the forces of labour, direct, all further incentive to curtailment of taxable tillage disappeared, since now it became the case that the *krestianin* had to pay the single round sum of seventy *kopaki* whether he ploughed two *desiatini* or four. The extent to which this measure succeeded is plain from the ensuing century's record of the fortunes of Russia's rural industry, since, as evidence of what the country had then come partially, if not wholly, to owe to Peter's souls-tax, we perceive that whereas, when the tax had been running for a little while only, Pososhkov's dream of an ideal State was limited to a State whose peasant homesteads ploughed no more than six *desiatini* on a three-strip rotation (that is to say, one-and-a-half *desiatini* per soul of the average four-souled peasant *dvor*), the close of Pososhkov's, the eighteenth century, would have made plots of that extent look comparatively small, since the average peasant homestead had then come to plough ten *desiatini*, or more. Wherefore against the fact that early

[1] See vol. ii. p. 249, and vol. iii. p. 225, et seq.

Russia's direct land taxation tended to divorce peasant labour from the soil we may set the fact that Peter's legislation, by transferring that taxation to souls, effected a re-attachment of that labour, and a re-attachment growing ever closer and closer. Indeed, it is not too much to say that one effect of the soul-tax—if not of the tax itself, at all events of the tax's help— was to cause the lands of eighteenth-century Russia to become tilled as they had never been tilled before, and that the principal significance of the tax lies in the fact that, though not a legal revolution, it brought about one, and a profound one, in the popular industry of its day. True, that was a result which the *ukaz* of ordination did not foresee; but at least it shows that, dense though Peter's juridical purview was, that purview was not so dense as wholly to cloud his juridical instinct—or that, if it did cloud it, fate, which so often rounds off even the most hazardous of legislative experiments, rescued him from his dilemma.

CHAPTER VI

Commerce and industry—The plan and scope of Peter's efforts on their behalf—Invitations to foreign artists and craftsmen—Dispatch abroad of Russian workmen—Propaganda through legislative means—Industrial companies, loans, subsidies, and exemptions—Inducements to engage in trade—Industrial failures and successes—Commerce, and means of communication.

WE have seen that there resulted from souls-registration, firstly, a multitude of new taxpayers, and, secondly, an increased aggregate of tax-paying labour. Similarly did Peter's application of measures to industry and commerce aim at increasing both the quantity and the output of tax-paying labour. And as soon as the Swedish War was over he let these measures, this department of reform, preoccupy him to the exclusion of all else. He did this the more because it was a department of reform peculiarly consorting with his bent and character. And his efforts in the direction of industry proved as effective as his military efforts had been—they displayed a like clarity of vision, a like breadth of view, a like fertility of resource, and a like tirelessness of energy, and proved that Peter was a true successor of the old hereditary Tsar-proprietors who had known so well how to acquire and to enlarge an empire, and enabled him to develop into a master economist pre-eminently capable, first of all of creating new financial resources, and then of introducing those resources into the people's daily round of toil. The only thing against him was that his forerunners had bequeathed to him little beyond theories and principles for the purpose, and that therefore he had to invent his own ways and means.

Already during the seventeenth century certain of the leading political intellects of Moscow had had dormant in them, and waiting to bear fruit, an idea that there were defects in the State's fiscal system, and that those defects were militating against the State's welfare. The system in question was one strictly of exaction of imposts in proportion to the State's needs, and therefore of laying burdens upon the popular labour without at the same time helping that labour to become more productive. But now Peter proceeded to base an economic policy upon the idea that, once he could effect an increase in production, a corresponding increase of Treasury resources would follow as a matter of course. In other words, he now set himself to accomplish the dual task (1) of furnishing the popular labour with improved technique and improved instruments of production, and (2) of introducing that labour to industries calculated to develop the country's hitherto almost untouched natural wealth. And in the process he extended this dual task to well-nigh every branch of the people's industry and during its performance ran a penetrating eye over every province of production, no matter how insignificant, but most of all over agriculture, every department of which he tackled, from stock-breeding and the culture of silkworms to horticulture, vine culture, and the management of fisheries. First and foremost, however, he worked to bring about an increase in his country's manufactures and technical industries, and to render its mineral resources effective, in that he knew these last to be vital towards the conduct of war. Accordingly, there was no useful technical process, however modest, that he overlooked—always he would halt in his stride to enquire into its details. Thus, there is a story that, when he was visiting a French village during his second foreign tour, and saw a priest working in his garden, he, after questioning the curé at length, said to his staff: "I too must constrain my slothful priests thus to labour in gardens and fields, that they may win both their daily bread and a better chance of the future life." And when he came to study Western Europe in detail he stood fascinated with the industrial progress which had been made there, and took minute note of the manufactures and handicrafts practised in such industrial centres as Amsterdam, Paris, and London, and eventually recorded his impressions of what he had seen. He paid this first visit to Western Europe at a time when both the State and the popular industry of that quarter were ruled by a mercantile system based upon the notion that, if a nation wishes to avoid impoverishment, it must itself produce all that it requires, and not rely upon foreign labour for the purpose, and, for amassment of wealth, export as much, and import as little, as possible. And, on thinking out all that he had observed in Western Europe, Peter decided to make this theory his own, and to do his utmost towards encouraging home production. To the same idea his devoted admirer Pososhkov gave able expression when he wrote that, though the first few years from the adoption of the system were bound to see the home-made article cost more than the imported, the former would need but to gain a footing for the original outlay to become redeemed. Also, in this financial policy Peter had two prime beliefs behind him: and the two beliefs in question were (1) that Russia was in no way inferior to, but, on the contrary, superior to, the rest of the world in untouched and undiscovered natural resources, and (2) that only the State could properly develop those resources, and that it must do so with the help of compulsion.

He embodied those beliefs in more than one *ukaz*. For example, he wrote: "Truly doth this Our State of Russia abound over many another land, so blessed is it with metals and minerals which, though not yet sought with diligence, are nevertheless meet for use." Whence Peter's two supreme objects in his popular-industrial policy were (1) establishment of such utilitarian industries as silk-weaving and the manufacture of wine, and (2) discovery and development of new and hitherto untouched excisable articles. Which things, he said, he sought "to the end that the blessings of God lie not vainly in the earth." Verily he was an extremely careful steward, for he peered into every item, and stimulated labour upon every virgin resource, and appraised the value of each resource, and, if need be, protected it from fraudulent manipulation and senseless exhaustion. Particularly did he keep an eye upon the country's shipbuilding timber, for he knew all too well the recklessness with which Russians will squander wood; whilst equally personal was his attention to the getting of coal and peat and charcoal, and to the consideration of uses to which their waste products could be put— as when he ordered all billets and odd pieces from the shipping yards to be turned into axletrees, or burnt for the sake of their potash: a petty instinct for saving which reminds us of Ivan III. on the occasion when that monarch, after ordering some sheep to be sent for a foreign ambassador's entertainment, commanded that their fleeces should duly be preserved and returned. In fact, Peter's eagerness to conserve all timber suitable for the construction of ships led him even to cut across a very common popular desire, a desire never before opposed either by the law or by religious piety, the desire to be put to rest, after death, in a coffin made of a single-piece block of oak or pine. And to this end he sent his *Ober-Waldmeister*, his Chief Superintendent of Woods and Forests (a subordinate department of the Admiralty), an "Instruction" that from the date of its receipt single-block coffins were to be constructed exclusively of red fir, birch, or alder, save that pine might still continue to be employed if the coffins fashioned from it were not whole-block, but made up of clamped-together strips. Thus did Peter strive to awaken the country's slumbering forces. And he took the more care to see personally to every detail because he distrusted both voluntary and private enterprise, and knew that in the industrial field especially reliance upon those agencies would spell little or no progress in the face of the Russian reluctance to adopt anything novel without official compulsion. Once he wrote: "Howsoever a work be good and necessary, yet will our people not perform the same, unless constrained thereto, if also the work be new." The same reason led him to bid his College of Manufactures transact business with lessees of State factories "both through the method of propounding matters unto them and with a strengthening of the same with instructions, implements, and the like," and also to support industrial *entrepreneurs* in such a manner that, "having thus beheld the favour of the Tsar, they shall, no matter of what rank and sort, bind themselves, with all goodwill, into companies for their greater security." For Peter habitually treated his people like children whom he knew would at first refuse to sit down to the hornbook, and then sulk when compelled to do so, and, finally, thank their tutor for his insistence. And in 1723, looking back over thirty years of activity, Peter soliloquises: "What though everywhere were things done for a while with illwill, yet may there be heard certain thanksgivings of to-day for much whence fruit hath proceeded." Wherefore his general method of development of Russian industry was to reinforce with results of his observation of the industrial processes of Western Europe his personal reflections and experiments. Let me briefly enumerate his means to the desired end.

I. *Invitations to foreign craftsmen and manufacturers.* In the year 1698 Russia began to be visited by a host of artists, craftsmen, and skilled workers contracted into the service of Moscow. In Amsterdam alone Peter engaged a thousand; and everywhere he charged his Foreign Residents to secure alien artificers for employment in Russia, so that in 1702 Germany, in particular, was set ringing from end to end with invitations to local capitalists and manufacturers and artisans to proceed to Muscovy on highly advantageous terms. In fact, a wholesale invasion of the country by skilled industrial and professional foreigners set in, for such experts were only too glad to accept the conditions offered, and never failed to find that punctilious fulfilment followed upon the Russian Government's promises. Especially did Peter value French craftsmen and trade hands, artists who had been famous from the days of Colbert [1] onwards: and inspection of the famous Gobelin factory at Paris led him so greatly to fancy its tapestry that on his return home he did his best to establish a similar institution in St. Petersburg. But though he invited the necessary Parisian craftsmen to the Russian capital, and also the famous architect Leblanc, whom he called "mine absolute marvel," and dowered with a splendid mansion on a three-years lease, with an annual salary of 5000 (40,000) roubles, and with a five-years licence for free travel, goods and chattels included, within the Russian Empire, the new tapestry had scarcely achieved establishment before lack of the proper sort of wool for such fabrics became apparent, and the enterprise had to close down. But always at this period Peter paid more attention to foreign artists than he did to his country's own, and an "Instruction" to the College

---

[1] Jean Baptiste Colbert (1619–83), Minister to Louis XIV., and famous for his reform of French industry, legal administration and finance.

of Manufactures enjoins that, should a foreign artist desire to leave Russia before the expiry of his contract, he should be safeguarded against all hindrance or molestation whilst doing so, and that if he should show any sign of displeasure, or, still worse, open dissatisfaction, he should be compensated, and the responsible party or parties sternly punished. At the same time, privileges of the sort were always granted on the condition that "these same foreign artists or craftsmen likewise do instruct our Russian folk, and without concealment, and as best may be befitting."

II. *Dispatch of Russian subjects for foreign study of handicrafts.* During Peter's reign every European industrial town of any importance remained thronged with bands of Russian students for whose instruction the Russian Government paid generous terms. As regards the students for nautical matters, they went first to Holland to be trained, and then moved on to Turkey, the Indies, and other countries, until, to quote Kurakin, "they lay scattered the earth over"; whilst, in the matter of industry, there was not a quarter of Europe not visited by Russian subjects, nor an art, nor a handicraft, not studied there—from "the philosophical sciences and the doctoral" to the trade of the potter, the mysteries of the *salon* decorator, and the calling of the maker of bedsteads. But unfortunately, though Peter paid this attention to technical instruction, he engaged for the home instruction of his Russian youth a class of foreign preceptor who performed his duties so grudgingly, and observed his contract with such negligence, that not infrequently his pupils "were left with their learning unfinished." Wherefore a suspicion arose that, before leaving home, professors of the sort swore to their compatriots that that should in very truth be how they would perform their duties when once they had reached Russian soil: and the result was that at last Peter had to bid his College of Manufactures change the system, and substitute for it exclusively a system of dispatching handicraft students abroad, subsidising them with Government funds, and granting their families privileges in proportion to the students' educational progress.

III. *Propaganda by means of legislation.* In those times a result of State tutelage added to ecclesiastico-pastoral ministration was to nourish in the Russian citizen a dual conscience: a public conscience, a conscience designed for display before its owner's fellow citizens, and a private conscience, a conscience designed exclusively for its owner's, and his home circle's, contemplation. Of which two consciences, the former asserted the individual's personal dignity and honour, whilst the latter was responsible for all else so long as once, or more often, a year it received priestly shrift. Unfortunately, the duality in question acted as a prime hindrance to industrial progress. In those days the urban-industrial-commercial class had to support a heavy burden of taxation assessed "according unto tradings and under-takings"—that class had, besides paying a direct duty upon their urban resi-dences and business premises, to render a five per cent. toll upon their turn-over, whilst also they stood charged with the performance of certain at once honorary and responsible Treasury services. Moreover the *Ulozhenie* had caused every person who pursued an industrial calling in an urban area to belong to some urban-tax-paying union for the purpose of meeting the town's taxes, whereas it had left such of the upper classes and institutions as sena-tors, the clergy, and the richer monasteries free to engage in trade without paying a toll at all, and so further to restrict a market already hampered at once with State trading and with impoverishment of the rural population. Yet, though the privileged dignitaries were not ashamed of being industrially employed, they were yet too proud to become industriously efficient, and, through a lack of the civic sense, despised and depreciated their humbler mercantile colleagues, and dubbed them "the base populace," and accused them of seeking to better their sorry circumstances with such tricks as the use of false scales and measures. But although we find foreign observers of the day declaring that the roguery of Muscovite merchants was so proverbial as to be expressible only by the formula, "Cheat not, and thou wilt not sell," the *Zemskie Sobori* of the seventeenth century, and especially the *Zemski Sobor* of 1642, and its accompanying conferences between the corporate classes and the Government, have shown us that at that time the industrial-commercial stratum constituted, through its elected representa-tives, the one social section evincing signs of the political sense, the one social section grasping the commonweal idea, the one social section admitting entry to the civic instinct. It is not without justification that the writings of Pososhkov, a peasant-industrial who had already learnt much that lay hidden from his social superiors, voice a note of professional irritation that *dvoriané*, *boyaré*, boyaral *dvorovie*, military officers, church servers, Govern-ment clerks, common soldiers, and *krestiané* should one and all of them be able to engage in business toll-free, and so take the bread out of the mouths of the toll-crushed merchant proper. And another obstacle to the genuine Russian trader was that he had to compete with an astute, well-organised body of immigrant foreign traders whom the corrupt authorities invariably protected at the native's expense. "It is high time," incisively remarks Pososhkov of certain senatorial and other highly-placed traffickers, "that such fellows did lay aside their ancient arrogance. They had done better to scorn us at the season when our Monarch himself did not trade, as now, but the *boyaré* still ruled all things!" And, further: "Behold what foreigners do come into Russia, and then thrust upon those who may be in authority first one gift of one hundred roubles, and thereafter another gift, in order that with a few hundreds of roubles they may win for themselves a profit of roubles to half a million! Yea, and this is because our *boyaré* do appraise us merchants at but an eggshell, and would barter us all for a groat!" In these words we see a passage that was the more likely to please Peter (for whom the work as a whole was written) in that he himself preached tirelessly the "honour-ableness" of labour, and declared that engagement in industrial and artisan pursuits did the State good service, and proclaimed by *ukazi* that, so far from a man being degraded by such pursuits, they advantaged both the Empire and himself to a degree equal to State employ or military skill, and so merited equal respect. Again, many a *dvorianin* must have frowned as he perused the *Ukaz* on Sole Succession, and read in it that "cadets" (younger sons in receipt of no portion of their deceased father's property) were to cease to remain idle, but "seek their bread either through service, or through teaching, or through a trade, and the like," and that such action on their part should be guarded against being thrown in the teeth of their families and themselves, whether verbally or in writing. Indeed, a private list of Peter's, a list of legislative schemes and projects which he had in con-templation, shows us that once he sent a mission to England to study even the humble crafts of bootmaking and whitesmithery. Also, in 1703, shortly after the founding of St. Petersburg, he had a workhouse for vagrants and unemployed built in Moscow, and specified the trades to be carried on there, and added to the ordinance a clause that illegitimate children similarly were to be taught crafts, and that institutions were to be erected for the purpose —an ordinance showing that I. I. Betski, the statesman of Catherine II., was not the first to conceive a scheme for compounding the inmates of foundling hospitals into an intermediate social status, or to think of making the innocent offspring of frailty the basis of a future *bourgeoisie*. In short, the then level of Russian tastes and ideas called for much strength of mind and civic temerity on the part of the Soldier-Artisan-Autocrat, for his legis-lative acts had to give shape to middle-class conceptions hitherto looked down upon by Russian lawmakers, and to make it clear that every pru-dently conceived and boldly carried out industrial enterprise did a service to the State by increasing the aggregate of utilitarian labour, and swelling the amount of subsistence available for the indigent. For Peter's fiscal instinct divined unerringly the true basis of civic, public life; and though posthumously, during Catherine II.'s philosophical reign, he incurred cen-sure at the hands of certain refined pedants of the type of Prince Dashkov for having devoted so much of his time to artisan and commercial and in-dustrial "trifles," he would have been accorded more indulgence by the

Prince if the latter had remembered that Peter had had to send abroad for instructors to teach his Russian boors their every handicraft, from ship-building to the making of besoms, for the reason that though the Russian clergy had been curing souls for the past seven hundred years, it had never occurred to them, during all that time, to build a single cheap and easily accessible rural school, but only institutes for teaching ikonography which scarcely deserved to be called schools at all, but turned out painters of a sort which led Pososhkov to observe that "they are fellows who inscribe only eyes and a mouth where a whole head should be, and, having fixed divers other points, conceive that they have made an image!"

IV. *Industrial companies, loans, subsidies and exemptions.* Eventually Peter's commercial-industrial efforts towards teaching his upper classes not to abhor industry and the workers of industry bore fruit, for we begin to see men of weight and eminence, and bureaucratic magnates, associating with plain traders as contractors, manufacturers, and proprietors of work-shops. And the supremely potent spur towards furthering industrial enter-prise of which Peter made use was his system of exemptions, fixed subsidies, and loans, as a system calculated at once to bring Russian industry into harmony with his administrative schemes and to utilise what he had learnt from inspection of Western European industrial methods and customs to-wards teaching capitalists to unite their funds, and bind themselves into joint-stock companies. But even before Peter's day ancient Russia had evolved certain forms of industrial combination, for, to take one example, merchants of the larger sort had established the form known as the *torgovi dom*, or trading-house, as a commercial association of three or more "portion-less" (landless through parental testament) kinsmen in whom usually there were included either a father and his sons or an elder brother and that brother's brethren or nephews, on a basis of the concern being not a capitalist partnership, nor yet a joint agency, but an enterprise which its senior member operated with the aid of a non-divisible sum of family capital, and for which he stood responsible to the Government both for all the partners ("trading sons," "brethren," or "nephews," as the case might be) in the concern and for any *prikazchiki*, or overseers, in its employ. An instance of such a house is found at the close of the sixteenth century, in the shape of the Brothers Stroganov, salt boilers, who were reckoned to have at their command a working capital of 300,000 (15,000,000) roubles; whilst an equally well-known late seventeenth century establishment of the kind was the house of Bazhanin, which had shipbuilding wharves at Archangel and on the Northern Dvina. Again, we encounter, during the same century, the *skladstvo*, which was a business union for, primarily, the disposal of commodities, and, secondarily, their production, and a representative member of which paid periodical visits to local markets, and there collected goods from the goods' producers, and sold them along with those of the *skladstvo* itself, on an agreed commission, as bailee. A particularly strenuous advocate of the introduction of the *skladstvo* was Ordin-Nastchokin, since he considered that smaller traders must always combine with larger if Russian merchandise was to maintain a continuously high level of export prices. Thus the *torgovi dom*, or trading-house, was based upon kinship, and concerns operating under the *skladstvo* system were based upon credit. To *arteli*, the old-established combinations of labour and capital, we need not here refer since Peter, after considering them, left them to their own devices, for the probable reason that, whatever other merits they might possess, he deemed them imperfect instruments for the especial purpose of the fight against foreign commercial-industrial competition. So on 27 October, 1699, simultaneously with removal of the *posadskie*, or urban-taxpaying dwellers, from the jurisdiction of *voevodi*, and with general accordance of local self-government, an *ukaz* ordained that thenceforth all engagers in commerce were to transact business as business was transacted in the other States of Europe. That is to say, they were to do so as members of companies "holding amongst themselves a commission from a common council for the disposal of merchandise." This edict particularly alarmed the Dutch colony in Russia, which scented in it a challenge to that colony's market supremacy; and though the Resident for Holland sought to reassure his compatriots by recalling that the Russian merchant was notoriously bad at embarking upon a new enterprise, and declaring that the scheme would fail, Peter so utilised exemption-grants plus sheer compulsion as at least to succeed in setting the project upon its legs, and keeping it there. Always the concerns which he endowed with the most generous grants of tax-exemption were industrial companies designed to foster manufacturing and engineering enterprise; and to promote this end he would relieve founders of factories and workshops not only of Treasury and municipal dues, but also of other obligations, and accord licences to those founders' "portionless" sons and brothers and *prikazchiki* and craftsmen and craftsmen's pupils both to sell goods and to purchase material toll-free for given periods, and advance them non-returnable subsidies and non-interest-bearing loans. Again, he charged his College of Manufactures so to watch over the fortunes of company-run enterprises that, on the first sign of their declining, the College should be at hand to "assign them capital and aid." Another of Peter's devices to protect his industrial undertakings from foreign competition was organisation of such a system of import duties as should cause those duties to grow in proportion with the native production of a given article until, on the volume of the home manufacture of that article at length coming level with the volume of its foreign manufacture, the import duty upon the article should precisely balance the foreign article's costs of production. Also, even before the College of Manufactures was founded in 1719, industrial companies are seen receiving grants of legal jurisdiction over their employees in civic and labour matters, until those grants were compounded and transferred wholesale to the College itself, and the College granted jurisdiction in these matters over the masters as well. Moreover, Peter's solicitude for the industrial interests of his country led him even to the point of contravening his own *ukazi*. For example, although he was constant in his vituperation of the unfortunate *krestianin*, and enjoined his immediate restoration to his master if he should abscond, and ordained infliction of fines upon anyone who should harbour or receive him, an *ukaz* promulgated on 18 July, 1722, expressly forbade that factory hands should be given up in the same way, "even though they be fled serfs." Lastly, by *ukaz* of 18 January, 1721, Peter conceded owners of factories and workshops the hitherto exclusively *dvorianin* right of acquiring "villages" (lands settled with bonded *krestiané*), on condition that those "villages" were used for the benefit of the industrial establishments concerned, and that "inalienably those villages should pertain unto the said foundries." In other words, the merchant-manufacturer now acquired the *dvorianin* power of owning bonded working hands; and the fact that he came to be conceded such a privileged position alone shows how thoroughly his Sovereign believed the calling of the proprietor of a factory or a workshop to be a service to the State, or something more. Had this not been so, that Sovereign would never have allowed industrial establishments to harbour absconded serfs the property of service landowners, or have granted the peasant capitalist the *dvorianin* privilege of himself owning serfs and lands. Lastly, be it said that to a certain degree the Petrine factory, or workshop, succeeded the Russian monastery as the leading moral-administrative institution in the country. For in a whole series of *ukazi* we find one or another industrial establishment being designated as a place to which, for correctional purposes, "women and young maids in error" should be dispatched!

But although the old order of *boyaré* gave place to an order of dignitaries founded upon the "Table of Ranks," to an aristocracy based upon the furnace and the loom, how far did Peter attain the end aimed at by his national-industrial policy, the end of stimulating Russian commercial enterprise, and developing the country's untouched resources, until the home market should stand clear of foreign competition? That Peter and the more patriotically disposed of his contemporaries believed that end to be possible no doubt whatsoever exists. In particular had Pososhkov a profound conviction that though Russia would be able to get on without foreign-made goods, the foreigner would fail within ten years unless he could resort to Russian merchandise. "Wherefore doth it behove us the more to surpass foreigners, and make of them, as it were, our slaves." Yes, clearly that is why Peter urged both *dvoriané*, State officials, and ordinary merchants to band themselves together in industrial companies, so that even such men as the brilliant Menshikov (who once had sworn that he would pluck any trader by the beard) joined with some plain mercantile folk in forming a scheme for harvesting the White Sea's produce of cod, porpoise, and the rest. Yet though even the widest of social distinctions did not prevent men from pacing the industrial field together, a few prominent examples of their doing so must not lead us to exaggerate the industrial success achieved by the average "*interesent*" (the name given to a member of one of Peter's companies). For instance, although he hired some silk weavers from France in 1717, and then invited two *tsaredvortsi*, Vice-Chancellor Baron Shafirev and Privy Councillor Count Tolstoi, to join Prince Menshikov in organisation of a silk company based upon extensive privileges, and dowered with sufficient initial resources to enable its founders to arrange for a grandiose establishment, it was not long before there arose quarrels necessitating Menshikov's retirement from the directorate; and though to him there succeeded Grand-Admiral Apraxin, and the concern was accorded fresh exemptions, even to a right of duty-free importation of silken wares, the founders had eventually to make over the concern's assets to a group of private merchants for 20,000 roubles, and to abandon an enterprise which, whilst costing the Treasury an immense sum, and leading to a squandering of the whole of its initiators' personal investments, achieved such failure to attain its designed object as not to have brought about the establishment of a single factory. The end was that Peter had to desist from pampering his beloved factories with exemptions, to cut them clear of Western European models, to side-track them from the line of free enterprise, and to reshape them on distinctively Muscovite lines. For the Russian spirit of venture had failed to meet his expectations: he had found that, instead of his *ukazi* peremptorily commanding capitalists to build factories, and form companies, and assemble shareholders and directors, those *ukazi* must issue polite invitations to do so. Hence, from now onwards he made it his rule to build factories and workshops only at the Treasury's expense, and then either to lease them to companies on terms of exemption or to have them compulsorily managed by *entrepreneurs*. Thus, in 1712 the Treasury established, by his orders, some cloth factories, and let them out to a group of traders whom he had forcibly collected into an association for the purpose. "And should the same not be willing to trade, then let things be done under a bond, yet with but moderate takings of yearly moneys from the factories,[1] to the end that the men therein may trade the more willingly." Thus the establishment of a new factory or the formation of a new company came to represent a capital act of State service, and a manufacturer or a trading company to approximate to a State institution. Yet Peter still utilised the old system as well, with its conditions overhauled and adjusted to suit the Treasury's new requirements. Hitherto the Treasury had exploited the State's customs and excise, as revenue-producing articles, either by submitting them to open auction or by delegating the collection of them to covenanted agents; but now, seeing that new sources of production had come into being, and these were articles of revenue of a kind termed by the *ukaz* on companies "things meet to restore the ingatherings of Our Treasury," and called for revised methods of exploitation, Peter introduced into his factories and companies a combination of compulsory enterprise with productive monopoly. Unfortunately, the fact that such nourishment of industry by the Treasury entailed, in addition, Governmental interference, and therefore Governmental regulations and irritating administrative supervision and a great display of official business incompetence, led to volunteers showing a reluctance to come forward. Moreover, industrial progress met with another obstacle in a similar (and not unnatural) unwillingness to take risks on the part of Russian capital in general—lack of rights at the bottom and excessive power at the top having rendered it so timid that the possessors of it shrank from putting their savings into circulation, and both *krestiané* and industrial hands buried their nest-eggs in the ground rather than disclose them to a master's eye, or declare them to a Government reaper of taxes and excise, whilst the *dvoriané*, adhering to their usual rule of shearing their serfs like sheep, stored in coffers gold which, otherwise, they might just as well have drawn from the more lucrative sources offered it by Peter. In fact, some of the more knowing members of the *dvorianstvo* even sent hoards to be banked in London, Venice, and Amsterdam; and in the first-named city Menshikov alone is said to have had 1,000,000 roubles lying on deposit. It goes without saying that, as a result, the nation's industry lost a huge amount of working-capital. Also, this widespread withholding of capital from its proper function of growth through circulation caused the Government to regard all capital withheld as parasitical, to treat it as a Treasury despoiler in respect of the Treasury's lawful profits of "tenth money" (a toll of five per cent. upon all

---

[1] That is to say, with the Treasury taking only a moderate proportion of the annual profits.

monetary circulation), to prosecute it as contraband, and to declare it subject to police forfeiture. Soon after the beginning of the Northern War an *ukaz* proclaimed that, should any person conceal money, and another person inform against him, and so lead to the money's recovery, that informant should receive one-third of the money, and the State the remainder, and that the Government Department or Departments concerned might require any members of the commercial-industrial community to declare their annual income and their current resources, and assess those two assets, and add them to the general rendition of taxes; and in this manner layings of information with regard to hoardings came to be the Government's principal source of financial control, and, as such, to be much valued. In a village on the Oka named Diedinovo lived some brothers named Shustov—law-abiding men, seemingly, and men who had never engaged in industry, but subsisted solely upon a stock of private means annually "declared" by them at two or three hundred roubles. But in 1704 a knavish merchant went and told the Government that the brothers, in reality, were wealthy folk to whom their forebears had bequeathed a fortune, and that, instead of increasing that fortune, they were spending it upon riotous living: and, sure enough, when Moscow instituted a search a vacant room in the house was found to contain, squeezed between the rafters and the ceiling, ducats and Chinese gold to a weight of 4 *pudi*, 13 *funti*,[1] and silver to a weight of 106 *pudi*.[2] Wherefore, translating this bulk of gold and silver into Petrine currency, and from Petrine into modern, we shall see that the Shustov brothers had inherited a sum of capital amounting to the equivalent of 700,000 modern roubles! And, naturally, the Government confiscated it, on the ground that it had not been lawfully declared. Thus at one time we see capital intimidated, through the prevailing lack of orderliness, from performing the function which the Reformer had assigned it, and at other times we see capital prepared to perform its function, but failing to so do through inability or an act of negligence on the Reformer's part. Once, before a campaign, he ordered a quantity of cavalry saddlery and other stores, enough completely to fill two large warehouses in Novgorod; yet eventually the whole had to go to waste for want of an *ukaz* as to its disposal, and, when thoroughly mouldy and rotten, to be cleared out with pitchforks! And in 1717, in the same way, some oaken timber which he ordered to be conveyed to the Baltic Fleet *via* St. Petersburg and the Vishnii-Volochok water system (with beams of it, in some cases, worth, reputedly, a hundred roubles apiece) was left to toss about the shores and islands of Lake Ladoga until it had become half-buried in the sand, all because the original orders had failed

---

[1] About 155 lb. avoirdupois.   [2] About 3810 lb. avoirdupois, or 1·07 tons.

to include an instruction that Peter's jaded memory should be jogged when the time for the timber's actual disposal should arrive, and he had, in the meanwhile, been touring Germany, Denmark, and France in an endeavour to settle the Mecklenburg affair. Yet though these things show us the reverse side of the medal, it is the fact that invariably a large scheme of building leaves much litter behind it; and though much of what was good in Peter's hastily conceived schemes ran to waste, not a few of the more impressionable and superficial observers of his national-industrial undertakings rejoiced at the wastage, since they desired to see Russia become one huge workshop, and her terrestrial bowels everywhere denuded of their latent riches to the sound of axe and hammer, and foreign professors and master-craftsmen invited to come thither with their books and tools and machinery, and Russia's monarch acting as supervisor of it all; whilst even of foreign observers there were not a few who, though glancing askance at Peter's industrial achievements, were glad to acknowledge that, for all the failure of certain productional enterprises, others had come not only to satisfy the home demand for sail-cloth, iron, and the like, but also to supply some of the foreign markets for those articles. In all, Peter left behind him 233 factories and foundries devoted to industry. The department interesting him beyond all others was the department of production of commodities connected with military clothing—of linen, broadcloth, and ordinary cloth; yet though in 1712 he ordered his textile factories to be organised with such efficiency that within five years from that date it should no longer be necessary "to buy even one uniform from the foreigner," it was not until he was dead that that result came to be attained. What really made the most progress in this regard was the metallurgical branch of the country's industry, since eventually four provinces, the provinces of Tula, Olonetz, the Urals, and St. Petersburg, came each of them to have its own large group of metal works. Of these four provinces, the two first-named had seen mining operations first begun within their borders during Alexis' reign; but since that time the operations had declined, and Peter now revived them, whilst, for the smelting of the ore, two iron-masters named Balashev and Nikita Demidov not only leased foundries from the Government, but also established private ones of their own. Also there arose in Tula a Government arms factory, a huge arsenal, and more than one township solely for the benefit of the smiths and other hands employed. Again, near Olonetz, on the margin of Lake Onega, an iron-smelting and iron-casting concern developed, by 1703, into a township named Petrozavodsk, whilst Povientz and other localities started iron and copper works for the execution of Government and private contracts. The scene, however, of the greatest diffusion of the metallurgical industry was the present Province of Perm; and in this connection the region of the Urals in particular may be said to have been Peter's peculiar discovery, since he it was who, just before his first foreign tour, had the locality surveyed for ores, and in 1699, on bringing back with him the necessary mining engineers and mechanics, ventured, on the strength of researches and experiments whereby the local ores had been shown to yield nearly half their own weight of iron, to build, on the river Neviansk, in the *uezd*, or canton, of Verkhotursk, ironworks subsidised by the Treasury to the amount of 1541 roubles, and by the local peasantry (for hire of the above staff of foreign artisans) to the amount of 10,347. And earlier, that is to say in 1680, there had been transported to Preobrazhensköe some hundreds of *potieshni* muskets [1] manufactured by a Demidov who, twenty-two years later, is seen obtaining a concession to build ironworks on the Neviansk, and so effectually contracting to furnish all such artillery pieces and artillery requisites as the Government might require that by 1713 his warehouses in Moscow had come to be stocked with 500,000 hand grenades (to mention only one article), whilst by the time of Anna's accession the contract prices of the day had come to be such as t） enable Demidov's son to draw annually from the Treasury a sum of over 100,000 (900,000) roubles. And upon the establishment of the Neviansk works followed the rise of many other metallurgical establishments, both Government and private, until all the region had become devoted to an industry which had its directorate centred in Ekaterinburg-on-the-Iset, a township named by General Henning, Peter's chief inspector of foundries and gunnery expert, after Catherine I. In time, too, this township came to be considered so important as to be allotted a special peasant guard of 25,000, for its protection against raids by Khirgizes and Bashkirs, and, before Peter's reign came to a close, to be comprising within its boundaries nine Government iron and copper foundries, and twelve private concerns of the same sort, with five of them belonging to Demidov. All of which factors brought it about that by the year 1718 the total annual output from Government and private smelting works was an output exceeding 6,500,000 *pudi* [2] of iron, and 20,000 [3] of copper, and that Peter now could furnish his field forces and fleet with muskets exclusively of Russian manufacture and Russian material, and that on his death he left behind him over 16,000 heavy guns.

But Peter did more than stimulate industry of production: he also devoted much thought to industry of disposal, and to internal trade, and,

---

[1] Muskets for Peter's *potieshnie*, "toy," soldiers.
[2] About 108,000 tons.   [3] About 3000 tons.

above all, to overseas commerce, a department in which Russia hitherto had been dependent upon Western shipping alone. Indeed, his prime motive in going to war with Sweden was to win for his country a trading harbour on the Baltic. Hitherto his every scheme had stood clouded with the problem of ways of communication. Even before he could enter upon the Pruth campaign he had to arrange for the southward transport of his troops and military stores by constructing, at an appalling cost to the local peasantry, a network of metalled roads radiating outwards from Moscow; whilst though, after his founding of St. Petersburg, he spanned the 500 versts between the new capital and the old with a sinuous, unmetalled turnpike, its mire and crazy bridges were such as once to cause a foreign ambassador to spend five weeks upon the journey, whilst frequently its system of posting necessitated a delay of eight days at a stagehouse during the procuring of a fresh team of horses. And though he afterwards attempted to straighten the road by lopping off from it a piece of 100 versts, and also rebuilding the first 120 versts out of St. Petersburg, the difficulties presented by the forests and swamps around Novgorod proved so insuperable that the attempt had to be abandoned. Hence, checked in road communication, Peter turned his attention to rivers, and concentrated his marvellous powers of intellect upon the unique network of ever-moving, ever-serviceable waterways which nature offered for the benefit of Russian commerce. For long past there had been germinating in his mind a grandiose scheme for linking up the country's splendidly carved river basins with a complete system of canals; but always the chances of the scheme being carried into execution had been marred by the fluctuations of his foreign policy. Quite early in his career, when Azov had just been taken, and he was thinking of consolidating his southward position by organising a commercial traffic system with the Azovian ports, and constructing a fleet on the Black Sea, he set about connecting that sea with the central waterways of the country through means of a canal designed to join the Kamishinka with the Slovina (both of them tributaries of the Volga), and then, passing through Lake Ivan, to link up that lake also with the Don and the Shat, and with the Upa and the Oka—at the same time canalising, clearing, and deepening lake and rivers alike. For years tens of thousands of workmen toiled at the scheme, and for years an immense quantity of material (on the Ivan canal alone twelve stone-constructed locks were built) went to waste; but in 1711, when his attention had to be diverted to the Northern War, and Azov was lost to him, both the canal project and the ruinously costly Azov-Don works-building scheme had perforce to be abandoned. Next, St. Petersburg having in the meanwhile come into being, he conceived an idea of connecting the new capital with waterways to the central provinces, and hugged to himself the notion that one day it would be possible for a voyager to embark upon the Moskva, and to disembark on the Neva, without once transshipping *en route*. So, in company with an educated peasant named Serdinov, he surveyed the fastnesses of Novgorod and Tver, and followed up the local rivers and lakes; until finally, pitching upon the water system of the Vishnii Volochok region, he set about cutting a second canal between the Vertsa (a tributary of the Volga) and the Tsna, the river which broadens into Lake Mstino, and issues thence as the Msta, and eventually falls into the Ilmen, and for four years employed 20,000 workmen upon the task, and by 1706 saw the task completed. Yet before a further ten years had elapsed the negligence of an inspector caused one of the locks of the system to become silted up, and it was only with immense difficulty that the fairway was cleared. Another constant impediment to Volgan-Nevan traffic was the turbulent Lake Ladoga, the hurricanes of which were only too apt to get the better of the flat-bottomed craft designed solely for navigation of the shallow waters of the Vishnii Volochok system, and to send them to the bottom, and cause serious loss. So in 1718 Peter conceived that it would be possible to avoid these disasters by cutting a canal right round Lake Ladoga, and so enabling vessels to pass from a point near the mouth of the Volkov direct to Schlüsselberg; and, having decided upon the scheme, and, with a party of engineers, surveyed the whole of the region between Ladoga and Schlüsselberg, he entrusted the affair's further working to Prince Menshikov, since, although the Prince stood ignorant of every possible subject, he was not the man to shrink from thrusting his nose in anywhere. The result was that he and his colleagues executed the scheme in such a manner as to throw 2,000,000 (16,000,000) roubles to waste in aimless tasks of excavation, and to exterminate labourers by the thousand through hunger and disease, and to accomplish nothing at all. And even though Peter transferred the affair to a hired foreign engineer named Minich, it was not until after his, Peter's, death that the expert himself succeeded in bringing the last hundred versts of the canal to completion. Peter's scheme had originally included also a second canal for uniting the Volga with the Neva through means of a bisection of the watershed of the Vitegra, a tributary of the Volga falling into Lake Onega, and then of a waterway following up the Kovzha, a tributary of the Volga falling into the Lake Bieloe Ozero, which in the nineteenth century was to see the Marzinski system constructed; whilst surveys also were made for connecting the White Sea with the Baltic; but none of these projects materialised, and the only canal system out of the six planned during Peter's day to be carried to a finish was the unambitious Ladogan enterprise. In any case, however, it was not rivers and canals alone that could render the new capital accessible and capable of being provisioned: and the same was true of the Baltic harbours which Peter desired to acquire as muster-points for his foreign commerce. Of these harbours the number was raised by the Northern War, eventually, to seven, for Kronstadt and St. Petersburg (which, of course, Peter himself had built) had added to them by the contest Riga, Pernov, Revel, Narva, and Viborg; but earlier than that, as early as 1714, if not earlier still, the question of acquiring them gave rise also to the question of whether it would not be advisable to divert to them the stream of Western European commercial traffic which hitherto had passed through Archangel and across the White Sea, owing to the fact that hitherto Archangel had been the Muscovite Empire's sole maritime outlet. Accordingly, after founding St. Petersburg, Peter worked not only to consolidate his position on the Baltic, but also to transfer Russia's foreign trade from the circuitous route of the White Sea to the route of the Baltic, and so, incidentally, to make that trade draw in upon the new metropolis. And though this commercial revolution was thought likely to collide with certain vested interests, and with certain fixed habits of usage, so that the Dutch opposed it because they had long regarded Archangel as their peculiar stronghold, and it was equally little favoured even by native merchants because they had become so used to following the route of the Northern Dvina, and the Senate supported both parties, and Admiral Apraxin, for his part, declared that the scheme would ruin the country's mercantile community, and involve its author in "everlasting, quenchless repining," Peter replied to these objections that, though it is always difficult to put principle into practice, all interests gradually come to accept an accomplished change, and then continued the struggle for eight years more until he had won over the opposers to his way of thinking, and St. Petersburg had become so entirely Russia's leading port for foreign trade that, whereas the number of foreign vessels which arrived at Archangel in 1710 was 153, the number which reached St. Petersburg in 1722 was 116, and, in 1724, 240; whilst the grand total for the Baltic ports (exclusive of Pernov and Kronstadt) for the same year amounted to 914. Hence Peter had been a true prophet when he had said that eventually all interests would become reconciled, and now he stood in the position of having met with such success in the first half of his dual task towards reorganising Russia's external trade that during the next two years after his death Russia exported to the value of 2,400,000 roubles, and imported to the value of 1,600,000. But, owing to a lack of capable *entrepreneurs*, less success befell the second half of his commercial task—the problem of bringing a

Russian mercantile fleet into being, and of wresting the country's foreign commerce from the alien hands in which it had long reposed. In this connection we can the better understand Peter's pertinacity in seeking to divert Russia's commerce from Archangel to St. Petersburg when we remember that, though St. Petersburg and her outwork Kronstadt arose primarily to serve as military posts in the face of Sweden, the conclusion of the war would have left the former in danger of altogether losing her right to be regarded as Russia's capital if Peter had not set himself to create for her a new position as the centre of the commercial relations with Western Europe for whose consolidation the war had been fought. For, left to herself, St. Petersburg could never have continued to exist as a mere stronghold for *chinovniki*, or as a mere camp for the Guards Regiments which always lay quartered, two on the Moscow-ward side of the capital, and four as a garrison on the Islands; whilst, in addition, the work of building the new capital had entailed a vast expenditure of monetary levies that needed to be recovered, as well as of human labour—men had been impressed thither from every province of the Empire, and supplies for those men's maintenance during the years of construction had had to be furnished from various quarters, and, even when nine years of strenuous toil had elapsed, fresh labourers to the number of 5000 had had to be rounded up from eight of the provinces already called upon for the purpose. Indeed, it is probable that there is not a campaign in our military history which despoiled the country of soldiers to the extent that the rearing of St. Petersburg and Kronstadt despoiled it of civilians. True, Peter himself used to call his new capital "Paradise," but for the people it meant a gigantic grave. For consider the price that must have been rendered for the place's mere laying out and initial provisioning! The method adopted was that, first of all, the staffs of such Government departments as either became established in or were transferred to the city had to build for themselves each some sort of a shelter, and that then, by *ukaz*, there were removed, rather, driven, thither a multitude of *dvoriané*, merchants, and artisans, all of whom, with their families, required to be lodged and fed thence onward, so that for a while the settlement resembled a gipsy camp, and even Peter had for his abode only a leaky-roofed barrack hut. Moreover, since the city's immediate environment was too barren to provide the supplies for such an accumulated multitude, distant court *sela* and the farms of rural *pomiestchiki* had to keep dispatching thither, along winter-bound roads, tens of thousands of waggon-loads of grain and other produce for the use of the Court and the *dvoriané*, and towns of the inland provinces thousands of waggon-loads of ordinary merchandise. And this sort of bivouac, hand-to-mouth existence perforce continued until at least the close of Peter's reign, and left a lasting impression upon the life conditions of the Nevan capital. Be it remembered that Peter was an administrator who, once he had considered a scheme, stinted upon it neither money nor human lives. The number of workmen who died merely during the building of a harbour at Taganrog (subsequently the clauses of the Turkish treaty compelled that harbour to be pulled to pieces again) ran to hundreds of thousands, even allowing for an exaggeration of the estimate; and the same in the case of the Baltic ports. Also, as regards the harbours of Kronstadt and St. Petersburg, both of them suffered from the threefold disadvantage of liability to become frozen for months at a time, of a freshness of water which injured the wood of which the hulks of vessels were then universally built, and of a shallowness of fairway; and though Peter long lavished labour and money upon efforts to remove at least the first and the third of these hindrances, at last he had to seek a more suitable harbour for his Baltic fleet, and eventually selected Rogervik, near Revel, which possessed an excellent roadstead. Yet even at Rogervik, it was discovered, the fleet lacked sufficient shelter from westerly gales; and though, to furnish the necessary piles, the forests of Livland and Esthland were almost denuded of their timber, and huge caissons were made, filled with packings of rock, and lowered to the bed of the ocean, storms repeatedly destroyed the whole until, in despair, Peter had to abandon the enterprise.

CHAPTER VII

Finance—Difficulties incidental to finance—Measures for those difficulties' removal—
New taxation—*Donositeli*, or informers—*Pribyltschiki*, or "profits men "—" Profits "
—The *Monastirski Prikaz*—State monopolies—The souls-tax—The tax's significance
—The Budget of 1724—Summary of Peter's financial reforms—Impediments to
those reforms.

HAVING studied Peter's measures for increasing the volume, and improving
the quality, of the people's labour, and thereby multiplying the sum of the
sources of the State's income, let us review the financial results of the measures
in question. In no sphere did Peter meet with greater difficulties than in the
sphere of finance, even though those difficulties were partially of his own
creation, or at least of his own maintenance. And in no sphere did he display
less aptitude for difficulties' removal. Indeed, late in life, he himself confessed that no other administrative province had given him so much trouble
or so consistently evaded his powers of comprehension. True, he knew well
wherein lay the sources of a nation's wealth, and never failed to remember
that taxation ought to be introduced without an overburdening of the
people; yet, as regards actually putting those ideas into practice, he never
progressed beyond the point of propounding to his Senators the at once in-
contestable and futile verity: "Money is the heart of war. Do ye gather
in all that ye may."

In 1710 he ordered a retrospective estimate of State revenue and expenditure for the last few years to be framed, and the estimate disclosed, amongst
other things, the fact that though, during the years 1705–7, the mean
annual income from the salt-boiling profits tax had amounted nearly to
3,330,000 roubles, the army and the fleet had absorbed 3,000,000 of those
roubles, and other expenditure 824,000—with the result that now there was
in being a deficit of 500,000, or 13 per cent. of the State's expenditure as
a whole. Hitherto it had been customary to balance deficits with remnants
left over from one or more preceding years, but at the present time no such
remnant was available. Accordingly, to mask the lacking roubles, the newly-
framed estimate proposed to levy an additional *poltina* (four modern
roubles) upon every taxable *dvor*, as the long-recognised (it had been
so recognised even before Peter's time) expedient for raising, in case of

emergency, what constituted, in reality, an internal loan neither carrying with it interest nor standing liable to be repaid. As a matter of fact, however, it was the only expedient possible, since neither at home nor abroad was anyone likely to give the Russian Exchequer credit if he could help it. And, that done, Peter, with a view to obviating a similar difficulty in the future, had the country's taxpaying capacity revised throughout. Hitherto all direct taxation had stood based upon the *podvornaia perepis*, or homestead census, of 1678; and though we do not find in any Act of Peter's reign a full, or a concise, summary of that census, there remains the fact that, at the time of the census' taking, the number of taxable *dvori* in the country was given as between 787,000 and 833,000, with tax-ratios per *dvor* varying in like proportion. Unfortunately, the subsequent lapse of thirty years had rendered the register so obsolete as to render it unusable even by a Petrine Government, and leave even a Government of that stamp powerless to assess direct taxation for the year 1710 from a census-list of 1678; and therefore, on discovering the deficit, Peter had an entirely new census taken —meanwhile flattering himself with the conviction that during the past thirty years a considerable increase of taxpaying population must have materialised. But the financial *débâcle* now met with rivalled the military *débâcle* at Narva, for by 1714 the Senate reported that its census-taking efforts had brought to light a shrinkage of taxpayers amounting to a fourth of the entire population (though be it added that in M. Milukov's careful and circumstantially detailed study of Peter's economy of State we find this panic-stricken estimate reduced to a fifth) and that, by implication, the culprit primarily responsible for this depopulation was Peter himself—his conscriptions of recruits for his military forces, added to his impressments of labourers by the ten thousand at a time for building his wharves and canals and new capital, having brought about a wholesale diminution of the taxpaying population, not to mention the hundreds of thousands of persons who had fled the country to escape his police measures and new fiscal levies, or else had taken advantage of the Treasury's difficulty in securing con-scientious tax-collecting agents altogether to secrete themselves from registra-tion. For Peter had his own fashion of envisaging the economy of a people's taxpaying powers, and held to the maxim that, the closer one shears a sheep, the more wool one obtains from its back: wherefore his later homestead censuses (of 1716 and 1717) revealed, not diminutions, but added in-creases, of taxpayer shrinkage—Kazan alone being reported by the Senate to have lost 33,000 *dvori* since 1710, or nearly a third of that year's registered assessable inhabitants!

Equally grave financial difficulties became manifest when the Northern

War had begun. Under Peter's elder brother [1] direct taxation had consisted exclusively of the class levies represented by (1) "posting money" and "prisoners money," which were imposts incident upon *kriepostnie liudi*, or serfs, alone, and by (2) "*Strieltzi* money," which was an impost of much greater weight, and fell upon the whole of the rest of the taxpaying population: and though Peter continued to collect these imposts at the old rates, the fact that his regular army and fleet began wholly to call for new resources gave rise, eventually, to the war taxes of "dragoons moneys," "recruits moneys," "ships moneys," and "moneys for conveyance"—the first being a levy for the purchase of cavalry horses which, falling upon everyone, even upon the clergy, amounted to six (modern) roubles per rural *dvor*, and nine per urban. And scarcely need it be stated that Peter did not dispense with the indirect taxation so dear to the hearts of the old Muscovite financiers, but even resorted to a new expedient in order to exploit this alluring source still further. Hitherto the supreme driving-force in the working of the State had been the Tsar's inspirational authority, and Peter himself long had shared this view, and probably he did so to the very end of his life, since it was in that view that he had been cradled and nurtured in the Kremlin; but now stern necessity drove him to add to that authority the general intellect: and, since, fortunately, the form which his activities had assumed throughout had had the effect of breeding his public to a political tendency which returned a gratifying response to his call for help, we see appear before us, at this period, men whom nowadays we should call publicists, but who were known, rather, in their day, as *donositeli*.[2] The members of the band included men drawn from every class of society, and ranged from an aristocrat named Saltikov, and a certain Colonel Urlov, and a son of Peter's old tutor, Zotov, to a plain burgher named Muromstev and our industrial peasant, Pososhkov; whilst their duty was to submit for Peter's consideration *prozhekti* (written schemes or suggestions) on every subject under the sun, from lofty questions of organisation of State to suggestions for the manufacture of rope—this last emanating from an artisan named Maxim Mikulin, whilst Pososhkov, for his part, forwarded to the Tsar an at once bold, vivid, and sombre picture of Russia's position, and appended to it some suggested expedients for a betterment of things. And with the framers of *prozhekti* worked men who, though sometimes known as *pribyltschiki*, or "profits men," and sometimes as *vymishlenniki*, or "devisors," were competent to play either rôle, and included a score of well-known names, and also names otherwise unknown. Every *prozhekt* Peter carefully scanned, and

---

[1] Tsar Theodor.
[2] Properly speaking, informers or accusers, but here used to denote furnishers of administrative suggestions.

every framer of a *prozhekt*, no matter how worthless that *prozhekt*, he rewarded, "in that," said he, "all of these folk have laboured for my good, and
do wish me well." Wherefore the functions of a *pribyltschik* came to represent
a sort of financial charge or commission, and to lie (to quote one of Peter's
own *ukazi*) in "sitting and ordering profits for the Tsar," that is to say, in
discovering for him and the State new sources of revenue. Particularly
noticeable is it that most of these functionaries came of the serf status.
Yet this is not so surprising when we remember that the *boyaré* of the day
maintained huge retinues, and that those retinues might well include menials
superior even to their masters in literary intelligence. To cite an instance,
it happened in 1699 that a *dvorovi* named Kurbatov was accompanying
his master through foreign parts, and heard that certain foreign States had
established a tax on stamps or dies. Upon that he waited until he had returned to Russia with his master, and then sent Peter an unsigned letter
begging the Tsar's favourable consideration for a species of writing-paper
which the writer of the letter called "eagled paper." [1] And so well did the
tax upon this paper succeed in its object that almost at once (says Kurakin)
it brought in to the Treasury 300,000 roubles a year (though the statement
may be exaggerated in view of the fact that at all events by the year 1724
the tax was bringing in only 17,000 roubles), and led to Kurbatov being
rewarded, first with a post as Director of a new Office of Commerce and
Industry, and then with the Vice-Governorship of Archangel—where he
died just as he was going to be arraigned for embezzling Government funds!
And to Kurbatov, as practically the founder of the order of *pribyltschiki*,
succeeded Ershov, Vice-Governor of Moscow; Nesterov, Comptroller-
General, and a daring indicter of Treasury thieves in high places, though
himself eventually convicted of peculation, and broken on the wheel;
Varaxin; Yakovlev; Startsov; Akinshin; and others. The function both of a
pribyltschik and of a *vymishlennik* was to search for new taxatory articles
which hitherto had escaped the Treasury's eye, and, on making any such
discovery, to establish and direct the special "chancellory" which always
was instituted to deal with the newly discovered article. And whilst such
non-taxable articles as contingent landed amenities and private industrial
establishments continued, as before, either to be made over to the Tsar or
to be converted into Government property (an example being fishery
rights), or else to be assessed to a tithe of one-fourth of the article's hitherto
profit (which course was adopted with regard to mills and public lodging-
houses), all articles already taxable were reassessed to a higher scale. For
the most part, Peter's *pribyltschiki* rendered their master good service. At

[1] That is to say, paper stamped with the Russian Imperial emblem, the two-headed eagle.

all events, they caused new imposts to begin trickling down upon the Russian taxpayer like water from a leaky sieve, so that the year 1704 alone saw introduced new taxes upon land, upon weights and measures, upon agricultural teams, upon varieties of headdress, upon boots, upon peasant souls, upon stage drivers' earnings (a tenth), upon sowings, upon reapings, upon horse and cattle hide-tannings, upon bees, upon bathhouses, upon mills, upon taverns, upon rents, upon market stands, upon timber fellings, upon ice cuttings, upon graves, upon fountains, upon stove-pipes, upon marine arrivals and departures, upon ships, upon firewood, upon sales of provisions, upon water-melons, upon cucumbers, and upon (to quote from a list of the day) "nuts and other such small ingatherings." Besides, there came into being certain taxes which even the unfortunate Muscovite who had to pay them can have understood but imperfectly, liberal though we may assume the education, rather, scarification, administered to his faculties by heretofore systems of assessment to have been. For now to taxation of industries and landed amenities there became added taxation of religious beliefs! Yes: besides having his material property taxed, the citizen had an impost levied upon his conscience if that conscience happened to lean towards religious dissent, since, though dissent was tolerated, it was considered to be a barely permissible luxury only, and, as such, an attitude properly assessable at a most onerous rate. Also was toll taken of the beard and whiskers through means of which the Russian of old was fain to assimilate his features to those of the Deity, and an *ukaz* of 1705 rated beards according to social grade—that of a *dvorianin*, or of a *Prikaz* official, at 60 (480) roubles, that of a first-guild merchant at 100 (800) roubles, that of an ordinary merchant at 60, and that of a serf, or of a church attendant, and the like, at 30. Only the *krestianin* might sport a beard for nothing; and even he had to pay a *kopek* (equal to eight modern *kopeki*) whenever he left his rural fastness to visit a town! But later (1715) all beard taxes were consolidated, and thenceforth every hirsute-visaged Russian, irrespective of his social grade, or of whether he was Orthodox or a Dissenter, rendered, for the beard privilege, fifty roubles. Next followed an obligation upon bearded folk to wear only the ancient costume of Russia. Indeed, amazement fills the breast as one reads the accompanying *ukaz* of ordination. Forwarded to the Senate by Peter in 1722, the document was the final outcome of his cogitations on freedom of conscience, and bade the Senate, bade it gravely and emphatically, "both confirm for ever Our former *ukaz* touching beards, to wit, that men should every year pay fifty roubles upon the same, and ordain that henceforth both bearded men and *Raskolniki* [1] shall wear only the raiment of

Dissenters.

yore, which is a *zipun*,[1] a straight [2] *kozar* [3] of buckram, a *ferezi* [4] and an *odnoriadok* [5] with an *ozherelie*." [6] Moreover, should any bearded person present himself for work in a Government office in non-prescribed costume, he was, "with no excuse received, yet not with complete dismissal from his task," to have his raiment mulcted to the tune of fifty roubles, even though he might already have paid his dress-licence fee; whilst impecunious individuals who landed themselves in a like unpleasant predicament were to be sent to work out the fine in the galleys at Rogervik, and anyone who "spotted" a bearded individual in non-regulation costume was to be allowed then and there to seize the culprit, to hale him before a justice, and to receive half the fine plus the offending attire!

Hence, great were the powers of invention displayed by *pribyltschiki*, and perusal of a list of imposts, "yielded profits," which sprang from these functionaries' wits shows that the inventors worked to rope-in the community at large, and succeeded especially well with the small manufacturer, the trades hand, and the skilled craftsman. But there remains also the fact that sometimes sheer virtuosity of skill in the pursuit of fresh Treasury increment led *pribyltshchiki* to cut across sound reasoning. For, since Peter's "projectors" and "profits men" proposed taxes upon births and marriages, and especially upon the nuptials of Morduines, Cheremissians, Tartars, and other non-baptised aliens, and suggested, for some reason, that the resultant chancellory should be attached to the Chancellory of Honey (which institution was presided over by a *pribyltschik* of the name of Paramon Startsov, raised to the post because he had been the first to think of, and to collect, a toll upon bees), how came those *pribyltschiki* to overlook the idea of a tax upon funerals, seeing that, whereas either an *ubrus* [7] or an *izvodnaia kunitza* [8] had long been the mulct upon a wedding, and was intelligible enough in that marriage is at least a minor luxury, it was, surely, a financial inconsistency to tax a Russian for having dared to enter the world, whilst letting him leave it tax-free? But at all events, the Church has since stepped in to rectify the inconsistency.

And since "profits" were so numerous and so varied, chancellories for their collection were numerous and varied in proportion. We read of a Chancellory of Fisheries, of a Chancellory of Bathhouses, of a Chancellory of Taverns, of a Chancellory of Honey, and of many others; whilst at the head of all stood Menshikov's Chancellory of Izhor, so-called because he was

---

[1] A sort of peasant's under-jacket.   [2] Stiff.   [3] Cravat or stock.
[4] Elsewhere described as "a festival garment."
[5] A sort of coloured smock or cloak.
[6] Either a necklet or a girdle—probably the latter.
[7] The pearl-studded frontlet rendered to the State by a bride.
[8] The export marten skin rendered by a bridegroom.

Governor of that locality. For the same reason these levies were known also as "chancellory dues." Yet though yet another name for them was "minor dues," they at one period brought in some very substantial sums—the Chancellory of Fisheries alone collecting annually (according to Prince Kurakin) 100,000 roubles, and the Chancellory of Honey 70,000. But towards the close of Peter's days the *pribyltschik* system began to evince two signs of impending failure; firstly, a falling-off in the returns, and secondly, a change in the popular attitude. To note the faults of the imposts Pososhkov was one of the first, and, in enumerating a list of them, he wrote heatedly: "Never will the Treasury be filled if only such mean bazaar tolls as these be used, in that they cause disturbance unto men, and are sorry in very truth." Without doubt the dues in question tended to put an ever-growing strain upon the taxpaying resources of the country, and to arouse resentment not only against their severity, but also, and still more, against their number, which, in the end, reached nearly thirty, and dogged the taxpayer's steps like a swarm of vicious gadflies. The imposts' final demise came of the fact that, in proportion as their productiveness declined, the State's deficit increased: and though in a list of imposts for the year 1720 they are to be found assessed at rates below some of the earlier rates quoted by Kurakin (the tax upon bath-houses alone excepted), the estimates for the same year disclose the fact that none of the sums from the imposts were collected in full, but to no more than 410,000 roubles out of the 700,000 originally budgeted for. The least successful impost of all in that year seems to have been the tax upon beards and illegal raiment, since, though estimated to bring in 2148 roubles, 87 *kopeki*, it eventually was collected only to the sum of 297 roubles, 20 *kopeki*. So in the end the Treasury had to abate its demands, and by *ukaz* of 1704 ordained that thenceforth *dumnie luidi* and first guild merchants should pay upon their bath-houses only three (24) roubles a year, and plain *dvoriané* and ordinary merchants and the rest only one rouble, and *krestiané* only fifteen *kopeki*. Yet, even so, twelve months had not elapsed before many of the more needy members of the intermediate taxpaying categories, such as soldiers, church cantors, and wafer bakers, found themselves unable to meet even the reduced exaction, and, after having been vainly stimulated with *pravozh*,[1] had to have their bath-houses reassessed to the next lower, or *krestianin*, scale. And so things continued until in 1724 Peter altogether deleted certain items from the list contemplated for the ensuing year; and, in general, the interest contained in the functions of a *pribyltschik* is confined to the fact that they serve to

---

[1] Caning a debtor over the shin-bone. For a fee the culprit could emulate the modern schoolboy's device of a copybook, and insert a thin plate of metal between leg and garment.

illustrate Peter's fundamental financial maxim, the maxim that, to obtain as much as possible, one should demand the sheerly impossible.

Another source of fiscal revenue towards which military requirements pointed a finger even before the *pribyltschiki's* entry upon their activities was the Church's landed wealth. True, *pribyltschiki* included in their proposed schemes of operations a series of taxes upon ecclesiastical establishments, and we have seen that after the fight at Narva Peter melted down a large number of church bells for cannon; but on 30 December, 1701, an *ukaz* also despoiled monasteries of their right of independent disposal of their otchinal revenues, of their revenues from their entailed estates, on the pretext that the period's monasteries had failed to follow the example of the older religious houses, and broken their vows by suffering their labours for the destitute to take second place to selfish subsistence upon the labours of others. The actual task of revenue-collection from monasterial *otchini* Peter delegated to an institution known as the *Monasterial Prikaz*, originally founded by Alexis, (in 1649), to serve as a legal-administrative Department for management of the spiritual authorities' secular affairs, but suppressed by Tsar Theodor, and now re-established by Peter. And under it Peter placed not only the Patriarchal and the Episcopal lands, but likewise those of persons in ecclesiastical employ, and bade it set aside for the State, out of monasterial incomes, a proportion of all monetary and cereal donations to monasteries equal to, per monasterial inmate independently of spiritual rank, ten monetary roubles, or ten cereal quarters, and allocate the remainder to hospitals, or to religious houses sufficiently pious not to be owners of *otchini* at all. Whereby, according to Kurakin, the *Monastirski Prikaz* ended by presenting the Treasury with from 100,000 to 200,000 roubles a year. But twelve months before the close of the Swedish War Peter transferred the institution to the control of the newly established Holy Synod, and thus enabled the Hierarchy to regain its old right of managing its own *otchini* and landed inbringings; so that Peter's ecclesiastico-financial measures amounted to a system of levying toll upon the Church's wealth whenever the State was in a difficulty, and then of secularising that wealth.

Another of Peter's fiscal expedients was to add to his already established Treasury monopolies in pitch, potash, rhubarb, gum, and the like, a set of Treasury monopolies in salt, tobacco, copper, tar, fish oil, and oaken coffins—the last of which commodities, the ultimate luxury of the prosperous citizen, he removed from the hands of private vendors in 1705, and committed exclusively to the State, which, so long as the stock of coffins held out, sold them at four times their original price, and then forbade their manufacture altogether. In the same year an *ukaz* proclaimed that, though salt might continue to be furnished to the Treasury under free contract conditions, the Treasury alone might do the re-selling, and re-sell, with that, at a price double the original contract terms, and so make a profit of a hundred per cent.! Unfortunately, the salt monopoly was so badly managed that at last even the deferential Pososhkov felt moved to call for free vendition, on the ground that, owing to the scarcity of salt in the country's remoter districts, where the price of the commodity had risen to over a rouble a *pud*, and to the fact that in Moscow the contract price was still the original one of twenty-four *kopeki*, large numbers of provincial folk were consuming their victuals without any salt at all, and dying of scurvy in consequence. Nay, for purposes of revenue, Peter's Government even went so far as to exploit certain of humanity's passions, for it next converted into monopolies *vodka*, tobacco, playing-cards, dice, chessmen, and other such appurtenances of diversion, and then farmed out the monopolies. "Only after a rendering of tolls now may men sport," a contemporary writer comments. Yet neither he nor anyone else could have gainsaid the fact that during the very first year of the monopolies' farming-out they presented the Exchequer with 10,000 roubles. And another important new article of revenue was a sub-division of, and a counterfeiture of, the State's own coinage by the State itself. Before Peter's day currency had consisted solely of silver *kopeki* and half-*kopeki* which, known together as *dengi*,[1] were, for purposes of computation, combined into units of *altini* (three *kopeki*), *grivni*, *poltinniki*, *polupoltinniki*, and roubles. But by the year 1700 this silver coinage had become so scarce that people in the remoter districts of the country had taken to settling accounts with leather tokens; and for this reason the Government issued small copper coins named according to the above computative units, even as were the existing coins of silver. Unfortunately, the latter tended, as ever, to lose weight and standard, and this led to the currency having infused into it, for the first time, the element of credit. For that matter, contemporary financiers had for long past contemplated the idea with a patriotically daring eye, and Pososhkov, particularly, had felt convinced that in a land like Russia (though nowhere else) the circulation might safely be left to the Sovereign's sole management, seeing that such a Tsar as Peter need but bid a *kopek* become a *grivna*, and a *grivna* naturally that *kopek* would become. And another suggestion (this time by a professional "devisor") was that the military expenditure should be masked, as frankly as fraudulently, with a ten per cent. monetary debasement, "to the end that, with disturbance unto none," a check might be put upon the export of specie. But such a specious device was too much for either the loyalty or the simplicity of the

---

[1] This word now means money in general.

money market; and though, by the close of Peter's reign, the Government's various financial bureaus were forwarding to the Treasury an annual collective profit of 300,000 (2,000,000) roubles, these roubles were merely an empirical profit, merely a skinning of the flint, for the coinage, meanwhile, had so deteriorated, and the cost of commodities become so artificially raised, that, taking grain values as a standard of comparison, the silver *kopek* had come to be worth only half the silver *kopek* of fifty years earlier, and to stand at about eight of our *kopeki* of modern times, whereas the silver *kopek* of Alexis' day had equalled at least fourteen or fifteen to-day's *kopeki*.

Thus, in Peter's time direct taxation underwent a radical revolution. For a long time past "homestead numbering" had constituted an unsatisfactory basis for assessment, and Peter's chancellory system had made the case worse, not better, and apportionment of taxes according to the census lists of 1710 and 1717 was sheerly impossible, since in each case these documents had brought to light a large decrease in homesteads as compared with the census of 1678. Now, therefore, the Statistical Department conceived a highly ingenious plan for conserving the Treasury's interests, the plan that upon the province division of 1719 there should be based a new homestead census-list compiled, not from a single census-list of earlier date, but from more than one, and with new figures introduced to meet the case. And the brilliant result of this brilliant expedient was that, though the census list of 1678 gave the number of the country's taxpaying homesteads as 833,000, that figure could, by multiplying the subsequent increase by two, be shifted to 900,000, without including urban homesteads at all. Unfortunately, another effect of this statistical imbecility was practically to stultify homestead assessment altogether: wherefore once more the search for a convenient unit of assessment had to be resumed. In reality, the desiderated unit was standing ready to hand in the census lists of 1710 and 1717, since both of those lists evinced the interesting phenomenon since expounded in M. Miliukov's treatise, the phenomenon that in certain rural localities the average male *personnel* of the taxpaying *dvor* had so marched with the increase in population as to come to stand at the figure of 5½ per *dvor*, as against the earlier one of 3 or 4. Yet though, owing to the existence of homestead assessment, and to the Government's hitherto failure to recognise the superior advisability of poll assessment, that growth of male taxpaying *personnel* had conferred no benefit upon the Treasury, this does not mean that the idea of poll assessment had never yet occurred to Muscovite financial intellects, for it had cropped up as early as the Sophia-Golitzin *régime*, and more than one of Peter's "devisors" had ventured to suggest male taxation per head

IV—K

as a means of correcting the manifest irregularities due to assessment per *dvor*. But the first Muscovite financier actually to agitate for poll-assessment was *Oberfiskal* Nesterov—he began his agitation in 1714; and he was followed by others who advocated transference of taxation variously from the homestead to the individual, and from the homestead to the family. As for Peter's own view of the proposal, he seems, whilst disregarding equally its juridical bearing and its possible effect upon economic development, to have kept his attention riveted solely upon its intendencial aspect, and looked exclusively to the efficiency of his army and fleet, and treated as altogether negligible the question of whether the proposal would ever effect a balance between military expenditure and popular-tax-paying capacity. Indeed, it was scarcely to be expected that a ruler who always looked upon his crushed renderers of imposts as an inexhaustible fiscal reservoir would let such a question trouble his head. Even when, in 1717, certain of his "projectors" and "profits men" told him that his "lowly subjects" had become tax-burdened beyond endurance, and, if burdened further, would emigrate wholesale, he merely wrote to the Senate (he was in France at the time): "If it be possible to take yet more moneys from the payers, and great oppression be not thereby caused, do ye then take those moneys," and ordained as the means of obtaining the needed cash, a continuance of taxation of industry, the imposition of a poll-tax upon the towns ("otherwise will the State be undone"), and strict care that any attempts at peculation "straightway do be visited with inquisitions and executions." These commands alone show how little Peter understood the comparative advantages and disadvantages of the *dvor*, the family, and the working-hand as taxatory units, and how completely his purview of human entities was limited to the soldier who needed to be supported, and to the *krestianin* who compulsorily must support the soldier. And it was for the same reason that in November 1717, when presiding over the Senate, he, in his usual cursory style, a style probably wholly unintelligible to any-one less used to it than a Senator, indited an *ukaz* ordaining that "ye appor-tion unto Our *krestiané* both Our land forces and Our marine recruits, and also the payment unto the same, and their victualling, and unto every soul, or unto every *dvor*, as of the twain We shall find the more expedient, Our foot soldiers, and Our dragoons, and Our officers of all ranks save that of general," and that "ye so apply yourselves unto these levies that they shall be allotted strictly according unto these presents, and Our *krestiané* be released from their other labours of every sort, and from all dues save these alone"—the rigmarole, of course, meaning that direct imposts now were to give place to a composite military tax either per *dvor* or per poll as Peter

might eventually select, and that the tax was to fall upon the *krestiané*
according as estimates still to be made might be found to assess the cost of
military upkeep. And since Peter eventually decided in favour of assessment
"per poll of working persons," the Senate, on 26 November, 1718, debated
the *ukaz* announcing the decision, and then prescribed the taking of a complete census of the male agricultural population, "from the most aged unto
the last stripling," and carried out that taking with the delays, and the
stoppages for verification and revision and re-revision, which we have seen.
Nevertheless, though variously dated items concerning the census which
have come down to us are confusing because they return the number of
registered male souls at figures fluctuating between 5,000,000 and 6,000,000,
there have come down to us also (1) the Senate's estimate of poll-tax for
the year 1724, (2) a list of the sums actually collected during that year
(ordered to be appended to the foregoing estimate in 1726), and (3) a specification of taxatory arrears according to provinces, as the three items of data
which, in 1724, guided the Senate in its task of quartering regiments according to locality, and of assessing the necessary taxation. For these documents
afford us at least some indication of how the poll-tax worked during the
year; which, as things turned out, was both the first year of the tax's operation and the last year of the life of the tax's instituter. And the documents
do so none the less because they stand clear of the changes which the system
underwent after Peter's decease. According to them, the taxpaying population of the country, inclusive of the country's 169,000 urban taxpayers,
amounted, in 1724, to 5,570,000 souls, whilst the ratio of fixation of
assessment rate per soul was proportioned to census results—being at first
calculated at ninety-five *kopeki* per soul, and then receding to seventy-four,
with the incidence equalised through the *krestianin* having his dues to his
pomiestchik replaced with a supplementary tax of four *grivni* in the case of
State *krestiané*, and of one rouble, twenty *kopeki* in the case of urban-
taxpaying *krestiané*.

But what specially gave rise to trouble with regard to the poll-tax was
the question of how the term "revisional soul" ought to be interpreted
as a unit of assessment, and even such an ardent adherent of the Reformer
as Pososhkov is found looking for no good to come of the scheme, and
avowing that he can make neither head nor tail of it, "in that a soul is a
thing impalpable, not to be apprehended, so that of it there is no power of
appraisement. What alone ought to be mulcted is chattels of the soil "—by
which the peasant scribe meant landed estate. But of course Pososhkov was
viewing the matter from the popular-industrial standpoint alone, a standpoint alien to Peter's intelligence, so that the writer believed the industry

of a people to lie, not in souls, but in the two aggregates capital and labour, and that only actual workers should pay State dues, and the aged and the very young should be exempted. As a matter of fact, if Peter really had wished to assess taxation according to working capacity, he could have found a model ready to his hand, for there was already existent in East Zealand a peasant tax falling upon the whole body of workers between the ages of fifteen and sixty; but, unfortunately, he cared less for a rational assessment than for a possibility of being able to receive tax returns un- encumbered with arrears. Besides, no rational system of assessment could ever have succeeded against the limited scope of his executive-financial ideas; and, for the rest, there remained the fact that it was impossible to effect an exact registration of the nation's productive forces, and therefore he had to fall back upon the composition of a purely arithmetical estimate of the nation's males. This estimate he duly composed. He carried it out to the point of including in it males only recently arrived in the world! Hence his "revisional soul" was merely a fictitious, computative, average- able assessment unit, since his first consideration was not a popular- industrial policy, nor a financial policy, but firstly, the *Kammer-Collegium's* book-keeping, and, secondly, the Treasury's record of tax returns. The task of actually investing his fictitious unit with a meaning he left to the tax- payers, and that task the taxpayers eventually performed, and thenceforth the revisional soul popularly connoted the ratio between the taxpayer's working capacity and resources and the taxpayer's portion of taxable land (or industry) and its ascribed taxation. In which sense it is that we find *krestiané* speaking of halves, or quarters, or eighths of souls, without in the least meaning to controvert psychological facts. Yet though the poll-tax became the successor of the *dvor*, the household, or homestead, tax, the latter also was levied so long as Peter was alive, and had, meanwhile, for its basis the obsolete census-list of 1678. Nor, as it lasted for a very long while, even until our own times were reached, did the homestead tax fail lastingly to impress the popular imagination, and to lead the payer of it frequently to wonder how it had originated in the past, and why he should have to dis- charge it in the present. Even in Pososhkov's day, he tells us, the *dvoriané* could make nothing of the *krestianski dvor* as a taxatory unit, since whilst some made it their rule to count their *krestianskie dvori* by the entrance- gates of those establishments, others reckoned them by the hearthstones, and both parties failed to grasp the idea that a peasant homestead could be a *zemlenoe vladenie*, or landed chattel, at all. Still more unintelligible did people find the revisional soul. But, putting aside the masses' ingenious interpretations of Peter's financial institutions, there remains the question why Peter's official world devoted so much attention to the creation of taxpayers who could not meet their liabilities, and regarded the tax-assessment imposed upon them as a mere arbitrary demand on the part of a red-tape, and alien, and anti-popular Government. Such a condition of things was at least a poor school, the poorest possible school, towards inculcating duty to the State, and one bound eventually to evolve "Chichikov" and his "dead souls" as the inevitable epilogue to what Pososhkov incisively terms "the State's unconscionable takings of souls dues." And Peter's fiscal reforms in actual execution only heighten our wonder. True, their latter-day apologists insist that the poll-tax had a double end in view—the end of placing all the Tsar's subjects on an equality for purposes of fiscal rendition, and the end of increasing the revenue without an over-burdening of the people; but also there remains the objection that the *ukaz* of the tax's ordination neither explains the revisional soul's *raison d'être* nor indicates whether that soul was to be regarded as a computative unit, or whether it was to be accepted as a reality. In the *ukaz* of 1722 for regulating collection of the tax from urban dwellers we find it commanded that "men in towns shall be rated amongst themselves according unto the substance of their towns"; but from the rural population the tax was gathered strictly in accordance with the tax's name [1]—though estimated according to local totals of souls, it was collected from individual souls regardless of whether those souls were working-hands. And this gave rise to innumerable complaints of "oppression and inequalities amongst the people," since, to take only one example, a poor *krestianin* who had three male children might have to render twice as much as a well-to-do *krestianin* who had only one male child. The net result was that, though the system purported to levy a level and uniform tax, it only accentuated the existent disparity between family-numerical *personnel* and social status. Yet to make a precise estimate of the weight of the tax's incidence as against the incidence of the old homestead levy is not an easy matter, for they were incommensurable as assessment units, and details are lacking. All that we can say about it is that, though the useful notes on the subject which Mannstein collected during the closing years of the reign should be looked upon as cursory, casual deductions rather than as an exact reckoning, he probably gave a correct summary of the best opinion of the day when he wrote that the one tax must have brought in to Peter twice as much as Peter collected through the other. As a matter of fact, the homestead tax varied according to locality of allotment and to category of payers: it rated the *dvori* of urban and Court *krestiané* more highly than it did the *dvori* of "black-ploughing" *krestiané* and Church

---

[1] *Podushina*, or tax per soul.

krestiané, and the *dvori* of the latter more highly than the *dvori* of privately-owned *krestiané*. And whereas, as regards locality, it imposed upon the *pomiestchichi dvor* of the province of Kazan an average rate of forty-nine *kopeki* per *dvor*, it imposed upon the same *dvor* in the province of Kiev an average rate of one rouble, twenty-one *kopeki*. Yet, glaring though this inequality was, the inequality stood largely neutralised by differences of local economic conditions, since, besides that the huge shrinkage of *dvori* in the central and northern provinces which the census of 1710 brought to light alone would have rendered equalisation of incidence impossible, long continuance of homestead assessment under the census of 1678 at length led to those provinces' *dvori* paying almost double in compensation for the *dvori* vacated, whereas in provinces like Kiev, Kazan, Astrakhan, and Siberia, where there had been an increase, rather than a decrease, of *dvori*, a diminished rate of impost became the rule. Naturally, these complicated and intricate conditions caused also the poll-tax to fall upon different classes of payers with a non-uniform incidence, and in some cases, to augment the burden of direct taxation only by a slight percentage, and in others to augment that burden by as much as two or three hundred, or more, per cent., so that in, for example, the provinces of Kiev, Kazan, and Archangel the mean rate levied upon the average four-souled peasant *dvor* was barely half the amount of the poll-tax—the exact proportion being 190:296. But the worst sufferers from the system, as well as the individuals least able to bear that suffering, were the *pomiestchiki's krestiané*, since, whereas hitherto the homestead tax, as a direct impost, had largely spared those *krestiané* because of the weight of their financial liabilities towards their masters, the amount of poll-tax exacted from them so marched with the amount levied upon the more prosperous Court and Church *krestiané* as eventually, in some localities, to become trebled, or even quadrupled. Wherefore the demand of equity for an abatement of the *pomiestchik's* levies at length became clamorous, and the Government seems to have expected that that abatement should be made, and itself strove to effect greater equality by assessing State *krestiané*, as a category exempt from seigniorial exactions, to a due additional to the general tax, "to the end that *pomiestchiki* may receive from their *krestiané* only what is befitting, and without distress unto persons." This additional due from the State *krestiané* the Government fixed at forty *kopeki*. But *pomiestckiki* were not going to rest satisfied with a mere four *grivni*; they at once shifted on to their *krestiané* both the increased expenditure which their, the *pomiestchiki's*, liability to perform State service entailed, and their fiscal payments on behalf of their non-income-producing household serfs. And they did this in full measure, and with interest, whilst also raising the *krestianin's obrok*, or seigniorial tithe, as it had never before been raised, in the sure and certain knowledge that no legal norm existed whereby the rate of that tithe could be reduced again. In fact, Pososhkov says that during this revisional period it was quite a common thing for a peasant's *dvor* to have to pay to its *pomiestchik* "unto eight roubles or over," whilst Weber, the Resident for Brunswick, an observer who collected much reliable information on Russian affairs between the years 1714 and 1719, notes in his *Das veränderte Russland* that certain *krestiané* even had to pay *obroki* amounting to from ten to twelve roubles, and, in a few instances, to twenty! Whence, if we take seven (60) roubles as the average rate paid per *dvor*, we shall see that, assuming the average *personnel* of the peasant household to have consisted of four souls, the *pomiestchik obrok* ended by doubling the poll-tax, and by becoming nearly five times the amount of the *pomiestchik's* legally recoverable forty *kopeki*. It remains a problem how any single *krestianin* in the country contrived to scrape together the necessary money; and the problem becomes no less when we remember how greatly his outside field for paid labour was restricted. And though we may remember, too, that fully half his renderings to his *pomiestchik* could be paid in grain or in *barstchina*, the poll-tax balanced its lessening of certain inequalities of tax-payment by introducing fresh ones, and by subjecting to a single departmental standard the many variations of taxpaying capacity which came of differences of locality, social class, and working-life conditions, and that, by assessing the people to a uniform ratio of crushing direct taxation, it debarred itself from achieving the very objects which it professed to be aiming at, the objects of, firstly, equalising fiscal liability, and, secondly, augmenting the Treasury's revenue without concurrently exhausting the people's strength. We gain a clear idea of this from an official return issued by the *Kammer-Collegium* in 1724, which document states that during the past twelve months the collection of poll-tax had failed to the tune of 848,000 roubles, or eighteen per cent. of the entire year's estimate, and adds plaintively: "With respect unto the arrears owing unto us, both governors and vice-governors and *voevodi* and *Kämmerer* and district commissaries do say in their intelligences and their reports that nowhere can souls-tax moneys be collected in full, by reason of the leanness of the peasantry, and of the mischances of the harvest, and of needs to sub-tract sums which have twice and thrice been inscribed in the tax-books, and of abscondings not pursuable, and of seizings of men for recruits, and of the case that many persons are grown old or halt or blind, or are orphaned babes, or are *bobili* lacking *dvori*, or are sons of soldiers with no land meet for ploughing." In all of which we see a fitting posthumous testimonial to

Peter's poll-tax rendered by the very agency, by the very organ of financial control, which gathered in that tax!

In other of Peter's imposts as well, both assessed and non-assessed, we see repetitions of the phenomena of (1) exaggerated demands on the part of a necessity-driven Treasury fixed in its belief that money was always to be found when wanted, and (2) a huge and ever-growing deficit, as the tacit response to those demands rendered by the taxpayers. For even the zeal of *pribyltschiki* (of which so much was displayed that by 1720 those functionaries had forced up the 1,500,000 roubles collected during the year 1701 to a total, of 2,600,000) could not prevent successive returns from showing a balance on the wrong side as inexorably as the above-cited case did, where we see an adverse figure of 500,000 roubles, or twenty per cent. below the estimate. But we can best gauge the ill-success of Peter's financial measures from the closing Budget of his lifetime, the Budget for 1724, the Budget for the first year of the tax's collection, a Budget made up partly of poll-tax, and partly of customs, excise, industrial tolls, and the like. It will be sufficient to quote the document's principal item of expenditure, the military item:

REVISIONAL SOULS

Kriepostnie liudi (privately owned serfs) . . .	4,364,653	(78 per cent.)
State *kriestiané*	1,036,389	(19 ,, ,,)
Urban taxpayers	169,426	(3 ,, ,,)
	5,570,468	(100 per cent.)

Poll-tax collected from the above, at 40 *kopeki* per soul	4,614,637	roubles
Other revenues	4,040,090	,,
	8,654,727	roubles

MILITARY EXPENDITURE

Upon the land forces (defrayed out of poll-tax) . .	4,596,493	roubles
Upon the fleet	1,200,000	,,
	5,796,493	roubles

Of course, these figures are not complete, whilst also they are based upon minima; yet at least they are instructive in that, though the returns for subsequent years show increased totals, the totals change little in their interproportions, and the above particularly well illustrate the connection between Peter's financial reforms and his military—which were the mainspring of his financial. For the table shows that the expenditure upon the army and the fleet for 1724 amounted to 67 per cent. of the whole estimated revenue, and to 75·5 per cent. of the actually realised revenue, and, in particular, that by that year the army had come greatly to exceed in cost the army of forty-four years earlier, which had required to have spent upon it less than a half-year's ingatherings. Besides, in spite of the fact that we perceive the estimated revenue for the year 1724 to have been nearly three times as much as the estimated revenue of the year 1710 (the year when the deficit had begun), owing to the poll-tax having swollen the Treasury's income by over 2,000,000 roubles, we perceive also, from the above-cited report by the *Kammer-Collegium*, that the very first year of the tax's imposition produced an adverse balance of 848,000 roubles, and therefore that, by 1724, fifteen years of struggling with a deficit which, in 1710, had amounted to thirteen per cent. only had swelled that deficit to a shortage of eighteen per cent. in poll-tax alone, and also worked grave injury to the instrument with which the financial struggle had in the meantime been waged. And though also it is clear that by the close of Peter's reign the State had become twice as rich as the State ruled by Peter's elder brother had been (for, if we translate the Budgets of 1680 and 1724 into modern currency, we shall find that the former works out at 20,000,000 roubles only, but the latter at 70,000,000), Peter's State owed its enrichment to a break in the fiscal system which I have shown to have resulted merely in taxation becoming deflected to another quarter. Direct taxation had, for the most part, yielded to indirect before Peter arrived at all; yet though, owing to his solicitude for commerce, industry, and industrial traffic, we might have expected to see indirect taxation grow thenceforward, things were otherwise, and the poll-tax held its own so stoutly as eventually to cause it to constitute fifty-three per cent. of all the Budget's revenue. For the same reasons, the reasons of lack of capital, and of insufficient currency to which taxation could penetrate, the weight of taxatory incidence, falling exclusively upon the labour of the indigent masses, of the already over-burdened working-hands, so oppressed that labour as to become unbearable. And this although both native and foreign observers adjudged that, in view of the Russian Empire's vast area and boundless natural resources, the Tsar should have reaped thence a far larger income than he did, and yet not have strained his people too far. And curiously enough, Peter too, seems to have thought the same. At all events, no matter whether the opinion were borrowed or spontaneous, the *Reglament* issued to the *Kammer-Collegium* in 1719 remarks that, "the world holdeth nowhere a State which might not lessen its burden of taxation if, in respect of its incomings and its outgoings, it did look unto justice alone, and unto equality according unto worth."

It was Peter's misfortune that he never succeeded in properly envisaging that indispensable "if." Every observer of his day declares that always there stood arrayed against his Treasury and his people's welfare two foes who, whilst holding "justice and equality" of no account, wielded a power greater even than that of the Tsar's own pitiless and ponderous hand. Which two foes, say these observers, were the *dvorianin* and the *chinovnik*, despite that in each case those members of the community owed their creation to the authority which they so poorly served. For the *dvorianin*, the observers remark, had for his one preoccupation the task of relieving his *krestiané* of their State obligations, and instead of lightening those *krestiané's* position, diverting the pecuniary value of their obligations to his own income— an end to attain which he stuck at nothing; whilst of the *chinovnik* the observers say that he was a veritable virtuoso in peculation, and could reap profits to almost incomputable amounts without letting himself become a whit more easy to detect than, to quote Weber, "it would be easy to drain the ocean dry." Prominent above all others in this way were the *Landrath* representatives of the *dvorianstvo*, the persons selected by that class to act as its directors or officials in the local tax-collection offices. Indeed, Weber compares these *Landräthe* to birds of prey outright, and says that they regarded their commissions to function as so many permits to suck the *krestianin's* blood, and to make his ruin a stepping-stone to their own prosperity—so much so that though, on taking up a Government post, a *chinovnik* might possess no more than the clothes on his back, he would, within four or five years at the most, have so thoroughly skinned the peasantry committed to his departmental care as, still a man drawing an official salary only of forty or fifty roubles a year, to be able to build for himself a fine stone mansion. And even if we suppose that this and similar impressions represent the views of prejudiced, splenetic foreigners, we still must recognise that Pososhkov was a Russian, and a tolerant one at that, and that he considered the magistrates and the *podiachie* of his day to stand below, in point of honesty, the very thieves and brigands with whom it was their duty to contend, and that other Russians of the period, Russians with a like knowledge of the *chinovnik's* wiles, habitually asserted (no matter whether in jest or in earnest) that, of every 200 roubles collected by the officials, 30 at most reached the Treasury, and the rest were shared by those officials to compensate them for their trouble. Moreover, we find observers, when expressing surprise at the Reformer's titanic energy, expressing also surprise at the vast areas of unworked, but fertile, land, comprised in Russia, as well as at the vast numbers of peasant plots either perpetually vacant, or roughly worked, or worked only from a distance, or at least never put through the full agricultural routine. And when such persons pondered upon the causes of this wastage they usually considered those causes to lie principally in the loss of population born of protracted campaigns, and in the doings of the pestilential swarm of *chinovniki* and *dvoriané* which discouraged the masses from ever pulling themselves together, and falling to work in earnest. Particularly does Weber paint the peasant's outlook as having become so darkened, through a despondency born of servitude, as finally to have left him unable to discern where his advantage lay, or to peer at anything beyond the wretchedness of his daily life. Wherefore we may say that in his financial policy Peter resembled a coachman whose only idea of extracting speed from a sorry horse is constantly to jerk at the reins. Peter himself it was who most hindered his own poll-tax. True, it was a tax heavy as compared with the homestead exaction upon which it followed; yet, even so, its weight was not extreme, and we shall realise that when we remember that, though the normal *personnel* of the then peasant *dvor* amounted to four persons, the tax which stood based upon that number amounted only to three roubles. Even Pososhkov, for all that he was one of those who constantly demanded either a land tax or a revised homestead impost, did not allow his dislike of the souls-tax to keep him from admitting that the due upon the "full" peasant *dvor* and plot of six *desiatini* could always, with justice, be raised by a third. But, of course, this view stood confined solely to the monetary portion of the homestead levy; and that portion by no means exhausted the whole, since the peasant's obligations in kind were heavier still, as well as had superimposed upon them all those contingent or extraordinary exactions which a period of war never failed to rain down upon the peasant's head like snow. Think, for example, what the *krestiané's* contribution towards the mere laying of St. Petersburg's foundations must have been, and then towards the many-years process of raising an Egyptian pyramid upon a swamp, seeing that for that process myriads of labourers had to be brought from all quarters of the Empire, and hundreds of thousands of roubles to be spent upon the maintenance of those labourers, and wholesale commandeerings of grain and wagons and horses to be imposed upon those labourers' fellow *krestiané* and *dvorie* at home, added to such monetary contributions, both voluntary and compulsory, towards the feeding and the lodging of the men and horses commandeered as in some cases to leave upon a given province, through the extraneous taxation necessitated, a taxatory deficit equal to a third of that province's entire assessment, and to entail a local imposition of supplementary taxes proportioned to the local number of *dvori*, and in 1707 to cause Kurakin (who himself was a large landowner) to remark in his autobiography that "from the *krestianski dvor* now there are commonly taken, each year, up to sixteen roubles." Wherefore, though it might be supposed that exactions per homestead equal to from 120 to 130 modern roubles were impossible, here we have an actual owner of those who had to pay them bequeathing us reliable testimony to the contrary. True, it was the official idea that, once the Swedish War could be brought to an end, the poll-tax would serve to lighten the taxatory burden which the struggle entailed; but inasmuch as the only result of the tax's first few collections was a huge deficit, the Government merely stood confronted with an exhaustion of the people's taxpaying labour. Also, although Peter left behind him not a *kopek* of State indebtedness, we know that shortly before his death the financial position was so bad as to lead a Russian manufacturer who resided abroad to suggest issuing five millions' worth of wooden credit-tokens, on the ground that currency of the sort would prove more durable than paper, Also, we know that though, in 1721, Peter bethought him of enlisting the help of the notorious banker-speculator John Law, in the hope that, in return for a Treasury subsidy of 1,000,000 roubles, he would accept a concession for organising a commercial corporation in Russia on (to the Government) attractive terms, the fact that the nation's debased forces, moral and fiscal, called for a heavy rate of interest, and that it was unlikely that that interest would be recoverable even if eventually Peter should conquer, not only Livland and Ingria, but also Sweden herself (or, for that matter, half a dozen Swedens), caused the scheme to be dismissed from further consideration.

CHAPTER VIII

Peter's administrative reforms—His system of military upkeep—The *Boyarskaia Duma* and the *Prikazi*—The reforms of 1699—*Voevodskie tovaristchi*—The Muscovite *Ratusha* and Kurbatov—Preliminaries to *gubernia* reform—The *gubernia* division of 1708—*Gubernia* administration—The defects of that system—Institution of the Senate—The Senate's origin and status—Informers—Peter's Colleges.

OF Peter's phases of activity perhaps the most striking and distinctive of all was his reform of the country's administrative system. Yet though historians, in appraising his work, speak more of this reform than of any other, they seldom stress sufficiently the slow and difficult preliminary process as Peter reconstructed his governmental institutions—they concentrate too much upon the final shape which the institutions, as reconstructed, had assumed by the close of the reign. Peter's administrative reforms were preparations for an end rather than an end in themselves: their aim was to create in the present such general conditions as, in the future, might ensure successful execution of other reforms. Yet is was not until the two fundamental reforms, the reform of military affairs, and the (partial) reform of finance, were already in working that Peter's Administration acquired a suitable setting for further operations. Let us see, therefore, how this discrepancy between means and ends affected his reforming activity as a whole. In this regard we come upon the usual features of the Petrine reforms—their piecemeal character, their lack of symmetry of aim, and their dependence upon current and changing demands. And, as usual, we find those features throw difficulties in the way of our study, and incline us to wonder what is the best way of dealing with them—whether, in order to leave no Petrine innovation overlooked, we had best review the innovations chronologically, or whether, to give them a coherence otherwise apparently lacking, a systematised review would be advisable. Well, the interests of exact study will, perhaps, best be consulted if we follow Peter's own example, and pass haphazardly from one administrative sphere to another, instead of attempting to investigate his reforms on the theory that he himself observed any plan. And though, for the time being, such a course may leave us under a certain impression of confusion, that impression will become corrected when, at the close of our survey, we summarise what

149

we have studied; and the more so if in the meanwhile we observe the rule observed by all textbooks on State Law, and divide administration into central administration and local, and again subdivide both. For a start, therefore, let us follow the trend of Peter's own activity by turning first to central administration.

During the twelve years (or rather less) which elapsed between the fall of the Tsarevna Sophia and the *gubernia* reforms of 1708 (which were the difficult years, the years of Peter's preparations for his radical reforms in the spheres of war, of industry, and of finance) neither the central nor the provincial system of administration underwent any fundamental change, but was worked still under the old institutions, and on the old lines of operation. Meanwhile there stood as controller at the centre the *Boyarskaia Duma*, a body sometimes functioning in the presence of the Tsar, but more frequently in his absence, and in no way changed from the past save that the *boyaré* no longer "sat above concerning affairs,"[1] but "gathered all together in council." And under that body there still functioned the old Muscovite *Prikazi*, though now either amalgamated with one another, or split up into additional, re-named Departments, or carrying on business with new *Prikazi* constituted on the ancient model—such *Prikazi* as the *Preobrazhenski Prikaz* (a Department for managing the Guards and the Secret Police), the *Admiralteiski Prikaz* (the Department for directing the fleet), and the *Voenni-Morskoi Prikaz* (a sub-Department for administrating Peter's new foreign-hired sailors). But into this mouldering, antique form of administration gradually there crept tendencies not so much new as strengthened and revivified by the constant strife amongst one another of (1) the Court parties of the various Tsaritsas, (2) the existent ruling class (the impoverished *boyarstvo*), (3) a throng of immigrant, lowborn *parvenus*, and (4) adherents of the two chief political standpoints of the day as represented by the Westerners and the Conservatives. And the result of the struggle (which in reality was a threefold struggle) was to pave the way for personal rule, and to militate against rule by institutions, and to make it possible that during the Regency of the Tsaritsa Natalia even such a nonentity as her brother Lev could be appointed Director of the *Posolski Prikaz*,[2] and therefore come to be the head of all the Ministerial Body save T. Strieshnev, Minister of War and of the Interior, and Prince B. Golitzin, President of the *Kazanski Prikaz*, and Governor of the Volgan Provinces—where, says Kurakin, "he did rule as though he had been Tsar," and eventually laid his territories waste. Again, the result of this predominance of timeservers was "to make the *boyaré* sit in the Council Chamber but as spectacles," and

[1] See vol. ii. p. 261.   [2] *Prikaz* of Ambassadors, or Foreign Office.

to intimidate even Peter into preceding his departure upon his foreign tour in 1697 by recommending his *boyaré* and Directors of *Prikazi* to wait upon Prince Romodanovski (then Administrator of the *Preobrazhenski Prikaz*) "whensoever they may list," and "take counsel with the same"—in other words, to make themselves dependent upon a man who, according to Kurakin, was "an evil tyrant, and drunken all his days," and, according to Kurbatov, "a fellow mean in the conceit of others, but absolute in his rule," and, for the rest, an ex-*stolnik* of non-*Duma* rank, even though, through his powers as *Chef de Cabinet* and President of the *Duma*, he could of his own initiative institute political prosecutions! In short, the old legislative formula, "Thus the Tsar hath commanded, and thus the *boyaré* have decreed,"[1] underwent virtual abrogation, since now Strieshnev and Romodanovski had the whip-hand of the *Boyarskaia Duma*, and the latter's members had ceased to have articulate utterance. And another tendency—to be more exact, another inevitable phenomenon—of the day is seen in the new administrative competency which the *Duma* acquired. In 1699 the cares entailed by calls for new expenditure, and a desire to ascertain exactly what pecuniary resources lay at the disposal of the swarm of *Prikazi*, led to Peter establishing also an institution which, known sometimes as the *Schetni Prikaz*, or Office of Accounts, and sometimes as the *Blizhnaia Kantzeliaria*, or Privy Chancellory, and designed to serve as a central organ of financial control, was a Department to which all other Departments had to furnish both weekly and annual statements of their incomings and outgoings, with reports upon the various staffs and buildings subject to their jurisdiction—the whole being meant to serve as a basis whereon the *Schetni Prikaz* could subsequently frame abstracts of the Treasury's receipts as a whole. Such a set of documents, a set for the years 1701-9, M. Milinkov quotes in his well-known work, and from them we can gain full material for a study of Peter's State economy. Up to the time when he himself assumed control of the military affairs and foreign policy of his Empire the *Duma* devoted its energies solely to the Imperial, and, above all, the military, departments of the administrative machinery; but as soon as Peter had established the *Blizhnaia Kantzeliaria*, and made it the office of control for both, it inevitably became, in addition, the *Duma's* own chancellory and meeting-place, and caused certain changes to occur in that Council's composition, competency, and character. For though originally it had been composed exclusively of men of birth, the *Boyarskaia Duma* now ceased to be purely *boyarin*, and, as its *boyarin* element declined, became only a petty section of the State's chief Council, and a section bereft of its genealogical basis,

[1] See vol. ii. p. 260.

and shorn of its social prestige. Formerly the *Duma* as a whole had been a body sitting under the Tsar as its president, and acting as the Crown's inseparable partner in administrative work; but now the fact of the Tsar's frequent absences causing it frequently to have to act alone led to its becoming of dispositive importance only, and competent to decide none save such matters as might be forwarded for its consideration by one or another *Prikaz*, and merely to elaborate, and to put into initial execution, such hastily framed commissions with regard to internal government as might be delegated to it by the Tsar. And this empowering of the *boyaré* to act in Peter's absence, nor always to need to refer to him for instructions when he was absent, brought about a growing divorce between the *Duma* and its President, and, consequently, a realisation that there was needed a system which would at once obviate joint action of, and retain the joint responsibility of, the two: and at length, in 1707, Peter ordained that, to that end, the *Duma* should furnish to him, when he was absent, reports of all its debates, and append to those reports the signatures of all who had been present, "nor in any other wise determine any matters whatsoever, lest the foolishness of any Councillor stand not revealed"—which was scarcely a respectful injunction to lay upon councillors charged with a State's gravest affairs!

Owing, therefore, to the new Office of Financial Control becoming the *Boyarskaia Duma's* private chancellory, and the *Duma* itself becoming merely a small and largely non-*boyarin*-constituted dispositive and executive body —practically a Committee of Ministers, or a Board of Chief Administrators for matters of military policy—the trend of Peter's policy in the general-administrative sphere becomes plain, and we perceive that the ulterior motive of his administrative reforms was the upkeep of his new fleet and new regular army, and their immediate motive the upkeep of his new military money chest. To attain the latter, the first step was to utilise the existing system of local government for acquiring an increased aggregate of State revenue. We have seen that during the seventeenth century certain local communities petitioned that the functions of their arrogant *voevodi* should be transferred to certain *gubnie starosti*[1] to be selected from amongst the local *dvoriané*,[2] "in that," to quote Tatistchev, "there are *voevodi* of cantons who thieve with an altogether excessive daring"; and under Tsar Theodor this idea led to an idea of delegating the actual election of *voevodi* to local *dvoriané* of districts, in the hope that those *voevodi's* subjection to, firstly, selection and, secondly, supervision by their own electors would finally check the robbery practised by such supposed guardians of legality. But as a matter of fact, things did not, for the time being, go beyond a trans-

---

[1] Headmen of rural districts. [2] See vol. iii. p. 153 *et seq.*

ference of the collection of "*Strieltzi* moneys" and other indirect imposts from *voevodi* to certain *starosti* and *golovi*[1] "chosen apart from the *voevodi*," and responsible only to their electors; and only on 30 January, 1699, did an *ukaz* carry the matter a step further, and (at least so far as the metropolis was concerned) deliver the public from further spoliation at the hands of *voevodi* and officials of *Prikaz*, by ordaining that thenceforth all persons who were engaged in trade or industry should have a right to vote for "such *burmistri*,[2] good men and true, as may be desired," as local officials commissioned to have the management of their electors' assessed renderings and civil and commercial suits, whilst to all towns other than the metropolis, and to communes of "black-ploughing" and Court peasantry, there was accorded the concession that, "owing unto the many wrongs endured by towns and communes at the hands of *voevodi*," the latter were to cease to superintend the local collection of taxes, and, instead, the towns and communes concerned were, "if they shall so will," to have their fiscal dues and legal differences managed solely by representatives elected of the local *miri*, and functioning under the local *izbi*, or headquarters of self-government. But this was only to be on condition that the towns and the communes paid double in taxation! And, not unnaturally, the portion of the taxpaying public affected came to the conclusion that, after all, there was nothing much to choose between the State and the *voevodi*, and it was no better off than before. We can trace a clear resemblance between this scheme of the *ukaz* of 30 January and the manner in which Ivan IV. introduced his local institutions, since Ivan similarly offered to wrest the taxpayers from the clutches of the *kormlentschiki* if, but only if, those taxpayers rendered a special tithe to the State.[3] And we see from the fact that even a century and a half had not availed much to advance the rulers of Russia in point of administrative resource. As it was, the majority of the urban taxpayers decided that the proposed concession and its attached condition were too costly to be pleasing, and eleven towns alone, out of the seventy, accepted them—the remainder replying that, in the first place, to pay the double rate was beyond their power, and, secondly, they lacked any suitable persons to be elected as *burmistri*, whilst a few even went so far as to declare that their "just" *voevodi* and *Prikaz* officials had been giving every satisfaction! Hence the Government had at last, whilst cancelling the stipulation as to a double taxatory rate, to make the change compulsory, and the fact in itself shows us that institution of urban self-government mattered to the Government far more than it did to the towns themselves, as the

[1] Urban mayors. [2] A corruption of the Swedo-German term *Bürgermeister*.
[3] See vol. ii. chap. xv.

accompanying *ukaz* bluntly admitted when it said that "by reason of the waywardness and the excessive ingatherings of Our *voevodi*," there had resulted a serious shortage in State revenue, and, through that, again, a grave accumulation of taxatory arrears—both of which could be converted into a State profit only by thoroughly responsible and disinterested *burmistri*. The truth is that the administrative reforms of 1699 were but one of the many symptoms of a century-old administrative malady, the malady represented by the constant struggle between the Governments of Russia (or between the State of Russia as Russian Governments, as yet, understood it) and the organs of those Governments—organs of sorry quality, but at least the best that the State could find. And the main result of the administrative reforms of which I am speaking was that the *voevodi* everywhere lost their juridical and administrative authority over the commercial-industrial urban populations of their districts, and had left to them only the management of the local State service class, and of the *krestiané* owned by that class, whilst in the maritime regions of the North, where neither the class nor the *krestiané* mentioned had ever existed, the local *voevodi* altogether disappeared.

However, in localities where *voevodi* did continue to retain some sort of a position the Government met the necessity of binding their greedy hands, and those of their associations of *dvorianstvo*, with an *ukaz* of 10 March, 1702, which, after declaring the *dvorianstvo*-elected *gubnie starosti*, or guardians of the law in cantons, abolished, obviated the necessity of leaving the local *dvorianstvo* associations wholly without a share in the administration of their localities by prescribing that "henceforth all matters from the *voevodi* shall be supervised by *dvoriané* who also shall be *pomiestchiki* or *otchinniki* in towns of their regions, and men of good standing, and men chosen of the other *pomiestchiki* and *otchinniki* in the towns," and that the "chosen" *dvoriané* in question should vary in number from two to four, according to sizes of cantons. And, that done, it was only logical to follow up the foregoing grant of Collegiate-elective administration to the urban-commercial-industrial communities by granting the same to the rural land-owning class of the cantons, a class the corporate administration of which the *ukaz* of 1699 had left vested in the hands of the *voevodi*. But unfortunately, there went with the Government's administrative-logical instinct a total inability to comprehend, or to apprehend, certain existing facts the origin of which was as follows. When Peter's regular army was created the old Muscovite cantonal *dvorianin* associations, associations which had been instituted with the territorial composition of the heretofore *dvorianin* contingent for their basis, fell into dissolution through the fact that now it became the rule to enrol all *dvoriané* without exception (even to the point of haling the recalcitrant ones from their rural places of refuge) in the new, the permanent, regiments, and to send them to serve in localities remote from their homes, and to leave unmolested in their retreats only *dvoriané* retired because of military inefficiency, and *nietchiki*,[1] or persons altogether evading service. Hence, even as an idea, the Government's plan of instituting a system of rural self-administration by *dvoriané* was rather futile, seeing that for the basis of that system it had only *dvorianin* "unfits" and *lezheboki* (men who, for failure to "join up," might at any time lose their class rights altogether); and from certain archivial documents on the working of the system adduced by M. Milinkov when treating of *voevodskie tovaristchi* [2] we see how faulty the system's results in practice did indeed prove to be. For, as things turned out, the new associations of rural *dvoriané*, of *dvorianin* remnants lurking in remote rural manors, either declined to recognise the proffered right or elected no more than a sprinkling of *voevodskie tovaristchi*; and eventually the business had to give place to nomination of *voevodi* variously by one or another metropolitan *Prikaz*, or by the Tsar in person. Yet, even so, it still remained to define by regulation the limits of those *voevodi's* authority; and this, again, led to so many quarrels between *voevodi* and their *tovaristchi* that, after an existence of eight years, or nine years at the most, the experiment, an experiment interesting to us rather than important, expired by imperceptible degrees.

Of greater moment, and fraught with far graver consequences, was a change effected in the financial organisation of the urban commercial-industrial class. Hitherto the urban taxpaying communes had stood linked with the metropolitan *Prikaz* in the point that the *Prikaz Bolshoi Kazni*, or Chancellory of the Exchequer, had been the institution unto which the provincial towns had had to pay their quotas of funds collected through direct taxation—the only exception to this being that their contributions towards "*Strieltzi* moneys" had gone to the *Strieletski Prikaz* direct: but now the Government decided that, for the purpose, the provincial towns should be placed under the upper mercantile class of the capital, and that class thus made to act as the Government's central financial staff. Also, it was to fulfil certain important duties with regard to the actual organisation and collection of the provincial towns' taxes, and in 1684, as a first step, a committee of metropolitan *gosti* [3] was ordered to fix a rate of "*Strieltzi* moneys" for those towns according to capacity to pay; after which, through the reforms of 1699, that temporary order became converted into a standing

---

[1] What we should now call "slackers" or "shirkers."
[2] "*Voevodi's* comrades" or "assistants," the name given to *dvorianian* and other elected representatives of rural communities.
[3] First guild merchants.

one, and by *ukaz* of 30 January it was commanded that, for tax-collection purposes, all urban *zemskia izbi* [1] and elected *zemskie burmistri* should thenceforth become subject to the *Ratusha*, or Metropolitan Municipal Council, and to *burmistri* elected by the first guild mercantile association of the capital, and that to this joint body there should be rendered all sums of taxation collected from the provincial towns, and that annually, for the auditing of those sums, the provincial-urban *burmistri* of customs and excise who had collected the sums, during the preceding twelve months, under their local *zemskie burmistri* should be summoned to sit with the joint body as assessors, and, lastly, that, as the supreme control organ for administration of the urban commercial-industrial class, the Metropolitan *Ratusha* should have the right of presenting its reports direct to the Sovereign, and apart from the Heads of *Prikazi*. Whereby the Metropolitan *Ratusha* became, in reality, a Ministry of Towns and Urban Taxation, and had committed to its sole care the dues formerly forwarded to no fewer than thirteen different *Prikazi*, the dues represented by "*Strieltzi* moneys," customs, excise, and so forth. And though at one time those dues had amounted only to a little over, 1,000,000 roubles, increment swelled them, by 1701, to 1,300,000, or over one-third, nearly one-half, of the *Ratusha's* whole estimated ingatherings for that year. The purpose of these taxes seen to by the *Ratusha* was the upkeep of the army; and when Kurbatov, the well-known "profits man," was set over the *Ratusha's* staff, and made President of the *Ratusha's* Committee of *Burmistri*, the activity of the joint body began still further to develop. For though, originally, only a household serf who had gained the Civil Service, and, through it, been promoted to a Government Ministerial appointment, Kurbatov brought to his grandiose functions anything but a serf-like spirit, and, on finding himself wallowing in the sink of bribery and peculation which had become formed as a result of the Tsar's frequent absences from the capital, initiated a campaign for the State's benefit which never slackened, and took no account of persons. Thus his every letter to the Tsar either indicted an abuse or informed against a highly-placed rascal, and in one of them, in particular, he took it upon himself to apprise his Sovereign that both Moscow and the towns of the provinces were sheer nests of tax-peculation, that his *podiachie* even of the *Ratusha* were incurable thieves, that the provincial towns' elected *burmistri* were the same, and that the the *burmistri* of Yaroslav in particular had made away with 40,000 roubles, and the *burmistri* of Pskov with 90,000. And when an *ukaz* issued for those peculators' impeachment was frustrated through the payment

---

[1] Headquarters of local self-government, or local municipal offices. Throughout it will be remembered that the adjective *zemski* means local or territorial.

of a huge bribe to Narishkin, Kurbatov went on to attack more powerful personages still, and eventually to inform against the worst offender of all, *Obermeister* Prince Romodanovski. In fact, the only highly placed personage whom he spared was his own private patron Menshikov—who was more than suspected of being the worst Treasury despoiler of the lot! As a last step of all, he told the Tsar that the evil would never be rooted out entirely unless he, Kurbatov, was given absolutely dictatorial powers of punishment, even to "a licence to condemn the doers of such robbery unto death," whilst at the same time he seized the opportunity to chant (as he always did) his own self-praise, and to mention that he had added so many hundreds of thousands of roubles to the *Ratusha's* income that that income now stood at a million and a half. Yet, whether or not this last was true, we at least know that the *Ratusha* had great difficulty in satisfying the State's military expenditure, and that this continued to be so until Peter's *gubernia* reforms [1] brought both the *Ratusha's* rôle in finance and Kurbatov's activities in the *Ratusha* to an end.

The real cause of the *gubernia* reforms of 1708 was a special bent of Peter's activity which itself owed its cause both to events external and to events internal, to events connected directly with war and to events connected only indirectly with war. In general, his predecessors had always remained seated in their capital, and never left that capital save to go upon a campaign, or, very rarely, to make a pilgrimage; and for this reason their administration had, throughout, been of a centralised character, and all local renderings to the Exchequer, direct and indirect, had filtered through the Tsar's *voevodi*, then made their way to the metropolis, then accumulated in the metropolis' various *Prikazi*, and, lastly, disappeared altogether, save for such portions of them as might be needed to pay provincial officials, or to meet local expenditure. But to this antiquated and stagnant system of financial centralisation Peter administered a first check by abandoning the ancient capital, the centre of the country, and moving outwards to the circumference, and then so touring the furthest confines of the land as, either with his red-hot vigour or with the popular upheavals resultant from that vigour, to galvanise every province visited into life. Never did the trail of his military activity leave any locality, whether inland or on a frontier, quiescent. Invariably it left the people of that region brought with a start to their feet, and engaged upon new and onerous undertakings. Thus, as soon as he had concluded his first expedition against Azov he set to work to construct his Voronezh flotilla of ships—meanwhile making over to a

---

[1] That is to say, the scheme of reforms by which Peter re-divided the country into *gubernii*, or provinces, with new *gubernia* institutions.

local *Admiralteiski Prikaz* which he instituted for the purpose a group of towns in the Don basin, and commandeering thousands of workmen, and, over the heads of the metropolitan *Prikazi*, allotting the local taxes exclusively to his shipbuilding operations. The same, again, when Azov was finally taken— he then re-allotted all the local taxes and man-power to the purely local purpose of building a harbour at Taganrog. Similarly, on conquering Ingria at the other end of the country, he set about the dual task of rearing St. Petersburg and (for the benefit of his Baltic fleet) laying out a port at Olonetz. Again, in 1705, on his innovations bringing about an outbreak in Astrakhan, he crushed the rising, and then reorganised the region throughout—transferred the task of local revenue-collection from the institutions of the centre to those of the locality itself, and assigned the proceeds purely to local requirements. And, lastly, when King August of Poland was forced to make peace with Charles XII. in 1706, and Peter suddenly found that Charles was overrunning that country, and developing a threat on the Russian flank, he drew upon the funds of the Central Administration, and, with their aid, formed of Kiev and Smolensk two new chief administrative districts, to serve as buffer regions. All of which events gradually brought him to realise that it would be far better if the taxatory ingatherings from the provinces ceased to be sent to wander about amongst the metropolitan *Prikazi*, and, instead, were forwarded direct to new provincial administrative headquarters instituted for the purpose, and furnished with an increased competence of local chief administrative officials. And so, though the provinces subsequently known as *gubernii*, or governments, had not yet come into existence, he accorded the leading administrative workers of localities the title of *gubernatori*, or governors, and was enabled the more easily to develop his ideas in this direction through the fact that already certain pertinent experiments had been made, in that for some time past Moscow had had in operation four "District *Prikazi*," as institutions designed to exercise independent financial control over their respective areas, the four areas represented by Kazan, Siberia, Smolensk, and Little Russia, with a partial military jurisdiction added; and that therefore, in so far as these four areas at least were concerned, all that required to be done was to transfer their departmental heads of *Prikazi* from the metropolis to the actual regions which those *Prikazi* administered. Yet the immediate cause of Peter coming to realise that all such officials had better be brought into direct contact with their administered populations was less any necessity of facilitating local administrative management than Peter's own self-created position, the position born of his war-makings, a position through which he had learnt how impossible it was to superintend diplomatic negotiations, to conduct military campaigns, to see to domestic affairs, and to tour the country all at one and the same time, and had had brought home to him that even to attempt to continue doing so would soon shatter his efficiency as an administrator. In fact, he appends to the letter in which he apprises Kurbatov of his institution of *gubernii* the remark that "both to learn of and to govern all things, even unto things which do lie beyond a man's actual vision, is indeed a hard matter!" Subsequently, on finally losing hope that his central *Prikazi* and the *Ratusha* would ever be able to cope with military expenditure, he placed the more important of the provincial districts under commissioned *pomiestchiki*, under the idea that merely those officials' local social position would suffice to accomplish his ends; and from that, led, as always, by his essential bent to place his trust in persons rather than in institutions, he went on to devise a scheme whereby it should be to the actual districts themselves which these commissioned *pomiestchiki* were provisionally administering that the army's upkeep and budget should be assigned. And since, in addition to having this dim perception of the advantage of "all administration being gathered into one," and evolving such a scheme for a unified Exchequer as Kurbatov had more than once submitted to him for his approval, he shared the generally prevailing view that each item of expenditure ought to be allotted its own source of income (when explaining to Kurbatov his theory of *gubernia* reform, he wrote that "all warlike and other payments should so be apportioned unto *gubernii* as to let every man concerned know whence each sum hath come,") he ended by placing this plan at the basis of his reformed system of province-division.

He effected the initiation of that system through an *ukaz* of 18 December, 1707. Worded in his usual obscure and laconic style, the *ukaz* merely assigned certain towns to Kiev, Smolensk, and other provincial centres; but next year the *boyaré* of the *Blizhnaia Kantzeliaria* recast this preliminary scheme to the extent of distributing the whole of the 341 towns of the provinces to eight new chief areas—to *gubernii* of Moscow, of Ingermanland (subsequently the *provintzia* of St. Petersburg), of Kiev, of Smolensk, of Archangel, of Kazan, of Azov, and of Siberia; whilst in 1711 the particular group of towns in the *gubernii* of Azov which had been allocated to Peter's shipbuilding enterprise appeared independently as the *gubernia* of Voronezh, and so raised the number of the new *gubernii* to nine, a number the same as that of the old *razriadi* (military districts [1]) which had been delimited in Theodor's reign, though the coincidence does not extend beyond a similarity of plan of military-administrative adjustment—more precisely, of administrative organisation into military-administrative areas. For the territorial

[1] See vol. iii. p. 156.

delimitation of Peter's new *gubernii* marched neither with that of the old *razriadi* nor with that of the existing *okrugi*, or areas administered by the "District *Prikazi*" of the metropolis, since in places a *gubernia* would coincide with two or more *okrugi*, and in others a *gubernia* contain within it portions of *okrugi* the bulk of which lay within others. This was because Peter made allocation of *gubernia* boundaries depend variously upon distances of towns from gubernial centres and upon the topography of means of communication—an instance being that he assigned to the new *gubernia* of Moscow all the towns situated upon the nine trunk roads which radiated outwards from Moscow towards Novgorod, Kolomna, Kashir, and elsewhere. Another feature was that this administrative re-shuffle lent itself to personal claims as regards nomination to the office of *gubernator*, for those new posts are everywhere seen becoming filled by such personages as Menshikov, Strieshnev, Apraxin, and the rest. And when the new *gubernii* had been demarcated they needed to have allotted to them their respective shares in provision of military upkeep, and, on total aggregates of future military expenditure having been calculated, to have those aggregates imposed in proportion to each *gubernia's* capacity. These points show the *gubernia* reforms' fundamental purpose. Further development of the scheme Peter delegated to the *Blizhnaia Kantzeliaria* and the new *gubernatori*; but so long did the debates over it drag on in the *Duma*, and at gubernatorial conventions, that it was not until 1712 that definitely the new administrative machinery could be set in motion. Hence Peter's *gubernia* reforms not only took a long time to prepare, but called for four years' strenuous work before they could become effectively operative. And, even so, they did not at once work altogether smoothly, for the *Blizhnaia Kantzeliaria*, the chief pertinent institution of control, altogether forgot, when distributing the regiments to their respective *gubernii*, that nineteen corps existed at all. The truth is that though Peter had been considering means of allocating the cost of military upkeep to the best advantage ever since the winning of Poltava, and daily expecting, as he thought out his plans for quartering regiments, that peace would soon arrive, he had kept being disappointed in this respect, and, as a matter of fact, the struggle went on for eleven years longer.

A peculiar feature of the *gubernia* reforms was the thick coating of administrative varnish which they, incidentally, laid upon local government. For each *gubernator* had accorded to him, according to a Staff List of 1715, a *vitz-gubernator* to assist him with respect to a portion of his area, a *Landrichter* to supervise the judicial matters of his *gubernia*, an *Ober-provientmeister*, sundry *Provientmeister*, to collect the *gubernia's* grain dues, and a squad of commissaries of the ordinary kind. Whence the *gubernator's*

authority was far from being a unipersonal authority, and the less so in
that, in spite of the fact that the experiment of appointing *voevodskie
tovaristchi* to help the local *dvorianin* associations in the task of local government had proved a failure in the cantons, Peter now repeated the experiment on a larger scale than before, and by *ukaz* of April 24, 1713,
prescribed that gubernatorial staffs also should have posted to them a
number of *Landräthe* varying according to *gubernii*, from eight to twelve,
and authorised to let no matter be decided without their cognisance, or save
by a majority of votes. In short, the *gubernator* was "not so much a ruler
in his *consilium* as its president," and the more so as his vote there had but
the value of two *Landräthe's* votes. The office of *Landrath* Peter borrowed
from East Zealand [1] after conquering that region; and at first the Senate
selected the holders of the office strictly according to duplicate lists furnished
it for the purpose by *gubernatori*; but later (probably through having discovered by experience that appointment of a *gubernator's* advisors solely
on that *gubernator's* nomination was scarcely an advisable step) Peter
thought further on the subject, and, by *ukaz* of 20 January, 1714, prescribed
that "*landratori* henceforth be chosen in Our towns and *provintzii* by all
the *dvoriané* there, and from amongst the chief men thereof." And as the
Senate calmly left this mandate unfulfilled, and went on, as before, to select
the concerned officials solely on its own account, and to make gubernatorial
lists the basis of their selection, Peter, in 1716, substituted for the ordinance
which the Senate had been disregarding for two years past a command
that thence onwards the Senate should appoint to act as *Landräthe* only
military officers who had been retired for old age or wounds, and by this edict
made of the *Landrath* less an elected representative of a given locality's
dvorianin association, or an official attached exclusively to the *gubernator's*
staff, than a *chinovnik*-commissioner attached equally to the *gubernator* and
to the Senate. Which, of course, was, really, the story of the *voevodskie
tovaristchi* repeated. However, even before Peter's promulgation of this
ukaz, the *ukaz* conferring the office solely upon wounded officers, the office
in question had diverged somewhat from its original form. Be it remembered
that Peter's *gubernii* covered areas which in every case were as large as two
or more of our modern *gubernii*—his *gubernia* of Moscow, for instance,
comprising not only the whole of the present-day *gubernia* of that name,
but also portions of the present-day *gubernii* of Kaluga, Tula, Vladimir,
Yaroslav, and Kostroma; whilst subsequently the old *uezd*, or canton, was
revived, and subdivided the *gubernia* further—the *uezd*, for the most part,
being an area of small dimensions. Hence at last the disproportion between

---

[1] The Swedish provinces south of the Baltic.

administrative fractions and administrative wholes became such as to evoke a demand for an intermediate unit, and the year 1711 saw *uezdi* begin to be mutually combined into *provintzii*. Yet, even so, the measure was neither general in scope nor simultaneous in initiation, but one carried out by degrees, and only in accordance with local and other considerations—an example of this being that eight *provintzii* were formed out of the *uezdi* constituting only a portion of the *gubernia* of Moscow. And later Peter accentuated still further the system's complexity by adding to subdivision of *gubernii* into *uezdi* and *provintzii* a third form of subdivision. This was because, since *gubernii* differed greatly amongst themselves in numbers of taxpaying *dvori* (for example, the *gubernia* of Moscow contained 246,000 such *dvori* as against the *gubernia* of Azov's 42,000), they also differed greatly amongst themselves in revenue-producing powers: and when assessment per *dvor* became too minute a process to be convenient Peter, as a man who cared for none but the simplest of mathematical problems, set himself to reduce the variations in *gubernia* dimensions to a financial common denominator through the method of inventing a purely computative unit termed the *dolia*, or "portion." To each of these *doli* he ascribed exactly 5536 *dvori*, on the arbitrary assumption that the Empire as a whole contained with equal exactitude 812,000 (probably the assumption came of the census-list of 1678); and when this had been done he commanded that by the number of *doli* ascribed by him to each *gubernia* there should be determined the contribution of each *gubernia* to the general tax-rendition. Next, the office of *Landrath* instituted, he converted the *dolia* from a purely computative unit into an actual administrative area by subdividing into *doli*, not the total numbers of *dvori* in each *gubernia* as those numbers stood in the financial estimates, but the *gubernii* themselves. Moreover, on it becoming clear, by the year 1711, that the system of joint administration by *voevodi* and *voevodskie tovaristchi* was a failure, and, as the result, *gubernia* institutions being introduced, there resulted the situation that though in localities where the *voevodi* had survived the reforms of 1699 those officials reappeared under the name merely of *Kommandaten*, they reappeared in possession of all their old financial and judicial authority over the populations of both their rural and their urban *uezdi*—an abrogation of urban self-government with regard to which it is difficult to determine whether it came of a dispensation from above or of action (through the working of usedness or custom) from below. And no sooner had *uezdi* become grouped into *provintzii* under *Oberkommandaten* and *Kommandaten* than an *ukaz* of 28 January, 1715 annulled the old subdivision into *uezdi*, and also the superimposed subdivision into *provintzii*, and the commissions of the staffs of *Oberkommandaten* and *Kommandaten*, and, instead, divided the *gubernii* into *doli*, and set over those *doli* a number of *Landräthe* armed with financial, police, and judicial powers—but only over the rural populations, not over the urban, whom the *Landräthe* were forbidden to "molest," whether in their public affairs or in their private. This *ukaz* of 28 January, therefore, carried the process of reconstruction of the provincial administrations to the point of once and for all abolishing their old-established basis the *uezd*. True, in some cases we find new *doli* coinciding with *uezdi* which they had replaced, but in other cases the boundaries of a new *dolia* are seen to enclose within themselves two or more extinct *uezdi*, or else to have broken up an *uezd* in defiance both of history and of geography, and according solely to symmetry of arithmetical plan. Also, in actual practice the authorities found it impossible to parcel out *gubernii* into blocks precisely corresponding with the 5536 *dvori* which each *dolia* was supposed to contain, and therefore a fresh *ukaz* had to empower *gubernatori* to assign to any *dolia*, "as may be found most expedient, and always as having respect unto distances," either more or less than the normal unit of 5536 *dvori*. The result was that, whereas a given *dolia* might contain 8000 *dvori*, a neighbouring *dolia* might contain only half that number, and the aggregate of *doli* as a whole was made to differ greatly from the corresponding aggregate of normal units, even though it was by this number of *doli* that the share of each *gubernia* in the general discharge of State obligations was determined. This discovery, the discovery that *dolia*-numbers determined those shares only haphazardly, "and according unto the judgment of the *gubernator* alone," made hay of the Imperial Legislator's figurings, and accordingly he had in certain cases correspondingly to increase the local *Landrath* personnel—an example being that in the *gubernia* of Moscow the *doli* originally estimated to constitute the area's proper complement had to have added to their original thirteen *Landräthe* a further batch of thirty-one. In 1715 yet another *ukaz* dissolved the *gubernator's* council of *Landräthe*, dissolved the organ which until now had constituted the *gubernia's* central administrative body, and, whilst leaving the *doli* with their heretofore attached quotas of *Landräthe*, yet considering it inadvisable for the *gubernator* to administer his area altogether without attendance and supervision, prescribed a system by which two *Landräthe* should always be in waiting upon him for a one, or a two, months turn of duty per pair, and that at the close of the year all the local *Landräthe* should repair to the local capital to audit the *gubernia's* accounts for the past twelve months, and to render a final decision upon any matter which called for a full conclave's decision. Unfortunately, the result was an ambiguous relation between *Landrath* and *gubernator*, in that, though the *Landrath* administered only a portion of his particular *gubernia*, and therefore was his *gubernator's* subordinate, he was also a member of the local Council of *Landräthe*, and therefore his *gubernator's* colleague. Naturally, the former of the two relations won the day, and the *gubernator* thereby acquired a sort of plenipotentiary status, as chief administrator of his area, and took to treating his *Landräthe* "as though he had been full ruler, and not only the region's overseer"—he took to ordering them about, and to commanding their attendance upon him out of turn, and even to subjecting them, although they were his colleagues, to arrest. Thus there resulted from an over-hasty process of remodelling the provincia institutions a radical disorganisation of service discipline, and from this over-abundant conferment of authority an inducement to those who stood subject to that authority to respond to it with disobedience. A particularly striking instance of this is seen at the close of 1715, when the fact that the country's staffs of *Landräthe* were still fresh to the work of administering their *doli* did not prevent Peter from laying upon them also the task of taking censuses of those *doli*. Naturally, to add this huge charge to the already existent labour of local administration had the effect of hindering both, and the taking of the censuses dragged over into the year 1716, and then into the next year. Indeed, in spite of the Tsar's and the Senate's best efforts to accelerate the affair by issuing instructions that when the staffs of *Landräthe* presented themselves in the capital, in the ordinary course, at the close of 1717 they were to do so with their census-lists all ready in their pockets, not a *Landrath* turned up before the year 1718, and even then but a few appeared, and one in particular had to have as many as thirteen Imperial missives dispatched to him before he reported himself, and another so far flouted the command that a *Landrath* showing himself recalcitrant in the matter should be forwarded to the capital in chains, and have his local staff arrested on warrants, and placed in detention, as not only to continue absent, but insolently to reply that anyone laying a finger upon his staff should receive, in return, a sound thrashing.

In short, Peter's legislation with regard to his *gubernia* reforms displayed neither carefully considered theory nor swift constructive calculation. For the purpose of that legislation was exclusively fiscal: his design with regard to his *gubernia* institutions was solely that they should act as a press for the taxpayer, and squeeze him dry of his money—they were not intended at all to benefit the popular weal. And, true enough, the Treasury's needs kept constantly increasing, and *gubernatori* not at all bestirring themselves to overtake them, even though by 1715 the fleet alone was costing almost double what it had cost in 1711, and lack of means for getting minerals was hindering the Baltic battleships from putting to sea, and detachments of the land forces were failing to receive their pay, and converting themselves into armed bands of brigands, and no money was available for the country's ambassadors to foreign courts, whether as personal salary, or as the wherewithal to meet the usual secret service expenses. And this although Peter goaded his executive officials with "harsh *ukazi*," and told supine *gubernatori* that if they "still did run so greatly after liquor" they would find themselves "treated not with words alone, but also with the hand," and bade the Senate "spare no mulctings of *gubernatori* who seek to find new springs of money only through an oppression of the people," and commanded that *Landräthe* who should fail to forward their ingatherings in full tale should refund a year's salary (120 roubles), and that, however much commissaries of *gubernii* (financial middlemen between the Senate and the *gubernatori*) should stand personally exonerated for any failure to produce the local amount of taxes, they should nevertheless receive three doses of *pravozh* [1] per week until the taxes appeared—which instructions show us that even under Peter, the State's staple methods of heartening an executive official had not progressed beyond "mulctings" and the rod. On the other hand, there were cases in which a zeal to acquire "profits" for the State's benefit led *gubernatori* to stick at nothing at all. Thus Apraxin, brother to the Grand-Admiral, and acting *gubernator* of Kazan, had it spread abroad that a new source of fiscal revenue had come to his knowledge, and followed up the intelligence by presenting Peter with 120,000 (1,000,000) roubles-worth of "profits." But though, to justify his claim to financial inventiveness, he subsequently, in addition to extracting the 120,000 roubles from some miserable aliens who resided in his *gubernia*, made 18,000 for himself by forcing those aliens to purchase Treasury tobacco at a price equal to two modern roubles a pound, these "profits" to the State eventually cost the State more than double their sum, owing to the fact that the above-mentioned persecuted aliens departed out of the *gubernia* in such numbers as in the end to leave 33,000 *dvori* tenantless, and so, despite the Treasury's efforts to restrain the movement, to deprive the Exchequer of a taxatory sum nearly three times Apraxin's privately pocketed gains. The mere fact that the Government had thus to turn hither and thither, and to strive to reduce expenditure in one quarter, and introduce extraordinary or temporary imposts in another, whilst all the while reaping only a third or so of those imposts' amount, meant, really, that there was nothing left to gather in, and that, in his chronic apprehensions of a chronic deficit, and in his utter distrust of his mouldering *Prikaz* Administration, and

[1] See footnote on p. 134.

in his constant endeavours to get rid of these difficulties through the method of decentralisation, of transference of the State's fiscal institutions from the capital to the provinces, and in his growing realisation of the expedient's futility, and in his constant, spasmodical reboundings to the centre with his administration, Peter was but re-enacting the well-known fable of the musicians.

The peculiar features accruing to the *Boyarskaia Duma* during Peter's reign were shared by the administrative institutions with which he replaced that conciliary body. Originally his Senate was meant only to be, firstly, an occasional, or an *ad hoc*, commission empowered to sit apart from the *Duma* during absences of the Sovereign abroad, and, secondly, a temporary committee into which the *Duma* might at any time resolve itself whenever he was absent anywhere at all, whether temporarily or protractedly, as when, in preparation for the Turkish campaign in 1711, he on 22 February issued an *ukaz* saying curtly that, "to the end that We may withdraw Ourselves hence, We have determined to institute a Senate for the work of administration," and when, on another occasion, an *ukaz* varied the phrase with, "We have determined to institute an Administrative Senate for withdrawals of Ourselves during the present war." In short, the Senate, at first, was a body organised "only for a season," since never at any time can Peter have meditated absenting himself *sine die* as frequently as was done by Charles XII. of Sweden. The next thing was that an *ukaz* fixed the newly instituted Senate's *personnel* at nine, a number equal to that of the still surviving members of the once multitudinous *Boyarskaia Duma*, and then that an *ukaz* transferred to the Senate a third of that *Duma*, in the shape of the Counts Mussin-Pushkin, Strieshnev, and Plemiannikov, and, finally, that on 2 March, 1711, the whole had imposed upon them the duty of taking general charge of affairs during absences of the Sovereign, and particular charge of (1) the judiciary, (2) the State's expenditure and revenue, (3) the enrolment of *dvoriané* and their retainers as military officers, (4) the commercial assets of the Treasury, and (5) the workings of exchange and trade. Also, the Senate's authority and responsibilities were defined—an *ukaz* commanding that thenceforth all officials and Departments of State were to obey it equally with the Sovereign himself, and to receive the penalty of death in case of disobedience, yet at the same time intimating that, should the Senate itself be reported to him for any irregularity before his return, he would, after his return, make the Senators account to him fully for their proceedings. And thence onwards there were occasions when, even though Peter was sojourning in foreign parts, he would send the Senate instructions on administrative irregularities "which, owing unto this distance and unto this grievous war, I cannot of Myself observe"; whilst on one occasion in particular he appended an intimation that the Senators must superintend things the more strictly "in that ye have no other business save the business of administration, which, shall ye not perform it with care, shall, before God, suffer you to escape judgment neither here nor hereafter!" Frequently, also, Peter summoned his Senators to such temporary halting-places as Revel or St. Petersburg, and bade them bring with them "clerks who may be meet for reckoning what hath been done under Our *ukazi*, and what hath not been done, and, of the latter, the reasons why it hath not been fulfilled." Yet the Senate's original competency shows none of the legislative powers which the *Duma* had possessed, since, though it was a conclave of Chief Administrators, it was less the Tsar's Council of State than merely a supreme dispositive institution responsible for the transaction of current Government affairs, and for execution of such commissions as the Sovereign might choose to entrust to it, during the Sovereign's absences—when, but only when, it became "a Council in room of his Majesty's own person." On the other hand, though its competency included neither military operations nor foreign policy, the Senate did inherit from its predecessor, the *Duma* or State Council, the Departments represented by the *Raspravnaia Palata*, or Hall of Justice, as the Senate's own chancellory for legal dispensation, and by the *Blizhnaia Kantzeliaria*, as the Senate's own chancellory for assistance in the task of revising the State's income and expenditure. The net outcome of it all was the Senate's temporary commission of 1711 became, in time, a commission held by a permanent Chief Institution, even as the *ad hoc* Staff-Office on the banks of the Neva became, in time, the Imperial capital, and as Alexander Menshikov, the *uriadnik* (senior sergeant) of the Preobrazhenski Regiment, became, in time, the *Hertzog* of Izhor, and a functionary described by Kurakin as "a very autocrat in his rule."

Further, we can trace a close connection between the origin and evolution of the Senate and the *gubernia* reforms of 1708. In the first place, those reforms nullified, or at all events undermined, the old *Prikaz* central-administrative system by abolishing the *Prikazi* of Siberia and Kazan, transferring their jurisdiction to the Provinces whence they took their respective titles, and transforming certain other *Prikazi* from institutions of the State at large into institutions of the *gubernia* of Moscow only—a particular case being that of the Muscovite *Ratusha*, which descended merely to filling the position of Moscow's Municipal Board. And from this process there resulted a State of very peculiar construction, since it was made up of eight large satrapies based, not upon a geographical centre, not upon a capital (as a matter of fact, no such capital was then existent for them to be based upon, seeing that Moscow had ceased to be a capital, and St. Petersburg had not yet become one), but upon a personal, movable centre that was for ever starting off along its own radii towards its own periphery—upon, in other words, Tsar Peter himself. Moreover, the chief administrative council in that State was a council so fortuitous of session and composition, and so irregular of procedure, that whereas a members' list for the year 1705 shows the number of its *dumnie liudi* and *boyaré* and *okolnichi* and *dumnie dvoriané* to have been thirty-eight, early in 1706, when Charles XII. unexpectedly made a sally from Poland with the design of cutting the Russian communications at Grodno, and decisive measures had at once to be considered and adopted, Peter found that he had with him in Moscow, for his assistance, only two Ministers of the necessary *Duma* rank, since the remainder were all away "on service," that is to say, making official tours of their districts. Also, though the few *Prikazi* of first-class grade which Peter's scheme left functioning in Moscow included the four Departments empowered to deal with requistions and expenditure (the *Voinski Prikaz*, the *Artilleriski Prikaz*, the *Admiralteiski Prikaz*, and the *Posolski Prikaz*), and though the old capital still remained the centre for tax-reception, the scheme deprived that capital of any headquarters institution to direct the reapers and the reaping of the financial harvest—to direct, that is to say, the *personnel* and the work of the new *gubernia* administrations. In fact, no longer was there any real Chief Administrative system at all in being, for Peter's absorption in military-strategical-diplomatic operations blinded him to the fact that even when he had got his eight *gubernii* organised, and had fitted them out with their several complements of pay-offices and recruiting-offices designed to maintain and support the army during the struggle with Russia's dangerous external foe, the State was still without a central administration for home affairs, and the Sovereign had no one standing duly empowered to interpret, and forthwith to put into execution, his autocratic will. Least of all was the Senate, though a conclave of Chief Administrators, and one having for its place of session the *Blizhnaia Kantzeliaria*, such a suitable executor, since it lacked both regularity of competency and permanency of composition, not to mention that its members also had other duties to perform, and that, even so, they stood bound to sign their assembly's minutes of debate, for fear lest acts of "foolishness" on their part should escape their President's notice! Wherefore what Peter really needed in this connection was not so much a State *Duma*, whether legislative or advisory, as a small, plain directorate of prudent statesmen who could at once divine the Imperial will, grasp the idea lying concealed beneath the laconic, cryptic wording of an *ad hoc*, hastily framed *ukaz*, develop that idea into an intelligible, workable ordinance, and authoritatively put that ordinance into execution; a directorate strong enough to be generally feared, yet also sufficiently responsible itself to be capable of fear; a directorate qualified to figure in the popular eye as the Tsar's *alter ego*, yet permanently conscious that over it there stood the Tsar's *quos ego*. At all events, these were the theoretical considerations by which a creator of a Senate for the State would have been governed if Peter had allowed anyone but himself to be that creator.

According to the rules, all Senatorial decisions had to be arrived at unanimously: and for fear lest any such decision should be extorted through means of personal pressure, Peter introduced into the Senate none of his chief coadjutors—no men of the type of Menshikov, Apraxin, Sheremetiev, and Golovkin. True, he allowed them to render him intimate assistance in the two extra-Senatorial spheres represented by military affairs and diplomacy, and so qualified them to rank as "highest lords" or "principals," and in certain matters to stand above the Senate's jurisdiction, and have power to write to that body "by order of his Imperial Majesty in person"; yet even Menshikov once received a broad hint that, however much he might be Prince of Izhor, he was, as *Gubernator* of St. Petersburg, bound to obey the Senate equally with the *gubernatori* of the provinces. Thus we see two systems of administration cutting across one another, and possessing interlacing competencies, and standing subordinate to one another, and standing mutually independent! The fact that the period's political sense actually could accept two such incompatible sets of administrative relations came of the circumstance that the period's statesmen neither could nor would think out political matters to a logical conclusion. And in any case the Senate's body was made up, primarily, of second-rate ex-officials only—Samarin, for example, had held merely the office of Military Treasurer, and Prince G. Volkonski that of Director of the Government's factories at Tula, and Apukhtin that of Quartermaster-General. Yet this is not to say that such men had not as good a capacity for the conduct of war as their so-called "principals," or that, if entrusted with it, they would not have made it the prime object of their senatorial solicitude; whilst, as regards peculation of funds, neither they nor anyone else could well have surpassed such "principals" as Menshikov and Prince M. Dolgoruki; of whom the latter could not write his own name, and the former could do so only by laboriously, painfully tracing its several characters.

Hence there were two conditions which were the outcome of administrative needs, and caused the Senate to become established as a temporary Commission, and then to have its continued existence confirmed, and, lastly,

IV—M

to have its composition, jurisdiction, and status defined. Which conditions were (1) the disruption of the old *Boyarskaia Duma* and (2) the Tsar's frequent absences from the capital. Of these, the condition of the disappearance of the old Central Administration evoked a need for a supreme administrative institution which should stand possessed of a permanent *personnel*, and also of a definite jurisdiction with regard to such matters as might be assigned to its exclusive charge; whilst the condition of the Tsar's frequent absences ended by creating an institution dispositive and supervisory, but not possessed of any consultative standing, legislative authority, or, since its powers were temporary only, liability to be called to account.

The Senate's most important task, at all events the task looming largest to Peter when he instituted that body, was the supreme supervision and conduct of the administrative system. For its assistant in framing the annual Budget it usually had the *Blizhnaia Kantzeliaria*, but one of its first acts in setting its administrative house in order was to establish a second organ of financial control, and through *ukaz* of 5 March, 1711, to secure for itself the necessary authority to select a prudent, upright man as "*Oberfiskal*" to keep an eye upon financial affairs in general, to enquire into any official's legal irregularity "in collecting moneys for the Treasury or otherwise," and to hale Treasury peculators before the Senate "no matter how eminent they may be," and there indict them, and, if the charge was proved, annex half the fine, or, if the charge was dismissed, disclaim responsibility for the acquittal, "nor have the same imputed unto him under pain of cruel punishment and despoilment of goods." And since also this *Oberfiskal* was to control a network of financial agents and *Fiskale* covering every district and every district-administrative department, with, according to the *ukaz* of ordination, every town (and Russia's then towns numbered 340) having at least one *Fiskal* appointed to it, and sometimes two, it follows that the total corps of metropolitan, provincial, and provincial-urban *Fiskale* cannot have amounted to much fewer than 500, and that the network must have grown larger still when the fleet also evolved an *Oberfiskal* and a staff of *Fiskale* of its own. Unfortunately, lack of responsibility led these functionaries to indulge in arbitrary acts, and at length even the *Oberfiskal*, Nesterov, though hitherto stern in his prosecution of irregularities, and bold in accusing members of the Senate itself, of the law's supreme guardian, of his own directing agency, and going to the lengths of indicting no less a man than Prince Y. T. Dolgoruki, whose official integrity had passed as a proverb, and of bringing to the gallows Prince Gagarin, *Gubernator* of Siberia—yes, at length Nesterov himself had to be impeached for accepting bribes, and was found guilty, and broken on the wheel!

And though it had always been the case that judicial procedure had permitted initiation of prosecutions on *donos*, or secret information, alone, the fact that the weapon had sometimes proved double-edged through the necessity, if the accused was submitted to torture and then acquitted, of the informant himself having to undergo torture, led the Government, whilst establishing *Fiskale*, also to establish *donos* as a regular State institution, and thereby obviate the risk to the informant—thus introducing into the administrative system and the community alike an unsound moral motive. Nor, at all events so far as Great Russia was concerned, did the Hierarchy break silence on the point—the Great Russian episcopate was too indifferent to public affairs, as well as too incapable of morally educating even its own flocks. Only in Little Russia did Stepan Yavorski, the local Metropolitan, and guardian of the local Patriarchal Throne, at length find the situation so intolerable that in 1713 he seized the occasion of the Tsar's nameday to preach before the Senators a sermon denouncing as "a vicious law" the *ukaz* through which *Fiskale* had come into being, and making some transparent allusions to certain features in Peter's private life. Yet though the Senators forbade Stepan ever again to preach in their presence, Peter took no action at all against his distinguished accuser, and possibly even had Stepan's homily in mind when, by subsequent *ukaz* of 1714 he placed the whole body of *Fiskale* upon a stricter and more responsible basis, and charged them also with the procuratorial duty of investigating "all such matters of the people as already have existing for them no right of petition." And in any case another prelate of Little Russia, Theofan Prokopovitch, subsequently atoned for his liberal colleague's outburst by (albeit rather shamefacedly) inserting into his "Spiritual *Reglament*" an injunction that thenceforth the *zakazchiki* (lay deans) of Little Russia were to account themselves "decorous persons appointed to act as spiritual *Fiskale*," and, in that capacity, to acquaint their bishops with any ecclesiastical irregularities or superstitious customs of which they might hear. And all too soon the newly-instituted Senate itself laid aside its scruples, and, in imitation of the "Spiritual *Reglament*," introduced into each of its subordinate Departments persons not merely "appointed to act as spiritual *Fiskale*," but persons in very truth appointed such, and gave them an organisation similar to that of the lay corps of *Fiskale* save that they bore the title, not of *Fiskale*, but of (here the Senate drew upon Catholic terminology in order to render itself more intelligible to the spiritual ear) "inquisitors." At the same time, no one was to be appointed an inquisitor unless he was a "man clean of conscience," and also of monasterial standing; whilst for the post of Inquisitor-in-Chief there was selected a *hieronomakh* named Pafnuti, builder of the Danilov Monastery near Moscow. Thus, so far from restricting *donos* to the sphere of official relations only, Peter's legislation helped *donos* to enter upon a yet wider field of action. Legally, his *Fiskale*, as a corps, represented one of the Senate's auxiliary instruments: yet always (and, perhaps, the more so because sometimes *Fiskale* informed against Senators themselves) the Senatorial body treated it with coldness and contempt, and Prince Dolgoruki once dubbed it "a band of antichrists and rascals." So at last, realising that the office was not exactly a bed of roses, but a distinctly unpopular one, Peter took the fraternity under his peculiar protection, and then set out to enlist enthusiasm for *donos* through an *ukaz* which, ostensibly purporting to combat fraud, or attempted fraud, against the State's interest, proclaimed that thenceforth no man—"none, even from the highest unto the tiller of the soil"—need fear at once to approach the Tsar whensoever such a one should hear that anyone had robbed the people, or, indeed, committed any act against the Imperial advantage. And for this denunciation the *ukaz* went so far as to prescribe a season, from October to March, whilst for his "services" in denunciation the *bona fide* informant was to receive the denounced's movable and immovable property, and also his *chin*, or rank. Wherefore, the system being such, it became possible that if, say, a *krestianin* belonging to Prince Dolgoruki laid a "true report" against his master, and the law was strictly implemented, that *krestianin* could forthwith receive not only his master's manor, but also his master's position as *General-Kriegsplenipotentiar*! The only unpleasant point about the *ukaz* was that also it commanded that any person detecting an infringement of the law without reporting the same to the authorities should "be beaten without mercy, or put to death." In general, the ordinance led to both the *Fiskal* and the plain individual looking upon *donos* as "a service done unto the State," or even as a natural duty, and to men's consciences being commandeered for the Treasury's benefit even as horses were impressed for that of the War Department. And, stimulated and refreshed with fines, the pursuit of engaging in detective work, of promiscuously laying information, became a regular trade or livelihood, and acted as the law's most active guardian, as the prime protagonist of good order. For example, although hitherto the Russian clergy's threats of posthumous retribution had lamentably failed to make their flocks respect either their priest or their parish church, so that the flocks had persistently brawled during hours of divine service, and chattered throughout the Liturgy, those flocks fell to silence on learning that to pastoral menaces there had become added an Imperial injunction that thenceforth all men should hold their tongues during performance of the sacred offices, and that "worthy persons" had been appointed to see that this was done, and that to any brawler in church there was to be meted out, first of all ejectment from the building, and then a fine of a rouble.

In this manner the Senate became at once the chief custodian of the State's legal dispensation and the chief overseer of the State's fiscal economy. Yet from the first it had at its disposal only faulty, inferior instruments, since at the time that it was instituted the administrative centre was still lying heaped with antique Muscovite and Peterburgan *Prikazi*, Chancellories, Offices, and Commissions whose jurisdictions overlapped, and whose inter-relations were indefinite and fortuitous, whilst the provinces had posted in them eight *gubernatori* who were not over ready to obey either the Tsar or the Senate, and, as yet, the Senate possessed for its legal departments only the old *Raspravnaia Palata*, or Court of Justice (staffed from the Council of Ministers), and the *Blizhnaia Kantzeliaria*, or Privy Chancellory. And though, also, at this time, the Senate's principal functions still were "the collection of as much money as possible" and the task of auditing the State's expenditure, and obviating as much of it as might be prudent, it kept happening that various localities would fail to render their accounts punctually, and on one occasion some years passed during which the Senate could not make out what ought to be credited to receipts, and what to be debited to outgoings, and what represented balance, and what represented deficit: of which faulty book-keeping during the height at once of a war and of a financial crisis the ultimate result was to make even Peter see for himself the necessity of a thorough reconstruction of the central administrative system. And as he did not feel equal to undertaking this particular branch of statecraft in person (since, for one thing, he lacked absolute theories or views on the subject), he followed his usual precedent at such junctures by resorting to foreign experts and models, even as earlier he had sought new sources of State revenue by calling to his aid the inventive genius of home-grown *pribyltschiki*. His first step was to collect every possible item of information concerning the central institutions of foreign countries, and their organisation; and when he had done that, and found the administrative system operative in Sweden, Germany, and elsewhere to be the Collegiate system, he had notes on what might be the best method of introducing Colleges into Russia compiled, and considered how best he could adapt that particular administrative form to his own administrative machinery. Eventually, by 1712, he found himself able, tentatively, and with foreign assistance, to make a first beginning with a College of Commercial Affairs—the particular reason for his use of foreigners being that, as he put it, "their trading is beyond compare better than our own." And his next step was to send Russian agents abroad to gather information on other Colleges as well, and to collect text-books on jurisprudence, and, last but not least, to invite foreign State officials to come and hold Collegiate posts in Russia, "in that if we shall have only the books, and not the men, nought will come to be accomplished, seeing that books never do write of all the circumstances." So long and energetically he had Germany and Bohemia scoured for learned jurists, expert clerks and secretaries, and, above all, *Slavonic* clerks and secretaries, since these last, as knowing the language already, would be the more competent to get the desired institutions into working order. For the same purpose he invited to enter his service some of the Swedes whom he was holding as prisoners of war. And at last, when all that was possible had been learnt about the Colleges of Sweden, and they had been found to hold the highest reputation of any in Europe, he definitely (in 1712) decided that they should become his model. He had the more reason for this adoption of a foreign example in that neither the past history of the Muscovite Empire, nor the statesmen by whom he stood surrounded, nor the bent of his own political thought were such as could well furnish the material necessary for the construction of a central State-institutional system by native hands. As a matter of fact, his own view of State institutions was the view of a shipwright. Always he, as it were, said to himself: "Why should I design a purely Russian ship when I have sailing before my eyes, both on the White Sea and on the Baltic, the goodly ships of Holland and Britain? Are not my own rotting at Periaslavl?" However, as things turned out, the scheme followed the usual course of Peter's reforms, and hasty decision was succeeded by tardy performance. First of all he had further inquiries made about the Swedish Colleges, and dispatched thither, for the purpose, a Holsteiner named Fick, and, as Fick's assistant, a Silesian baron named von Luberas who already possessed an expert knowledge of Sweden's Collegiate institutions: and in due time these emissaries forwarded to him books of regulations, and other items, by the hundred, together with their ideas as to how best the Swedish regulations could be adapted to the requirements of Russia. Next, von Luberas, touring Germany, Bohemia, and Silesia, hired a further batch of 150 volunteers to serve in the contemplated Colleges. Lastly, he and Fick—but principally Fick—set about bringing those Colleges into actual being. The first thing that the pair did was to draw up a schedule of organisation precisely specifying for each College its *personnel*, from the president and the vice-president downward, but at the same time empowering each such College to frame for itself additional rules modelled upon those of its Swedish prototype, and also, "according unto its judgment," to substitute new Russian rules for any clauses in the Swedish regulations which might not go well with the new *milieu*, "nor be in concord with the circumstances of this Our present State." Next, the presidents appointed, those presidents were bidden to have their new Colleges prepared, and ready to begin work, by the time that the current year, 1718, should come to a close: and though, subsequently, constant postponements and alterations prevented some of the Colleges from getting into working shape before the year 1719, and a few before the year 1720, at length the desired end was attained. Originally they numbered nine, and in an *ukaz* of 12 December, 1718, we find them set down in the following order, and under the following titles: (1) the *Collegium Chuzhestrannich Diel*, or College of Foreign Affairs, (2) the *Kammer*, or Department of State Revenue, (3) the *Justitzia*, or Department of Justice, (4) the *Revision*, or Exchequer of Income and Expenditure (Head Office of Financial Control), (5) the *Voinskoe Collegium*, or Department of War, (6) the *Admiralteiskoe Collegium*, or Admiralty, (7) the *Kommerz*, or Department of Trade, (8) the *Collegium Berg und Manufactur*, or Department of Mines and Manufactures, and (9) the *Collegium Staatskontor*, or Chief Pay Office. The list points clearly to the interests of State-given precedence, as considered to stand in most need of administrative development. For, of the foregoing, no fewer than five Colleges are seen to have had for their design the supervision of the State's and the people's economy, industry, and finance. And as regards the principles which chiefly distinguished these Colleges from the older *Prikazi*, they were (1) a greater amount of systematisation, and concentration of sub-departments, and (2) the fact that in them all business was transacted on the consultative system. Then, with regard to their fields of activity, only two of the nine coincided, in activity, with the *Prikazi* replaced by them—those two Colleges being the College of Foreign Affairs, the scope of which coincided with that of the old *Posolski Prikaz*, and the *Revision*, the scope of which coincided with that of the old *Schetni Prikaz*; whilst the rest were in every case newly compounded Departments, and Departments standing wholly clear of the territorial element peculiar to their predecessors, which for the most part, had possessed jurisdictions confined exclusively to some one portion of the Empire, or to some one *uezd*, or to some particular group of *uezdi*. Already Peter's *gubernia* reforms had abolished some of these *Prikazi*, and now the last of them became extinguished as Peter's reforms became extended to every sphere of Collegiate activity, and covered the Empire as a whole, and either combined an outlived *Prikaz* with one or more Colleges, or placed it in subordination to the same— an example being that the College of Justice absorbed into itself heretofore *Prikazi* to the number of seven. The general effect was not only to render departmental division at the centre at once more simple and more compact, but also to bring into existence some new *Kontori* and *Kantzeliarii* either operating under given Colleges or formed into independent administrative centres. A new institution of the sort was the College of War, whose operations thenceforth were carried on in company with those of three minor chancellories known as the *Glavnaia Provientskaia Kantzeliaria* (Chief Office of Commissariat), the *Artillereiskaia Kantzeliaria* (Office of Artillery), and the *Glavni Komissariat* (Department of Military Clothing and Recruitment). The foregoing also shows us that Peter's well-meant Collegiate reforms failed to produce as simple and solid a departmental system as might reasonably have been expected. This was because he failed to make his new system accord sufficiently with the hereditary addiction to administrative segments and squares and fractions of squares which from the first had been sedulously cultivated by Moscow's State builders in imitation of actual architectural work. Not that he did not aim at a system of equal and systematic assignment of public business to particular Colleges, and carefully subject his scheme to practical alteration and amendment. For example, he soon found that, owing to pressure of pertinent business, he must convert his *Pomiestni Prikaz*, or Office of Service Estates, an institution at first placed under the College of Justice, into an independent *Otchinnaia Kollegia*, or College of *Otchini*, and also divide his College of Mines and Manufactures into two separate Colleges, and merge his *Revision*, or general organ of financial control, with the Senate, and make it act as a financial check upon that body, and the more so because, as the *ukaz* of mergement frankly stated, the original plan of making the *Revision* an independent Department had been "ordained without due circumspection, and in error." Hence by the close of his reign his Colleges had come to number ten. And as regards the difference between the new Colleges and the heretofore *Prikazi* (that the former exclusively adopted the consultative system for transaction of business) be it remembered that that system had not been wholly unknown under the old *Prikaz* administrative *régime* as well, since, by orders of the *Ulozhenie*, the old *Sudi*, or Directors of *Prikazi*, had been wont, for the decision of certain matters, to sit in council with one another, and with one or more *starshie diaki*, or head clerks of Departments. The difference lay in the fact that this old quasi-Collegiate *Prikaz* system never was properly regularised, and therefore gave way as often as heavy-handed *Sudi* had put excessive pressure upon it. Accordingly, when Peter re-introduced the system, and, for a beginning, made it apply to the Council of Ministers, to the cantonal and provincial administrations, and to the Senate, he can have done so only in the laudable determination to establish it upon a sounder basis. And since the absolute authority of a Tsar craves advice rather than law ("Through counsel alone," remarks Peter's *Voinski Ustav*,[1] "can the best ordering be accomplished "), and one person can screen an illegal act more easily than can a whole band of colleagues any one of whom may at any moment betray the rest, Peter made each Collegiate Board consist of eleven members—of a President, a Vice-President, four Councillors, four Assessors, and a Councillor or Assessor appointed from amongst the foreign section of the community much on the same principle as that by which every Collegiate chancellory always had two foreign leading secretaries placed upon its staff, and decide each item of business by a majority of votes, and then delegate that item to be further reported upon by the College Board's Councillors and Assessors, each of whom stood at the head of a minor chancellory for the purpose, and a chancellory so organised that it and its fellows together constituted an individual division or section of the College as a whole. The reason why foreigners formed part of the Collegiate *personnel* was that the presence in Colleges of alien directors of experience already acquired was thought likely to aid Russian novices in their work, whilst a like motive must have inspired Peter to furnish each of his Collegiate Presidents with a foreign Vice-President—Menshikov, President of the College of War, being set to act with a General Wied, and D. M. Golitzin, President of the College of State Revenues, with a *Landrath* from Revel, one Baron Nirot, and the College of Mines and Manufactures being headed by an artillery expert named Bruce and the von Luberas whose acquaintance we have made already. But in 1717 an *ukaz* made permissible a system whereby Presidents of Colleges might "make and name their own *Collegien*"—in other words, constitute their own Boards, and select their own councillors and assessors, from a list of candidates guaranteed to be neither kinsmen nor "creatures" of the President of the given College, but solely officials previously balloted for at a general Collegiate convention.

To sum up, therefore, Peter's division of the administrative system into Colleges differed from the old *Prikaz* system in that it (1) included special departments for special affairs, (2) enjoyed a certain field of institutional activity, and (3) brought into play a new manner of transacting official business.

[1] Army Act, or Army Regulations.

CHAPTER IX

THE changes which Peter's Collegiate reforms effected both in the chief administrative system and in the subordinate were all of them notable changes; but quite the supreme change was the change which those reforms brought about in the position of the Senate. During the first nine years of its existence that body acted, firstly, as the Government, and, secondly, as the central administrative system, and one of its principal clerks is found writing that in his day every Government Department was dependent solely upon "my Lords the Senators," and constituted a Senatorial-Departmental chancellory. The duties of the Senate, at that period, were that, on receiving an Imperial *ukaz* on current matters of finance, or on military policy, or on recruitment, or on exchange, or on a liquidation of State indebtedness, it should expound that *ukaz* to the central and the provincial institutions, and indicate the measures to be taken for the *ukaz'* fulfilment. Also, it had to examine and to resolve such judicial and administrative points as might be forwarded for its official consideration by public institutions or private individuals. And from this it follows that, of the Senate's then powers, the one which it had most constantly to exercise was the power of disposition and execution. "Now have I laid all things upon them, and only upon them," comments Peter meditatively by *ukaz*, when bidding all and sundry consult the Senate rather than himself upon administrative matters. "Yea, now have I committed all things unto their care." But in time the Colleges relieved the Senate of some of the rougher part of the work, subject to the condition that always the newly-acquired measure of individual and independent authority of a given College should not stray beyond that College's peculiar jurisdiction: and this gain of leisure by the Senate enabled the latter *pari passu* to increase its inspectory and supervisional powers. The Colleges began by being institutions standing directly and solely in dependence upon the Senate, and therefore standing bound to submit to

Senatorial revision any matter soever which transcended their competency, and to have their Collegiate decisions appealed from by private persons, and revised by the Senate, as said; but in time—and this came about the more because at length even Peter came to have a better understanding of the theory and the practice of the right working of a State, and to cast his ordinances in more strictly departmental form—there arose a demand that all such ordinances should be subjected to a process both of preliminary review and of subsequent legislative elaboration, and, in consequence, we see *"ukazi* for fulfilment forthwith" begin to give place to *ukazi* merely ordering that a given point or proposal should be examined before the point's or the proposal's possible fulfilment later. And the effect of this was to change the Senate from a mere responsible executant into an institution competent to advise the Sovereign, and at the same time remain, as hitherto, both the chief dispenser of the law and the chief overseer of the State's economy. In which evolution of the Senate into the State's adviser upon, and scrutineer of, new laws the principal factor was Peter himself, in that he of his own accord began to drop out of his *ukazi* the old dictatorial tone, and, instead of demanding "instant fulfilment" of them, to request but tentative formulation. Instances are that by an *ukaz* of 1720 he, whilst prescribing that children of an absconded *krestianin* should cease to be surrendered along with their father, but "abide where they have been born," added, "Yet whether or not it shall be done thus, or whether it shall be done otherwise, must first be set forth in writing in council of the Senate, lest hereafter confusion arise," and that by an *ukaz* of 1722 he ordained that in future, whenever the Tsar was absent, a current matter calling for decision, but transcending the Senate's competency, should, nevertheless, first be scrutinised by the Senate before being remitted, for final action, to himself, and have appended to its protocol the written opinion of every Senator present, "to the end that his Majesty may find it less difficult, later, to adjudge upon the same." Also, Peter took to sitting with the Senate in person, and supplying it with legislative ideas by word of mouth. For example, in 1718, when he was striving to carry through his scheme for a Ladoga canal, and could not secure the necessary means to the desired end, he said, eventually, to his Senators: "Herewith, O Senators, do I submit unto you my manner of thinking, and surrender it unto your judgment. Wherefore render ye your voices, either for or against, upon the same." And from a subsequent *ukaz* we see that the Senators did so "render their voices"—and, at that, if not wholly "against," at all events not wholly according to Peter's views. Wherefore, whilst still continuing to act as the head of the subordinate administrative system, as that system's dispositive and supervisory authority in connection with laws already given, the Senate came also to work in company with the chief administrative machinery, and to figure as the recognised institution for submitting legal advice to the Sovereign. And this, again, led to a demand both for legal formularies of, and for a system of distinguishing between, laws and administrative orders, and this, yet again, to Peter renouncing, both on his own behalf and on that of the State, the right of issuing *ukazi* solely by word of mouth, and to a "General *Reglament*" of 28 February, 1720, undertaking that thenceforth the Tsar should "inscribe" *ukazi* only jointly with the Senate, and regard them alone as binding upon the Colleges. This was an innovation which, when put into actual and practical interpretation, caused *ukazi* "for action of performance," or "for instant fulfilment," to differ from *ukazi* "for conception of action alone" (for establishing means for those *ukazi's* possible later fulfilment) through the fact that, though the latter could still be issued by the Tsar "by word," they also had to undergo debate in the Senate, and then be confirmed with corresponding written *ukazi* before they could acquire effective force. Only in the event of a pressing emergency arising was that confirmation to be dispensed with; and then it was to be dispensed with only by the Senate sitting jointly with the Synod. Thus, when writing to the Synod from the Persian military field in 1720, Peter says of certain matters that were pending that he could not deal with them "on sight alone" (that is to say, without previously consulting the Synod and the Senate), and, with regard to certain other matters, that they must similarly be postponed, "so that, if God shall will, We Ourselves may resolve the same after that We shall have returned," and, with regard to certain other matters, matters which could not possibly be postponed, that, whilst a written report upon them must be sent him by the Senate, "to the end that We at least may know of the same," the actual decision of those matters must be undertaken solely by the Senate, and "whether or no We approve of the same, in that ye are Our Senators, and how can We Ourselves, at this distance, issue *ukazi* for the like concerns?" Whence the letter really constituted an *ukaz* "for action of performance," and not an *ukaz* "for conception of action alone," in that it gave an anticipatory promise, with regard to the last-mentioned matters, that the Tsar would sanction any decision whatsoever at which the Synod and the Senate might arrive, and also any action which might follow upon that decision. But of course this is on the assumption that had not the non-postponable matters already lost their urgency, had not provisional action subject to subsequent amendment already been taken. This compound Senatorial rôle as legislator, as supreme administrative organ, and as a body vested with executive authority subject only to existing law, finds additional expression in the Senate's structure. Peter recast the Senate's composition more than once—and in after days confessed that he had been gravely to blame for such vacillation. In the beginning he, when instituting his Colleges, ordained that their Presidents should sit also in the Senate, and thereby make of the latter a sort of Committee of Ministers; and though we do not know Peter's motive for doing this, we know that a system of the sort already obtained in Sweden that Peter's foreign *pribyltschik*, Fick, had proposed it for Russia as well, that, similarly, the old dispensation by *Prikazi* had included a custom of Heads of *Prikazi* sitting with the *Boyarskaia Duma*, and that the successor of the *Duma*, the Council of Ministers, had been solely a gathering of departmental chiefs. The misfortune of the new step was that it gave rise to a cross relation which at length became apparent even to Peter: to the cross relation that Heads of Colleges, whilst inferior to themselves in their co-capacity as Senators, stood, as Senators, over themselves as Heads of Colleges! And for this reason, and because it was found that these composite Collegiate-President-Senators could not deal properly with Senatorial business and Collegiate alike, an *ukaz* of 1720 ordained that though the Presidents of Colleges were to retain their seats in the Senate, their places in their respective Colleges were to be taken by new, elective Presidents—the *ukaz* incidentally remarking that, "inasmuch as this matter was not in the beginning wisely ordered, it must now be set right," and that, since a Senator's business lay exclusively "in State ordering and in just judgment," [1] he should not also be director of a College, but be set clear of that College, "whereas until now Our Senators have been abiding in Colleges in this manner, and how can a man exercise right judgment over himself?" Only on special occasions might the Senate call Presidents of Colleges into consultation; and then no more of them than the Presidents of the three chief colleges—the College of Foreign Affairs, and the two Colleges concerned with war. Lastly, if we study the Senate's varying composition we see that, four months later, and by way of a final change, Peter sought to tackle the prevailing dearth of suitable Senatorial candidates, sought to deal with "the present scarcity of just men," by restoring Presidents of Colleges to the Senate on an understanding that they should attend there two days per week less often than had formerly been the case.

The Senate also had vested in it wide plenipotentiary powers. Originally summoned only for "labouring stedfastly towards a due ordering of the State," for re-adjusting an administrative system that, as yet, was anything but "well-ordered," the Senate later developed into Peter's chief director

---

[1] That is to say, equitable dispensation of the law.

of the administrative reconstruction carried out during the closing years of his reign, and into the wielder of at least as much institutional authority as any governmental organ under such a ruler as Peter could have looked to wield. In other words, the Senate came to be competent not only to dispense justice, but also to fashion juridical norms, and to introduce imposts for the "collection of all possible moneys," and to lick the Tsar's ebullient *ukazi* into shape, and pre-natally to divine his legislative ideas. Hence it became the situation that only with the Senate's consent could anything be begun upon, or anything really be finished, since, in Peter's absence, the Senatorial body stood "substitute for his Majesty's own person," and therefore was, from the legal standpoint, a body equal to the country's two supreme wielders of the law under God—to the Tsar, and to "the whole honourable estate of this land." Unfortunately, it still remained difficult to raise the Senate's status and *personnel* to a plane of legal definition so lofty as this, or, for that matter, to any plane of definition not stripped of every vestige of rhetorical colouring; for though the Senatorial body was the executor of the Autocrat's will, it had no independent will, but ranked only as an authorised steward of State, with powers that represented a responsible commission, not a self-acting right, an administrative mainspring, not an effective political force. This is best seen from the fact that to Senatorial failures or Senatorial errors there were meted out, not threats of dismissal outright, but threats merely of punishment. "In this taking of bribes after the manner of your ancient follies have ye done amiss, and when again ye shall present yourselves in Our presence ye shall be chastised indeed!" However, the Senate's *personnel* was quite in keeping with this rough and ready treatment, since never from the first did it have appointed to its ranks anything much better than second-rate *chinovniki*, nor did its stamp of member improve even when the Colleges were instituted, and it was joined by such aristocratic personages as Menshikov and Prince D. M. Golitzin, and so forth. In fact, no administrative organ of the day required more careful supervision than it did; and naturally, when it came to considering the question of instituting a higher institution yet, an institution which should be competent to supervise the Chief Administration itself, the matter proved a very ticklish one, since supervision of the sort would need thoroughly to harmonise with the two existent forms of responsibility as represented by the Tsar's power to command the Senate, and by the Tsar's power to fine any or all of its members equally with a peccant chancellorial official (as when, in 1719, he fined a fifth portion of the Senators for having returned a non-regular decision). Not that I mean by this that those two forms of responsibility tended to exalt the Senate, as an institution, as an office, in its subordinates' eyes, for, on the contrary, they lowered it there, whereas it had always been Peter's desire that, however heavily he might come down upon the Senate's faults in private, its authority should be preserved in public, as an essential factor towards the success of his administrative efforts in general. In fact, his anxiety to preserve an all-round standard of administrative-service discipline was such that at times he would resort to a method of chastising a peccant official that was as patriarchal as it was unobtrusive, since it meant his taking the official offender into the privacy of the Imperial workshop, and then and there laying on with a cudgel (Menshikov himself once got treated in this way), and, lastly, when the threshing was over, inviting the victim to dinner as though nothing had happened! But whilst seeking to substitute private and summary correction of Senators for public and lasting exposure of those functionaries, and trying and re-trying every means of keeping Senatorial procedure in due order, Peter continued to find his *chinovniki* flouting both the orders of their superiors and his own *ukazi*, and coming to constitute an administrative plague-spot worthy of the truculent *diak* of Moscow who replied to a fifteenth *ukaz* requiring him to dispatch a *podiachi* for the disposition of a grave matter: "Nevertheless, and despite the *ukaz* of your great Majesty, no such *podiachi* will be sent." And as fines proved useless, and the same with threats of degradation, or of "absolute dismissal," or of committal to the galleys, Peter, when the year 1715 was reached, appointed what he called a Revisor-General, and charged that official with the duty of scrutinising the Senate's decrees. And, for a beginning, he bestowed the post upon a son of our old friend Nikita Zotov (now President-General of the *Blizhnaia Kantzeliaria*, and Peter's "Jester-in-Chief"), since he was a man of some education, and had studied abroad. Said the *ukaz*: "As Our Revisor-General, this man shall have his own table in the place where sitteth the Senate, and take note of all decrees made by the same, and ensure that those decrees be fulfilled, and report unto the Senate any *chinovnik* who brawleth amongst them, and declare unto the Tsar any Senator who similarly beareth himself." For as yet the *ukaz* was not going to extend the Revisor-General's powers against the Senatorial body further than that. But since the Revisor-General's duties thenceforth included the task of "ensuring that everything be duly fulfilled," gradually and insensibly (we see this from reports framed by the first holder of the office, Zotov's son) his inspectional eye came to detect that, though the Senators stood bound to punish any *chinovnik* whom they found guilty of any act of malfeasance, they themselves were just as bad, or even worse, since, according to Zotov's son's reports, they shirked their duties three days out of the seven, and once took three years to decide three questions, and at all times refused to pay their fines, and invariably flouted both Peter's *pribyltschiki* and members of the assembly when either of them put forward a new proposal. So in 1720 Peter tightened up the brakes by once and for all telling his Senators that during their times of session they were to "do all things in order only, and without turbulence, shoutings, and the like," and, to that end, to observe the following procedure. "When the matter in hand shall have been recited, let there be held, for one half-hour, both considera-tion of and discourse thereon. And if it shall prove difficult, and demand stay for thought, then be it set aside until the morrow, or, if not able to be set aside, considered for an half-hour yet, or even for an hour, or even for three hours, if need be, but not more. And when the sand clock shall have shown that the term hath expired, then let paper and an inkhorn be brought, and every Senator inscribe his manner of thinking on the matter, and add unto the same his name. And if the Senators shall be unwilling to do so, then let everything be stayed, and speed made unto the Tsar wheresoever he may be." Yet the man whom Peter now commissioned to enforce this routine for the preservation of orderliness in debate was not the Senate's *doyen*, or senior member, but a man named Stchukin who until then had been merely *Obersekretar* of the Senatorial Chancellory, and Reporter to the Senate. And, before this functionary had been twelve months in office Peter trans-ferred his post to a number of Guards officers, of "Staff-Officers-in-Waiting upon the Senate," whom he charged to act as policemen over the assembly for a month each at a time, and, in the event of any Senator brawling or otherwise misbehaving himself, to throw the delinquent into prison, and then let the Tsar know what he had done: whilst in the event of the officer himself proving negligent in his duties, that officer was to be stripped of his property, or else "despoiled of his honour" (of his rights as a soldier), or else outlawed, or else even executed. But, as before, this arrangement lasted only for a year and Peter next took it into his head that the best and most suitable guardian for his Senatorial bantling would be a *Prokurator-General*, and, after further thought, set forth the result in an *ukaz* of 12 January, 1722. This *ukaz* was a document which, for once, abandoned the usual pro-cedure of improvisation by the Sovereign before further elaboration by the Senate (probably because in this case the Senate itself was the target aimed at), and one for whose preparation Peter's zeal had led him to con every possible *prockt* on the question, and all his own *ukazi* on the subject. And, the result having been more than once re-cast and re-issued, only on 27 April, 1722, did the final fruit of those labours emerge in the form of an "Instruction to Our *Prokurator-General* of the Senate." Repetitive of much that had been said already, but likewise containing some new and important features, the *ukaz* began by defining the essence of the new post, by stating that "it is to be a *chin* to serve as Our eye, and as Our *striaptchi*, in all matters of State in the Senate" (meaning that the holder of the new office was to be the Supreme Power's representative during sessions of that body), and then went on to specify that the *Prokurator* was also to preside over the Senatorial Chancellory (thus converting the Senatorial body into a limbless trunk possessed merely of a sand clock and the right to demand a twenty-four hours' "stay for consideration"), and to lay before the Senate all matters which lack of capacity or the necessary power might at any time prevent a College from deciding independently, and to forward to the Senate all *gubernatorial* or *voevodal* reports on extra-Collegiate points, and to preside over the corps of *Fiskale*, the Senate's principal taxatory-supervisory instrument, and to act as general go-between as concerned the Senate and its subordinate institutions, and to superintend the Senate's order of procedure, and to preserve order and decency in debate, and to censor, if necessary, what was done by the Senate, and to point out any unfairness or animus in a Senatorial opinion or decree, and, if the Senate should then not see eye to eye with him on the point, to call a halt to business until he could report the matter to the Tsar whether at once, or only after consulting with "whomsoever he may deem best," provided that the delay involved did not exceed a week. Also, the *ukaz* lessened the risks of the *Prokurator-General* colliding with the Senate with the discreet clause that, should the Senate only *unintentionally* commit a breach of duty, the Tsar would "not impute the same unto these Our Senators, nor at all blame them for it, in that better are errors come of speaking than errors come of speaking not." But this saving clause was not to cover any repetition of an error, and from this we may assume that, though Peter makes no reference to the fact, he was not blind to the possibility of his "eye" in the Senate one day proving to be a crooked organ of vision. Lastly, this *Prokurator-General* of Peter's was to hold the legislative initiative in the Senate. Earlier the *Boyarskaia Duma's* procedure in the matter of propounding legislative questions had followed the peculiar rule that all such questions, whether come from the Tsar above, or from a director of a Department (who had usually been a *dumni diak* as well) below, had been treated by the Sovereign and by the *Duma* on the basis that he and it were not two separate authorities, but one authority indivisible, and supreme, and dispositive of the legislative authority in equal shares from its two organic portions: but, as we have seen, the antiquated, decadent *Boyarin* Council gradually lost its legislative power, and when Peter instituted the Senate he, whilst according that body a wide dispositive authority, retained the function of

IV—N

actual legislative inception in his own hands, until, on his work coming to
be carried on in a setting which forbade of his continuing to fill the legislative
rôle, and on his foreign and military policies necessitating his attention so
completely as to render his simultaneous direction of the State's domestic
affairs and formulation of the State's military and financial demands and
legislative problems a matter of impossibility, he decided that, whilst
still relying upon his *vymyshlenniki*, or "devisors," for assistance in the
invention of new taxes, he would impel the Senate, which stood nearer
to current affairs than he did, still further in the dispositive direction, and,
whenever absent from the capital, no longer issue *ukazi* on legislative points
unless they had first been delegated to the Senate for scrutiny. Nevertheless,
so many were the Senate's futile quarrellings and bickerings, and so timid,
or so careless, were its ways of transacting the State's business, that questions
of State accumulated and accumulated until, by the year 1722, they had
reached a total of 16,000, and rendered the Senate powerless to take up
the threads of domestic government in earnest. Hence, as we have just seen,
Peter seized the first available leisure moment to confer the legislative
initiative upon a personal representative of himself in the Senate, and,
by creating a *Prokurator-General*, to leave to the general Senatorial body
only the task of legal elaboration. Thus the procedure in the Senate became
that, as soon as there arose a point not already embodied in a law, the
Prokurator-General reviewed the point in question, and then invited the
Senate to frame an explanatory *ukaz*. Such an *ukaz* has come down to us.
Let us examine it. It is dated 17 April, 1722, treats of the maintenance of
civil rights, and was ordered to be laid on the table of every tribunal in the
realm, "from the Senate's own table unto those even of the least of Our
places of law, to the end that the *ukaz* may serve alway for a mirror unto
them who do sit in judgment, and restrain them from sporting with the law
as with cards, and sapping the law's fortress." Its contents set forth, precisely, programmatically, the routine to be observed by the assembly and
its members during the elaboration of a legislative proposal. On such a
proposal being raised in the Senate, the *Prokurator-General* was to make notes
of it for the benefit of the members, and then to leave them, in joint session
with the Presidents of Colleges, "to take thought," and "engage in debate
under oath," and, finally, declare their opinion; after which the *Prokurator-
General* was to remit that opinion to the Tsar, and the resultant "Resolution"
by the Tsar was to constitute the required Law. Of this procedure the
immediate outcome was to make the *Prokurator-General*, and not the Senate
at all, the State's administrative driving-wheel, even though he formed no
part of the Administration proper, and had no vote in the Senate, but served

merely as the assembly's acting president for the purpose of preserving order in debate, tabling legislative questions, giving rulings on correct functioning, helping the "sand clock" to time the assembly's discussions, and, in short, converting the Senate into a house built of the same material. And from now onwards certain other powers of the Senate also underwent restriction, and there was a period during which it even had to put up with the presence of a *"Rechtmeister"* and a *"Heroldmeister"*; of whom the former had charge of "the orderings of affairs of petitioners" (the reception and scrutiny of appeals from Collegiate errors, and complaints concerning Collegiate delay in legal suits procedure), and could compel any College to decide a given suit within a given period, and enquire into allegations of judicial animus, and act as petitioners' counsel, and, notwithstanding that the Senate was still the supreme guardian of legal equity, take Collegiate appeals out of the Senate's hands, and refer them to the Tsar for consideration and endorsement before referring them back to the Senatorial body; whilst the *Heroldmeister*, a lineal successor of the old *Razriadni Prikaz* (now become part of the Senate's private Chancellory), was charged with superintendence of the *dvorianstvo* in all matters of State service, with the presentation of members of the same order for posts in the service "whensoever a call for men may come" (in order that those posts might never fall vacant, or the commissions to them lapse), and with enforcement of the rule that, though the Senate was to retain a power of nomination of candidates to both superior and inferior posts in the service, it was to exercise that power solely in accordance with lists tendered it by the *Heroldmeister* —such lists each to consist of two or three names only. Hence the manner in which the two subordinate institutions attached to the Senate were made to work brought it about that, though those two institutions were, nominally, auxiliary instruments only, they so fettered the Senate, so cut it off from the rest of the community, and so hedged about "the fortress of the law," as actually to hinder that fortress's extension.

Further, Peter's reorganisation of his central institutions gave rise to reorganisation of his provincial institutions, since otherwise administrative unity could not have been achieved—the centre had been recast on Swedish lines, and Peter could not but bring the rest into harmony, and the more so seeing that the *gubernia* reforms of 1708 had by no means answered his expectations, and, for peculation, taxatory dilatoriness, and general abuse of functions, *gubernatori* had proved no better than the earlier *Prikazi*, and, in particular, Prince Gagarin, *Gubernator* of Siberia, had had to be hanged. So in 1718 Peter had extracts from the regulations governing the provincial institutions of certain other lands compiled, and submitted to the Senate, "to the end that thought may be taken as to how best those customs may be joined even unto our own." And when eventually the Senate decided upon the provincial institutions of Sweden, Peter confirmed the decision with an Imperial Rescript of 26 November, 1718, and ordained that to the new institutions there should forthwith be furnished "all possible instructions and courses of Swedish rule — though, peradventure, with amendments of the same in case of need," and that the institutions in question should be ready to enter upon their labours by the year 1720. And as a next step the Senate set about reconstructing the system of province-division, and in the task had Fick to assist it as its principal expositor of, and interpreter of, Sweden's provincial-divisional methods. But Fick would have it that, as in Sweden, the dimensions of the new administrative areas, together with the amount of official business transacted in each of them, ought to correspond with the quotas of administrative *personnel* available for service in each; and this necessitated the Russian departmental eye viewing matters, for the first time, from an unfamiliar standpoint, since everywhere and always the Russian *chinovnik's* bugbear was not so much a plethora of official business as a deficiency of the same, and, as a result of such a deficiency, a shrinkage in chancellorial "contingencies in respect of labour performed" (in other words, official perquisites), and a risk lest the larger districts should come to do no better in that respect than the smaller. Nevertheless, and although the provincial-administrative areas of Sweden and of Russia were so absolutely incommensurable as to render division of provinces in both on an identical system a matter of sheer impossibility, a vast effort was made, and, at last, the tight administrative uniform of Sweden dragged on to the huge Russian frame. The resultant system, as evolved by the Senate, was as follows. The *gubernia*, though it had no parallel in the Swedish model, was retained as the largest territorial unit, but retained with this difference: that the Senate's new system divided off from the *gubernia* of Kazan a new *gubernia* of Nizhni Novgorod-Astrakhan, and divided off from the *gubernia* of St. Petersburg a new *gubernia* of Revel—thus raising the total number of *gubernii* to eleven. Also, the *gubernia* now underwent an alteration in its unit status, for it became merely a military-judicial area, with its constituent portions standing subject to the local *gubernia* administrative system solely in those two relations, and, in all other relations, becoming re-modelled to the form obtaining in Sweden. That is to say, the *gubernia* now became divided into *provintzii* and into *distrikti*. Of these two units, the *provintzia* was the successor of the old *Landrath*-administered *dolia*, but embraced a larger territorial area than the *dolia* had done, and ran to an average of 50 per *gubernia* as against the *dolia's* 146$\frac{3}{5}$. Moreover, though the *pro-*

vintzia had existed as a unit under the earlier *gubernia* system as well, it only now for the first time became the prime, the universal, unit of the system; and whereas the *Oberkommandaten* administering the earlier *provintzii* had been officials dependent throughout upon their *gubernatori*, a gubernatorial list of 29 May, 1719, says of the local *gubernator's* new *provintzii* that the latter "mostly stood apart from him"—that is to say, were subject to him in his capacity as military administrator of the locality and president of the local tribunal, but in all else were purely self-contained. Over these new *provintzii* stood *voevodi* entrusted with superintendence of the finance, the police, and the popular industry of the same, but remaining responsible in these matters to the central institutions, not to the local *gubernator*, who, so far as they were concerned, was merely, and ranked merely as, administrator of the *provintzia* constituted of his local capital town. And the resultant duality of the *gubernator's* position was concisely summarised when a *gubernator* of the sort remarked: "In their *provintzii* my *voevodi* do stand apart from me, nor are subject unto me in any sort soever,"—his meaning being that, whilst, as *voevoda* of the *provintzia* constituted of his local capital town, he stood outside of his own jurisdiction as *gubernator* of the *gubernia*, he yet, as holder of the latter office, could not administer himself as *voevoda* of his *provintzia*! To each *voevoda* of a *provintzia* there was allotted, firstly, a *zemskaia Kantzeliaria*, or local chancellory, secondly, a colleague for inspectional and supervisory purposes known as the *zemski Kämmerer*, or local superintendent of taxes, or manager of the *provintzia's* revenue, and, thirdly, a *zemski Rentmeister*, or local superintendent of grain dues—these last two officials also joining to run the *zemskaia kontora*, or local tax-office. Lastly came the *distrikt*, the third and lowest unit of the new system of province-division. The curious fact about the *distrikt* was that, though a symmetry-loving Senate allotted to this unit a hard and fast total of 2000 taxpaying *dvori*, that symmetry found no support in fact, since the boundaries of some *distrikti* coincided with the boundaries of *uezdi*, and others ran with two or more *uezdi*, and others split an *uezd* into fractions. For the rest, the duties of the *zemski Kommissar* (local commissary, or administrator) of a *distrikt* were the management of its finance, police, industry, morality, and education. But above all he had to collect the local taxes, to act as local representative of the *provintzia's Kämmerer*, and to form, with the latter, a local *Kammer-Kollegium*. And, lastly, at the bottom of the scale of officialdom in provincial administration stood the old rural police agents, the *sotskie* and the *desiatskie*,[1] functionaries who continued to be elected at conventions of local

[1] See vol. ii. p. 274.

krestiané, but derived their warrants of authority from the local *voevoda*, and, whilst forming no part of the local *chinovnik* hierarchy proper, assisted the local *zemski Kommissar* in his duties. As for the smallest Swedish unit, the church parish, it alone, with its peasant-elected beadles, and peasant-elected justices of first instance, was left disregarded, and not transplanted to the Russian administrative field, since the Senate considered that, "inasmuch as our *krestiané* of the *uezdi* include not sufficient men of able wit," the Russian *selo*, or peasant village, lacked the necessary element of meticulously official intellectuality for the purpose, even though that sort of intellectuality was common to *pribyltschiki* come of the *krestianstvo*, and Pososhkov once wrote: "Now do our governors in Russia reck but little of the Russian *muzhik*. Yet those governors will ever die for a groat, even though they care nought for the loss of a thousand roubles." For the rest, the lands held by private possessors still retained for their sub-unit the seigniorial manor, which had become that unit in the seventeenth century; and was to remain that unit for a century and a half after Peter's death.

From the foregoing one might have supposed that, what with *gubernii*, *doli*, *provintzii*, and *distrikti*, the provincial population of Peter's day now had undergone a sufficiency of administrative shuffling and re-shuffling. But no—it still remains for us to study a fifth unit. We have seen that with the introduction of the poll-tax in 1724, there went a system of quartering regiments locally, and that that system introduced into the local government principle certain institutions which were essentially alien to that principle's nature. The fifth unit referred to, therefore, was the *polkovi distrikt*, or regimental district, as the area in occupation by the number of revisional souls locally assigned to a regiment for that regiment's upkeep. But the cost of upkeep of garrison and field corps varied always according to circumstances, and ranged from some 16,000 roubles a year to 45,000, and therefore soul-assessments had to vary similarly, and regimental districts similarly to differ in aggregates of area and taxpayers, and not necessarily to coincide with *provintzii*, or with *distrikti*, or with *uezdi*, but to be formed of two or more *distrikti* or *uezdi*, or of portions of two or more *distrikti* or *uezdi*, or of portions of *distrikti* or *uezdi* added to portions of *distrikti* and *uezdi* belonging to another *provintzia* altogether. And, naturally, the system complicated both local administration and province-division, and in 1723 led to the collection of poll-tax and "recruitment moneys" in *gubernii* and *provintzii* being transferred from those units' local authorities to special commissaries representing the *dvoriané* of each regimental district, save only in the case of the maritime regions of the North, where there were no *dvoriané*, and where the representatives in question were elected by associations of taxpayers grouped according to *uezdi* of the local regimental districts. At the same time, we know from documents cited by M. Bogoslavski in his well-known treatise on Peter's provincial reforms that we must draw a careful distinction between the *Kommissar ot zemli*, (the "commissary elected by the land"[1]) and the *zemski Kommissar*, or local commissary placed over each *distrikt* by the *gubernia* reforms of 1719, and forming, with the local *Kämmerer*, the local *Kammer-Kollegium*. For both of these functionaries were operating then, and only in a very few cases did the one come to replace the other. Also, additionally to assist the Government in its important task of supporting its regiments, Peter created *zemstva* (local councils or communes) which are not found at all in the earlier reforms of 1719, even though those reforms had been strongly addicted to embellishing the names of provincial posts and provincial institutions with the term *zemski* (local, "of the land"), in order to distinguish them from posts and institutions of the centre—the term "*zemski*" being, in reality, no more than a literal translation of the term found prefixed to such East Zealander administrative titles as *Landkommissar, Landrentmeister*, and the rest. Yet the fact that Peter created these new *zemstva* to help in the task of local administration did not in any way bring about a revival of the earlier cantonal associations of *dvoriané*, for these associations had so sunken beneath the pressure of his military reforms as now altogether to lack an inter-connecting link in the form of class solidarity, or of mutual responsibility, or of a mutual corporate interest, and nothing of the kind was to be looked for from a mere obligation to meet the local regimental colonel once a year, and, with him, receive the accounts of the outgoing local commissary, and select a successor to that commissary, whilst such a result was rendered less than ever possible by the fact that the local commissary's prime duty was collection of cash and stores for the benefit of a regimental horde which had had its headquarters pitchforked into the locality to serve thenceforth practically as the centre of a grasping, overbearing police-financial jurisdiction, harassing and hampering the local authorities, and causing the peasantry of the neighbourhood to view its quartering in their midst as a raid carried out upon them by a brigand band of their fellow countrymen.

In passing, the *gubernia* reforms of 1719 are particularly interesting for a new and unwonted type of judicial institution introduced by those reforms into the administrative system of the provinces, even though the interest arises from the fact that the institution concerned affords a good illustration of Peter's notions of reform in general rather than from the fact that it in any way constituted an actual factor in the reorganisation of his

---

[1] That is to say, by the given locality.

State. For on 8 January, 1719 an *ukaz* ordained the creation of nine *Hof-gerichte*, or "aulic courts" as documents translate the term; whilst later there became added to these nine aulic courts two known specially as the Court of Enissa and the Court of Riga. But only in five cases did these courts' jurisdictions coincide with *gubernia* boundaries, whilst, of the other six courts, two each were allotted to the *gubernii* of Riga, St. Petersburg, and Siberia, and the *gubernii* of Archangel and Astrakhan received none at all. Moreover, the same reforms instituted two categories of *nizhnie sudi*, or inferior courts, courts of first instance, in the shape of (1) Collegiate courts known as *provintzialnie sudi*, organised in the larger towns only, and consisting of assessors under an *Oberlandrichter*, and (2) Collegiate courts known either (as the case might be) as *gorodovie sudi* or as *zemskie sudi* (town or local courts), organised in the smaller towns and those towns' *uezdi*, and consisting of a magistrate sitting alone. And from the mere fact that Peter adopted these particular Swedish tribunals we may infer that his true object in the matter was separation of the judicial authority from the administrative. Not but that, let us remember, it is always dangerous to attribute to past ages the ideas of to-day: and though Peter's framers of "projects" and "instructions" are almost certain to have been at least theoretically acquainted with this separation of the two authorities, it is improbable that Peter himself ever attained the view that a legal tribunal ought to be a specialised, independent organ of State government upon which no external pressure can exercise an effect, still less, that, as he was what he was, he ever at any time abjured the old Russian idea of a court of law being a mere administrative offshoot. On the other hand, there can be no doubt that provincial offices concerned exclusively with legal dispensation existed as early as when the *Prikaz* system was in force; and though eventually the particular *Prikazi* with which those provincial offices were connected were absorbed into the College of Justice, and that institution was made to include the State as a whole, it would seem as if the *gubernia* reforms of 1719 contemplated, if not absolute separation of the Judiciary from the Administration, at all events the utmost possible ramification of the latter according as local pressure of State business demanded. In other words, Peter's primary consideration in the matter seems to have been executive efficiency, and his immediate object the furnishing of each chief College with its own organ of local and internal administration. And the same with regard to his *Kammer-Kollegium* and his College of Justice: in each of these cases he worked to separate the dispensation of law from the management of State much as he worked to separate the local *Kämmerer*, the local collector of monetary revenues, from the local *Proviantmeister*, the local collector of imposts payable in cereals, seeing that always he found it easier to borrow a foreign institution than to borrow that institution's theory. This difference all the history of his contrivance of legal institutions for his *gubernii* goes to illustrate. In 1719, first of all, he introduced into the provinces eleven aulic courts under eleven sets of local-administrative heads—eleven *gubernatori*, eleven *vitz-gubernatori*, and eleven *voevodi* of *provintzii*; until by 1721 this had everywhere become the system obtaining, and, by 1722, had altogether annulled the *nizhnie sudi*, or inferior courts, and transferred their authority to *voevodi* either sitting alone or sitting with assessors. But inasmuch as these imported notions clashed with native custom, separation of local tribunals from local administrations eventually bred a feud between the two, and caused *gubernatori* and *voevodi* so to interfere with the College of Justice that as early as 1720 we find the college complaining that officials of the kind did but "desire to stir up contention, contumely, and impediments in the affairs of this college." All of which means that though, earlier, the *voevodi* of *uezdi* had been found to be so corrupt as to render their removal imperative, Peter's latest imported experiments in organisation of State only rounded a circle, and brought back the State to its starting-point, save that, in the meanwhile, its *voevodi* had been transferred from *uezdi* to *provintzii*.

Peter's Collegiate and provincial reforms were followed by a foreign-modelled, but home-adapted, reorganisation of the urban social classes. We have seen that the *gubernia* reforms of 1708 reduced the *Ratusha* of Moscow to the position merely of the city's Municipal Board, and, in doing so, deprived the industrial-commercial communities of the provincial towns of their heretofore *zemski izbi* and elected *burmistri*, of the only institutions which until then had served to unite them; but now Peter proposed to restore that unifying centre, "to the end that all Our scattered company of Russian merchants do once more be gathered together." And, of course, he believed at first that the task would prove easy, and in 1718, on Fick's suggestion, gave orders that civil magistracies should be appointed, and provided with rules of procedure—the Resolution running that "in all our towns it shall now be done as hath been done already in Riga and Revel." Yet a year and a half passed, and nothing materialised. Then in 1720, he commissioned Prince Trubetskoi at least to form a magistracy for St. Petersburg, and, next, to organise corporate and Collegiate institutions in the provincial towns. But another year passed without anything having resulted. Then he issued a *Reglament* definitely bidding the now formed magistracy of the capital, as the model and principal institution of the sort in the realm, co-operate with its president, Prince Trubetskoi, in establishing everywhere magistracies, drawing up magisterial rules, and acting as those magistracies' supervisor: but another year (1721) passed, and nothing was done. Only at the beginning of 1722, when a vision of the galleys had extracted a promise that the matter should be completed within six months, did the supine Trubetskoi definitely enter upon his task, and so perform it that two-and-a-half years later Peter at least was able to promulgate his first "Instruction to Magistracies." His organisation of magistracies included division of the superior stratum of the urban taxpaying populations into two guilds: into a guild of bankers, "eminent" merchants, doctors, apothecaries, and skilled artisans, and into a guild of small traders and ordinary craftsmen, with the latter, again, organised into *tsechi* (trades clubs), and the general mass of workers, of people who lived by wages and labour, into a homogeneous aggregate of *podlie liudi*, or persons dubbed by the "Instruction to Magistracies" "citizens not added unto the citizens truly eminent"—a class lying *pod*, under, the upper social strata, rather than ranking as *podli* in the present unpleasant moral sense of the term.[1] The effect of this consolidation of the urban communities and creation of magistracies was wholly to alter the character of urban administration. The *ukaz* of 1699 had ordained election of local *burmistri* for one year only, but now the successors to those *burmistri*, the members of the new magistracies, were to be elected indefinitely, and even for life; which shows, amongst other things, that there had now arisen a demand for a greater stability of *personnel* in urban administration, and this is additionally clear from the fact that whereas the old local *burmistri* had been elected by the citizens as a whole, elected at urban conventions composed of every social class, the new magistracies were to be chosen solely by *burmistri* and "the first men of *miri*," and drawn solely from the two leading urban guilds. For the rest, a chief town magistracy was to include a president and a given number of *Bürgermeister* (or *Rathmänner*[2]), and its field of action to be larger than had been that of the old *zemskie izbi*, and its judicial authority to equal that of an aulic court in civil and in criminal cases alike, to be one needing only to have its sentences of death confirmed by the magistracy of the capital—which magistracy, again, was to constitute a general court of appeal for all the minor town magistracies. Also, the principal town magistracies were to oversee the municipal economy and police of their towns, to extend encouragement to local manufactures and handicrafts, and to establish elementary schools, hospitals, and, in general, public institutions. Further, the "Instruction to Magistracies" empowered them sometimes to sit with open doors, and transact business in company with

---

[1] Base or vile.　　　　　　　　　[2] Aldermen.

the local citizens, or with representatives of those citizens, and to permit the guilds of their town to elect *starshini* (with those *starshini*, in their turn, co-opting certain *starosti*, or headmen), and send those elected spokesmen of theirs to help the local magistracy "by giving civil counsel in" any more than usually important matter. Lastly, those magistracies were to be free to accept from the *starosti* of their local guilds any pertinent proposals for the town's welfare which those functionaries might see fit to offer, and to allow *starosti* and *starshini* alike to re-assess tax-calls, and to permit "the citizens, all together consenting" to choose their own taxgatherers. But for the very reason that these conferences between citizens and magistrates on matters "touching all the burghers" were to be attended, nevertheless, only by first guild citizens and *starosti* and *starshini*, and that, even so, these representatives of the guilds were to have an advisory voice only, whilst the plain workers, "those not added unto the true citizens," or citizens of full rights, could do nothing save request the "true citizens" and the *starosti* and *desiatskie* to make representation to the magistracy on their behalf—for this very reason of this very feature of Peter's magisterial reforms, the guild citizens inevitably became a sort of local ruling class or urban patriciate. In fact, the substantial result was that the upper mercantile stratum now had legally established for it the position which it had long ago gained for itself, through the various financial systems whereby that stratum had had imposed upon its shoulders the bulk of the responsibility for the taxatory assessment common to all, and been utilised, owing to that tenure of a commission to fiscal duties, as the class to be weighted with the heaviest burden of State services. For since the stratum's ability to guarantee its fellow citizens' taxes came of the stratum's holding of monetary capital, the stratum could not, in point of fact, fail to gain the loudest voice in the communities of its several towns. Hence Peter's magisterial reforms established between magistracies and local communities a relation which, without actually supplanting the old elected urban authorities, the *starshini* and *starosti*, but still leaving the magistracies bound sometimes to consult those authorities, led magistracies to avail themselves of the fact that they were the administerers of both parties, and, with that, irremovable, and become rather directors of, than elected representatives of, their fellow-townsmen. Indeed, both a *Reglament* of 1721 and an "Instruction" of 1724 roundly term magistrates "acting governors"; and it follows that a setting of the kind could not but convert alike magisterial presidents, *burmistri*, and *Rathmänner* into *chinovniki*, and not the less so seeing that the law extended to such officials a prospect of *chini* in the "Table of Ranks" on their retirement, and to presidents, particularly, of elevation to the *dvorianstvo*. Wherefore the members of the new urban magistracies inevitably came to stand apart from their fellow citizens, but most of all from the working classes.

We see, then, that by beginning his reorganisation of urban administration with class *zemskie izbi*, and ending it with class-bureaucratic-departmental magistracies, Peter made a complete round of a circle. The cause of this was a process leading to a change in his outlook upon urban self-government. In 1699 his sole object was organisation of the best and most lucrative system of collecting urban revenue whilst at the same time protecting the providers of that revenue from the high-handed rapacity of *voevodi*; but by 1720, the year when he first set about considering his magisterial reforms, his views had expanded, and the standpoint of Treasury gain given place to the broader standpoint of popular industry, since, as an administrator, he had now come to understand that the sources of a State's income should be deepened and widened rather than exhausted, and that no amount of financial jugglery justifies their complete drainage. But inasmuch as the loan of an outfit of boring apparatus was required before a shaft could be sunken to the richer and deeper veins whence those sources were fed, Peter sought and found that apparatus, or perceived it when pointed out to him, in the urban magistracies which contemporary Western Europe was finding at once efficient and practical, and, filled with the idea that only through thorough organisation can a people be made to endow its State's money chests with a good and assured income, charged his magistracies not only with the task of local tax-collection, but also with such economic and reconstructional functions as encouragement of local manufactures, diffusion of local learning, and administration of local charity, and the more so because he had found those tasks to overweigh the masses and the elected *burmistri*, and conceived that all urban affairs had best be transferred to the hands of "good men and true," drawn from the upper mercantile stratum, in order that, armed with indefinite warrants, they might, in those respects, help the similarly class-staffed Colleges. And the further "to the end that they may come to be both heard and respected," Peter, in his "Instruction to Magistracies," bade all magistrates "bear themselves decently, and with honour," and "come to be as exalted, and to be held in as much reverence, as are the magistrates of other States." And though, as he wrote, he evidently had flitting before his mental vision the wealthy and influential *bourgeoisies* of the West, and was fated to see his calculations with regard to his own *bourgeoisie* prove abortive, it was not his fault that in the end his new corps of magisterial *Bürgermeister* turned out no better than the corps of *zemskie burmistri* had been.

So much for our review of Peter's administrative reforms—a review which I have not cared to shorten. In them he met with many failures, and in them he made not a few mistakes; yet though those mistakes were not fortuitous, transient happenings, but phenomena destined to become the chronic malady of our State life, and to be repeated by rulers until they had come to be regular State habits and addictions, they actually have been hailed as sacred bequests of Peter's! Hence we must walk warily when attempting to determine whence originally came the administrative conditions and principles which clung to Russian State life for nearly two centuries after Peter's departure: and the more as during those two centuries they had ceased to be justified by the existence of the conditions to which they had owed their original creation.

Let us start from the point of the dinner-table conversation between Peter and his coadjutors in 1717, the conversation during which Prince Y. Dolgoruki told him that, despite his military and diplomatic exploits, he had as yet done little for legislation and internal reconstruction: for from that year it is that we see set in such a marked stressing of his legislative labours that within the next five or six years he accomplished more in that respect than had been done by his predecessors during five or six decades, or than his successors were to accomplish during a like period of time. And it was from his organisation of Colleges, and from his reconstruction, rather, fiscal construction, of the Senate, and from his second *gubernia* reforms, and from his new judicial institutions, and from his magisterial improvements that there resulted the factors eventually forming the administrative system which we see in existence at the time of his death. And ever throughout the fluctuations, the variously retrograde or devious movements, of his variously partial or reactionary administrative and departmental work of reconstruction we keep catching glimpses of, now a well-considered principle, and now a gropingly apprehended idea, and at least may ascribe to the number of his achievements (1) more precise inter-delimitation of the central and the provincial administrative systems, a process, nevertheless, sketched out for him in advance by some of Russia's earlier rulers, (2) an attempt to effect systematic definition of the respective jurisdictions of the central and the provincial administrative systems according to business transacted, and a series of experiments towards giving judicial business its own sphere in the structure of the administrative edifice, (3) an attempt to rebuild his administrative institutions on Collegiate lines— successful at the centre, but less so in the provinces, (4) some success in the direction of substantiating the idea of creating for the central Colleges provincial executive organs, and (5) a process of province-division thrice repeated.

But Peter did more than demarcate the central administrative system from the provincial. He attempted also to effect reconstruction of both. The inducement to him to do so was the peculiar social composition of the public institutions of the Muscovite Empire: and in this connection we must distinguish carefully between the two standard administrative systems of the day: between the corporate-aristocratic system, a system under which one or more ruling classes predominated over the rest through the agency of class-chosen representatives of their own, and the bureaucratic system, a system which took no account of social origin, but left the Supreme Power free to delegate the administrative task to whomsoever might be, or might be reputed to be, familiar with that task's conduct. Of these two systems, the former had for its prime concern advancement and consolidation of the interests of the State's ruling classes, whereas the latter concentrated, theoretically if not actually, upon advancement and consolidation of the interests of the State and the people alike. But in ancient Moscow the prevailing system stood further complicated with peculiarities of that system's composition, structure, character, and scope, both with regard to the Tsar's particular manner of administration and with regard to the administered community's peculiar nature. The then Muscovite system resembled a bureaucracy rather than a system of the corporate-aristocratic type, because its head officials were *chinovniki* appointed by the Crown, yet performing their functions purely on chancellorial lines, and and in no way sharing them with the community at large, or, if doing so, only to such a very small, passive degree, that during our study of the seventeenth century we have seen popular institutions, from a *zemski sobor* to a *volostni starosta*, cease to be autonomous, fall into decay, and perish. But on the other hand, the old Muscovite system was corporate-aristocratic as regards its *personnel*, for the dominant element in that *personnel* was an hereditarily privileged service class which stood quite apart from the general mass of departmental-bureaucratic *diaki*, *podiachie*, and similar officials of purely chancellorial position, and from their assistants, elected or co-opted representatives of *zemstva* (taxpayers' associations), men who officiated only as the Government happened to accord them temporary, casual commissions to do so. And, of course, these various circumstances communicated to the administrative system of the day a certain duality of composition, and rendered the Civil Service a what I might call "class-bureaucratic" institution. For the same reason Peter set himself a dual aim. That dual aim was (1) to place the State's military forces and financial resources upon a proper basis, and (2) to act likewise as regards his people's industry, in that he knew that only an increase of the productivity of that industry could bring about attainment of the first, the military-financial, aim. But since the two tasks were wholly different in essence—the first being fundamentally a task for the State, and the second being fundamentally a task for the community in general, this difference led him radically to recast the governmental system which once he is found describing as "ill-ordered," He did this, not by abolishing the existent class-bureaucratic basis of the system, but by setting himself to weld together the two prime elements of that basis, and then, having made the one sufficiently "bureaucratic," and the other sufficiently "class," to assign the result its place in the administrative sphere. The first step that he took to this end was to impose upon the Central Administration the dual function of promoting and consolidating the State's general interests, and of organising, in particular, the State's military forces and their upkeep. But a requisite was that the administrative organs employed for the purpose should first be educated up to a certain standard of administrative knowledge and experience; and for this reason he prescribed for his proposed executants a course of preliminary technical training which, regardless of those executants' social status and origin, should bureaucratise the system without also involving popular participation in the administrative task, or, on the other hand, converting the Civil Service into a purely class aggregate. The same reason led him to fill the higher administrative posts indifferently with an aristocratic *boyarin*, with that *boyarin's* major-domo, with a *dvorianin* genealogically indefinite, with a "son of fortune and no family," with an ex-*podiachi*, with a nondescript alien. But, as he considered the direction of the people's economy to be a different matter altogether, a task pre-eminently proper to the provincial local administrative bodies (always supposing that it was carried on under central-administrative superintendence), he assigned the dominant role in that economy to the landed *dvorianin* class, and to the class of superior urban merchants, as the two classes which held concentrated in their hands the whole of the country's land and landed industry, and, therefore, the two fundamental forms of capital lying at the base of the people's economy, and most needing to have labour expended upon them if the economy of the State too was to attain sound establishment. Thus, whilst handing over the country's superior interests to the care of his central administrative system and its executants, Peter also consulted other interests of the country which, though but auxiliary to the first, were nevertheless vital to national-industrial development, by placing the two leading social classes at the head of the local-provincial administrations, and so linking up the hands of the *dvorianin* of the *selo* and the rural fastness with the hands of the urban guild citizen as to communicate to each of the two classes a bureaucratic complexion, and to convert them into a joint social force capable of efficiently helping the organs of the central administrative system to control the people's labour. Whence Peter's administrative reforms were not so much political as technical, in that he introduced no new principles into the machinery of government, but compounded old ones into fresh combinations, borrowed administrative forms from other States on the advice of alien experts, and distributed the resultant compound of new administrative elements amongst his administrative branches as the varying character of those branches' activities demanded. Wherefore his administrative edifice, though new of construction, resembled his other re-creative enterprises in being old of material.

The series of reforms just described was Peter's last, but a series carefully thought out, and accompanied with rules and instructions for every post and institution, from the Senate down to such subordinate officials as commissaries and *Waldmeister*. Those rules and instructions were, for the most part, translations of, or recasts of, Swedish and East Zealander rules and regulations, and had at their basis such a strict view of the nature of a State as shows Peter now to have attained a thorough understanding of State problems, so minutely and so precisely do they set forth for every department of his new administrative system that department's composition, scope, duties, responsibilities, and mode of working. Also, despite their foreign origin, they afford us a good view of Peter's maturer political bent, since, though we cannot suppose that he read every single "project" and note which Fick and von Luberas framed, or every single charter and abstract which they borrowed from Sweden's Collegiate regulations, he undoubtedly took both a personal and an active part in composing the necessary *Reglamenti*, and personally superintended the progressive development of his administrative reforms. Another point interesting to us is that through those labours he was led to become acquainted with problems and ideas which he had never before had the leisure to consider, and, on realising from them that he was falling behind the times, to grow more ready both to recognise his mistakes and to respect others' opinions. Again, these mental workings so revolutionised his political sense that, though he had begun by putting his trust exclusively in persons, he ended by acknowledging the virtue of State institutions, and grasping their importance in a people's political education. True, something of the sort had dawned upon him earlier, since an *ukaz* of 1713 expresses the opinion that wilful infringement of State interests can be obviated "only if We do truly set forth in this *ukaz* what are the interests of a State, and enable all men to learn of the same in full"; but it was only now that he came also to understand that such a "setting forth in full" were best done through duly formulated laws, and through institutions so organised that their very structure would check official licence, and their very practice instil instinct for legality and the common weal. And of the fact that finally he deemed that result to be most surely attainable through Colleges and new legal tribunals we have evidence in the circumstance that he more than once bade all men resort to his Collegiate institutions for justice, and not to himself, and assured them that they would never need to appeal from those institutions to the Crown.

Nevertheless much of Peter's confidence proved premature, for his *Reglamenti* and "Instructions" on State tasks failed to influence their intended beneficiaries as much as they influenced himself. Nor, for that matter, does modern legislative science itself attribute to those *Reglamenti* and "Instructions" more than a purely academic importance: it looks upon them as political tracts, and has never thought it worth while to develop them into administrative norms. True, history can show instances of improved administrative institutions improving those institutions' administrators, but, for all that, Peter's innovations were ill-fitted to contemporary shoulders, and in any case needed for their working a trained and disciplined body of workers such as was not to be discovered amongst the stock of officials available. Moreover, Peter's manner of introducing them was very much that of a well-meaning mother who thrusts unduly large clothing upon her offspring with the remark, "The children will grow to the clothing, and then it will fit": for long before Peter's mob of Privy and Acting and Collegiate Councillors and Assessors attained the necessary growth they tore their new administrative garments into shreds. In fact, from minutes compiled by his administrative institutions themselves we see only too clearly how those institutions failed to justify their founder's hopes. For one thing, it was not easy to find a sufficient number of competent native officials, and for a long time Peter had to resort to hired aliens—only in 1718 was he able to respond to representations on the subject from Fick, and issue a Resolution to the effect that inasmuch as indentured foreign assistance was needed no longer, quest might be made for "men near at hand, and for them only." And the quest began, and every likely native who presented himself at an inspection of *dvoriané* was earmarked either for an aulic court or for something similar, whilst the Senate's *Heroldmeister* also was bidden to consult the requirements of the Colleges by compiling lists of suitable young members of the *dvorianstvo*. But the real need was for a permanent reserve of State workers, and at last Fick suggested to Peter that he, Peter, should ordain "some such simple instruction of our Russian youth" (including special schools) as should serve to afford that youth a general preparation for the civilian branch of the State's service, and Peter replied to the suggestion, "Be it so. Let such academies be formed," and saw to it that Russian professors were secured, and foreign treatises on jurisprudence translated, and every other means towards the same end taken. Nor did he scruple both to cozen and to flout class prejudice by selecting military officers from amongst educated slaves, and chancellorial secretaries from amongst the petty *shliachetstvo*, and by posting "*Junker*" (minor sons of *dvoriané*) to Collegiate-administrative apprenticeships. And this introduction of an added degree of complexity into the scale of service statuses was made worse by the rivalry which long had subsisted between the service's military branch and its civilian. True, the *dvorianstvo* continued to provide the bulk of the candidates for the civilian branch, but as the majority of that class's best and most efficient members were usually taken for regimental duty, there remained behind for the chancellories and the legal tribunals few workers save *dvoriané* on spells of regimental leave, or in permanent retirement, or in evasion of their military duties. Besides, the posts which the new institutions introduced were so numerous that in a statistical treatise entitled *The Prosperity of the Russian Empire*, and compiled by a Senatorial *Obersekretär* named Kirillov in 1717, we find the administrators, *Prikaz* officials, and *Fiskale* serving in the Government's offices and chancellories of the day set down at a total of no fewer than 5112, And probably even this estimate was less than the actual total. Further, it still continued to be the case that the Government's expenses were hampered with "contingencies," or winked-at official perquisities, or, in plain words, bribes, and to an amount which, notwithstanding the prevailing scarcity of ready cash, the receivers of those bribes, the great brotherhood of *chinovniki*, themselves once calculated to be equal to twenty-five per cent. of the State's whole salary list! Nor was the position rendered easier by the fact that the *Ulozhenie* of 1649 was now obsolete, and buried beneath new legislative strata, and that, consequently, no adequate compendium of the country's laws existed. Eventually, to meet the difficulty, Peter appointed a Commission, and charged it to frame a supplement to that *Ulozhenie*, and the Commission began its work in the year 1700, and laboured industriously until superseded in its ordained task by the newly-instituted Senate. But as, again, the Senate, though as industrious as its predecessor, achieved no practical result on these lines, Peter, at the close of 1719, at the height of his mania for all things Swedish, gave that body fresh instructions—this time to carry out a parallel examination of the *Ulozhenie* and of the Swedish Code, and select thence any apparently suitable jurisprudential clauses, and, lastly, compound the latter into *"punkti,"* or points, or *casus*, against emergencies pertinent to the same, and to have the whole ready and completed by the following October. That is to say, Peter commanded that the Senate should do in ten months what its predecessor in the task had failed to do in twenty years! And of course the task failed both then and for the next hundred years. And during the Senate's labours at it there was nothing in the way of careless procedure and official indiscipline that it did not flaunt before the eyes of its subordinate institutions. To give only one instance, we perceive from some provincial statistics which the Senate compiled in 1719 that the ordinary posting route, when official documents were being conveyed from St. Petersburg to Vologda, ran through Archangel![1] Moreover, daily the Senate's meeting-place itself was the scene of virulent quarrels and unseemly brawls, since *Oberprokuror* Skorniakov-Pisarev was chronically at loggerheads with *Prokuror-General* Yaguzhinski, and Sub-Chancellor Baron Shafirov with Chancellor Count Golovkin, and Princes Golitzin and Dolgoruki with the brilliant, but plebeian, Prince Menshikov, whilst all and sundry reported to the Tsar personally their individual and party grievances. In fact, these wranglings degenerated to such depths that once a member called another a thief, and on an occasion in 1722 when certain high dignitaries of State met together at the house of the *Prokuror-General* to celebrate the taking of Darbent, the *Oberprokuror*, after having two passages of arms with the *Prokurator* of the College of Justice, and then almost having the same with the Sub-Chancellor, reported his antagonist to the Tsar and the Tsaritsa, and was similarly reported by his antagonist, and only after a long time could be brought to confess that both the one and the other had been at fault, in that he himself had been "very merry," and his opponent "merrier still." Naturally, doings of the sort militated against the Senate's dispensation of sound justice, and on one occasion Prince Menshikov himself felt bound to remind a conclave of his colleagues that he and they were occupying themselves with trifles when they ought to be attending solely to the State's interests. Again, few Senators escaped suspicion of, if not conviction outright for, fraud, and this happened even to Prince Y. Dolgoruki—nay, it happened even to Menshikov, although, as a rule, he was first and foremost in denouncing his colleagues, and had been dowered with immense wealth by his Sovereign. In vain did the Tsar chide this favourite of his, this virtuoso in peculation. In vain did he thrash him soundly, and actually threaten him with death. Menshikov and his ever-growing army of *chinovniki* merely continued to increase their gains at the

[1] That is to say, the documents, instead of being sent direct, a distance of 400 miles, were sent over the two long sides of the triangle connecting the three places—a distance of about 1000!

Treasury's expense. Only when Korsakov, *Vitz-Gubernator* of St. Petersburg, was, with Chief Secretaries Princes Volkonski and Opukhtin, given a public flogging with the *knut* did Menshikov think it advisable to escape the same punishment by pleading in excuse his longstanding friendship with the Tsar, and, through discreet utilisation of certain incidents in Catherine's past, procuring also her intercession. Yet, even so, the Tsar flung back at her pleadings: "Verily was this Menshikov conceived in lawlessness, and hath been reared in sin, and will for ever remain a knave! If he amend not, of a surety he will lose his head!" And in point of fact we find a contemporary writer computing that Menshikov's dishonestly-amassed fortune cannot have amounted to less than what would now be equal to 10,000,000 roubles. Naturally, the very fact that the only authority in the State which stood above the Senate extended to official bribery and corruption, not punishment, but its protection, caused those offences to increase the more, and to attain dimensions never before equalled, and never since surpassed: until, in his distraction and perplexity as to how best he could arrest fiscal sums from "leaking as it were through sleeves," Peter reached the point that on an occasion when he was presiding over the Senate in order to receive reports on this very matter of official malfeasance he then and there drafted an *ukaz* ordaining that any person who should be caught robbing the State of so much as the value of a rope should with a rope be hanged. And only when the *Prokurator-General*, the Tsar's "eye" in the Senate, Yaguzhinskii, exclaimed: "Then doth your Majesty desire to find himself bereft of all his subjects, in that all of us do steal, only some of us more openly than the rest?" did Peter, with a laugh, command that the *ukaz* should remain inoperative. During his later years, however, he gave increased attention to this question of Treasury embezzlement, and appointed a special commission. Moreover, there is a story that when *Oberfiskal* Manunin was detailing to him sundry such matters, and enquired: "Wilt thou that I cut but a few branches from the tree, or that I lay mine axe unto the roots thereof?" Peter replied: "Fell the tree in whole—branches and roots alike." And, says Fokkerodt, when narrating the story: "Had the Tsar lived but a few months longer, verily would the world have heard of many and great punishings." The same reason accounts for evidence of a new spirit creeping into Peter's *ukazi* during his closing years, for those *ukazi* are altogether unlike his usual short, sharp utterances—rather, they, with the diffuseness of a homily, complain of the prevailing service laxity, and bewail the fact that disregard of Imperial Rescripts is threatening to lay the Russian State beside the ruins of the Greek Monarchy, and lament that the Tsar's subjects accord him not a moment's respite from petitions, and remark that even a Tsar cannot see to everything at once during the throes of a strenuous war—"no, not even if he be an angel, in that even an angel cannot be in all places at one and the same season, but, even as I, must abide in one place alone, and, if he be anywhere present, be there, and no-where else." Somehow, as we read this tone of sorrowful resentment we are vividly reminded of the look of despondency to be seen on Peter's face in the later of the two portraits described.

In short, Peter's new administrative offices were institutions which, torn from their original moral and theoretical settings, and arbitrarily trans-ferred to an atmosphere of autocracy and force, found the soil of their new home lacking in their indispensable nurture. An example is that, though the "Instruction to Magistracies" hopes that the Russian magistracies may come to enjoy the respect accorded to magistracies in other countries, the magistracy of Kolomna once had a very different story to tell. For as this magistracy consisted only of a *Rathmann*, three *burmistri*, and a *starosta*, and one day one of its *burmistri* was ridden down, and nearly killed, by a certain General Saltikov, and, another day, a second *burmister* and the *Rathmann* and the *starosta* all were treated in the same fashion by an *Ober-offizier* Volkov who was acting as escort to the Persian Ambassador, the one in-tact *burmister* had at last to report to the Tsar that, as all his colleagues were lying maimed, and could not attend the local court, he was single-handed, and the court's business could no longer be carried on. Yet the public still possessed two resources against administrative ignorance and pride: and those two resources were violence and fraud. An example of this is that when the census lists came to be revised it was found that entry of no fewer than 1,500,000 souls, or twenty-seven per cent. of the country's whole tax-paying population, had been omitted by those souls' masters, whilst another example is that, however much a series of insistent *ukazi* might command absconded serfs to be looked for, whole bevies of these runaways would form themselves into colonies on the larger estates around Moscow, and there abide, or else betake themselves to the wilds. The same reason accounts for our reading, at this period, of a general growth of brigandage, and of deserters from the army commonly riding forth in well-disciplined, well-armed, and well-mounted bands, and "ravaging thereafter in regular order," and sacking villages, and arresting tax-collection, and even penetrat-ing into townships—so much so that in one case a *gubernator* dared not tour his own district, and in another Menshikov, *Gubernator* of St. Petersburg, and the man who once had thought himself capable even of constructing the Ladoga canal, had to inform his colleagues that to deal with the marauders in his area had passed beyond his power. Hence brigandage in the depths answered to despotism on the heights, and, whilst insensibly stereotyping incompetence and illegality on the one hand, confirmed hopeless despair on the other. Nor could it have been otherwise when a dishonest metropolitan official, or a galloping provincial general, or a service-shirking rural *dvorianin* could throw the Reformer's menacing *ukazi* out of window, and join with the forest brigand in disregarding the fact that operative in St. Petersburg there were a semi-autocratic Senate and nine (later ten) colleges organised on the Swedish model, and armed with systematically prescribed and regularly-defined jurisdictions, and constituting—well, constituting a false façade to a sorry legislative structure.

CHAPTER X

THE foregoing represents a by no means complete outline of Peter's activity as a reformer, for, as yet, I have not touched upon his measures in connection with social organisation and popular enlightenment, nor upon the changes which those measures wrought in his people's morals and ideas, that is to say, in his people's spiritual life. For in every case it befell either that those measures and those changes had no connection with the more pressing reform problems which Peter encountered, or that their action did not become apparent in whole during Peter's lifetime, or that, even so, they affected only a portion of the country's social classes. But in due time I will rectify these omissions of mine. I have said that Peter's reforms were, both in origin and in final aim, military-financial, and have confined my review of them to such factors as, though born of that dual significance alone, nevertheless reacted upon the community at large; but now, I believe, we can utilise those factors for forming a general appreciation of the character and the significance of Peter's reforming activity in at all events a few of its aspects.

For all of us the question of the significance of Peter's reforms hinges, first and foremost, upon how far we have developed the historical sense. For nearly two hundred years Russian historians have been writing principally about Peter's career, and still more people have been principally discussing it: and the reason why this is so is, first and foremost, that reference to Peter's career has always been thought indispensable when the subject in hand has ceased to turn upon historical factors alone, and passed to the inter-connection of those factors. That is to say, anyone who has ever essayed to survey the past of Russia from the philosophical standpoint has always deemed it a matter of scientific decorum to pass judgment upon the Petrine reforms. Nay, in some cases writers have compressed the whole of the philosophy of Russian history into an appreciation of those reforms, and so, through a sort of scientific foreshortening, caused that history's whole significance to centre upon the significance of Peter's achievements, and upon the relation of the new Russia of his creation to the Russia of his predecessors. And, in its turn, this has led to Peter's reforms being taken as the one turning-point of Russian history, and at once a summary of our past and a presage of our future (which view at least simplifies matters by dividing Russian history into two periods, into an ancient, a pre-Petrine, period, and into a modern, a post-Petrine one). Yet, though many different opinions have been voiced concerning Peter's career, it was long before that diversity began to proceed from a proper study of, or a proper comprehension of, his record, since during the 150 years between his death and the year 1864 (the year when the fourteenth volume of Soloviev's great work appeared) almost nothing whatsoever was done towards radically investigating his reforms. True, towards the close of the eighteenth century a merchant of Kursk named Golikov spent the years 1788–98 in publishing a compendium of materials and appendices for a Petrine biography, under the title of "The Acts of the Great Peter"; but the effect of this compendium upon the historical sense of its author's contemporaries was small only, for, to quote Soloviev, the work was "but a thirty-tomed hymn to the Reformer," and in any case too voluminous, cumbersome, and panegyrical to attract the active study of a reader, whilst its very laudatoriness militated against a true understanding of its subject. Hence real light from within has never yet fallen upon the Petrine reforms, for their study-method has never been anything but a one-sided method, and writers upon them have appraised them mostly through their contemporary impression, despite that that impression was one dependent alike upon transient popular moods and upon a social atmosphere largely due to extraneous influences.

Yet for long after Peter's death the community affected by his reforms and his magic personality maintained towards them the attitude almost of a cult, so that we find a plain cabinet-maker deducing from twenty years' experience of Peter's rule the opinion that, "though no longer Peter the Great is abiding with us, yet is his soul within ours, and we who have had the felicity of dwelling under such a monarch will die true to his memory, and bear our ardent love for the Lord of the World even unto the tomb," and Lomonosov saying that Peter was a "man like even unto God himself," and Derzhavin speculating whether "the Almighty did indeed descend from Heaven in him." At the same time, even in Derzhavin's day certain people were beginning to be influenced by French philosophy, and to have their eyes changed with regard to the Reformer's work—to have their minds attuned to purely abstract attitudes on social questions, and to subtleties purely of academic *moral*. And, naturally, observers of the kind found it no easy matter to accept a policy which throughout had confined itself to concrete details of military administration and governmental routine, and could not but see in such a policy an earthy, materialistic outlook equally unworthy of Peter's intellect and derogatory to his position. This standpoint the holders of it were wont mostly to express by depreciating the Petrine reforms as compared with the achievements of Catherine II., as when Kheraskov sang: "Peter did give unto his Russians bodies, but Catherine hath given unto us souls." Well, the brilliant society of a period whose delight it was to welcome and enthrone a bevy of philosophers could scarcely be expected to feel drawn towards a working-man Tsar; and its appraisements of Peter's reforms gained further complexity through the fact that sometimes popular-moral considerations were imported into those appraisements' composition, as when Prince Shtcherbatov stated, in a treatise entitled *The Decline of Manners in Russia*, that, though the Petrine reforms had at least been "necessary," they had also been, in large part, "excessive"—meaning that, though they had in part met the people's needs, they had met them too radically and heterogeneously. Nevertheless Peter was not the man to rest satisfied with a bare minimum of legislative, military, economic, and educational innovations, but strove to correct also his people's individual, private life, and to introduce a human touch into his age, and to soften its rude manners. Unfortunately, this process of softening led to licence, and licence to an extremity of moral deterioration, until long afterwards, at a dinner party given in Vienna by the Princess Kaunitz in 1780, one of the guests, Princess Dashkov, after censuring Peter's passion for ship-building, and such artisan pursuits, as trifles to be deemed beneath a monarch's dignity, took it upon herself to say that if Peter had really had anything of the legislative instinct in him he would have let time and nature evolve the improvements which he introduced by force alone, and have placed too much value upon the name of his forefathers to sully it by introducing alien customs—a dictum which, with the preceding one, shows us that even a Director of the Academy of Sciences and a fine lady "intellectual" could express views of Peter's rough and ready labours quite as sordidly "patriotic" as those of the mob. But with the entry of the nineteenth century came other intellectual tendencies, and, with them, other appraisements of Peter, for the French Revolution had inspired Russian society with a dread of political upheavals, sent it harking back to antiquity, and converted Karamzin, the once brilliant defender of revolt, into a daring upholder of a conservatism so effete as to denounce Peter's sharp break with

Russia's past as a movement of an almost iconoclastic tendency. Yes; though Karamzin had, in his younger days, combated the cosmopolitan thesis that Nationalism is as nothing when compared with Humanism, and glorified Peter's educational reforms, and deprecated the harsh jeremiads condemning him as an actual alterer of the Russian character, as an actual blurrer of Russia's moral countenance, he still could, twenty years later, indite a dour lament on the subject, compare old Russia favourably with the new, and bewail a change in Russian manners and institutions the inception of which he ascribed to Michael's period, and which he alleged then to have progressed smoothly and uninterruptedly until, under Peter, it rudely suppressed the popular spirit, and broke the State's moral mainspring, by leading to acts illegal even for an autocratic monarch. "True, at that time we did become citizens of the world, but also, through Peter's fault, we did cease in some sort to be citizens of Russia." The general effect of Europe's then rebound towards antiquity, a rebound born of hostility to the doings of the French Revolution and the French Empire, was everywhere to evoke a nationalist movement on the part of crushed or disintegrated European peoples, and incite them to attempt recovery of their political independence or their political solidarity, and, as the nations fermented more and more, to throw Peter's reforms into such an added measure of discredit that by the thirties and the forties of the nineteenth century the dispute over old and new Russia had developed into a regular European feud. On the one hand were the "Westerners," who said that Russia's true road lay in the cultural path trodden by the rest of Europe, and that Peter had been the first to set Russia's foot upon that road: on the other hand were the Slavophils, especially Khomiakov, who merely repeated the old charges against Peter, and underscored Karamzin's accusation that his reforms had interfered with the moral life of his people, and prevented Russia's native customs and traditions from continuing to be carried on and upheld by the more enlightened men of Peter's day (whom Khomiakov used to liken to a colony of Europeans stranded amongst savages), for the reason that the best life-principles were to be found neither in Western Europe nor (where Shtcherbatov and other lovers of "true Russia" looked for them) in Russian antiquity and the pre-Petrine age, but in such of Russia as had survived untouched by Peter's "enlightenment."

Hence for two centuries Russian historical thought has split upon the rock of the Petrine reforms, and accusation followed upon accusation as there waxed and spread the dual process of idealising pre-Petrine Russia and of elaborating a cult, a quest, of "the people's hidden spirit." And, in the absence of ultra-profound scholarship, the process has forged ahead the more, since intelligent guesses have been taken for historical facts, and leisured dreams become popular ideals, and scientific investigation of the true significance of Peter's reforms lowered to the level of drawing-room or journalistic disputes on old and new Russia, and those two Russias', mutual relations, and two contiguous historical periods made to figure as two irreconcilable life principles, and historical perspective replaced with two hard and fast philosophico-historical attitudes concerning the differences between the Russian and the European cultured worlds. At all events that is how Soloviev sums up the controversy as he prepares for, makes preliminary sketches for, his erudite study of the reforms in question, and comes into view as the first Russian historian really to place the investigation of those reforms upon a documentary basis, and one that stands related to the progress of Russian history in general. Only need one read the close of Chapter III. of Soloviev's eighteenth volume (published in 1868), the passage in which he finally sets forth his views, to stand filled with admiration of his breadth of outlook and sustained loftiness of tone. And even though he does not express that exposition as fully as he might have done, it is one that represents something more than the fruit of erudite study, since it constitutes at once a polemical rejoinder, a defence of Peter's works, and a challenge on those works' behalf. The principal features of it are as follows. Never in the world's history has any people accomplished what the Russian people accomplished under Peter; never in that history has any people experienced a reformation so great, so many-sided, so complete, and so fraught with prodigious consequences both to the people's life and to the people's place in the life of its fellows, of, that is to say, the world at large, as fell to the lot of Peter's subjects. For in Peter's epoch there became imported into those subjects' workaday round certain new principles of civil and political adjustment, and there was put into the community's hand the weapon of a power of independent action springing from, as its immediate causes, (1) his introduction of the Collegiate system, (2) his introduction of the elective principle, and (3) his introduction of urban self-government, whilst through his enactment of an oath of allegiance to the State as well as to the Sovereign the Russian people acquired a *motif* calculated to inspire it to a realisation of the State's true meaning, and through his measures for protection of the person in private and civil life, and through his attention to State service, to imposition of poll-tax, to prohibition of marriage merely at the behest of parents and serf-owners, and to female emancipation, release of the subject's personality from the shackles placed upon it by the country's close-locked hereditary class.[1] Of which reforms (says Soloviev) the general

---

[1] That is to say, the class of serf owners.

historical results were, (1) that at last a nation hitherto weak and impoverished and practically unknown definitely set foot upon the European cultural stage, and acquired an influential share in the political life of its fellow nations, and (2) that the fact that the two hitherto separate halves of Europe now became united in a joint activity of which the Slavonic stock bore its proper share caused the essential representative of that stock, the Russian people, to become an actor in the affairs of Europe in general.

Thus Soloviev's view. But at the same time it should be added that included in that view stand other opinions which have found expression in our literature from time to time—opinions at once skilfully presented by their authors, and carried to a high degree of development, and partially accepted even by persons otherwise hostile to Peter and his works. Which opinions may fundamentally be summarised as assertions in various terms that Peter's reforms at least effected a profound revolution in our national life, and a basic, radical, and complete national renovation of our people describable only as Soloviev described it—"notable, and even awe-inspiring." Nevertheless, whilst some historical students of this way of thinking treat the revolution accomplished by Peter as a universal human service, others declare that, at least as regards Russia, it brought in its train only misfortune. The lineage of the latter view derives directly from some of Peter's own contemporaries and helpers, from men who, though not in active sympathy with his work, at least felt that, in assisting him to re-cast the nation's life, they were contributing towards the consummation of a critical phase whence that life was bound to draw new principles and new forms. And this impression of those men was no more than an impression at once natural and intelligible, since it is the inevitable tendency of persons caught up into the whirlwind of great and resounding events to derive from the retrospect of those events an exaggerated idea of the events' dimensions and importance. For example, at the time when Nepluev, one of the ablest of the younger generation of Peter's helpers, received the news of the Reformer's death he was residing in Constantinople as Russian Minister to Turkey, and in his memoirs we read the entry: "The monarch now gone from us did place our country upon an equality with other countries, and also teach us to know ourselves as men. And even as whatsoever may now be beheld in Russia did come of him alone, so must we henceforth draw from the same source the wherewithal for the doing of what yet awaits us"; whilst, earlier, Chancellor Golovkin had said in a solemn address which he presented to Peter on the occasion of the Nystad Treaty festivities of 22 October, 1721: "Only through thy tireless labours and direction have we been brought from the darkness of ignorance, and set upon a glorious stage before the world, and led from non-existence to existence, and added unto the company of political nations." Which utterances show us how completely the scientific views of Peter's reforms which Soloviev did not voice until a century and a half later were nevertheless the views widely held whilst men still were living under those reforms' immediate influence. At the same time, do we ourselves find those views satisfactory as they stand? No, they contain points still indeterminate, still calling for consideration.

To begin with, how came Peter to be a reformer at all? True, we need but mention his name to find our thoughts turning in reform's direction, so inseparably are the two connected, and so inevitably do the words "Peter the Great and his reforms" represent to us both Peter's established sobriquet and his historical destiny; but, however much we may assume that Peter had reform in his mind from childhood, and regarded it as his predestined historical calling or *métier* in history, it was long before he himself adopted such a view of his personality—he at least spent the whole of his boyhood and youth without dreaming that he would ever come to rule the most unpromising of unpromising States for reform, and grew up under the impression that, however much he might be Tsar in name, he was, in reality, a refugee monarch, and, so far from knowing power, was likely to find even bare existence difficult so long as his sister and the Miloslavskis should hold the reins. But then there came, and came before very long, the time when his sportings with ships and soldiers ceased to be merely boyish diversions suggested to him by his *entourage*, and he divined that if ever he should win through to manhood and attain rule in earnest, a real army and a real fleet would be his first two requirements. And though, at first, he seems to have been slow in deciding upon those instruments' immediate purpose, he gradually came to understand, as Sophia's schemes grew clearer, that his soldiers' principal task would be subjection of the *Strieltzi*, and set himself to do what immediate circumstances demanded to that end, and troubled himself little about the future—regarded his every task as a current necessity rather than a permanent reform, without, meanwhile, noticing that in reality his every act was helping to change his environment, and to affect both systems and persons. Yes, even from his first foreign tour he derived no actual concrete ideas for schemes of reform, but only some cultural impressions, a fancy to transplant to Russia a proportion of the things beheld abroad, and a project of declaring war upon Sweden in retaliation for having deprived his grandfather of the Baltic littoral. Only during the last decade of his fifty-three years' career was it borne in upon him that he had done anything new, let alone anything excessively new. And that tardy realisation of what he had done itself was no more than a mental reflex process proceeding less from thoughts of the contemplated than from thoughts of the accomplished: which means, in other words, that Peter, in becoming a reformer, did so only involuntarily, automatically, and unawares. The prime factor first introducing him to reform, and then permanently impelling him in the same direction, was the factor of war. True, the life of States furnishes few instances of inter-association of external conflict and internal reform, since these two conditions are conditions mutually opposed, and the former acts as a drag upon the latter; but throughout our own history the correlation has stood otherwise, in that a Russian war carried to a successful issue has always helped to strengthen the previously compounded order, or to confirm the previously compounded position of affairs, whereas a Russian war carried to a disastrous issue invariably has evoked such a volume of popular dissatisfaction as has wrung from the Government of the day a larger or a smaller measure of positive reform, and compelled the authorities to overhaul domestic matters. And inasmuch as, during the time that it has been doing the latter, the Government of the day has always avoided external conflict, and even, for the same purpose, allowed the international position of the State to suffer, progress in Russia's political life at home has always been gained at the price of Russia's political misfortune abroad. Moreover, there fell to Peter's lot yet another correlation between external conflict and internal self-development, or internal self-organisation, since war, in addition to being the setting of his reforms, had an organic connection with his reforming activity, and was at once that activity's evoker and that activity's director, and so brought it about that, whereas other periods in Russian history have seen war act only as reform's cradle, Peter's day saw it become reform's school, and he himself termed it that. Not but that the union was an unnatural one, since it was a union of opposed forces, with war braking reform, and reform clogging the wheels of war by evoking, as one of its results, a degree of popular opposition, and even of open popular revolt, which long hindered the nation's forces from uniting together sufficiently to administer the *coup de grâce*, and obliged Peter to labour at his tasks within the ring-fence of the foregoing inter-linked contradictions.

Dispute has raged also over the two questions of (1) whether Peter's reforms had the way prepared for them in any respect, and (2) whether those reforms were designed to meet known popular needs, or whether they were thrust upon the people solely because Peter forcefully, autocratically willed that the people should accept them. In any case, no amount of disputation has ever illustrated clearly the nature of the preparations by which, as some allege, these reforms were preceded, or the point of whether the preparations were positive—represented the normal starting-point of our natural growth, or whether they were negative—represented the distress of a nation forced at last to feel about it for a remedy, for a way out, for a new path through, and a new manner of, life. We only know that it must have been in the latter sense that Soloviev understood the phrase "preparations for Peter's reforms" when he wrote that all Russia's previous history had led up to those reforms, and that they were "demanded of the people." Besides, there can be no doubt that during the periods successively of Peter's grandfather, father, elder brother, and sister those reforms had at least undergone a partial initiation, and more than one Western innovation had been borrowed, whilst also there is the even more important fact that long before Peter's time there had been sketched out an extensive programme of reforms with which Peter's subsequent puttings into practice largely coincided, but of which, in more than one instance, those puttings into practice fell short. True, it was a programme that could never at any time have been adopted in whole, for it was projected by intellects of the day which, as yet, had done no more than break clear of their day's ideas; yet also it was a programme that paved the way, if not for Peter's particular species of reforms, at all events for reforms in general, and, had events proceeded more smoothly than they did, might have achieved fulfilment gradually, through being spread over several generations instead of over one—spread over several generations as was the preparatory stage to the peasants' reforms of a subsequent day, which took a century to carry through, and as was a process which occupied the combined reigns of Theodor and Sophia, and eventually introduced what a contemporary writer terms, "*politesse* and the Polish manner," an innovation which found expression in carriage styles, in sartorial styles, in a desire to study the Polish and the Latin tongues, and in abolition of the long, loose, ungainly *okhaben*, or hooded court cloak (the latter a reform which, pushed further still, would probably have substituted the *kuntish* for the *kaftan*, and the polka-mazurka for the Russian dance, even as, a hundred and fifty years later, the old Russian beard came into its own again on the chins shaved by Peter the Great). In the first instance Peter introduced his reforms on the Dutch model; in the second he introduced them on the Swedish, and replaced Moscow with a swamp-born city, and dubbed that city St. Petersburg, and issued *ukazi* under which all *dvoriané* and merchants of St. Petersburg must there erect for themselves dwellings, and transported thither thousands of workmen from the interior provinces. Thus Peter's reforms were Peter's personal work, and though that work was as necessary as it was forceful, it lacked definite intent through the fact that the external perils threatening the

State eventually outstripped the nation's backward growth. On the other hand, there arose during the age of Catherine II. thinkers convinced that the Russia of Peter's day could not have been renovated with the help of time's slow, silent process alone. Thus, Prince Stcherbatov, whilst disapproving of the Petrine reforms, and discerning in their broad, insistent scope nothing but moral ruin for the community, and condemning the autocratic system as unconditionally harmful to its subject people, was also sufficiently led by his historico-literary instinct to embark upon, and competently accomplish, a chronological calculation as to "how many years it would have taken Russia to attain her present glorious and enlightened position if she had not received help in that respect from the Autocracy of Peter the Great, yet had at the same time enjoyed the most favourable possible of circumstances." And the result of the calculation was that, in the absence of the Autocracy, at least one hundred years from Russia's "half-finished condition" towards the close of the eighteenth century would have been required—that, without that Autocracy, no "enlightenment and glory" could have dawned upon Russia before the year 1892, nor even then unless meanwhile no external or internal setback had occurred—no Tsar had destroyed his predecessors' handiwork, and thereby additionally retarded the national regeneration already impeded by Sweden's (under Charles XII.) and Prussia's (under Friedrich II.) peculations of Russian territory. Hence it can scarcely be said that Stcherbatov's estimate of the period necessary for Russia to have undergone renovation in the absence of any assisting mechanical impulse ("through nought save her own people's bestirring") erred on the side of optimism, even though Stcherbatov was a man predisposed to idealise rather than to decry the features which most distinguished the life of his country during the Petrine epoch.

The most complex question, however, confronting us is the question of how far, and how deeply, Peter's reforms really exercised an effect. It is a question which includes also the basic point of the main question, the question of those reforms' significance, and, to decide it, we had best begin by dissecting its complexities, seeing that Peter's reforms involved so great a clash of interests and influences and motives that the internally prepared-for elements in them essentially need to be separated from their externally borrowed proportion and that, that done, the inevitably unforeseen must be differentiated from the actually foreseen. And no light except a one-sided light can be shed upon the question, nor will our views escape sharp distortion, if we confine our investigation to one series of conditions alone whilst overlooking all the rest. No, we must probe the conditions of the question from the threefold standpoint of (1) Peter's relation to Western Europe,

(2) Peter's relation to ancient Russia, and (3) Peter's work as it influenced later ages. As regards the third of these standpoints, it need not be regarded as strange when we remember how often the work of a strong man, surviving his departure, produces posthumous results. In fact, any appraisement of Peter's career which omits that career's subsequent repercussions is incomplete, despite that he was gone before those repercussions made themselves manifest; for in, respectively, what unreformed Russia gave to Peter, and in what he borrowed from Western Europe, and in what he bequeathed to reformed Russia, what, that is to say, his countrymen subsequently made of his work, we see the three constituent portions of our principal question, the question of the Petrine reforms' significance.

Other things bequeathed to Peter by ancient Russia were, firstly, a very peculiar composition of the Supreme Power, and, secondly, a no less peculiar adjustment of society. When the new dynasty ascended the throne the country recognised the Supreme Power thenceforth to be hereditary; but when that Power lost the private-proprietorial character pertaining to it from the old *régime* it lost also both its definite juridical guise and its duly regulated scope, and entered upon a process of either expanding or contracting its action according as circumstances and the character of its wielder happened to dictate. Peter, however, after inheriting this authority in its then form, proceeded to institute a Senate, and thus to enlarge his authority's scope until he stood rid of the old *Boyarskaia Duma*, and, with that *Duma*, of the last shadowy *boyarin* pretension. And when also he had abolished the Patriarchate he stood rid both of the perils involved by the Nikonian scandal, and of the soul-cramping, affected reverence traditionally paid to the œcumenical title of the "Patriarch of All Russia." Further, we may ascribe to him a first attempt to define his, as yet, formless, vague authority from the moral-political point of view. Up to his period the political sense of the people had, as regards public life, identified the State idea solely with the person of the Tsar, even as to this day, in private life, the master of a household stands juridically identified with that master's establishment or domicile; but these two conceptions Peter separated by legalising separate oaths of allegiance both to the Tsar and to the State, and insisting that the supreme and unconditional norm of any State system was the State's interest, even though that might involve the Sovereign himself, for all that he was the State's paramount dispenser of law, and the public weal's paramount overseer, playing second fiddle to that interest. Peter, therefore, considered his every act a personal service to the State and to the country, and it was as a *chinovnik*, a service official, that he wrote of his victory over the Swedes at Dobro: "Not since I first began my service as man-at-arms have mine

ears and mine eyes been greeted of such shooting and other excellent achievements of our soldiers as here." Under Peter, too, it was that the phrases
"State interest," "public weal," and "popular advantage" made their
début in Russian legislative ordinances. At the same time, since historical
tradition resembles instinct in operating unconsciously, it was unconsciously
that Peter, bowing to the force of that tradition, adopted the view that his
reforms were State and popular benefits, and went on to sacrifice to
the same supreme, self-assimilated law his only son. *A propos*, it was from
this last tragic event that there arose the *Ustav*, or Charter, of 5 February,
1722. In this document, an instrument designed to regulate the Succession,
we see the first semi-popular ordinance apparent in the history of Russian
legislation. According to it, "This *Ustav* We have decided to enact to the
end that, from this time forth, it may lie wholly within the will of the Ruling
Sovereign to grant the Succession unto whomsoever he desireth, and likewise to revoke the same should he perceive his successor-designate to have
aught of unworthiness in him." By which terms of self-justification the
Ustav, in reality, harked back to the occasion when Ivan III. made arbitrary
assignment of the Succession to his grandson, and then to his son. Before
Peter's time Russian jurisprudence included no law at all on the subject,
and it was left for one and another system to establish itself in that connection on varying bases of custom and of circumstance. For example, the
old dynasty considered the State its private *otchina,* and, up to the
year 1589, adhered to a system of father-to-son testamentary transmission,
whilst in that year a system of election of a Tsar by General *Sobor*, or Council,
came into force, and later, during the seventeenth century, the new dynasty
adopted a view of the State as at least something more than a personal,
hereditary dynastic chattel, yet, in doing so, discarded the old system
before the new one had become properly consolidated, and left the ruling
House to rank as hereditary for a single generation only, and the country,
though swearing allegiance to Michael's possible issue as well as to himself,
to swear no further. Hence, as, up to Peter's time, a fundamental law of
Imperial Succession had been lacking, and the throne been filled up
haphazardly (whether through election by *Sobor*, or through public exhibition
of the heir by his father in the Red Square, as was done by Alexis with the
Tsarevitch Theodor, or through the procedure adopted when the rebellious
Strieltzi and the counterfeit *Zemski Sobor* established Peter and Ivan upon
the throne as joint Tsars), Peter now replaced these various systems with a
Sovereign's right of personal appointment and re-appointment of his successor
(practically bequeathal), and thereby legalised the absence of a law on the
subject, and, in essence, restored things to their old *otchina* basis, in that

the governing idea of the *Ustav* of 5 February was precisely the same as the idea underlying Ivan III.'s well-known words, "Unto whom I will, I will give the Princeship." And the same tendency irresponsibly to reproduce echoes of the past as innovations entered into Peter's social measures, for those measures neither modified the bases of the social adjustment resting upon the *Ulozhenie*, nor modified division of classes according to obligations, nor modified serf-right, but, instead, further complicated the existing system of corporate obligations with new obligations, and, by establishing compulsory education for *dvorianin* youths, divided *dvorianin* State service into two categories, a military and a civil, and, as regards local government, clamped all the urban taxpaying statuses into a corporation administered by *zemskie izbi* (later, by magistracies as well), and, lastly, confirmed the liability of the superior urban guilds not only to perform the fiscal functions already allotted them, but also to discharge a new industrial obligation of forming companies to lease and work Treasury-established workshops and factories. In fact, we never in any instance see a Petrine factory or a Petrine workshop being carried on under private direction alone, or in the interests solely of the lessee, for enterprises of the sort were always State establishments administered by the Government through the Government's forcibly impressed agent, the guild citizen—to whom, nevertheless, be it repeated, the Government always took care to concede, no matter whether he was a merchant, or a manufacturer, or merely a workshop superintendent, the hitherto exclusively *dvorianin* privilege of acquiring for his concern's benefit villages and bonded working-hands, and applying to the same their labour. Again, though Peter left serf-right untouched in its essence, he changed serfdom's social composition by both juridically and economically fusing all the existent forms of bondage into a single category known as "*kriepostnie liudi*," a category constituting a solid, homogeneous class of bonded, taxpaying *krestiané*, and by assigning the *volnitza*, or non-domiciled element of the population, to, in towns, the inferior civic guilds ("to the end that thereafter all such wanderers may be led to seek a trade, and cease to walk abroad without any sort of labour"), and, in rural districts, to the army and bonded peasanthood. This was a simplification of society which, through annulment of the population's transitional and intermediate strata, and through those strata's forcible compression into self-contained and fundamental corporations, enabled Peter's legislation so to continue the work of the *Ulozhenie* as to cause the Russian community to assume the adjustment always aimed at by seventeenth century legislators, and to issue in a form at once clear-cut, ringed about with individual class lineaments, and intricately and extensively burdened with liabilities even more than the hitherto social categories of the country had been. Wherefore we may consider that Peter's general relation to the State and the social order of pre-Petrine Russia was what I described when treating of the individual manifestations of his reforming activity, since, without laying a finger upon the ancient bases of the existing order, and without introducing any new ones, he either completed processes begun by other hands, or modulated ready-made combinations of conditions by either segregating the constituent elements of those combinations or fusing those elements together until these methods had succeeded in creating for the State a position permitting of augmentation, for the State's exclusive benefit, both of the State's administrative institutions and of the people's working forces.

Meanwhile, what was Peter's attitude towards Western Europe? It was an attitude largely governed by the fact that amongst the tasks which he inherited from his predecessors there was included the task of "performing all things according unto the example of strange lands," of, that is to say, Western Europe in particular, and that this task, again, entailed upon him at once a vast amount of labour, no little disappointment with regard to the national forces, and a constant exercise of self-denial. And how, precisely, did he understand the task? Did he see in Russia's relation to Western Europe a relation worthy of permanent retention as a model, or did he conceive that the world of the West need be used as a temporary instructor only, and could be dispensed with on the instruction's conclusion? Well, already we have seen that, in his view, seventeenth century Russia's greatest hurt had been her loss of the Baltic Provinces, and consequent alienation from Western culture. Yet how came it about that his country so greatly needed communication with that culture? It is the custom of some to portray the Reformer as a blind, irresponsible "Westerner," as a man who loved things Western less because they were better than the Russian article than because they were altogether unlike it, and to declare that he desired more than approximation of the two—that he desired their complete assimilation. Yet it is difficult to believe that a ruler so purposeful as Peter can really have leaned towards such a purely platonic affection. No, we see the prime end for which he needed Western Europe when, in 1697, he organised, and under an assumed name, himself joined, a "Grand Embassy" designed to collect and import, for his country's benefit, every possible outcome of marine and general-technical skill. For Peter nourished no blind, indulgent passion for the Europe of the West. Rather, he never ceased to treat it with grave distrust, and had the less inducement to cultivate fanciful ideas about Russo-European spiritual relations in that he knew in advance the ill-will and contempt likely to be encountered there by Russia. It was for this last reason that long afterwards, in 1724, when he was drafting a solemn ode with which to celebrate the first anniversary of the Peace of Nystadt, he wrote that consistently the nations of Europe had striven to exclude Russia from the light of reason, and, above all, to restrain her from advancing in the art of war, but that now those nations had had dust thrown in their eyes as regards Russia's military progress ("there are certain matters which they are powerless to discern"), and that might be ascribed to a divine miracle, and verily that obfuscation of the nations should therefore be given the more lyrical prominence during the forth-coming festival, "and set forth at large, as a matter of much purport"—as, that is to say, a matter of much promise for a furnishing of new ideas. Gladly, too, would one believe a tradition which has descended to us from different sources, and avers that Peter once uttered, and Ostermann once recorded, the words: "For a few score more years only shall we need Europe. Then shall we be able to turn our backs upon her." All this makes it clear that Peter looked upon Russian approximation to the West as a means to an end rather than as an end in itself. And what did he hope to gain by that approximation? Before we can answer that question we must recall the purpose for which he sent his Russian youths abroad, and the species of foreigner whom he imported. The students dispatched abroad he dispatched thither for study of mathematics, natural science, shipbuilding, and navigation, and the foreigners hired thence he hired for service as military officers, shipbuilders, navigators, factory superintendents, and mining engineers (later, as, in addition, jurisconsults, departmental officials, administrative experts, and, above all, financial specialists) whose help might enable him to establish in Russia certain things which he had observed to be of utility in the West. For instance, Russia lacked a regular army, so he organised one. Russia lacked a fleet, so he built one. Russia lacked a sea route for her external trade, so Peter's army and fleet proceeded to re-conquer the Baltic's eastern shores. Russia's industrial production was weak, and her industrial development almost non-existent, and technical knowledge imperatively needed, so Peter equipped his capital with a Marine Academy, Schools of Navigation and Medicine, a training college for gunners and sappers, and seminaries for acquisition of mathematics and Latin, whilst allotting to the chief towns of his *gubernii* and *provintzii* elementary "schools of ciphers," and schools for the children of soldiers doing garrison duty. Again, Russia needed funds to cover her State expenditure, so Peter set to work, and tripled the State's revenue. Lastly, Russia needed a well-regulated administration which could manage his swarm of new and intricate institutions, so he engaged foreign specialists to organise a new central administrative system, and to put it into working order. Nor was this all, for the foregoing include only the tasks for which he sought Western European assistance, whereas, although technical training and skill in popular-industrial and financial and administrative matters constituted the principal sphere of labour in which Peter invited Western Europe to come and work whilst teaching his Russian people to do the same (for his object was not so much to borrow the fruits of Western technique as a temporary loan than to adopt them permanently, and to transplant their products, and those products' prime lever, technical culture, to Russia for good), he also assimilated and developed as no other Tsar had done before, or ever has since done, the idea to be seen flitting through more than one intellect of the seventeenth century, the idea that the productiveness of popular labour must be augmented before technical attainments can assist that labour to develop untouched natural resources, and to bear additional taxatory burdens. Wherein Peter stands alone in the history of our land, even as he stands alone there as regards his foreign policy, as regards the policy which made its chief end direction of the nation's forces to the question of the Baltic Provinces, as the question seeming most to bear upon the nation's economy. Yet, though he imported into the routine of popular labour an aggregate of new productivity almost beyond apprehension, beyond appraisement, such signs of a resultant enrichment of the country manifested themselves less in a heightened level of popular prosperity all round than in a generally heightened level of State revenue-collection, in that any surplus earnings realised by the people very soon disappeared into the gullet of war. For the same reason it was that popular-industrial reform had, in turn, to give place to financial reform, and progress in general to become progress exclusively in fiscal matters, so that when Pososhkov told Peter that the problem of filling up the Imperial Treasury was insignificant as compared with the problem of "enriching the people, which is a great and a divine task indeed," he voiced not so much a politico-economic truth as a despondent deduction which he and other thinkers of the day drew from observed events. Peter's generation, therefore, never toiled for its own benefit, but always for the benefit of the State, and, whilst performing more and better labour than preceding generations had ever done, issued from the task even poorer than they. But on the other hand it may be said that Peter bequeathed to subsequent generations not a *kopek* of State indebtedness, nor squandered a single working day at their expense: also, that he devised for them a store of State resources which long relieved them of the necessity of adding anything on their own account. Indeed, the fact that he made himself the creditor rather than the debtor of the future was what, more than all else, constituted his superiority to his successors. But as this last is a subject more apposite to the results of his reforms than to the reforms themselves, we will leave it until later, and, for the moment, say only that, in estimating the sum of Peter's efforts to secure the external security of the country rather than the State's internal position or the popular welfare, we must look for the fundamental idea of his reforms in his popular-industrial undertakings, and consider the course of those reforms to have been marked out by their failures of accomplishment, and their principal result to have been what he achieved at least in the financial sphere.

Thus the State forces represented by Peter's form of supreme authority, dispensation of justice, and corporate-social system were derived by him from ancient Russia, and his technical means for organisation of an army, a fleet, a State-economic order, a popular-economic order, and a new set of administrative institutions were borrowed from the West. Yet can we properly describe factors which communicated to the life of Russia new forms and principles (no matter whether those forms and principles were beneficent, or whether they were the reverse) as a revolution in that life, whether renovatory or destructive? That certain of Peter's contemporaries who helped to transmit his reforms to their successors regarded the phenomenon as a revolution lies beyond doubt, as also does the fact that, if the Petrine reforms did not renovate the country, they at least alarmed it, and stirred it to its depths. This they did, however, less through their novelty than through their conditions, and less through their character than through what I might call their "temperament," whilst the people whom they most of all affected were the people of the succeeding period—the people of the Reformer's own period mostly failed to apprehend their meaning, but realised sufficiently their practical conditions of working to derive thence an impression with which Peter more than once found himself forced to reckon. The conditions to which I refer developed even as Peter's character did, and ran both with the environment of his reforming activity and with his relation, arising out of that environment, towards his people's habits, circumstances, and ideas. In other words, Peter's reforms owed their peculiar setting to external warfare and internal discord. Yet though the former of these was their mainspring, it influenced both their course and their issue adversely, for it compelled them to be carried out amongst all the disorder and hubbub of military conflict, and, to meet the needs and diffi-culties which they evoked at every step, Peter had so to keep accelerating their pace as to communicate to them an unhealthily nervous, feverish pulse, and an excessive rate of progression. Only in his closing days, when at last he stood released from military cares, did he really find leisure to halt and survey the position, to weigh his projected measures, to consider those measures' possible development, and to await accomplished schemes' possible outcome. Another result of his ceaseless craving for immediate action and speedy results was to drive him to meet hindrances and delays with a use of the verbal goad, until at last his menaces insensibly lost their stimulating force. Indeed, there was not an offence against the law, from presentation of an inopportune petition for a permit to fell an oak tree or a "mast-head" spruce of more than the statutory height to the failure of a *dvorianin* to attend an annual inspection, or to a mercantile transaction in Russian cloth, for which he did not ordain, variously, confiscation of property, loss of civil rights, the *knut*, the galleys, or the gallows—either, that is to say, political extinction or physical death. And of this extravagance of legal chastisement the inevitable result was both to strengthen hardihood in wrongdoing and to bring about such a perplexity of the subject's mentality, such an intellectual neurasthenia, such a sense of spiritual oppression, as was well described by Apraxin, one of Peter's most zealous assistants, when, in 1716, he wrote to Makarov, Peter's private secretary: "We are wandering, in all things, like unto blind men, and know not what to do, in that everywhere there are coming about great undoings of men, and unto none is it known whither best they may turn, or how best they may act. From nowhere, moreover, can money now be gathered, for all things are estopped." In short, it fell to Peter's reforms to navigate such a sea of internal ferment as more than once, owing to their novelty, broke into a violent tempest. Four serious rebellions, and at least some three or four conspiracies, occurred, as upheavals endeavouring to defend the old *régime* and its prejudices and ideas. At the same time, they enable us to understand why Peter cherished such bitter hostility against the ancient order of things, and so disliked the people's existent mode of life, and so persistently persecuted the outward symbols in which the notions and the bigotries of the past still found expression. It was an attitude further accentuated by his early political education, which had caused his every political idea and sentiment to attain development amongst turmoil and conflict as, with the Russian community divided into two mutually hostile camps, the protagonists of innovation, the party advocating Western European exemplars and assistance, had warred with the politico-ecclesiastic, old-believing section. An institution particularly dear to the hearts of this section was the system of external distinction which, with the beard and a special sartorial mode as its leading signs, had from earliest times demarcated the ancient

Russian from the denizen of Western Europe; and though Peter cannot well have considered these features to be inimical to reform in themselves, he evidently regarded them as cover for certain convictions and sentiments, and found them smack of opposition, and symbolise protest, and therefore, being himself ranged on the side of innovation, yearned always to join issue with what he believed to cloak the conservative's cult of tradition. And he would attach the more importance to these trifles because of the impressions gathered during his boyhood, gathered during the period when trifles of the sort had figured exclusively on *Strieltzi* and Old Believers—on persons, that is to say, in rebellion against the State. Yes, that must have been the reason why he came so instinctively to view the old-established Russian beard as something beyond a mere physical feature of the masculine countenance, and to class it with the pristine long-skirted habit as a sign, as a mark, of a certain political attitude, of opposition to the State's authority. Nor can there be very much doubt that he also itched to clothe and shave his subjects after the manner of foreign parts because he believed such a course to be calculated to contribute the more towards those subjects' Western approximation, for when the news of a fresh *Strieltzi* outbreak in 1690 brought him hurrying back to Moscow it was then that, for the first time, he shaved the chins, and shortened the *odnoriadoki* [1] and the *ferezi*,[2] of his *entourage*, and introduced wigs. Well, at this distance of time we can picture to ourselves but dimly the legislative and police hubbub which must have arisen from such a forcible thrusting of exotic coiffures and raiment upon the Russian subject: yet still we can picture it. True, it affected neither the clergy nor the peasantry, since always those two classes have preserved inviolate their corporate privileges of Conservatism and Orthodoxy; but, with regard to the other classes, an *ukaz* of January 1700 proclaimed, to beat of drum through street and square, that the ensuing Shrovetide was to see every man vested in an Hungarian *kaftan*, and in 1701 an *ukaz* added that thenceforth every man was to procure for himself also a jacket of either Saxon or Gallic cut, and wear it over a costume of German small-clothes, waistcoat, breeches, gaiters, boots, and cap, and every woman to disport herself in German boots and petticoat and bodice and head-covering. Also, for the purpose of promptly "running in" anyone who should be found to be wearing a beard or an illegal garment, the gates of every town were to have stationed at them inspectors of such articles, empowered then and there to strip the delinquent (as regards at least the offending garment) and reduce the clothing to shreds, whilst upon any *dvorianin* presenting himself either bearded or whiskered at an Imperial inspection there was to be inflicted the

---

[1] Court uniforms.   [2] See footnote on p. 133.

penalty of being "beaten without mercy." Only Old Believers thenceforth might walk abroad bearded and in other than the regulation costume. Yet, even so, this was balanced by a vicarious penalty upon their wives, who, though naturally exempt from the beard-tax, had, because of their husbands' hirsute visages, to wear sleeveless robes and long-horned caps. Lastly, there was awarded to any merchant trading in old Russian clothing the *knut*, confiscation of the illegal merchandise, and hard labour.

To ourselves these and similar things may seem not a little laughable, but, unfortunately, an ugly feature of them was that temporarily they deprived Russian legislation of a befitting tone of gravity, and brought it down to the tonsorial and sartorial spheres. Conjecture as we may, it is doubtful whether we can really imagine the streams of popular invective which these whims of Peter's must have tapped, or the popular hostility which those streams must have represented, or the grave impediment which both together must have offered to reform. And to the same multitude of petty impediments we must attribute the glaring want of proportion between the scanty success of Peter's internal administrative reconstruction and the costs and sacrifices made to that end. For contemplation of the labour which he had to put forth before attaining even the most modest of advances leaves us as overwhelmed with astonishment as was his ardent devotee, Pososhkov, when frankly and finely he said: "Whatsoever material Peter may drag unto the heap, millions will remove it thence!" and as was one of Peter's lathe-turners, Nartov, when mournfully that craftsman attributed "all that hath been conceived against this monarch, and all that he hath had to bear and to suffer, and all that hath gone to grieve and to hurt him," to the fact that Peter had stubbornly sailed in the teeth of the wind at a speed automatically increasing that wind's resistance. Besides, there was this moral contradiction in Peter's policy, that his motives were directly at variance with the form of that policy, and always remained subject to the contradiction in question—yes, even though, as he left his unseemly youth behind him, and became so wholeheartedly and undividedly solicitous for his people's welfare as to surpass, in that respect, any other Tsar in our history, he hurled against that contradiction the whole force of his powerful, indomitable nature. On the other hand, this self-devotion of his rendered more than one profound thinker his devoted servant—it led men like Nepluev, Bishop Mitrofan, Pososhkov, Nartov and others to regard him with an unfailing goodwill behind which lay at least an inkling of the moral basis underlying his strenuous efforts. Thus Nepluev on one occasion adds to the term "earthly god" the remark that "no need have we to fear to call Peter our Father, in that of him we have gained great betterment and truth and quietude." But, as against this, there remained the fact that many people of an indifferent or an obdurate cast of mind could not but recoil from the methods and the conditions inevitably connected with an activity which sought attainment of its ends rather through authoritative might than through spiritual influence, and relied more upon moral compulsion than upon native instinct, and governed the State mostly from the post-chaise and the stagehouse, and thought always of affairs, and never of persons, and felt too assured of its power to be capable of indulgence towards passive resistance. In fact, Peter's bent in the direction of reform and his implicit belief in his all-embracing authority were like two hands not so much striking against one another as cramping one another, and paralysing one another's action. And so, ever seeking to make up for his lack of available resources by arrogating to himself an added measure of authority, he strove to do more than was humanly possible until at last his overawed and inexperienced executants became incapable of playing up to his forceful policy, and had to leave the reforms to pursue such a headlong, such an inexorable, course that the persons affected by them merely sank into a slough of stolid, passive resistance, and ceased to have the heart to value the efforts made on their behalf.

Hence, without exaggeration on the one hand, or belittlement on the other, the significance of Peter's work might be expressed thus. The origin of his reforms was certain State and popular needs instinctively divined by, as fate would have it, a man of subtle intellect, strong character, and abundant talent—in short, one of those rare natures which factors not yet wholly understood by us periodically evolve in our midst. And to that man's qualities, as time went on, fate, again, applied the torch of a sense of duty, of a stern resolve "in no way to spare my life for my country," and at the same time placed at the head of a people less historically fitted for his purpose than any other people in Europe! True, that people had been strong enough, towards the close of the sixteenth century, to put the coping-stone to an Empire destined to become one of the greatest on the Continent, but since that period the seventeenth century had elapsed, and the people in question come to realise its insufficiency of means, moral and material alike, for continued support of the structure raised during the past eight hundred years. Hence Peter had for the immediate aim of the reforms which he instituted, not the rebuilding of an established political or social or moral order, or an attempt to re-establish the life of his country upon an unfamiliar Western European basis, or the introduction of any new and borrowed principles, but the provision of Russia's State and people with Western-European intellectual and material resources, that the State might be restored to its old international position in Europe, and the productiveness of the labour of its people placed upon an equality with that people's dawning capacity for labour. Unfortunately, all this had throughout to be done in the teeth of dangerous, persistent struggles with external foes, and therefore done hastily, through methods of compulsion, in the face of popular apathy, against the deadweight of an inertia nourished by a rascally official class and a gross landowning caste, and in defiance of fears and prejudices instilled by an ignorant clergy. Hence, though originally but modest and limited of scope, and designed but to reorganise the military forces, and to extend the financial means, of the State, the Petrine reforms developed into an internal struggle stirring to its depths the stagnant pool of Russian life, and throwing every social class into a ferment. And though those reforms were begun by the Supreme Power, and subsequently carried on by the Supreme Power, merely in that Power's capacity as director of its people, the reforms eventually assumed the character and conditions of a sheer upheaval, of a revolution, of a convulsion which, though centred about the aims and the results of Peter's innovations rather than about their scope, impressed contemporary nerves and imaginations the more because of the novelty of the alterations effected. For it was not only that the Petrine reforms represented social change: there followed upon them the unforeseen, the undesigned, consequence of social shock.

In conclusion, let us attempt to determine the relation of the Petrine reforms to ourselves. In the contradictions in which Peter's work became involved, in his errors and fluctuations and phases of ill-considered decision, in the weakness of his civic instinct, in the inhuman cruelties which he was powerless to prevent himself from perpetrating, in his wholehearted love of country, in his stubborn devotion to his task, in his broad and enlightened view of duty, in his daring plans, in his creative subtlety, in his boundless vigour of execution, and in his successes, successes won through enormous efforts on his part, and through incredible sacrifices on that of his people, we see such a vast diversity of features as practically to render their composition into a single presentment impossible. Students who study those features may derive thence either an impression of light or an impression of shade; such students may bestow upon the features in question either biased eulogy or undue censure: but in most cases the latter will be the meed allotted. The reason of this is that even when Peter's doings were beneficent in intention they were accompanied with a repellent display of force, since his reforms were a threefold struggle between a despotism, a people, and a people's instincts, a struggle in which, using his authority as a menace, he constantly strove to spur a community of serfs into self-action, and yet to make of his *dvorianstvo*, that community's own enserfer, the introducer of European science and enlightenment, as the two factors which he considered indispensable before the people as a whole could act for itself, and its fettered bondsmen, in particular, engage in free and conscious activity. And though throughout the two centuries since his time we have been setting down this conjunction of despotism and freedom, of enlightenment and bondage, as a sort of political squaring of the circle, and endlessly debating it without ever resolving the problem, there were statesmen of the eighteenth century who did in some sort prove that Peter's reforms were reconcilable with human instincts. Thus, much though Prince Stcherbatov disliked autocratic rule, he still could devote a whole "discourse," or treatise, to an explanation of and a justification of Peter's arbitrary acts and constitutional failings, and declare that the writer had derived much benefit from Peter's enlightenment, and his colleagues the same, and that he and his could with the less justice decry the Petrine reforms in that it was thence that both the writer and his friends had derived all that they knew about the evils of government by an Autocrat. Moreover, Stcherbatov's treatise is an expression of faith in the miraculous power of education almost equal to Peter's own, a faith inspiring the writer to cultivate and reverence learning so far as he himself was concerned, and to desire to fire also the enserfed intellects of his fellows until the resultant cultural spark should glow into a yearning for rectitude and freedom. And eventually even the thinkers of Peter's day who voted autocratic rule an odious principle in politics, and one wholly unacceptable to the civic conscience, found themselves able to reconcile their minds to a personality which at least added to that unnatural political force complete self-sacrifice, nor spared its utmost efforts for its people's weal, nor shrunk from breaking itself against its own self-created and insuperable obstacles. The simile most commonly employed by these thinkers when treating of the Petrine dispensation was to liken that dispensation to one of those spring hail showers which, though boisterous enough to strip trees of their boughs, yet freshen the air, and stimulate growth.

CHAPTER XI

NEXT let us turn to the third section of the question of the significance of the Petrine reforms, and see what men made of them after their author's death. First let me recall that, in prefacing that significance as our immediate problem, I did so with the reservation that, since its revelation in manifestations observable during the Reformer's lifetime was only partial, any appraisement of the Reformer's work must include the results of the reforms displayed when the Reformer was gone, and the more so because the latter will shed light for us upon the reforms as a whole from an angle which for Peter himself had always to remain in shadow. Peter's reforms failed to attain all that he sought with their help, but to that must be added that they introduced, or, at all events, paved the way for, much which he did not live to see realised, or, for that matter, might not have approved if he had done so. The first step is to essay a picture of the Russian community as Peter left it on his decease.

To understand the mental attitude of the Russian people when it received the news that Peter was gone, it may be apposite to recall that he died soon after the second of the only two peaceful years of his reign had been entered upon, and when for the first time, the Persian War having been ended fifteen months earlier, the generation of the day saw its country standing at loggerheads with no one, even though until now constant introductions of new taxes and everlasting enrolments of new recruits had left that generation absolutely convinced that, whether with the Turks, or with the Swedes, or with the Persians, or with such sections of the Russian people itself as the peasants of Astrakhan and the Cossacks, Russia was fated for ever to be engaged in either external or internal strife. For by this time the Peace of Nystadt had rendered Russia's international position secure; and though that position was still delicate, and Russia's principal foe, Sweden, was continuing to bluster, and to talk revenge, she had no second Gustavus Adolphus, nor a second Charles XII., to go on with, but, since Charles's death, had re-established her aristocratic form of government under a Senate, and, by doing so, brought it about that her domains had degenerated into what the Russian Resident at Stockholm of the day called "a veritable Poland of anarchy." And for these reasons, and likewise because Russia and Sweden had concluded with one another a defensive alliance of 22 February, 1724, the right, the northern, flank of Russia's European position now stood cleared of peril, whilst later, during the August of 1726, a Russo-Austrian alliance guaranteed Russia's left, southern, flank as well, as a result of Catherine I.'s new Government refusing firmly to sacrifice Russian interests to French on the chance that Peter would successfully betroth his daughter to the young king of France, or to one of France's out-at-elbows Princes of the Blood —a consummation for which, as a matter of fact, the diplomatic world of Europe had grown weary of looking. Nor did either the fact that an Austro-Spanish Coalition had become compounded or the fact that England and France had subsequently followed suit seem to Russian patriots a reason for anxiety about Russia's international status, and the less so because by this time reformed and re-invigorated Russia possessed military forces of Poltavan reputation to act as her backing in the direction of the west, and because the Russian fleet at least would have to have its crown of Hango laurels dissipated before Russia would come again to be regarded as a second-class marine power, and St. Petersburg would lose her new position as the headquarters of Eastern European diplomacy. The unfortunate point was that Russia's cultural relations with the West had proved less successful than her diplomatic, and new-European Russia now had at her disposal for competition with the Europe of the ancient Roman-Germanic standard, and of old-established and highly developed forms of public life, and of norms so long elaborated as to be clear of all prejudice and custom, and of stores of learning and thought, and of savings accumulated ever since the suckling of the twins of Rome, only some promising possibilities and a huge reserve of military and commercial raw material. Thus Russia still lacked any solid cultural resources, and her public life had for its basis only popular inertia, and that inertia for its basis only the popular conviction that it was unthinkable that ever a change could take place in Russia's inherited traditions. Nor did she possess a social system, but only, instead, a habit of yielding to the first chance internal *émeute*. Nor had she any learning—only a newborn taste for knowledge. Nay, her very juridical sense stopped short at a shadowy idea that justice was a social necessity, and her conception of wealth at an ability to perform more or less prolonged labour of an arduous kind. Yet although the two mutually incommensurable historical entities, Russia and Western Europe, were rivals as well as neighbours, and constantly impinging upon one another, and constantly coming into collision with one another, Western Europe could not well let her lack of sympathy with Russia lead to an open breach, lest, in addition, she should become Russia's victim. Herein, then, lay the interest which first brought ancient, Western, Europe into direct contact with the new Europe of the East, and it is in the highest degree important that we should make sure what the phenomenon meant—whether a relation between two widely sundered cultural orders (an advanced and a backward) which would keep the two permanently sundered by an age-long, dividing gulf, or a mutual confrontation of two historical growths of sufficiently unequal and fortuitous cultural standards to be bound temporarily to clash, but not for ever to remain separate. And that is why, as I have said, we had better attempt a visualisation of the Russian community at the time of Peter's death, and of the different views taken of his reforms by the various strata in that community, and of those views' inter-relation.

From contemporary eye-witnesses, native and foreign alike, we receive gloomy, and even terrifying, accounts of the demonstrations which the news of Peter's passing evoked amongst the people. Particularly graphic are the words of an eminent official chronicler when he records that at all the requiem services held for Peter in Moscow's cathedrals and churches "so great were the outcry and the lamentations," and "such the wailing and tears thereat, that even if those present had all been women, they could not more have grieved, nor more bitterly have wept, so that never since my birth have I heard or beheld such a consternation of the people." True, some of this display may have been no more than the stereotyped meed of tears considered to be *de rigueur* at the burial of a Muscovite Tsar; yet, for all that, the rest of what foreign observers noted shows there to have taken place a genuine military-popular tribute. The truth is that at least all had a feeling that gone was the strong hand which had grasped things so firmly, and that but slender, therefore, was the prospect of the present order continuing. Everyone involuntarily, anxiously asked himself: "What next?" For, be it remembered, Peter's reforms had, as yet, gained no more than an uncertain, unstable footing amongst the masses.

Up to the very close of Peter's career those masses remained restless and perplexed, for they could understand neither his intentions nor the trend of what he did, but regarded his aims as incomprehensible, and the origin

of his reforms as obscure. Hence from the first the reforms evoked
only a deadweight of opposition, and the more so because the masses
saw those reforms only in two of their most oppressive aspects—in the aspect
of the State exacting forced labour, and straining it to an excessive degree
of tension, and in the aspect of the State, for no ostensible purpose, infringing ancient customs, the country's old-established social adjustment, and
the people's time-honoured habits and beliefs. Not unnatural, therefore,
was it that these two presentments of the Petrine reforms should render the
people constantly suspicious of, and out of sympathy with, Peter's labours.
And this effect was increased by two popular impressions derived from
events of the seventeenth century. For during the course of that century the
inhabitants of the Muscovite Empire had seen some truly strange things
happen. To begin with, they had witnessed the rise and the fall of a whole
string of pretenders to the throne, and of illegal Governments which acted
sometimes on the lines prescribed for such bodies, and sometimes merely
in imitation of Governments armed with genuine authority based upon
precedent; whilst in the second place the inhabitants had seen file before
their vision a whole succession of legal rulers who acted less on the old lines
than on lines which bade fair to overthrow the existent civil and ecclesiastical
orders, to shake Muscovite antiquity to its foundations, to introduce Teuton-
ism into the State, and to thrust Anti-Christianism upon the Church. And
of these two categories of popular impressions the present joint result was
to instigate the above-described popular attitude towards Peter and his
reforms. Indeed, the people's view of Peter's activities was a view so poignant
and peculiar as spontaneously to evolve for itself two legends at once self-
explanatory and illustrative of how sorrily Peter's reforms won their way
amongst the people—one of the legends in question declaring him to be
a usurper, and the other one setting him down as Antichrist. Of the former
of the two legends the origin was as follows. On Peter perceiving that profound and persistent opposition was likely to be offered to his reforms, he
sought to crush it with the aid of a secret police institution known as the
Preobrazhenski Prikaz, deriving its name from the suburban village where
he had been brought up. From that institution we have inherited some
records which, besides being an interesting additional help in studying
the popular attitude of the day, throw especial light upon the origin, the
development, and the diffusion of the legends to which I have referred. In
each case the legends had an historical basis, and passed through given stages
of poetic evolution, and afford a striking example of the lengths to which
the popular mental-creative faculty can run, more especially if it issues from
a process of filtration through a police agency. The legend that Peter was a

usurper derived its original idea and fundamental *motif* from certain phenomena observed of the people during the early part of his reign. For the first thing that Peter did to impress the people with his activity was to add to the people's existent State obligations a whole category of new ones. From the earliest years of the century State obligations had been making the masses all too conscious of their weight, but formerly the people had laid the blame for them, not upon the Tsar himself, but upon his administrative agents, since invariably in those days the person of the Tsar had stood above and apart from the people, and he had shown himself before them so seldom as to lead the popular imagination to invest him with a sort of dazzling halo and unearthly majesty, and to attribute unpopular acts of the State exclusively to the administrative ring of *boyaré* and *prikaznie liudi* which stood between him and his submissive subjects. But now, in Peter's day, the Tsar descended from the cloudy eminence on which his predecessors had loomed, and for the first time brought the Imperial person into direct and independent contact with its subject people, and enabled that people to view it as it really was, and dissipated the political myth of the old-time Tsars. But this, again, led to the fact that now, when the people murmured, they murmured against the Tsar personally, for now all men could see that, after all, he was a human being like themselves, a Tsar sprung only from an earthly source. Besides, even at that, this particular Tsar was a Tsar extraordinary beyond description, a Tsar in an unwonted guise, a Tsar of unfamiliar manners and attributes, a Tsar who wore no crown, nor walked in purple, but, taking axe in hand, would thrust pipe between teeth, toil like a plain sailor, dress and smoke like a German, drink like a trooper, and swear and brawl like an officer of the Guards! And so, as Peter's people contemplated its extra-ordinary monarch, and saw how completely he differed from the pious Muscovite Emperors of old, involuntarily it began to ask itself: "Can this be the *rightful* Tsar?" And from this point some vigorous thinking led to some vigorous play of fancy, the successive stages of which the *Preobrazhenski Prikaz's* documents bring clearly before us, so that we can trace each phase of the people's imagination, and note how that imagination, fertilising the seed of thought, at last developed the latter into legend. Also, there was another factor helpful to the seed's free germination, to the growth, in the matter, of a strong popular faculty of invention: and that factor was the mass of popular discontent which existed. The first thing that caught the masses' attention was the question as to the Tsar's rightfulness; and that question led to gossip, and that gossip was overheard by certain police officials. On one occasion, for instance, some *krestiané* were heard to com-plain: "Ever since God sent us this Tsar for a ruler we have seen not a single day's prosperity, All our *mir* is overburdened with his ordained takings of roubles, and of *poltini*, and of loads of corn, so that never doth our brother *krestianin* gain a respite from the same"; to which a *boyarin* who had been listening thought well to add some class grievances on his own account, and say: "Speakest thou of the Tsar? Then look you how the Tsar now hath summoned our brethren of the *boyarstvo* to go forth and serve him, and seized our men-servants and our *krestiané* for recruits, so that no man escapeth, and some of them he even setteth afloat! Now, shall we kill this Tsar of ours? To kill him would diminish the services of the *boyaré*, and likewise lighten the burden of the common people." Here some soldiers' wives thrust forward a conservative-minded comrade to speak for them. "Verily what a Tsar is he!" she said. "For here hath this Tsar taken our husbands to be men-at-arms, and ravaged the peasantry and their homesteads, and left us and our children to weep for ever!" To which a *kholop* appended: "A Tsar, sayest thou? Nay, but a foe and a darkness unto our *mir*! So let him well look to it that, as he speedeth through Moscow, he lose not, one day, his head!" "An extortioner!" said others. "For see how, after devouring our *mir*, he is setting himself to destroy yet other goodly lives, as though only he himself, the villain, were not to be destroyed!" Class protests of the sort Peter himself helped to develop, and they passed from the point of speculation concerning his enigmatical personality to the point of seeking a solution of the enigma, and so to the point of discovering that solution. Thence the popular fancy gathered to itself yet ampler wings and achieved flights altogether unbounded. "For," said the people, "behold our Tsar's extraordinary manner of life and conduct!" Was he not a Tsar who himself had executed *Strieltzi*? And was he not a Tsar who had immured his wife and sister in a convent? Besides, that Tsar was never for a moment quiescent, but constantly engaged in drinking-bouts with his foreigners at Preobrazhenskoe! Also, actually, after the disaster at Narva, he had stripped churches of their bells, and converted them into cannon! Thus the ferment grew, and continued to grow, until at last an ecclesiastical dignitary gave it as his opinion that the only end of such happenings could be disaster, and from this the public derived the answer to the subsidiary question of the two which it had propounded to itself, and discovered that the persons by whom the Tsar had been corrupted from the first, were—the Germans! And this discovery gained the more popular support because the people knew of Peter's nervous seizures and fiery temper. "The Germans," the people explained, "have so gotten themselves about him that, though, in divers hours, all may be well with him, in other hours he only rageth and rendeth, in that he hath gone against God, and despoiled the churches of their bells." All of which really signified that at last the people had begun to resent the stream of foreign immigration which long and steadily had been adding to the growth of alien influence in Russia. But even so, the people still lacked a satisfactory answer to its main question, and at last met the difficulty by saying that Russia could not long harbour a Tsar warped, a Tsar who flouted his people's ancient customs. Then, as a secondary phase, it went on to answer the main question by fastening upon, and answering, the subsidiary question, "Is the Tsar even a Russian?" To which question some replied, "No, but the son of a German woman," and others, "The father of him was Lefort." And from this developed the further tale that only through usurpation had Peter gained the throne at all—people in general saying, "Once the Tsaritsa did bear a maiden babe, and exchange her for this German boy, this 'Peter.'" In particular, the Muscovite police overheard the following political utterance at a gathering of politically discontented *krestiané*. Breaking out into open invective, they cried: "A fine Tsar this! A Tsar born of a German outcast, and abandoned as a foundling! Aye, for before the Tsaritsa had left childbed she did say unto him: 'No son of mine art thou. Thou art a changeling.' And for yourselves can ye see that alway he doth wear German clothing! Known unto all men is it that he is one come of the Germans." And from this conception automatically there became evolved the legend's secondary portion: and that portion grew until it had come to embrace every pertinent phenomenon of the day. The factor first to give the secondary legend a lead, and facilitate its development, was Peter's first foreign tour, for it was then that he began to import foreign novelties—a shaving of beards, a Germanised style of dress, and so forth, and that he put away from him the Tsaritsa Avdotia Fedorovna in favour of a German wench, and ordered all men to smoke the accursed tobacco. Yes, the people repeated again and again, these things took place immediately after Peter's return from foreign parts. And possibly it was not only the Tsar's journeying to the lands of the Western, non-Christian peoples that furnished the masses of Russia with the link for further guidance in the legend: very likely, also, those masses had heard the story that in 1700, when Charles XII. of Sweden had left his dominions to make war upon Russia and her allies, he had appointed his sister, Ulrica Eleanor, to act as Regent, and she, on his decease, had succeeded to the Swedish throne, as also that in 1697 Peter had been flouted by the Swedish Government at Riga, and refused a permit to view the local fortifications; and in that case these two items in combination were such as might well provide the popular fancy of Russia not only with a legend, but also with a legend fused into a continuous, connected whole. At all events, as there could be no doubt that Peter had gone abroad at that time, the people now took to enquiring whether he had ever returned thence, and by the year 1706 had answered their own question thus. Whilst the Tsar and his *entourage* had been abroad they had toured, amongst other lands, the land of Germany, and reached a "Kingdom of Stekol," [1] ruled over by a young woman. And there the young woman had quarrelled violently with the Tsar, and caused him to be seated upon a hot gridiron, and then cast into a dungeon. But on the arrival of her nameday her princes and *boyaré* had approached her during its celebration, and said: "O Empress, we pray thee, in virtue of this day of thine, that thou wilt release yonder lord from durance," and she had replied: "Then first go ye and regard him, and, if so be that he is still alive, then I will release him for your sakes." And the princes and *boyaré* had gone and viewed the prisoner, and reported him to be "in a swoon." And thereupon the young woman had cried out: "In that case bring him forth," and the princes and *boyaré* had brought him forth, and set him at liberty. Yet, for some reason, even before he could leave the realm the same princes and *boyaré* had, after many crossings of themselves, fashioned for him a nail-studded chest; and only the fact that one of the Tsar's *Strieltzi* had learnt of what was pending, and run to his master, saying, "O Tsar and lord, I pray thee rise and be gone, seeing that I have beheld what they are preparing for thee!" enabled the Tsar to make good his escape. Meanwhile the *Strieletz* took his place on the bed, and the young woman's princes and *boyaré* entered, seized the *Strieletz*, shut him up in the nail-studded chest, and cast him into the sea. Thus the final legend. Yet, even so, it had a ragged end hanging out, in that it did not specify the Tsar's further fortunes: so later the people evolved as a climax: "This present man is not our Tsar, but a German, in that the rightful Tsar was he whom the Germans did place in a box with nails, and cast into the waters." Last of all, with Peter's decease—for after death men resurrected the Peter whom they had damned during his lifetime—the tale took on the addition that, whilst the recently departed Tsar had undoubtedly been a German, the true Tsar was still alive, since a Russian merchant long resident in "the Kingdom of Stekol," had, after all, enabled him to escape from his German prison. Yet, even so, it was not unusual for the narrative to wind up with the query: "Nevertheless, how cometh it that never again hath our true Tsar been seen in his realms?"

Of course, the real foundation for the legend was a taxatory *motif*, since it grew amongst the most heavily taxed social classes, and, above all, amongst that section of the masses which, after long enjoying exemption from State obligations, new *ukazi* had rendered subject to new fiscal burdens and

[1] Stockholm.

public duties. And of the legend that Peter was Antichrist we may say that it seems to have had its origin, or at all events its early development, amongst the ecclesiastical body, as a result of the ferment into which the Church had been thrown by the Nikonian innovations. Hence the two legends had two different sources of inspiration. As regards the second of them, Peter's activities seemed to the people to be a direct continuation of what it considered the aimless, unintelligible encroachments upon native faith and religious custom initiated by Alexis' Governments. And grievously wounded in its religious views though it was by such novelties as Peter's commands to shave the beard and wear foreign clothing, there appeared at the close of 1699 something transcending even tobacco and German raiment in vileness; and that something was an *ukaz* altogether abolishing the old Russian-Orthodox calendar, and bidding the years thenceforth be reckoned, not, as hitherto, from the Creation of the World, but from the Birth of Christ, and each individual year begin, not on the hitherto Orthodox first day of September, but on the European, the non-Orthodox, first day of January. And when this ordinance was extended also to cover the Church's whole system of chronological reckoning many persons who already abhorred Latinism with an abhorrence rendered possible only by the Nikonian period felt that once again they must stand up for the ancient faith, and thereby came to figure in certain incidents which are to be found entered in the records of Peter's police institution. Thus we read in those records that in 1703 a merchant named Andrei Ivanov actually made the long journey from Nizhni Novgorod to Moscow solely to lay a *donos*, or "information," against —against whom? Why, against the Tsar himself for having, with his orders to shave beards, and to don German clothing, and to smoke tobacco, infringed the ancient religious beliefs of his country! Yes, to arraign the Tsar himself did Andrei Ivanov tramp from Nizhni Novgorod to the capital! Also, we read that on Easter Day, 1705, when Dmitri, Metropolitan of Rostov, was walking home from his cathedral, he encountered two young men, and was besought for his advice as to the right way of treating the beard-shaving order—the young men declaring that they would rather lose their very heads than their beards. Countered the prelate: "Yet which of the twain, I pray you, would grow again the more easily?" And another record relates that once when the same dignitary was entertaining a party of superior guild citizens, a dispute arose concerning the peril to the soul which beard removal entailed, and left the learned ecclesiastic so moved by what had been said that immediately after his guests' departure he fell to work upon the inditement of a monograph on the human image and its divine model. These and other items alone show how heated the beard question became, even if it was not also known to us that anonymous pamphlets on the subject were broadcast throughout the provincial towns, with exhortations to Orthodox Christians, one and all, to rise on the beard's behalf. At the same time, persons of a deeper way of thinking there were, even if they were only a few, who refused to accept the alleged usurpation as the true cause of things, and deemed it necessary to probe further before it would be possible to discover the true source of Peter's reforms, with all their dangers and temptations. But as, whenever they remonstrated with Peter concerning such follies of his as his face-trimmings and his indecent "College of Drunkards," he rejected the advice proffered, such members of the community's more superstitious section at last had left to them, for debate, only the question of whether or not Peter's slightings of decorum portended the end of the world—in which case the only anticipatory means of salvation might be voluntary submission of the person to suffering. And in this way popular debates at last led up to a legend that the Tsar was no less a personage than Antichrist himself. The first occasion when we meet with the legend is in 1700, when Peter's police arrested a Muscovite amanuensis named Talitski, a man of some education, on a charge of having composed and distributed treatises prophesying the end of the world, and suggesting that between Antichrist and the Tsar there existed at least a connection. And, indeed, the treatise seems to have had force enough in it to reduce the Bishop of Tambov to tears, and to move the Prince and *Boyarin* Khovanski to inform the author of the work with some despondency that though hitherto he had been in a fair way to receive the crown of suffering, he had now dropped out of the running through, firstly, consenting to use a razor upon himself, and, secondly, "consecrating" a new mock "Metropolitan" for Peter's "All-Drunken Assembly." The regions where the legend spread most easily were the regions around Olonetz, and the country lying to the north of Lake Onega, since it was there that Old Belief had taken deepest root, and it was thither that the reign of Alexis had seen protagonists of the ancient faith most flee for refuge. And for the same reason those localities now (at the close of the seventeenth century) became the scene where fanatical refugees most sought to defend themselves from their Antichrist Tsar and his new and heretical Church by inflicting upon themselves the torturing death of self-immolation: where they did so in such numbers that a work by a contemporary member of the persuasion declares that during the period 1675–91 no fewer than 20,000 souls cast themselves into the flames. And inasmuch as news from the outer world reached the dense forests of those Northern and White Sea districts only in the distorted guise which an imagination spurred by fear readily converted into miraculous portents, it is not to be wondered at that one day when a priest and a cantor were leaving the church of a certain *pogost* in the *uezd* of Olonetz, they fell to speculating with each other upon events in the world without, and that a conversation on the following lines took place. Said the cantor to the priest: "To-day are we bidden to number the years only from the Birth of Christ, and to wear the raiment of Vengria";[1] and the priest responded: "Aye, and likewise I have received word in the *volost* that the Week of the Great Fast is to be lessened, and milk to be drunken on every Wednesday and Friday throughout the year from the Feast of St. Thomas." This brought back to the cantor's mind the means of salvation offered by suicide, and he remarked: "So long as *ukazi* of the sort come unto us, so long will the men of this *pogost* go to dwell in the forest, and burn themselves. I likewise am minded to go into the forest, and burn myself!" And to him the priest made eager reply: "Then take thou me with thee, now that for all of us life is drawing unto its close." We may assign this item to the year 1704. And it was during the same year that a *Strieletz* of Ladoga who was returning home from Novgorod chanced upon the Superior of a monastery, and fell into conversation with him. Said the Superior: "To-day we have indeed many a holding of worship, and what sort of a Christianity can it be that demandeth such a following of the Faith? I myself cleave unto the ancient Books. Yet, look you, they are to be burnt!" Then the subject passed to the Tsar, and the Superior continued: "A fine Tsar for Christian folk! But he is no Tsar at all—rather a man of the Latin Church who keepeth not the fasts, an impostor, the Antichrist, a son of an unclean woman! Look you, moreover, how, if he striketh his head against aught, or if aught causeth his foot to stumble, straightway he must destroy it with his foul spirit, and for the same cause hath punished even some of your own *Strieltzi* for being Christian men, and not infidels like unto himself and his soldiers—not a few of the which are unbelievers altogether, and keep not the fasts, and others are foreigners who do walk abroad in German apparel and periwigs, and shave their beards." At this point a recollection of his military office made the *Strieletz* feel that, after all, he ought to take up the cudgels in the Tsar's defence, and he remarked that, if Peter was nothing else, at least he was Tsar, and born of the Imperial stock; but this the Superior would not have at any price—he exclaimed: "And what was the Tsaritsa, his mother? Who, but a heretic who bore none save female children?" Also, we know that the utterer of these words was doing something more than preach adherence to the ancient piety. He himself was upholding that piety, for when the *Strieletz* asked him whence he had come he replied: "From the forest-

[1] Hungary.

country beyond Onega, whither only on *lizhi* [1] can a man come in winter time, and during the summer time he can come not at all." The story gives us a vivid picture of the mental attitude then most obtaining in Northern Russia, whilst in 1708 we begin to meet with the legend of Peter as Antichrist also in the South, and hear a priest say to a colleague in the *uezd* of Bielgorod (*gubernia* of Kursk): "God alone knoweth what now is passine in this our realm of Russia! For behold how the territory of the Ukraing lieth all undone with taxes which no man can reckon, so that they fall even upon our brethren, and do mulct both their bath-houses and their huts and their bees in a manner never known unto our fathers and our grandfathers. Can it be that no Tsar is abiding in the State?" And on another occasion the speaker was studying a treatise when he read in it that one day Antichrist would be born of an unclean woman, of a false virgin, of "the tribe of Dan." And as he was wondering what the words could mean, and where precisely the birth would take place, and whether that spot would be in Russia, there entered to him one Anika Akimitch Popov, sub-lieutenant of the local regiment of Bielgorod: and, on being told by the priest of the speculation as to Antichrist (the priest adding that "if verily things shall befall as written in this book, and Antichrist come to birth of a 'Tribe of Dan,' all my work will stand as nought"), Anika Akimitch took thought, and at last replied: "Antichrist is here already. He is reigning in this our realm as Tsar. For by 'the Tribe of Dan' there is signified the Imperial House, whilst known unto all men is it that Tsar Peter was born of an evil connection, in that his mother was a second spouse, and only a first one is lawful." And so we have the tale that Peter was Antichrist.

Scarcely need it be said that legends of the sort in no way lessened the popular hostility to reform, or aided reform's progress, since they turned the people's attention from interests which Peter was genuinely striving to meet to such individual aspects of his policy as, owing to his superstitious bent, he had a tendency to manifest mostly in anti-popular or anti-ecclesiastical forms. The result of this confusion of his mental attitude was to induce a popular view that reform was as unintelligible as it was oppressive. Only a few persons, persons who had actually seen the Tsar at work, felt it incumbent upon them to defend him from gossip and tittle-tattle. And (as certain records show) there were occasions when even the masses themselves derived a favourable impression from Peter's personality and toil. An instance is that when a certain peasant of Olonetz was relating how Peter had spent his days during a recent visit to the northern districts, the narrator added: "And he is indeed a Tsar, for so long as he was here he never did eat his

---

[1] Snowshoes.

bread for nothing, but did surpass even us *muzhiki* in labour." In fact, it was altogether unfortunate that the people as a whole never obtained a chance of deriving an impression like the foregoing, a chance of personally beholding the Tsar in working trim, and divining from the spectacle the fact that under the stern trappings of his Imperial authority, and behind the seeming aimlessness of his precipitate activity, there lay operative a moral driving-force. Amongst the rare instances of such divination may be mentioned a memorandum which a *pribyltschik* named Ivan Filipov presented to Peter, and in which, with all the acumen of a trained historian, Ivan remarks that "the Tsar is a much-thinking and never-resting lord, and understandeth all that maketh both for justice and for the safeguarding of his people." As regards the bulk of the population, however, as regards the huge aggregate of individuals whose limit of permitted thought was the *knut*, and what the priests might allow them to know, that bulk vested Peter in every odious guise furnishable from the rag-bag of popular fancy, and surrounded him with an invented atmosphere at once born of, nourished by, and morally sanctioned by a political discontent whose source, again, lay in the State's exactions, and in Peter's German novelties. How great that discontent became towards the close of the reign we know from native and foreign observers alike. Not that open rebellion ever threatened, for a leader capable of heading such a movement no longer existed, the masses were naturally servile and subservient, and the elements of popular militant force which had figured in the past had long ago become spent in the *Strieletz* risings, and in the *émeutes* of Astrakhan and Bulava. No, the feud between the State's authority and the people's will was carried on without the aid of weapons, and the court appealed to by that will was the conscience of the lay citizen. There is a story that shortly after Peter's death some Old-Believing members of the *Strieletz* had it given out that the Tsar, when dying, exclaimed: "Had I lived longer, the world would have cursed me"; and the story at least shows how completely, even by the time when he came to depart, Peter's great schemes and efforts for his people had failed to gain that people's understanding, but, terrifying all, mystifying all, had passed over the people's head as intangibly as a hurricane.

At the same time, the superior social classes of the community at least did not remain unaffected by Peter's reforms, for those classes possessed better qualifications for comprehending such things, and stood in a closer relation to the Reformer, and were induced to co-operate with his efforts by, amongst other motives, the fact that numerous threads linked them to the world of Western Europe which represented the source of Peter's impulses towards reform. Moreover, the very fact that those classes constituted Peter's governmental service laid upon them the greater an obligation to help Russia to win for herself an influential status in Europe, improve her diplomatic relations with the West, and strengthen, not weaken, her Western cultural ties. Again, to the same end tended certain changes in those classes' social and racial composition. True, still lingering in the administrative ring were a few survivals of the old Muscovite aristocracy like the Golitzins, Dolgoruki, Repnin, Stcherbatov, Sheremetev, Golovin, and Buturlin, members of the *boyarstvo* of the "Book of Degrees" who since that "Book's" day had become workers of State; but the real kernel of the administrative class of the seventeenth century was the upper grade of the metropolitan *dvorianstvo*, of the class known under Peter as *tsaredvortsi*, and inclusive of families like the Pushkins, the Tolstois, the Bestuzhevs, the Volinskis, the Kudivevs, the Pletchievs, the Novosiltzevs, and the Volkovs, with, later, the influx of provincial *dvoriané* best represented, in Alexis' time, by Ordin-Nastchokin, and, in Peter's, by Nepluev, and with, later again, the stream of "poor *shliachetstvo*" and "men below the *shliàchetstvo*" best represented by the Narishkins, the Lopukhins, Menshikov, and Zotov, and with, latest of all, an aggregate drawn sheerly from the ranks of the *kholopstvo*, and inclusive of *pribyltschiki* like Kurbatov, Ershov, and the merchant Stroganov (promoted, in 1722, to the rank of baron). True, the invasion of the official circle by these newcomers can scarcely be said to have increased that circle's *esprit de corps*, and in any case it helped to disintegrate the circle's social composition, both morally and genealogically; but at least the invasion in question fired the ruling class to a certain animation and rivalry, broke down the old *boyarin* pride, and shook up the stereotyped metropolitan-official system. And in proportion as homegrown *parvenus* of the new class completed their terms of service, there became established in the country, and reached important State positions, a multitude of alien immigrants of whom I may cite as types Baron Shafirov, a Jewish-born foreigner who embraced Christianity after being taken prisoner by the Russians, and later served, first of all as a menial in the household of a *boyarin* named Khitrov, and then in the emporium of a merchant of Moscow; Yaguzhinski, reputedly a swineherd by origin, and the son of a Lithuanian-Lutheran organist; Devier, a man who rose to be chief of the St. Petersburg police, but originally was a cabin boy on a Portuguese ship who absconded to Holland, and caught Peter's attention; Baron Ostermann, son of a Westphalian pastor; Count Bruce; General Henning (a noted organiser of foundries); and an engineer named Münnich. Lastly, there came from the remote fastnesses of Lithuania, and made their way into the ranks of the Russian aristocracy, the peasant kinsfolk of Catherine I., a conglomeration of individuals whom their Imperial relative hastened to load with titles, dignities, and wealth. Not but that it ought in fairness to be acknowledged that some of the newcomers, such as Bruce and Shafirov and Ostermann, turned out to be skilful and well-educated executants, and, so far from desiring to set Western Europe at loggerheads with their adopted country, displayed sufficient merit and culture to constitute a standing reproach to the native *boyarin* caste, most of whom were idle boors.

A further bond between the upper classes of Russia and the world of the West was the bond of elementary education. During the first half of Peter's reign, when, as yet, Russia possessed few schools, the principal road to learning lay through the system of dispatching Russian *dvoriané* abroad for technical training; and notes made by these travellers (either on their own account or compulsorily) show us how difficult that road was, and how barren of results it proved. For since the travellers in question were sent abroad as unprepared for as indifferent to the purpose of their journey, they merely stared open-mouthed at the manners, governmental systems, and public regulations of Western Europe without learning in the least to distinguish between culture and rubbish, or to derive any clear-cut idea from what they beheld. Thus, whilst a Muscovite prince whose name has not come down to us gives us a detailed description of a dinner which he enjoyed with a scantily-clad wench at a restaurant in Amsterdam, we find the same student admitting that all he could think of, when viewing the Cathedral of St. Peter in Rome, was to ascertain, by pacing, the external superficies of the building, and to note the hangings covering the interior walls. And even Prince Kurakin, though he had lived in Western Europe before, and, in particular, studied at Vienna, could find nothing better to record of the Erasmus Memorial in Rotterdam than that "here there standeth, fashioned in molten copper, a peasant with a book. The book signifies that he was learned, and did teach, and so doth the whole image"; whilst later, when Kurakin visited Professor "Bidlow's" (Bidloo's) anatomical theatre in Leyden, and saw the Professor "rend asunder" a corpse, and show his students the corpse's portions, and also exhibit a fine collection of "preparations within vessels of spirit," all that our Russian observer felt moved to do, as he watched the efforts of a Dutch scientist attempting to gain a knowledge of life through a study of death, was to jot down a recommendation that no intending visitor to Holland should miss Leyden, since a visit to "these curiosities" would afford the visitor "much diversion." Yet this lack of previous preparation on the part of his Russian students did not discourage Peter from basing high hopes upon their foreign tours, since he believed that the travellers would, in spite of everything, derive from their experiences abroad as much useful knowledge as he himself had done. And above all things he sought to force upon his *dvoriané* the nautical art, since in that art he descried the first and the soundest basis on which to build up his new State: and we know from persons connected with the Russian Embassy in Holland that, beginning with the year 1697, scores of young Russian aristocrats were dispatched to that country alone for nautical training. The unfortunate point was that the sea more than all else repelled the average *dvorianin* youngster, and moved one such lad pathetically to write home that he would rather be appointed "unto any land science soever" than to the science of the ocean, even though the "land science" might be but the lowest rank in the army, seeing that that rank would at least relieve the petitioner of having to remain in the naval profession. But later the programme of *dvorianin* foreign study underwent a considerable degree of extension, and though (as we know from his memoirs) even Nepluev, like his fellow students, set an indifferent example as regards making an intelligent use of his four years (1716-20) of foreign study , we at least gain from his writings an idea of what Russian youths of his class in society learnt abroad, and of how they lived during the assimilation of that learning. As a rule the *dvorianin* students were distributed only to such leading towns of Europe as Venice, Florence, Toulon, Marseilles, Cadiz, Paris, Amsterdam, and London, where they received academical instruction variously in painting, coach-building, mechanics, navigation, engineering, gunnery, naval architecture, seamanship, military law, dancing, fencing, riding, and such purely artisan mysteries as copper-smithery, joinery, and ship construction. But at the same time the students had an unfortunate habit of deserting science for Mount Athos, and hanging about "redoubts" (gambling halls), and brawling, and even killing one another, so that frequently it happened that the youths possessed of means, after dissipating their substance, escaped a debtors' prison only by disposing also of their landed property at home, and that students relying upon more or less irregular subsidies from the same quarter had, after periods of semi-starvation, to take service under the State in which they were temporarily residing. Naturally, therefore, the reputation of these students for "good cavaliership" [1] underwent a gradual deterioration. Besides, our youthful exponents of culture had seldom been long returned to their native land before their newly-imbibed customs and scientific impressions blew from off them like dust from a turnpike road, and left remaining only such an admixture of alien vices with native shortcomings as once moved a foreign observer to remark that, so far from that admixture helping to promote virtue and godliness, it simply hastened degeneration both

---

[1] In modern terminology, "good form."

moral and physical. At the same time, a few instances did occur in which, on issuing from a course of foreign study, a student did so with a few fragments of culture sticking to him. It was Peter's idea to make of his *dvorianstvo* his general agency for home dissemination of foreign naval and military technique; and though it was not long before he perceived that technique to sit awkwardly on the limbs of the class concerned, and seldom, and only with the greatest difficulty, to enable a Russian *dvorianin* to develop into a capable engineer or a capable sea captain (for in very few cases did students put their foreign-gained knowledge to any practical use after their return, and even Menshikov, one of Peter's co-workers as a mast-making apprentice in a shipyard at Saardam, never became anything more smacking of the sea than a dry-land Governor-General), in one or two cases a period of residence in various foreign countries did leave behind it a trace. Hence, generally speaking, there may be set against the fact that at this period compulsory scientific education failed to furnish Russia with scientific knowledge the fact that that education at least gave the Russian *dvorianin* his first introduction to enlightenment, aroused in him a measure of cultured appetite, and taught him, if not the particular things for acquisition of which he had been sent abroad, at all events something.

In addition, Peter took care to set on foot measures for reform in the domestic sphere. The first, the indispensable, thing to that end was to drag the Russian out of his native isolation, and project his vision beyond the limits of his own country. And the best means of doing this Peter conceived to lie in the newspaper, and in the theatre. Wherefore the month of January 1703 saw Russia's first-published periodical appear in Moscow. This first-published periodical was the *Viedomosti*, or *News*, and thenceforth, on every second or every third day (sometimes at longer intervals, according as a foreign mail came in) the journal issued one or more sheets printed in the old round, ecclesiastical type, and reproducing both "writings" (items) clipped from sundry journals of Western Europe and purely Russian items which Peter ordered the *Prikazi* to furnish. And he revised the production's opening number with his own hand, and had the type of it set up in the then State Printing Office, an establishment standing where Nikolskaia Street now stands; and amongst the intelligence communicated to the public by this opening number were the items that, "by command of his Majesty, the Schools of Moscow are to be enlarged, in that already forty-five scholars have heard dialectics therein, and now are hearing philosophy, and that the School of Mathematics and Pilotage hath in it three hundred students who likewise are gaining good knowledge; "that between the twenty-fourth day of November and the twenty-fourth day of December, three hundred and eighty-six male and female children were born in Moscow"; and that "from Olonetz cometh it in writing" that recently one Ivan Okulov, a priest, had enrolled a thousand volunteers, crossed the Swedish border, killed fifty Swedish cavalrymen and four hundred Swedish infantrymen, fired a thousand Swedish homesteads, and awarded the booty to his "army"—the whole with a loss of only two men wounded. Also, besides giving foreign news, the journal presented its readers with foreign-culled Russian items distinguished from those already described by having been subjected to no censorship or administrative colouring of any sort. An instance of this is that seven months before the completion of the founding of St. Petersburg an inhabitant of Nieumanetz-on-the-Neva sent the journal's first number word that "in this town of ours we are indeed dwelling in sorry plight, so greatly hath Moscow already worked ill unto these parts," and that the panic-stricken inhabitants were betaking themselves and their valuables wholesale to Viborg. The total number of issues published by the journal during its first year of existence was thirty-nine.

As early as Alexis' day a court theatre of a sort, staffed with a foreign troupe, was established: and though I should not care to speculate as to the precise effect upon the artistic taste of the privileged circles who received invitations to attend this first essay in histrionics, there can be no doubt that even at that period Moscow could boast of many dramatic devotees, and accorded the new form of recreation at least an adequate measure of support. Also, says Prince Kurakin, the household serfs of great establishments had long been used to celebrate holidays by performing "droll tales of every sort"; whilst from other sources we know that the students of the Muscovite Academy sometimes produced plays by invitation or command, and figured on the playbills as "State youths"—probably because amongst them there were not a few scions of aristocratic and official-aristocratic families. So when, during the early and more troublous days of the Swedish War, Peter returned home from Narva he set to work to organise, not a court, but a public, stage, and for 5000 *efimi* (20,000 modern roubles) hired the services of a troupe of German actors (mostly "*studiosi*" under one Kunst, actor and dramatist both), and as a next step consulted the entertainment of "all willing beholders" by building, on the Red Square, a free and open playhouse known as "The Mansion of Comedy," or "The Hall of Comedy," and providing three performances a week—performances at which one or more interpreters from the *Posolski Prikaz* translated into Russian, in unison with the given dramatic action, a repertoire made up of pieces of the type of a comedy based upon the story of Don Pedro and Don Juan, of a comedy entitled *Bajazet and Tamerlane,* of a drama entitled

Scipio Africanus, and of Molière's well-known *Le Médecin Malgré Lui*; whilst the musical element was represented by extracts or arias from "singing pieces" (operas), and the comic by "Hanswurst,"[1] the well-known buffoon-hero of the German popular stage—his name transmuted by the Russian official interpreters into "Zaiatchoe Salo"![2] And in no case did Peter omit to make these and all other imported artistes transmit their craft to his native talent, and, in particular, guaranteed Kunst a definite number of pupils solely on condition that, "with good zeal, and in all openness," he should instruct those pupils in "the mystery of comedy," and, for the purpose, receive them (they were mostly young *podiachie* from the Government Offices) at his residence in the German Suburb.

One of the strongest impressions which Peter derived from his first foreign tour—possibly it was the strongest of all—was a sense of astonishment at the fact that so many Western Europeans received an education of a nature qualifying them to become self-supporting. And so convinced was he that this represented cause and effect that as soon as ever he returned home he resolved to dower his country with a general university or polytechnic, of some sort. Hence, after exchanging views on the subject with the Patriarch, and expressing dissatisfaction because the already existent Academy had in it but a handful of students, and lacked proper supervision, he announced his intention of instituting a "school which shall send forth men meet for all necessities of service in the Church, and in the State, and in warfare, and in building, and in the physician's and the surgeon's arts," and should help parents desirous of obtaining "free learning" for their sons to dispense altogether with resort to the foreigner. Unfortunately, the eventual outcome was that, owing to lack of means, and to failure to take the right preparatory steps, this scheme dwindled down into the establishment merely of some minor primary-technical seminaries; and though even to these, during the opening years of the century, Peter devoted every possible moment which he could spare from the main portion of his self-imposed task of resolving the problems of war and finance, so that, according to Prince Kurakin's autobiography, not only were subsidised students dispatched abroad for "learnings," and a public theatre opened, and a daily journal founded, but also "mathematical schools" established, and colleges organised for teaching such arts and sciences as "fashionings of headwear, of cloth, of leather grounded on buckskin, of plaster figures, and of architectural erections,"—although all this was done, it proved constantly the case that popular reforms of the kind had to yield to naval and military necessities. In the same connection Peter had recourse, in 1698, to the

[1] "Jack Pudding."   [2] "Hare Sausage."

Scotch University of Aberdeen,[1] and, hiring thence a Professor Farquharson, allotted that preceptor the Sukharev fortress as a college for sons of *dvoriané* and the official world, and bade him, first and foremost, instruct those pupils in navigation: and in consequence of this it may fairly be said that the real founder of nautical-mathematical studies in Russia was this savant from Scotland, and we have additional confirmation of the fact in a statement by Kurbatov that Farquharson and a couple of Scotch assistants trained every grade of Peter's new navy, and conducted their school "in due order, and with all regularity," save for the one exception that, being, as said, Scotchmen, the trio indulged in occasional "celebrations," overslept themselves, and sought to excuse their dereliction of duty by saying that it would not have happened if their more ready-witted pupils had not outstripped the more stupid ones instead of waiting for the latter to catch them up! In 1715, however, Farquharson was transferred to an academy designed to obviate the necessity of sending young *dvoriané* abroad for study, whilst earlier, in 1711, there also became established a school of engineering, with a Lieutenant-Colonel von Strauss for its head, and a Colonel Liamkin for its lecturer, and, lastly, a school for instruction in gunnery. Hence, if we add to these a Slavonic-Greco-Latin Academy in Moscow, an establishment with a theological schedule designed to reform the clergy, we shall see that by now there had come into being two chief educational establishments for conferring instruction in general upon a few specified social classes, and three similar establishments for conferring upon the same classes a training of a professional-technical nature. Yet these five institutions must not be misunderstood—it must not be thought that they bore any more relation to their official titles than they did to our modern social and scholastic classifications, for all of them received pupils belonging to more than one social grade, and had an elementary *curriculum* plus, in each case, a single speciality—an example being that the School of Navigation's pupils included both princes and plain *dvoriané*, and that those pupils were collected only as military volunteers were enrolled, in proportion, that is to say, as additions might be needed "to complete establishment." At first the Muscovite School of Engineering had assigned to it twenty-three students only, but later Peter ordered the complement of the *personnel* to be raised to, firstly, 100, and then 150, on condition that two-thirds of that complement should consist of sons of *dvoriané*: and when the authorities replied that to comply with the condition was beyond their powers, they received a wrathful *ukaz* bidding them select the additional 77 pupils

---

[1] Subsequently the author speaks of Farquharson as hailing, not from Aberdeen but from Edinburgh.

from amongst the general public, but most of all from amongst sons of such *tsaredvortsi* as owned at least fifty peasant homesteads apiece. For the rest, the nature of the *personnels* and the *curricula* of Peter's scholastic institutions can best be studied from the Marine Academy, which was an establishment primarily *dvorianin* and technical of composition, with 172 pupils out of its total of 252 hailing from the *shliachetstvo*, and only 80 "commoner" *alumni*. In its higher classes the establishment taught "great astronomy" and "navigation plain and round," and its lower classes communicated the alphabet to twenty-five commoners, the Breviary to two sons of *shliachtichi* and twenty-five commoners, the Psalter to one *shliachtich's* son and ten commoners, and the calligraphic art to eight commoners. Yet numerous drawbacks hampered the Academy in its instruction, for it lacked both a charter and a proper inspectional system; and though Peter did not let even his cares in connection with war prevent him from giving the enterprise such attention as was possible under the circumstances, neither teachers nor taught found their tasks easy to execute. Nor did the scarcity and the costliness of educational appliances tend to lessen these difficulties, for in 1711, we read, the State Office of Printing, or Treasury Press, the institution which held a monopoly for the issue of scholastic works, had to pay a proof corrector named Harmann 17½ roubles for the mere task of revising an Italian-Russian lexicon that was "needed for school matters," and in 1714, on the School of Engineering applying to the Press for thirty treatises on geometry and eighty-three "books of sines," the Press could only reply that it must charge eight roubles a copy for the treatises, and that, as regards the "books of sines," it had not a single copy left in stock. Moreover, seeing that it had not yet become usual to familiarise Russian youngsters with the tongues of alien lands, we cannot but wonder in what sort of dialect Peter's imported instructors can have lectured to their audiences, and on what footing towards the latter those instructors stood. We merely know from a minute compiled by Count Ratviev, Chief Superintendent of the Marine Academy, that on one occasion the Director of that institution, a French baron of shallow attainments, so maltreated the young academicians that one of them felt driven to go and lay a personal complaint before the Tsar, on the ground that the director had first slapped him on the cheek, and then caned him before the whole school—an item which, taken with other indications, would seem to show that the general atmosphere of the educational province was at least one scarcely conducive to, if not actually militant against, a successful acquisition of culture. So for once let me break my rule of not risking the reader's impatience by setting before him a few of the educational features specially distinctive of the Marine Academy which Peter founded in 1715. The daily routine there began with an early assembling of the "naval guards" (as the institution's *alumni* were termed) for prayers—that they might beseech the Lord's favour for themselves, and His bestowal of success upon the Imperial arms: which ceremony, at the same time be it noted, was always carried out "under penalty." And when the ceremony was over all dispersed to the class-rooms to be—again "under penalty"—lectured to by professors who, in return for a due accordance of respect, were, "under penalty" as in the case of their pupils, to instruct the latter "in the best manner devisable, and with all possible diligence"—otherwise to be made to refund four times the amount of their hitherto received fees, and, in the event of the "transgression" being a second one, to be made also to undergo "chastisement of the body"! Inevitably a scholastic establishment thus converting human tutelage into a taming of wild cubs tended to arouse repulsion in the youthful breast, and to lead to the particular form of scholastic opposition which from earliest times has been the primitive resource of youngsters, finding themselves standing at loggerheads with their preceptors, and has never been improved upon. I need hardly say that that resource is the resource of playing truant. Whereby in Russia of that period military desertion and scholastic flight became the two chronic maladies afflicting State defence and popular enlightenment. Yet, for all the gravity of truancy as an offence, it is, at all events as regards Peter's day, partly intelligible when we remember, in addition to other causes, the laboured diction in which Peter's foreign preceptors must have lectured to their boorish and not very accessible pupils, and also those preceptors' own conditions of service—conditions never really inducing them to conciliate the objects of their instruction, but imposed by a Government which considered scholastic training to be less a moral need of the community as a whole than a natural obligation renderable solely by that community's youth before entering that Government's service. Indeed, the then Russian authorities looked upon the Russian school as a porch admitting merely to one of two places—to a barracks or to a chancellory, and that school's scholars looked upon their labours as a period of confinement in, as it were, a hulk or a penal cantonment, and upon escape from it as attainment of the highest good. So in 1722, with all the solemnity ordinarily accorded only to decrees invoking assembly of the State *Duma*, the Senate issued an *ukaz* to inform the public, on behalf of his Majesty the Emperor and Autocrat of All Russia, that, inasmuch as the Muscovite School of Navigation (an institution subsidiary to the Peterburgan Marine Academy) had recently lost 127 scholars through truancy, and thereby suffered in its funds, since "for a space of years past" many of the absconded pupils had "dwelt in receipt of recompense," the absentees referred to must now, by a given date, return and report themselves—otherwise, delicately added the *ukaz*, such of them as were sons of *shliachtichi* would be mulcted in fines, and such of them as were sons of lower ranks would be subjected to an even more poignant penalty. Lastly, the *ukaz* appended to this invitation a list of the absentees' names, and heartily commended those names to the public's attention. They included the names of thirty-three sons of *shliachtichi*, of one prince (A. Viazemski), of eighty-two sons of *reitari*, Guards soldiers, and commoners, and of twelve sons of boyaral slaves. And the mere fact shows us how various the social class composition of the Academy was.

In short, the dawn of Russian scholastic enlightenment broke dull and louring. Perhaps the most remarkable episode, as that enlightenment grew and spread, was Gluck's Academy. Gluck, a Saxon-born pedagogue and an active missioner, was a man who, after receiving a good education in theology and philosophy at certain German universities, made his way to the Livonian town of Marienburg in the capacity of pastor, and there set to work to learn the Russian and the Latin languages with a view to translating the Hebrew and the Greek Testaments into Russian for the benefit of the Eastern Livonian Roman Catholic and Russian population. And, of course, as regards the latter, he re-translated from the Slavonic dialect, of which the Russians of the day knew little. And, that done, he began to agitate to have Latin and Russian Schools established in the region, and went so far as to make a preliminary translation, for those schools' benefit, of a complete series of primers, but was taken prisoner by the Russian army on the town's capture in 1702, and forwarded to Moscow. Now, it so happened that he arrived in Moscow precisely when the Muscovite Department of Foreign Affairs was badly needing translators and interpreters, and doing all it could to obtain them by inviting foreigners to visit Russia and accept commissions for communicating their respective tongues at least to the official ranks of the metropolis. Hence, just as in 1701 a foreigner named Schimmer had been made director of a school in the German Suburb, and then transferred, as a translator, to the *Posolski Prikaz*, and allowed, meanwhile, to teach the German, French, and Latin languages to a few sons of *podiachie* with a view to those youths themselves becoming Government translators, so now Gluck had pupils entrusted to him at his residence in the German Suburb, and, in 1705, on the authorities learning that, in addition to an ability to teach languages, he could also "inform upon all the sciences of schools, and upon mathematics and philosophy, and in many and diverse tongues," had organised for him a sort of intermediate college which an official document terms "The Gymnasium," and was appointed the college's first director. In fact, Peter set so high a value upon this pastor (amongst whose domestic staff there was a Livonian peasant woman known to the local neighbours of the day as "Das schöne Mädchen von Marienburg," and later to the world at large as Catherine I. of Russia) that eventually he allotted Gluck's school an annual subsidy of 3000 roubles (25,000 modern). As a first step before starting the school, Gluck issued to all the youth of the Empire a showy and most alluring appeal which, beginning with a declaration that the young men of Russia were "as clay malleable, and meet in all respects for instruction," went on to beguile them with the words "Hail, ye fruitful ones, ye marvels who now would have stay and support!" and to furnish a detailed synopsis of the school's proposed *curriculum*, with a list of foreign *savants*, that *curriculum's* proposed executants—the founder himself heading the list as chief instructor both in geography, in ethics, in politics, in "Latin exercises, rhetorical and oratorical," in Descartian philosophy, in the French, German, Latin, Greek, Hebrew, Syriac, and Chaldaic tongues, in the Terpsichorean art, in "the steps of the German and the French graces," and in the mysteries of equitation and the schooling of horses; whilst from a document recently reproduced in facsimile, and dating from early in the year 1705 (the period of the school's formal institution by *ukaz*) we can piece together a fairly circumstantial record of this educational establishment's subsequent brief and most curious history. In the school's *ukaz* of institution it was set forth that it, the school, was to be ordained "for a teaching of languages, and of philosophical wisdom," principally to sons of *boyaré* and *okolnichi* and *dumnie liudi* and *blizhnie liudi* and other official ranks, but also to a given number of sons of the mercantile stratum; whilst other sources tell us that Gluck prepared, and used in teaching his school, a Russian compendium of geography, a Russian grammar, a Lutheran Catechism, a Lutheran prayer-book (the last versified into sorry Russian), and a guide to parallel linguistic study—the preliminary compiler, in this case, being a Bohemian pedagogue named Konianski, a man who already had issued a work entitled *Orbis Pictus*, or *The World in Illustration*, and seen it achieve a large circulation amongst elementary schools in the West of Europe. And though, when Gluck died in 1705, the "Rector" appointed in his stead, one of his own pupils, Paul Wernher by name, fell into speedy disgrace "through his much violence and corruption," and also through his habit of selling the school's books for his own benefit, and was dismissed, the original *ukaz* of ordination had empowered whomsoever might at any time be head of the school to apply to the State for all necessary tutorial assistance, and therefore by 1706 the institution's foreign preceptors had come to number ten, and were being lodged on the school's premises at the Government's expense, in a sort of club boarded by Gluck's widow, and receiving such enrolments in salaries and "table wine" as together, for all that the preceptors kept asking for more, amounted to from 48 to 150 (from 384 to 1200) roubles a year. Also, the school had its own official complement of horses and servants; and though only the tongues of Rome, Germany, Italy, France, and Sweden were taught out of the multitudinous studies included in Gluck's original and most pompous programme, the lecturer on Swedish, it was announced, would always lecture also upon history, and Gluck's son expound philosophy and "theological delights," and Remburg, the dancing master, instruct in "the elegancies of the body, and compliments after the French and German styles." As regards "form" grading, the school was divided into three classes only—into an elementary class, an intermediate, and an upper, but in each of these classes the scholars were promised equal advancement, whilst those of the scholars who took the course from end to end received an undertaking that as soon as their time for State service should arrive it should be left "wholly according unto their will" as to which branch of the service, whether the military or the civilian, they should enter, and that they should not have to enter either unless individual taste or social standing impelled. In the beginning, too, the school was voluntary, and pupils received nominations to it "only of their own seeking"; but in time this free academic principle split upon the rock of general academic indifference, until by the year 1706 the school had remaining in it only forty scholars. Upon that, and as its tutors considered the school's total holding capacity to stand at at least 340, the Government intimated to certain "eminent *chini*" that, as their younger sons were receiving no education, those sons might just as well "be ascribed unto the School without avoidance,[1] and instructed at their own cost and maintenance." Yet that this step failed to secure the desired complement would appear from the fact that, though there were included in the first batch of "ascribed" pupils such youths as the Princes Buturlin and Bariatinski and other scions of the aristocracy who were in a position to pay for their own upkeep, later we find the school being entered by members of comparatively obscure families—mostly as "scholars on stay," or scholars subsidised by the Government to the amount of, in modern currency, from 90 to 300 roubles a year, and consisting of sons of *Prikaz* officials, nominated through the directors of their fathers' Departments. In any case the result was to render the school's *personnel* a very heterogeneous one, for included in it now were sons of landless *dvoriané*, of military majors and captains, of common soldiers, and of urban tradesmen—all of them persons so moderately circum-

[1] That is to say, compulsorily, without evasion of the "ascription."

stanced that in one case a pupil whose father was on war service had to lodge with his mother in a garret in Svietenka Street rented of a *diak*; whilst we have further evidence that the *personnel* consisted mostly of pupils "on recompense," of pupils on subsidised board, in the fact that a list of scholars for the year 1706 gives at least a hundred of them as receiving "agreed payment," and standing to have that "payment" increased on attainment of the school's upper division, "to the end that thereafter they may learn with the more diligence and speed." Moreover, some of the pupils who lived at a distance from the school were allowed to have organised for them, by their tutors, a sort of club or system of common life, and to live housed in eight or ten huts in the building's forecourt, and so to constitute a miniature corporation privileged to approach the authorities direct. For the rest, we know from departmental documents that the instruction imparted in the establishment now followed a rigidly defined course, even though the original *ukaz* of ordination had stipulated that the scholars should "learn no sciences other than as each shall will": and this would seem to show that, the *ukaz* apart, the management had since come to conceive that regularity of sequence of subjects was desirable. Never at any time, however, did the establishment develop into an institution solid and permanent; it never was anything but a place which scholars soon left either for the Slavonic-Greco-Latin Academy, or for the School of Medicine which Peter had erected on the banks of the Yauza, close to where now stands the Military Hospital, and placed under a nephew of the celebrated Professor Bidloo whom we have met at Leyden, or for a course of technical study abroad, or for the Muscovite Office of Printing, or, in the case of sons of deceased *pomiestchiki* (provided that their mothers and sisters were willing) for the country estate of the departed parent. Until by 1715 matters reached the point that it was thought best to transfer the surviving remnant of the scholars to St. Petersburg, and enter them in the new Marine Academy. At the same time, though Gluck's seminary was a scheme hatched by a professor of Marienburg which even Peter himself came at last to consider futile and ridiculous, we see in it a first attempt, even if a premature attempt, to create for Russia a public school as we of the present day understand the term—and that in spite of the fact that the scheme's original idea was less to afford the general public education than to feed the *Posolski Prikaz* with translators, and that, developing thence into a sort of "foreign correspondence institution," it ended by being remembered amongst subsequent generations as no more than what Kurakin calls "a school of divers tongues and knightly skill on horseback and with swords." At all events, on its decease the only in any way "public" educational establishment remaining in Moscow was the Slavonic-

Greco-Latin Academy, an institution originally founded to meet ecclesi-astical requirements, and later reorganised wholly on a general professional basis, and now so admirably conducted as to earn Weber's hearty approval on an occasion when, visiting the place in 1716, that diplomatist beheld 400 students zealously acquiring learning under "learned monks who were also men of knowledge and of wit," and when one of the senior *alumni*, a youth of princely family, faultlessly delivered in honour of the visitor an address couched in highly complimentary terms. And since in similar fashion Kurakin records of the Muscovite School of Mathematics that, though an "Englishman" was at the head of it, the attached staff was made up ex-clusively of Russians, and that these Russians were imparting to their numerous young seekers after learning a scheme of first-rate and systematic instruction (the above-mentioned "Englishman" evidently being Farquhar-son of Edinburgh), the items together show that by now the plan of sending Russian youths to study abroad had not proved wholly unsuccessful, but, on the contrary, had enabled these two scholastic establishments to be staffed wholly with preceptors of native birth. The success was not the less notable a one in that its attainment had been attended with difficulties and blunders, and handicapped throughout by the fact that all too many of the students dispatched abroad on subsidy, especially such of them as went to England, drove their guardians nearly to distraction with their pranks, and at the end of their term felt so reluctant to return home and face the consequences that in 1723 an *ukaz* had to inform them that, never-theless, they could seek their native land again unperturbed, and, on arriving there, would even "stand pardoned of everything," assured of clemency, and receive, not punishment, but—"rewards both of recompense and of lodging!"

So, in general, we see from the all-class composition of the schools des-cribed that at all events in the two capitals, and in intellects influenced by Peter's reforms, popular education was now a permanently floating idea. Yet it is difficult to determine whether that idea was the outcome of a real ardour for reform, or whether it was a scheme still being thought out before being put into practice. True, in Pososhkov's opinion, compulsory education of the children of the country's peasantry by junior *diaki* would not take longer than three or four years at the most to organise, provided that the schooling was confined strictly to "letters," to reading and writing; and Peter too seems to have pondered the question of establishing national elementary colleges; but the first Russian disseminator of primary education was, as it turned out, the Muscovite School of Mathematics, an institution which made its appearance as such a disseminator when, in 1714, the *ukaz* ordaining compulsory education for *dvoriané* also ordained that to every *gubernia* in the country the School should dispatch certain "teachers for instruction of the *rebiatki* [1] of the people throughout," and that, in addition, every episcopal residence and chief monastery should establish on its premises an elementary "school of ciphers" under a tutor, and that that tutor should receive not less than a *grivna* per day, or 300 (modern) roubles a year. Yet so badly organised in some cases was the scheme that one of these new schools had no children at all dispatched to it, and the authorities had to collect the necessary quota by force, and to detain them forcibly on the premises when collected, or at least to keep them under surveillance. Hence six years elapsed before a single school of the sort obtained a genuine footing, and meanwhile we find a group of urban tradesmen begging the Senate to exempt their own youngsters from "ciphers," for fear lest the youngsters should thereby learn to despise their fathers' calling, whilst, of the total of forty-seven teachers dispatched to the various *gubernii*, no fewer than eighteen discovered there were no pupils to instruct, and therefore had no choice but to return to the capital. And even as late as the year 1722, eight years after the scheme's inception, we read of the Riazan "school of ciphers" having lost fifty-nine out of its ninety-six *alumni* through "flight," and of Chadaev, *Voevoda* of Viatka, having his efforts to establish a school in his *provintzia* so hotly opposed by the local clergy and the local diocesan authorities that eventually he could muster scholars only by having every *uezd* scoured by two commissaries charged forthwith to remove all children of school age to the *provintzia's* capital. In short, the "school of ciphers" effort proved, at first, a failure. Meanwhile those schools' *curriculum* stood limited to reading, writing, arithmetic, and a little geometry, for at that period these subjects embraced Russia's whole programme of elementary enlightenment; and though, by the end of Peter's reign, the schools had come to number fifty (since by then every capital of a *provintzia*, if not every capital of a *gubernia*, had one within its boundaries), Peter never succeeded in making them public establishments in the true sense, but only establishments designed primarily, or wholly, to educate sons of *diaki* and *podiachie* before those sons' entry into the Government's employ. Hence Russia's public instruction was introduced by fits and starts—through casual efforts on the part of such isolated zealots as the *Voevoda* of Viatka and the *pribyltschik* Kurbatov, the latter of whom, on being given the Vice-Governorship of Archangel, rounded up forty soldiers' orphans, established a school, and had his captives duly put to "letters," and to tentative courses in "ciphers" and navigation. A similarly casual element ruled home and private

---

[1] Young children.

education, as when, in 1715, Prince Kurakin, desiring to have his sons taught
the rudiments of the German language, had to pay the German tutor
engaged a hundred roubles, or eight times as much, for that one piece of
tuition, as he would have had now to pay for a course! But a particularly
useful agency in the tutorial sphere was found to lie in the body of Swedish
officers whom Russia was holding prisoner; and frequently influential citizens
would engage them for their children's education, and find them excel
native competitors in achieved results, not to mention that the citizens
enjoyed the additional gratification of feeling that their payment for such
labour was charity bestowed as a gift from God.

Thus, periwigs, the new clothing, shaven chins, Collegiate institutions,
primary and secondary schools—all these things were so many constituent
portions of the one broad, comprehensive scheme by which Peter sought
to reform Russia externally and internally, to transform the model on
which she had become cast into the model distinguishing more enlightened
lands, and to confer upon her inhabitants an administrative system, an order
of public life, a physical exterior, and a mental habit that should approximate as closely as possible to those of the European world with which her
historical destiny linked her. And, regarded from this standpoint, details
otherwise unimportant acquire peculiar significance, as when, conceiving
that by compelling his *dvorianstvo* to study technical science he would
automatically enable that *dvorianstvo* to become competent to render its
country acquainted with the amenities and *convenances* of Western Europe,
Peter ordained, by *ukaz* of 1708, that thenceforth all secular books must be
printed exclusively in the "civil" type, a type whose conformation resembles
the Latin in about the degree that the old Slavonic-Russian-Ecclesiastical
type resembles the Greek. And the first book of the new series to be issued
was a geometry, a "measurement of the earth," written in the Slavonic
tongue, and subsequently amended, in manuscript, by Peter himself—a
fact incidentally demonstrating that the work must have been produced
at a period when Peter at least could snatch the leisure for such censorial-
correctional labours. To which publication succeeded *A Course of Application, or How to Write Compliments of Divers Species,* translated from a
German *Complete Letter Writer,* or set of epistolary models for any and
every occasion, and, next, a *Book of the Alphabet* containing matter
amended by Peter's own hand, and displaying on the margin of its manuscript an injunction that "in these letters alone shall any books on history,
or on manufactures, henceforth be inscribed": which affords us at least
presumptive evidence that both the new type and the new clothing symbol-
ised an outlook which Peter desired to become the dominant one. The end

of it was that so many works on history, technology, and kindred subjects were translated and printed under Peter's direction that even until
he had been dead three years the Muscovite market remained stocked with
productions of the sort, and most of all with translations from the Polish.
In time, also, the Printing Press took to issuing manuals on polite, polished
correspondence, and the police authorities to doing the same with books of
regulations on decorous behaviour. In particular, *Oberpolizeimeister* Devier
marked the year 1718 by coming out with printed rules for conduct of the
assemblées which leading houses had now begun to hold for the benefit of
members of the *dvorianstvo*, of official persons not below the rank of *Ober-
offizier*, of prominent merchants, and even of artisans holding the grade of
foreman. These *assemblées* constituted, practically, both a social club, a dance
rendezvous, a place for discussing news and affairs, and a centre for card
play and music. Yet they called for no ceremonial, for no right of *entrée*,
for no introductions, and for no obligation to be amusing; anyone who pleased
might attend them, and sing at them, and eat at them what the host provided, and depart from them at the dictates of fancy. At the same time a
certain code of deportment did exist for their proper management, and
anyone who infringed that code stood liable to the prescribed penalty of
having to drain such an *orel* ("eagle" or beaker stamped with the Imperial
arms) of strong wine as left him for the rest of the time a helpless target
for the company's ridicule. *A propos*, in 1717, Peter issued either a command
or a commission for the publication of a translation of a foreign work entitled
An Honourable Mirror for Youth, or a Guide to Deportment. The ingenuous
object of this production was to provide the young spark of the period with
a complete code of social conduct calculated to win him success both at
court and in the greater world, and it propounded, as the youthful *shliachtich's* first rule in life that he should never emulate the rustic boor by getting
tipsy in the daytime, but always remember that membership of the *shliachetstvo* came, not of eminent name or lofty birth alone, but also of the grade's
tradition of honourable bearing, and of the three distinguishing virtues of
courtesy, of ease of manner, and of ability to refrain from wrath, in each
of which the *shliachtich* must perfect himself before he could become a
finished court *habitué*. Next, said the manual, he was to acquire languages,
to master the arts of riding, dancing, and fencing, and to render himself
nice of speech, well-read, capable of taking part in a conversation without
either disclosing the nature of his thoughts or letting anyone forestall his
remarks, and free from diffidence or want of initiative—this last in particular,
since the man who went to court shamefaced would probably return thence
empty-handed. Yes, the *Guide* declared one and all of these qualities to

be indispensable for the young *shliachtich* who would attain his natural life-ambition of becoming what we should call a polished popinjay, or a court coxcomb. Nevertheless, in Peter's day the production ran through three editions, and, after his day, through several more. Other directions which it gave were not so easy to compass. Yet also they were very much to the point, since they warned the young *shliachtich* not to walk along a street with head poked forward, or eyes cast down, or features attuned to super-ciliousness. Rather, he was to preserve, as he advanced, an air at once cheer-ful, polite, urbane, and firm, and, on being introduced to a new acquain-tance, to doff the hat at a distance of three paces, and, on passing an old one, to see to it that he did not overlook that acquaintance, and at all times to refrain from dancing in boots, and beyond all things to be care-ful, when forming one of a group of persons engaged in conversation, to spit, not into the middle of the group, but to one side of it. As for conduct under cover—indoors, or in church—he was to avoid blowing his nose loudly, or sneezing loudly, or picking his nose with a finger, or drawing his hand across his mouth, or leaning his elbows upon a table, or letting his hands stray, or shuffling his feet about, or licking his fingers, or gnawing a bone, or picking his teeth with a knife, or scratching his head, or champing his victuals like a pig, or speaking with his mouth full. For, said the manual, these things might well be left exclusively to the *krestianin*. Then, after enumerating for the benefit of damsels of virtue and refinement some twenty points particularly useful "for their bedecking," the manual, hark-ing back to the "young stripling," told him that never, when he was in company, must he converse in his native language, since otherwise a menial might overhear, and understand, his words, and set him down for a block-head. Nor, for that matter, was intercourse at all with menials to be en-couraged: rather, the young *shliachtich* was to treat such persons as though with distrust and disdain, and so "render them humble and lowly of spirit." And in this last injunction Peter's German-*dvorianin Mirror* hit right upon the root-nerve of the Russian *shliachetstvo's* then mental attitude, since whereas Peter himself stood above class prejudices and pretensions, and worked solely for the good of his people, the upper strata of the Russian society of his day had for long past been led by the course of affairs to turn their attention mostly to the question of how best they could turn the fruits of the Reformer's labours to their own advantage, and so put a greater gulf than ever between themselves and the "ignorant clowns" represented by the peasantry and the serfs. However, petty and ill-bred though this German manual was, it at least served the Russian *dvorianin* in so far as it gave him his first inkling of the meaning of good manners.

On the other hand, Peter's educational schooling did nothing to cause the ruling class to look clear-sightedly upon the work which he desired that class, and that class pre-eminently, to perform. Indeed, as regards understanding that work, and, above all, its essence, the ruling class stood little, if at all, above its fellows, and, though swift to apprehend its self-created difficulties when encountered, stood powerless to devise a single idea for those difficulties' removal. Besides, the class no longer had a source from which to derive such an idea, since, though its members were as much self-taught workers of State as was their leader, they were not in any respect as talented as he, and could only learn their rôle as they proceeded, from day to day, with no previous course of preparation, nor yet with the benefit of practice which might help them definitely to become used to reducing their tasks and their end to a common plan; whilst on the other hand, the fact that Peter's reforms gradually stripped them of their old-time clothing, and of the customs grown up with that clothing—of the rigid, finicking mode of life of ancient Russia in its entirety—gradually increased their sense of emancipation in proportion, and left them the more exposed to deterioration from the moral standpoint. For the old order had at least been able to hold in check their more evil propensities, whereas now those propensities could display unbridled licence. No other explanation than this loss of familiar standing-ground can suffice to explain such an almost incredible phenomenon as that in 1698, when Kurbatov, then a household serf, was touring Italy with his master, Sheremetev, he personally addressed to the Pope a petition praying, "as a true son of the Catholic Church," that his Holiness would furnish him, Kurbatov, with certain religious-dogmatical books, and asserting that ultimately the Catholic propagandist campaign in Russia would prove successful, advising the Pontiff to send to Russia none but men of education, and—and promising to secure for those men the *entrée* to Russia's aristocratic circles! Probably the truth is that, though such men as Kurbatov helped on reform involuntarily, they never were its adherents sincerely and in spirit, but supported, clung to, it primarily for their own advantage. Peter himself served his country wholeheartedly, but his assistants did not necessarily understand the term "service" as service of Russia, for the fatherland idea still lay beyond their comprehension, and had no connection with their civic intellectual growth—even those of them who stood nearest to the throne were virtually, as yet, only Peter's court and personal underlings, and little, if at all, fitted to act also as his agents in his reforms. Hence, strive as he might to regard his helpers as co-workers, it was an effort which only increased his sense of autocratic isolation, and left him with no idea in the matter save to thrash them soundly with cudgels. For example, Prince Menshikov, *Herzog* of Izhor, never at any time renounced his virtuosity in evasion, covetousness, and theft, or wholly cleared himself of a charge of forgery, and, as regards the rest (with the exception of Count Tolstoi, a man of an intellect which Peter himself recognised as forceful, comprehensive, and profoundly penetrating), Peter had to do the best he could with such workers as Apraxin, cousin to the Tsar, and an essentially dry-land Grand Admiral who never in his life evolved a workable idea, or even learnt the rudiments of his nautical profession—though also he never let a guest depart sober from his cheerful, hospitable mansion, or, for that matter, allowed his close association with the Reformer to prevent him from consistently opposing the latter's schemes, and from cherishing a deadly hatred of foreigners; Baron (afterwards Count) Ostermann, the son of a Westphalian pastor, a man who in early youth had been valet to a Dutch vice-admiral, and later, on becoming Admiral-in-Chief under Anna, became also so omnipotent in Russia as to earn the sobriquet of "Tsar of All the Russias," and to pass for a diplomatist sufficiently dexterous and lacqueyishly cunning never to want for the right word at an official juncture, even though when anyone asked him in private life whether it was, say, gout or biliousness that he was suffering from, he would at once tie himself up in such a mass of unintelligible verbiage as proved him beyond all doubt to be as stupid as he was treacherous, pusillanimous, and evasive; and Yaguzhinski, a fellow who was for ever quarrelling with someone, or getting drunk, or threatening some chance-comer with blows and insults, yet could play with distinction the rôle of "leading tragedian" in a stock theatrical company, and enact with distinction the grandiose part of Senatorial *Prokurator-General*. These, no better than these, had Peter for his leading workers, and to these, and to no better than these, was he forced, on his departure, to devise the fortunes of his Empire! And he had scarcely breathed his last before those workers began to play the fool, for, as early as on the evening of 31 March, 1725, only two hours after the close of the Tsar's solemn funeral service, Yaguzhinski, bursting in upon the all-night vigil that was being held in the Petropavlovsk Cathedral, extended a hand towards the spot where Peter's coffin was reposing in the centre of the building, and burst into a torrent of abuse against Menshikov on the score of some insult in the past: whilst next morning, to add to that, a sudden hubbub awakened all St. Petersburg—the supposedly disconsolate Empress having taken it into her head that, inasmuch as the day was 1 April, the capital might as well have a joke played upon it. The truth is that though, until now, the sheer force of the Reformer's iron will had kept people like these united in at least a show of labour, the fact of such a mere phantom of authority as Catherine succeeding to the throne at once led to those people ceasing to feel responsible to anyone but themselves, and proceeding, instead, to take stock of one another, and of their mutual relations, and of their several positions in the country which now they had independently to administer. And though their mutual affection was small, at least they had been acting together for a sufficient length of time to know how to convert that country into their prey, into their article of commerce, and to ensure that nothing important should be done without bribery, and to fix, each for himself, his tariff, and all to agree to maintain silence as to those tariffs' inbringings, seeing that they represented no more than the offspring bound to result from such a fiscal-police State as Peter's—a State which had reared them to an atmosphere of arbitrary rule, to general contempt for legality and the person, and to a blunted sense of morality which could lead even a responsible statesman like Artemi Volinski, one of the dead Peter's junior *protégés*, to see nothing shameful in laying *donos* or secret information, but only in the fact that even the most insignificant *dvorianin* should so far conform with the enactment as to confrontation as to stand up in court and prove his charge, in that such a course, he said, was "villainy," and any informer openly justifying himself "a churl, despite his right so to do." Men of the sort had neither the power nor the will to continue Peter's work: all that they could do was, if not to destroy it, at least to impair its efficiency. Hitherto they had been accustomed to march to the stroke of Peter's baton—and, for that matter, had cut a certain figure in the process; but now they were left standing by themselves, and, bereft of their number one in the line, figured only as ciphers. We see this especially in the fact that whenever they met to discuss any matter of moment, Ostermann, without whose consent the court of the new Empress dared not move a step, at once hastened to enhance his personal value by sending word that, owing to a sudden attack of one or another of his political maladies, he found his personal attendance at the meeting impossible; and upon that his fellow arbiters of the country's fortunes would cut short their deliberations, and, after quaffing a few beakers of refreshment, disperse to re-assemble around the Baron's board, and spend the rest of the day in endeavouring to dissipate the Peterburgan-Westphalian Mephistopheles' ill-humour. For though Ostermann's whole countenance bespoke the fact that its owner lacked intellect, learning, and industry, and all men despised him for an alien, all likewise feared him for his power of organising intrigues, and for his potential capacity as a rival. An instance is that once when he and Menshikov—the pair now become, respectively, Peter II.'s tutor and Peter II.'s father-in-law-elect—were hatching a court plot together, a sudden difference arose between them, and when, during the altercation, the Prince called the Baron an atheist, and declared him to be corrupting the young Monarch's conscience, and threatened to have him exiled to Siberia, the Baron effectually checked that by desiring the Prince to remember that, whereas he, the Prince, could not carry out any such threat, he himself, the Baron, could at any moment cause the Prince to pay the richly merited penalty of having his head removed from his shoulders. Yet, ignorant though these men were of the real meaning of Peter's reforms, they had the wit to discern that those reforms promised no benefit to their own class, or to the classes which stood linked with their own, and therefore, in their social administration, hastened to avail themselves of Peter's lack of legislative foresight in order to strip serf-right of its last restrictions, and at the same time to decline to shoulder the resultant responsibilities. Moreover, such opposition did they offer to foreign learning and usage and thought that when Nepluev and his student colleagues returned from their educational tour abroad they found themselves greeted with dislike both by the public and by their relatives, and everywhere, if they showed the least sign of "Europeanism" having crept into their mode of life, "derided with laughter and cursings." From all of which it came about that what Menshikov once called "the completion of the unfinished fane" was carried out very differently from what the departed Reformer had intended; and for the same reason Theofan Prokopovitch showed excessive optimism when he said in the celebrated funeral sermon preached for the consolation of Peter's bereaved countrymen: "At least hath the Reformer bequeathed unto us his spirit."

CHAPTER XII

As regards events after Peter's death, the period 1725–62 was remarkable for certain phenomena in Russian State life which, whilst leaving the bases of that life unaltered, were at once new in themselves, not apparent until after the Reformer's death, and closely related to the results of his activities. Incidentally, it is not impossible that, in reading the preceding chapters, the reader has wondered why the ends of Peter's reforms contained within themselves such a paucity of self-created means, and why his selected states-men stood so ill-qualified to continue his labours, and why his work evoked so little sympathy from the people in general, and from the leading strata of the people in particular, seeing that the factors named in each case promised little towards Peter's reforms being completed after his departure, or even towards their being carried on with the energy always desired by the Reformer. Well, the phenomena now about to be studied were certainly such as to justify any misgiving: and this I venture to say even at the risk of being accused of anticipating events, or of passing judgment before con-viction. For one thing, the Reformer's spirit and intentions already stood contravened by the fact that in a State in which an absolute, a supreme, ruling authority holds good the course of events is bound to be influenced largely by the fortunes of the throne; whilst in the same connection we should do well to recall the order in which the Supreme Power of Russia devolved after Peter's departure. At the time of his death the Reigning House stood split into two lines: into an Imperial line, and into a Sub-Imperial—the former being come of the Emperor Peter himself, and the latter of his elder brother Ivan. And from Peter the throne passed to Peter's widow, and she became Catherine I. And from Catherine the throne passed to the Reformer's grandson, and he became Peter II. And from Peter II. it passed to Anna Duchess of Courland, Peter's niece, and daughter of Tsar Ivan. And from Anna it passed to Ivan Antonovitch, infant son of Anna Leopoldovna of

Brunswick, Anna's niece, and daughter of Catherine Ivanovna Duchess of
Mecklenburg, and own sister to Anna Ivanovna. And from the infant Ivan
it passed, on that infant's deposition, to Elizabeth, daughter of Peter I.
And from Elizabeth it passed to Elizabeth's nephew, Peter III., son of
Anna Duchess of Holstein, Peter I.'s second daughter. And from Peter III.
it passed, when his wife dislodged him, to that wife herself, and she became
Catherine II. Wherefore never has any country seen its Supreme Authority descend in a line more broken than Russia's. The chief factor in
this disintegration was the heterogeneous manner in which the various
Sovereigns attained their ruling position. For in every case they ascended
the throne altogether independently of any legal or stereotyped system, but
either through some purely fortuitous circumstance, or through the agency
of some court revolution or palace intrigue. And the original, the primary,
cause of this calamity was the Reformer himself, in that, as we have seen,
his Law of 5 February, 1722, abolished the two hitherto operative systems
of succession, the system of succession through testamentary bequeathal,
and the system of succession through election by *Sobor*, and set up, instead,
a system of personal appointment by the throne's current occupant. Yes,
an ill-starred ordinance this Law was, and it sprang from a series of dynastic
mischances. Had the natural, or customary, order of succession continued,
the throne would, in the ordinary course, have devolved from Peter to
Alexis, Peter's son by his first marriage: but inasmuch as the son had always
threatened to undo his father's work, Peter, to preserve that work, felt
driven to sacrifice to it not only the son, but also the natural order of succession, and thus found himself, since his sons by his second marriage (Peter
and Paul) had died in infancy, left with no heir except his minor grandson,
heir to the unfortunate Tsarevitch, and therefore the Tsarevitch's natural
avenger. Also, since it was possible, even probable, that that minor's
grandfather would die before the grandson came of age, this brought
into the field also two possible female expectants of power in the
shape of Evdokia Fedorovna (*née* Lopukhina), a dour, cantankerous
nun-*divorcée* who, after taking the veil, had opposed every form of innovation, and of Catherine, Peter's peasant-woman Consort, an obscure alien by
origin who even now held but a doubtful legal standing as a wife, as well as
was of a disposition rendering it likely that, should she ever attain the
Supreme Power, she would at once delegate it to Menshikov, Peter's chief
favourite hitherto, yet also the ringleader of the Treasury's despoilers. Hence
we can imagine Peter's feelings during his later years (even though the burden of the Swedish War had now become removed from his shoulders) as,
plunged in the weariness and the depression born of a malady which even

an acute consciousness of an unprecedented renown and a well-earned greatness was powerless to combat, he pondered the future fortunes of his Empire. For looming before him he can have seen only a vast void, a prospect of having to leave his work suspended in the air, Russia's throne fallen vacant with no reliable candidate to fill it, and an eventual failure of his reforms through lack of adequate, stable support either from a band of coadjutors whose worth, or lack of worth, he knew only too well, or from fundamental laws which he knew to be non-existent, or from a people which had lost not only its pristine form of will-expression, but also all desire to express that will. In short, as Peter gazed ahead he must have seen that, for all his limitless power, he was absolutely alone, and so, true to his bent, resorted once more to that power, and sought to escape from the position of affairs with regard to the succession by vesting that power with unconditional authority to appoint its own legatee. Seldom, however, has an Autocracy brought down upon itself such a retribution as the Law of 5 February brought down upon Peter's. Once he remarked in an *ukaz* that "it is vain to inscribe laws unless those laws be fulfilled," and the Law of which I am speaking proved so absolutely and entirely "vain" that it failed to be kept even by its own framer, and, after a whole year's vacillation on the subject of his choice of a successor, he could but, with death at hand, and his tongue no longer functioning, jot down, "I surrender all things unto——," and leave unspecified the name which his faltering hand had proved powerless to indicate. For the Law of 5 February not only deprived the Supreme Power of its regular setting: it also cast to the winds of heaven the institutions created by the wielder of that Power, brought Peter's dynasty, as an establishment, to an end, and replaced it with an aggregate of personages belonging, true, to the Imperial stock, but lacking any definite dynastic standing. The throne therefore became the sport, the plaything, of chance, and for decades the Sovereignty never changed hands without making confusion worse confounded, in that each accession of a Sovereign was preceded variously by a court *émeute*, by a subterranean intrigue, or by an open blow. For which reason, indeed, we might call the period between Peter's death and the accession of Catherine II. "The Epoch of Palace Revolutions." Unfortunately, upheavals of the sort, in the eighteenth century, possessed a political significance passing far beyond the court's immediate purlieus, for they reached to, and affected, the bases of the State order itself. The chief factor which gave those upheavals their peculiar significance was a factor running through them like a single thread. Almost always it happens that if law be either absent from or inoperative in a State, political questions in that State tend to find resolution through resort to some force at once dominant and on the spot: and that force Russia of the eighteenth century found in the Corps of Guards, the more privileged section of Peter's recently created regular army. In fact, scarcely ever did the period named see a change occur on the Russian throne but the Guards bore a share in bringing it about. And though the Corps was a force consisting only of the Preobrazhenski and the Semenovski Regiments, added to, during Anna's reign, a new Izmailovski Regiment and a troop of our present Horse Guards, the Corps so bore itself that for thirty-seven years it practically made and unmade Russia's Governments. Let us briefly review the Governments in question.

Peter I. died on 28 January, 1725; but though he passed away without having nominated his successor, the men who had to dispose of the vacant crown were not left wholly without guidance in their procedure, since, verbally obscure though the Law of 5 February certainly was, that obscurity was not such as wholly to preclude self-interpretation. The *ukaz* in question was more than a personal behest of Peter's concerning the future successional system, or a specification of sole succession to the throne; it was also an *ukaz* motived and principled specially in correspondence with the sole successional principle, and establishing as the legal and testamentary rule with regard to the succession that, in the absence of a son or sons, the throne was to pass to an eldest daughter. But when Peter's eldest daughter, Anna, had become betrothed to the Duke of Holstein in 1724 she had renounced her right to the Russian throne not only on her own behalf, but also on that of any possible issue of hers, and allowed her place in the order of succession to pass to Peter's second daughter Elizabeth; and though on no successional basis whatsoever could a widow become Empress (the *ukaz* of 1714 had merely confirmed to Russia her agelong rule of ensuring that a widowed Tsaritsa with children should, for her lifetime, be supported by those children, and the rule of allowing that a widowed Tsaritsa should, if not succeed outright, at least be competent to act as Regent if, and so long as, the heir to the throne was a minor), there had now come into existence circumstances which essentially hindered precise fulfilment of the ordinary rules. This was because there were still surviving remnants of the old *boyarin* aristocracy, men like the Princes Golitzin, Dolgoruki, and others, who believed in the ancient successional order, and therefore considered the Grand Duke Peter to be the lawful heir, as the only extant male survivor of the Imperial House; whereas the official aristocracy which Peter himself had created, the official aristocracy which consisted of such men as Menshikov and Tolstoi, were opposed to the Grand Duke for the reason that his succession would mean that their and Catherine's past hostility to the Grand Duke's father, the ill-fated Tsarevitch Alexis, would bring upon her and themselves irretrievable ruin. Hence, as this latter faction viewed the matter less in the light of equity and legality than in the light of their own fortunes, they felt that win the day they must if they were not to see either exile or hard labour under the *knut* descend upon themselves, and a convent close upon Catherine and her daughters. And either because Catherine really feared her rival's grandson, or because she had suddenly awakened to ambition, at all events she voiced the idea that she would rather rule outright on Peter's death than become Regent, whilst also, as she conceived her daughters to be her potential rivals, she now vied with, or even surpassed, her fast-failing Consort in endeavouring, through marriage, to get rid of their threatened competition. Everywhere Peter sought for them brilliant matches: everywhere he put them forward as not only the offspring of an illustrious European potentate, but also (so foreign ambassadors of the day tell us) as in themselves no mean wits and beauties, even to marking down for them every eligible Prince in France, Spain, and Prussia, and sending the daughters' portraits impartially to Versailles and Madrid. Yet nothing came of this attempted auctioneering of his Imperial issue save increased difficulty as regards deciding the successional question, and its continuance in a vexed state. Taking, therefore, their cue from this, Menshikov and Tolstoi, on Peter's death becoming imminent, set on foot their agitation on behalf of Catherine and themselves, and, as a first step, sought to tamper with the loyalty of the army in general, and with the loyalty of the Guards in particular. And this, as it happened, proved to be no very arduous task, in that the Guards, already devoted to their creator, were inclined also to be devoted to his ex-*vivandière* Consort, whilst in addition they received a promise that their participation in the plot should ensure to them a monetary largesse, relief from certain disliked duties, and all their outstanding arrears of pay. After which, the preliminary measures taken, it remained only to conduct the Guards officers to bid the dying and speechless Tsar farewell, and then to procure with the Tsaritsa an interview during which the officers swore—many sobbed as they did so—that they would rather die at her feet than allow anyone else than herself to ascend the throne. Meanwhile the opposing, the Golitzin, faction remained sitting with folded hands, and did nothing; and even when, at a late hour on 28 January, the Senate and its fellow high dignitaries of State met together at the Palace, and entered upon a deliberation as to who ought properly to succeed the Tsar, and indulged in interminable disputes as to the dying Emperor's wishes, those Senators and the rest still committed the folly of not seeking light in the only quarter whence light might have been expected to come, namely, in the Law of 5 February, but kept sending for Makarov, Peter's private secretary, and asking him if *he* knew anything about the disputed question, and each time receiving a negative reply. But at last, just when the adherents of the Grand Duke had offered to strike a bargain with their opponents—had said: "We propose that the Grand Duke shall be raised to the Throne, but Catherine and the Senate rule until he come of age," and the wily Tolstoi had risen to ridicule the proposal with his usual dialectical skill, an interruption came from a corner of the conference hall in the shape of the entry of some Guards officers brought thither no one knew how, or by whom. And, having entered, these Guards officers fell to enacting the part of the Chorus in ancient Greek drama, of the bevy of stage characters which reflects aloud upon the play, but takes no part in the play's action. Nor were the opinions voiced by the officers so wanting in frankness as not to approach very closely to insolence, especially as regards a, for some reason, very frequently expressed remark that any *boyarin* who should be found offering opposition to "Our Little Mother Katerina" would have his head broken. Then from the square before the Palace there resounded a drum-beat, and in front of the building the two Regiments of Guards, summoned thither, like their officers, no one quite knew how, or by whom, were seen to be deploying into line. Upon this, Prince Repnin, President of the Collegium of War, exclaimed angrily: "Who hath dared send for these my regiments without the bidding of their Field Marshal, myself?" but the Semenovskis' commanding officer, Buturlin, calmly replied that the summoner of the troops had been himself, in pursuance of an order from the Tsaritsa, "unto whom let her every subject, including thyself"—a suggestive touch—"now render allegiance." What the Guards most relied upon for ensurance of acceptance of their action was a suggestion that, by having the Tsaritsa crowned during the previous year, the Tsar had meant to indicate that, under this Law of 5 February, she was to become his successor. So in due form the Senators proclaimed her "Autocrat Empress," and, having thus abrogated the Law of 5 February through their own interpretation of it, issued, on behalf of themselves, of the Synod, and of the General Staff (even though neither the one nor the other had taken part in the conference), a Manifesto in which Catherine's accession was set forth, not as a mere Senatorial-electoral act, but as an actual Senatorial interpretation of the deceased Tsar's will. And, that done, it remained only for the Senate to invest Catherine with the Crown and Imperial Unction, and then to publish a proclamation to the effect that the Senate desired all men to know what had been done, and, on the strength of it, render "Catherine, Autocrat of All the Russias, faithful service." Thus not a word was said about a *Zemski Sobor*, hitherto the legal and fundamental source of successional right in the absence of an Imperial heir. No, for the first time ancient usage was made to yield to present actuality, and the more easily in that, though it was to the time-honoured form of election by *Sobor* that Peter himself had owed his position, action on Peter's own part during his reign had rendered that assembly obsolete, and all men save the outspoken Pososhkov had forgotten it—Pososhkov alone venturing to recall the occasion of the assembly's last meeting, which had been when representatives of all the social classes had been summoned to frame the *Ulozhenie.* As things turned out, Catherine's reign proved to be a brief one only. Throughout it the Government never ceased to court the Guards, as may be seen from the Government's own notices in the Official Gazette, which show the authorities to have been so anxious to cultivate the Guards' favour that actually they induced the Empress to receive the Corps' officers in her tent at reviews, and tender them wine with her own hands! Against this there remains the fact that the favour shown to the Corps helped to make Catherine's two-years' reign a reign of peace; and to the same result contributed the fact that her interference in State matters was as scanty as was her comprehension of them—her prime solicitude being enjoyment of her private life, which was so irregular that, corpulent and unhealthy though she was, she would remain sitting at banquets with her intimates until five o'clock in the morning, and leave the administration of the country to look after itself. In fact, a foreign ambassador says of that administration that "in it there was not a man with a thought for aught else than what he might steal therefrom," and that especially as regards the closing year of her life, Catherine's various whims cost the country a sum approaching to an equivalent of 6,500,000 (modern) roubles. And all the time there were mal-contents drinking healths to the dispossessed Grand Duke. And all the time there were police carrying out daily hangings of incautious babblers. And all the time the representatives of foreign Governments were reporting these things to their principals.

Peter II. also had his road to the throne prepared by a Guards-assisted court intrigue. From Catherine the Catherine-Menshikov party, of course, wished to see the throne to devolve to one of the Empress's daughters, but public opinion supported the view that, as Peter I.'s grandson, the Grand Duke was the lawful heir, and when a feud threatened between the nephew's adherents and those of the aunts, that is to say, between the family of Peter's first wife and the belongings of his second (in other words, between the State's two agelong sources of trouble, sources bound to exist where the court resembled a fortified manor), the wily Ostermann sought to smoothe the contestants' hackles with a proposal that the twelve-year-old nephew should marry his own seventeen-year-old aunt Elizabeth. In fact, he even attempted to justify this consanguineous union with references to Biblical and primitive methods of race propagation, until Catherine herself could not but cold-shoulder the scheme. Then the brains of certain foreign ambassadors evolved a plan, and a still more brilliant one, for conciliating the two hostile parties: and it lay in a proposal that Menshikov should change over to the grandson, and, that done, endeavour to persuade the Empress to make him, the grandson, her successor on condition that he, the grandson, married his, Menshikov's daughter, who at the time was even younger, by a year or two, than the Grand Duke's seventeen-year-old aunt! And finally, when the brief malady preceding Catherine's death in 1727 seized her in its grip, the members of the three chief administrative institutions (the Supreme Privy Council created of Catherine herself, the Senate, and the Synod) assembled in the Palace, and, with the Presidents of Colleges and the commanding officers of the Guards (who had now come to be a sort of State corporation, and a necessary consenting party before any grave political matter could be decided), discussed the question of the Empress's successor: with the result that, as this conclave expressed a marked preference for the grandson over Peter's daughters, Catherine reluctantly appointed that grandson her heir—though during the last few days of her life, it is said, she again and again told Menshikov that she would much rather have bequeathed the throne to her daughter Elizabeth, and that she had submitted only because otherwise her reign might not end in peace. However that may be, a deathbed will was framed in haste, and as hastily signed, for the Empress, by the Princess Elizabeth: but though this will, an instrument having for its primary purpose a reconciliation of the two mutually hostile factions, or sets of adherents, represented by Peter's two families, nominated to the throne, alternatively, Peter's grandson, the Tsarevna Anna, the Tsarevna Elizabeth, and the Grand Duchess Natalia (sister to Peter II.), and, again alternatively, any possible issue or posterity of those persons, who were severally to ascend the throne if his or her predecessor died childless, the will has no real importance in the history of the Imperial succession, since with the death of the next-succeeding heir, Peter II., the throne began to change hands in such an order as even the most far-sighted Imperial testament could never have foreseen. No, the sole significance or status in the history of our Imperial successional legislation possessed by Catherine's will is due to the fact that it did at least import into that legislation, if not a new norm, at all events a new tendency, since at one and the same time it took its stand upon the Law of Peter I. and sought to fill that Law's legislative gaps—in both cases with a view to finally establishing a legal and permanent successional order, and to regulating the Sovereign's office in such a manner that the regulations themselves should constitute a fundamental law on the subject. In fact, the document openly says that it is such a law, and a law, at that, competent to remain operative and effective for ever, and at no time to be abolished. And, adding this to the fact that, on the morrow of Catherine's decease, the document was read to the Imperial Family and chief Officials of State assembled in solemn conclave, we may look upon the testament of 1727 as a direct precursor of the Law of 1797, whilst incidentally it is interesting to note, as bearing upon the history of Russian legislative theory, that the testament had its plan of exposition drawn up by Bassevitch, Holsteiner Minister in St. Petersburg.

In January, 1730, Peter II. caught a chill which, before he had long been suffering from it, threatened to become fatal: and as soon as that was perceived to be the case the timeserving Prince Alexis Dolgoruki and his son Ivan, prime companion to the young Emperor, decided to attempt a trick for laying their hands upon the Supreme Power, and therefore convoked a family council at which they propounded a will said to have come straight from the hand of the dying Tsar, and to be an instrument devising the Supreme Power to Prince Alexis' daughter Catherine, the Tsar's *fiancée*. And when Field-Marshal Vasilii Vladimirovitch expressed doubts as to whether such a shameless stratagem could possibly succeed, Dolgoruki retorted: "O Prince, art not thou commander of the Preobrazhenski Regiment, and is not thy son, the Prince Ivan, a major in the same, and will the Semenovski Regiment, any more than thine own, withstand this testament?" Which speech shows how completely by now the courtiers standing nearest to the Throne had come to take it for granted that, given the Guards' support, even the most important question of State would achieve a solution, and could in advance be counted upon to succeed. And, sure enough, when, on the passing of Peter II., the Supreme Privy Council essayed to cut across the true order of succession (and thereby to flout the authority of the chief administrative institutions which were the Council's fellows) by electing to the throne Anna, daughter of Tsar Ivan, and widow of the Duke of Courland, and limiting her power, the enterprise at once failed owing to intervention on the part of the Guards and the *dvorianstvo*. The details were as follows. Emboldened, at last, both by the assurances of the Privy Council and by the fact that Russian tongues had for ten years past been rigorously tied, the Regent Anna sought to forestall her death and her successor's ultimate coming-of-age (he was then an infant but two months old) by appointing Biron, Duke of Courland, Regent, and vesting him with a measure of autocratic authority: and since this constituted such a rude challenge to

Russian national sentiment as to take even Biron himself aback, and to remind the Russian people how, during the ten years in question, they had had to endure the sorry, galling spectacle of Anna's beloved German faction besieging the Russian throne like a troop of cats around a bowl of milk, and eating and drinking to repletion, and working off the resultant lethargy by scratching and biting one another, Münnich, on the night of 8 November, 1740, went to a friendly dinner with the Regent, and later, mustering the Palace guard plus a posse of officers and men of his own, the Preobrazhenski, Guards, dragged Biron out of bed, thrust his nightshift into his mouth, gave him a good thrashing, wrapped him in the bed's coverlet, and haled him to the guardroom; whence later, with a soldier's cloak thrown over him, he was sent to join his family at the Winter Palace, and thence to Schlüsselburg, whilst Anna Leopoldovna, the infant Emperor's mother, proclaimed herself Regent *vice* Anna Ivanovna, and the latter's Government went to pieces. Next, Ostermann again started upon his intrigues, and succeeded not only in dislodging Münnich from power, but also in setting Anna, a princess so barbaric of temperament that she would sit for days together unwashed and undressed, at loggerheads with her husband, Duke Anthony Ulrich of Brunswick, despite that the latter was of a mentality that would scarcely, in the natural order of things, have inclined him to fall out with his wife. All of which led up to the fact that on the night of 25 November, 1741, Peter's daughter, the Tsarevna Elizabeth, felt emboldened by the Government's weakness and her popularity with the Guards to enlist the help of a grenadier company of the Preobrazhenskis towards carrying out a new and original revolution. First she said her prayers to God. Then she took a vow to the Empire that if she should attain the throne she would never thereafter set her hand to a death warrant. Lastly, slipping over her bodice a cuirass, and walking with head bare, and carrying in her hands a cross in place of a halbert, and attended by no military or other escort—only by her elderly music-master, Schwartz, she set forth, like a new Pallas, and made her way to the barracks of the Preobrazhenski Regiment. And there, after reminding the grenadiers that she was a daughter of Peter the Great, she fell upon her knees, bade the grenadiers also kneel, held up the cross before their eyes, and cried: "Herewith do I swear to die for your sakes. Do ye also die for mine." And when a chorus of assent had answered her she placed herself at the soldiers' head, and led them to the Winter Palace, where, encountering no opposition, she succeeded in penetrating to the Empress-Regent's sleeping apartment itself, and aroused her with the words, "Come, my sister! It is time to arise!" And, on Anna drowsily enquiring, "Is it thou, Sudarina?" she laid her hand upon her in token of arrest, kissed the deposed infant Sovereign, and forthwith had mother and child removed to her own palace. Meanwhile, her grenadiers had similarly aroused the infant Emperor's father, wrapped him in a coverlet as he sat helplessly on his bed (even as had been done with Biron just twelve months earlier), carried him downstairs, and dispatched him to meet his wife at the Tsarevna's residence; whither soon also there arrived (though only after experiencing some rough usage at the hands of the soldiery who had arrested them) the chief members of the fallen Government, Münnich, Ostermann, and others, and such of the adherents of the new Empress as had known in advance that she was about to attempt seizure of the reins of authority. And so, greeted by the populace with the same enthusiasm as by the Guards, she, that night, removed to the now vacant Winter Palace, and, by doing so, finally broke up the camp which the Courlander-Brunswicker clique had pitched on the banks of the Neva for the purpose of seizing and retaining in its hands the Imperial Power bequeathed by Peter the Great to that clique's country of adoption; whilst a secondary effect of the revolution was once more to unloosen patriotic tongues, and embolden Church preachers openly to proclaim that, through Germanised administration, Peter's reformed dominions had until now been converted into a trading mart for the spoils of thieves. Thus the Teutonic faction not only failed to found a new dynasty in Russia, but itself slipped from the Russian throne into a Russian prison, and was replaced by a set of Holsteiner-Gotthorpers. Yet so close to one another did the palace and the gaol of eighteenth-century Russia stand, and so intimately did they uphold one another, and so easily effect exchanges of tenants, that though Elizabeth was succeeded by her nephew the Duke of Holstein, and he became Peter III., and ascended the throne without let or hindrance, half a year had not passed before Peter's wife and a posse of guards had dislodged him thence.

I repeat, therefore, that the Guards were responsible for almost every one of the various Governments which followed one another throughout the thirty-seven years covering the period between the death of Peter I. and the accession of Catherine II. And inasmuch as the same period saw the Guards participate also in some five or six *révolutions de palais,* the Guards' barracks came practically to rival the meeting-places of the Senate and the Privy Council as the country's seat of rule, and to succeed the old *Zemski Sobor.* Particularly did the Corps' intervention in questions of the Imperial Succession bring about very important political results. In the first place, the fact of that intervention itself came to influence the Corps' political attitude, and to lead it, from serving merely as a docile instrument for such personages as Menshikov and Buturlin, to aim at itself becoming an autonomous institution, and interfering in politics. For its preparatory training-ground in the latter it selected *révolutions de palais*, since the Corps was more than a privileged portion of the Russian army, a section segregated from its fellow regiments and the general public—it was also a body of men possessed of great social weight, a body close-locked within itself, and made up, and recruited, exclusively from the ruling class. So entirely was this the case that even its rank and file represented the flower of its social stratum, the stratum formed by Peter I. when he had compounded the ruling class's various layers into the whole known variously as the *dvorianstvo* and the *shliachetstvo*: and since of this stratum the Guards Brigade constituted the military service school, it all the more came about that though, in the first instance, it was court affairs only in which the Guards aspired to political ambitions and claims, those ambitions and claims soon ceased to be matters affecting merely the inmates of the Peterburgan barracks, and spread to every *dvorianin* establishment, both urban and rural, in the country. Not that certain personages in authority did not speedily scent the danger latent in this close political connection between the Guards and the ruling class, and make that danger clear. One of those personages, for example, was Biron. No sooner, after Anna's death, did he become Regent than he complained of the Guards' attitude in general, and of, in particular, the fact that they had decried a Courlander soldier of fortune for acquiring the Supreme Power in Russia through dishonourable means. In fact, he went so far as to call them "Janissaries," to aver that the root of the evil lay in their social *personnel*, and irritably to add: "Wherefore in any case soever need the Guards be of *dvorianin* soldiers? Let those Guards' officers be removed thence, and dispatched to corps of the line, and replaced with officers chosen from amongst the common people." Naturally, the threatened danger of finding themselves broken up and distributed to other formations incited the Guards against Biron the more, and against Münnich as well. Thus the Corps' participation in *révolutions de palais* brought about two important changes in the *dvorianstvo's* political attitude: the change that the political rôle imposed upon (and readily assumed by) the Guards, as the result of their activities at court, inspired the *dvorianstvo* at large to believe that the class was of paramount importance in the State, and the change that eventually the same notion combined with the circumstances of its birth to alter both the class's State position and the class's relation to its fellow sections of the community.

Another result of Peter I.'s labours was to evoke amongst the community a first and vigorous process of political thinking, since it so often happened, during the Petrine period, that men chanced upon unexpected situations, or encountered, and had to accept, unprecedented phenomena, and remained with unfamiliar impressions stamped upon their intelligences, that at last even the most irresponsive intellects could not but turn their thoughts to what was passing in the State. In outlining certain contemporary popular gossip about Peter, I indicated the eagerness with which even the humblest folk then canvassed phenomena which stood remote from their own prosaic existences; and, to the people's amazement, those strange, arresting phenomena did not cease even when Peter was gone. Never before, for example, had Russia seen a woman ascend the throne. Yet here, after the Reformer's death, was a woman actually doing so, and, at that, a woman hailing the Lord knew whence! And scarcely need it be added that such an innovation evoked some grievous misunderstandings, and that some of those misunderstandings were as comical as they were grievous—an instance being that on the day when allegiance to the new Empress-Widow had to be sworn many of the more simple menfolk of Moscow flatly refused to take the oath, on the ground that, "now that a woman is become Tsar, only women should kiss the cross unto her!" A similar line of political thought inevitably found expression amongst the ruling class, the *dvori-anstvo*, and the more so as that class stood nearest to affairs of State, and was the Government's executive organ. But the phenomenon showed itself in different ways amongst different strata of the *dvorianstvo*, for, whereas the rank and file of that body were men liable at any time to be dragged from the retirement of their rural manors, and allotted alternatively to regiments or to elementary training-schools and therefore inclined principally to whet their mental faculties upon invention of means for evading, as the case might be, military duties or a lettered education, the upper strata of the class, more especially the circles most connected with the administrative world, had in them intellects fully capable of applying themselves to higher matters, since they still retained remnants of the old *boyarin* aristocracy, a close-locked clique limited to a few families possessed of a special *motif* of political thought, a definite programme of political ends derived from that *motif*, and a class view of the most desirable order of State to be developed from that programme. Again, amongst the more specifically official section of the *dvorianstvo*, the conditions conducive to processes of political reflection were different. For one thing, that section had not yet wholly lost touch with the political traditions of the seventeenth century, the period when the *boyarstvo* of Moscow had made more than one attempt to limit the Supreme Power, and, during Theodor's reign, had nearly succeeded in doing so: and therefore such members of the section as had survived from that period would still be able to remember that approximate success, not to mention that, however little likely it is that the idea ever occurred to Peter

himself, his administrative decentralisation system of 1708 which created
eight *gubernii*, or vice-royalties, under eight plenipotentiary pro-consuls
must have brought back to such survivors' minds the *namiestniki*-aristocrats
of the earlier scheme of 1681. Also, to look at the matter from another point
of view, these recollections are bound to have been fanned by Peter's arbitrary
contempt for birth: and when we add to that the fact that all contemporary
chroniclers declare the closing decades of the seventeenth century, and
more especially the period of the Regency of the Tsaritsa Natalia, to have
been the time when the leading *boyarin* families began to undergo their most
marked decline, and persons to be promoted "even from the lowest and the
meanest *shliachetstvo*" to high rank and the style of "eminent and great
lords of State," it will not be difficult to imagine the view which minds
capable of looking back upon generations of registered ancestors were bound
to take of the antagonism between the old and the new aristocracies, and how
such minds would easily convert vivid remembrances of past tradition into
brilliant dreams of future power. And upon these described tendencies of
the country's political sense not even Peter's "projectors" were the men to
effect much of an impression, since the public at large never became familiar
with those functionaries' *prozhekti*, and, as it was, those *prozhekti* centred
too much around purely departmental-official matters, about matters of
finance and industry and public order, and largely gave themselves up to
searching the ordinances of Western Europe for "anything proper, it may
be, unto our own Autocracy," and never touched upon the State order's
actual bases. Nor, for that matter, need stress be laid upon any possible
intellectual effect produced by the political literature of the day, even
though, under Peter, the mass of works compiled, and translated, and
printed, and written was simply enormous, seeing that even a scholar like
Tatistchev could, whilst commending Puffendorf and Hugo Grotius as subjects for study, lament the growing influence of such "obnoxious" writers
as Hobbes, Locke, and Boccalini,[1] and aver that, rather than gain from
such productions injurious ideas concerning the origin of States and forms
of rule and sovereign powers, a man were better reading such a work as
Theofan Prokopovitch's *The Right of Monarchial Freewill*! Of this work it
may be remarked, in passing, that, though Western European of genesis,
and, in a degree, interesting as an encyclopædia of then State Law, it
achieved, during its first four years of circulation, a sale of 600 copies only.

[1] An Italian satirist of liberal views who, in a work purporting to describe an arraignment of the world's rulers before Apollo and a tribunal of "wise men" on the summit
of Mount Parnassus, represents that those rulers flouted the "bench" of deities for its
erudition, and declared that "the Prince of Muscovy" would be far preferable as a judge,
"in that he is a ruler sworn to combat all learning and enlightenment!"

And another cause of the tendency to political and intellectual unrest seen amongst the Russian ruling class of Peter's day was that certain of its sections then first began to gain a knowledge of the political systems and social manners of the West, as one of the inevitable results of Peter's scheme of dispatching scientific and diplomatic missions abroad. For, however cloudily the Russian observer may have envisaged alien life-systems as he pursued his travels, he cannot well have failed to bestow upon them a certain surprised attention, and the more so in that originally he must have left home filled with a fixed idea (an idea born of, and fostered by, the whole of his previous existence) that nowhere could either law or order or a social system be created or maintained without the help of a disciplinary Church and a minatory police force. See, for example, the astonishment with which Tolstoi, Peter's statesman, records in his diary that the Venetians customarily dispensed with Church and police alike in such a connection, "in that each man standeth free from abuse, and hath not cause to fear or aught or anyone, and may act according unto his will alone, and dwell in peace, and in freedom from insult, and in relief from overburdensome dues," whilst Mateiev, another of Peter's statesmen, beheld in France things still more marvellous—the record of this son of the Tsaritsa Natalia's enlightened guardian running: "There hath no great lord either reason or the means to conceive enmity against his fellows, even the lowliest, nor to put any such to shame, seeing that, as toucheth common dues, even the State's Autocrat Ruler himself may not take them either privily or by force, but only as Parliament first shall have adjudged the need—otherwise doeth he so at his own peril. . . . There also do sons [of noblemen] suffer no harshness either from their parents or from their teachers, but are reared in forethought, will, and daring, and, accordingly, learn their tasks without difficulty." Well, at least the Russian thinker of that period had his reasons for considering that persons who "acted according unto their will alone," and refrained from exploiting one another (not to mention "great lords" who, for all their greatness, thought twice before they dared insult their fellow men, and autocratic rulers who could not mulct their subjects without previous Parliamentary sanction, and youths who could be induced to master their studies without helpful stimulus of corporal chastisement), were almost impossible marvels, were phenomena hardly to be conceived as existing where sheer anarchy also did not exist, and least of all as existing, as they did in France, under the effective protection of rules the slightest infringement of which automatically entailed a civic scandal.

Hence the effect of political memories stored at home, and of political observations made abroad, was to awaken the ruling circles of Russia, if not to a definite notion of social freedom, at all events to a definite notion of personal security. Until finally, with the accession of Catherine I., those circles gained their chance of attempting once and for all to place a fence between themselves and the Crown's freewill, and to use new and (this time) durable institutions to consolidate their position. And since Catherine acceded as a Sovereign merely proclaimed by the Senate, and owed her position, therefore, less to legality than to Guards-exerted pressure, she found, when she turned for support to the men who had been surrounding the throne at the time of her Consort's death, that that support was not altogether forthcoming, so much did they fear any possible strengthening of the Menshikov influence. Hence from the earliest days of her reign there began to be rumours of conferences held between the official aristocracy and the Golitzin-Dolgoruki-Repnin-Trubetskoi-Apraxin group, with the object of those two sections obtaining a larger share of influence in the Government, or at all events a share sufficient to deprive the Tsaritsa of her power of deciding State matters without Senatorial co-operation. In fact, Peter had scarcely passed away before the Senate decided that the Senatorial body was now the principal extant organ of rule, and went on to gain further support for itself by taking the Guards under its immediate direction—measures which led that very astute foreign observer, the French Ambassador Campredon, to write home to his Government that a very weighty section of the Russian nobility was then (in January 1726) essaying to limit the Empress's despotic power, and had resolved not to wait for the Reformer's grandson, the Grand Duke Peter, to come of age in order to assume increased administrative authority, and reorganise the administrative system on the English model. However, Catherine's adherents displayed similar expedition in devising means of self-defence, and there spread abroad, as early as May 1725, a rumour that her Cabinet had it in mind to form a Privy Council exclusively of the Empress's plebeian friends under Menshikov, and even to confer upon it precedence over the Senate in State matters of prime importance. But when such a Council did appear its character and its composition were seen to be very different from what the country had been led to expect, and for the following reasons. We have seen that Peter failed to carry through his scheme for a Ladoga canal before his death. Accordingly, towards the close of 1725 Münnich demanded that the Senate should allow 15,000 soldiers to be sent to the spot for further excavation purposes, and the proposal gave rise to a heated debate—Menshikov declaring that such labour was bad and unsuitable for military men, and others contending that concession of the asked-for allotment of military would at least prove the cheapest means of bringing Peter's enterprise to completion. And at last, the opposers having had their say, Menshikov rose again, and unexpectedly closured the debate by intimating that, let the Senate decide what it might, the Empress did not intend to have a single soldier put to the task named: and, of course, this deeply offended the Senators, and set them murmuring against the Prince for having allowed them so long to debate the matter when all the time he could have made the statement just presented, and also for having failed to state what right he possessed to ascertain the Empress's will in advance, whilst certain Senators even threatened to withdraw their further attendance. But though, following upon this, a rumour flew through the capital that the malcontents were going to bring forward an alternative scheme of enthroning, with limitation of his power, the Grand Duke Peter, Tolstoi eventually managed to assuage the ferment by proposing a bargain of a kind calculated to allay, if not wholly to remove, the resentment felt by the old-established aristocracy because that aristocracy had been deposed from its heretofore dominant status in the administration by a band of non-aristocratic upstarts. And, following upon the proposal, an *ukaz* of 8 February, 1726, established a Supreme Privy Council of six members, with five of those members—Ostermann, Menshikov, Tolstoi, Golovkin, and Apraxin— belonging to the new, the official, aristocracy, and only one, Prince D. M. Golitzin, to the old, the *boyarin*, aristocracy of birth. Yet, as the *ukaz* of ordination itself stated, the Council was not a brand-new institution, since it included amongst its members Crown advisers who, as "First Ministers" and otherwise, had long been accustomed to consult together on important matters of State, and to act as ex-officio Senators, whilst three in particular, Menshikov, Apraxin, and Golovkin, stood at the head of the three chief colleges, the Colleges of War, of Marine, and of Foreign Affairs; and as a matter of fact, the *ukaz*' real aim was to get rid of the drawbacks entailed by the existing "over-plenitude of labour" entailed upon individual statesmen, and to convert "privy" conferences held periodically amongst the Crown's advisers into permanent sessions of those advisers when relieved of Senatorial duties. So in due course the Councillors submitted their "opinion" on their own *punkti* of ordination to the Empress, and she ratified this "opinion," and it became the *Reglament*, or Charter of Constitution, of the new administrative organ. That *Reglament* placed both the Senate and the Colleges under the Council's supervision, on the footing, as concerned the Colleges, that, whilst they were to retain their original bases as founded upon their charters, they were thenceforth to forward to the Council, instead of deciding independently, any primarily important matters which either transcended their powers of procedure, or could only be resolved by the Crown, or called for a new law. And from this we see that,

IV—T

though the Senate was to retain its powers of disposition within the limits of the existing system, it was to lose all legislative power, and the Privy Council, under the personal presidency of the Sovereign, was to act, as concerned its conciliary capacity, jointly with the Supreme Power. Moreover, inasmuch as the *Reglament* ordained that thenceforth no *ukaz* was to be promulgated until it had been subjected to "composition in full" (formulation) by the Council, and recited to the Sovereign, the two points best enabling us to understand the basic idea of the new institution will be found to be (for we may dismiss all the remaining points as so much technical detail for the basic idea's elaboration and development), (1) that the Supreme Power now renounced its power of sole action in the legislative routine— the purpose of this being to safeguard the governmental system from intrigues, from attempts illicitly to approach the Supreme Power, and from time-service and favouritism, and (2) that the *Reglament* drew, for the first time, a clear distinction between a current Administrative Order and a permanent Law—between the two State acts whose mutual confounding hitherto had, more than all else, tended to render the administrative system seemingly inequitable in its dispensation of justice. In fact, from that time onwards no matter of real importance was to be left to be acted upon by the Sovereign without the Supreme Privy Council, nor any law proclaimed without that body's previous consideration and sanction. True, certain foreign ambassadors attached to the Russian court believed the Council to be a first step towards changing the governmental form throughout, but as a matter of fact the Council involved no such thoroughgoing change as that —merely changes in the administrative system's essence, and in the character of the Supreme Power. Of these, the latter was to retain its titles whilst ceasing to be a personal will and becoming converted into a State institution; but though Acts of the period begin, consequently, to drop the term "Autocrat," there seems to have been some doubt about the direction in which things were trending, for in an *ukaz* of the year after the Council's inauguration we find appended to an explanation of the Council's fundamental idea a whole mass of cloudy reservations, secondary details, and direct contradictions—an example being that, whilst the *ukaz* ordains that before consideration of any legislative *punkti* they must be submitted to the Council, and that "from no person whomsoever shall the Council first accept any privy representations," the document adds the reservation, "Nevertheless shall it be competent for Ourselves, privy and apart, to give unto whom we will the authority necessary for any action"—which infringed the new Council's very essence. But at least all this prepared the ground for a further advance, and as a matter of fact the Privy Council soon waxed so greatly in importance that Catherine's testament appointed it to act as co-Regent during her successor's minority, and vested it, for the purpose, with almost autocratic-sovereign powers. Not that those powers availed much against the vicious young Emperor's whims, or against the highhandedness of his Imperial favourites; and the result of these two factors, coupled with others, was that once again the necessity of a restriction of the Crown began to make itself felt, even as it had been felt at the time of Catherine's accession, and that this time appeal for help was made to the better-class section of the hereditary aristocracy.

That section had expected much of Peter II., and been woefully disappointed. Its leader was the bold and cultured Prince D. M. Golitzin, a man who, in 1697, at the age of thirty-six, had been sent abroad for study with other young aristocrats, and resided in Italy and other foreign countries, and acquired thence a taste for observing European systems of State organisation, and reading European political literature. Yet throughout he had retained intact his inborn love for the antiquity of his own country, and recently consulted it by forming in his villa at Archangel (near Moscow) a splendid library. That library was disposed of on his banishment in 1737, but until it was so there stood included in it some six thousand foreign, or foreign-translated, works on history, philosophy, and politics, valuable treatises on Russian history, and text-books of Russian law. In fact, Golitzin had not omitted to add to the collection a single one of the more notable products of Europe's political thinkers of the sixteenth, seventeenth, and eighteenth centuries, from Machiavelli onwards, with ten monographs on Aristocracy alone, and ten on the English Constitution. All of which is clear indication of the bent of the collector's thoughts, and of the form of government most attractive to his ideas. Further, on being appointed Governor of Kiev, he had additional books by foreign writers translated into Russian by scholars of the local Academy, for the branch of contemporary political studies then most absorbing him (as it had absorbed Peter I.) was Puffendorf's Moralistic-Rationalistic School. First he had Puffendorf's *Introduction to a History of the States of Europe* translated and published, and then he did the same with Puffendorf's *A Treatise on the Duties of the Man and the Citizen,* and with Hugo Grotius' *De Jure Belli et Pacis.* A curious feature, however, is that he seems never to have possessed any translations of Hobbes's works, even though at that time that publicist was the leading Materialistic thinker, nor yet a copy of Locke's treatise on civil administration. The explanation of the omissions must be that, like Peter, Golitzin believed the only sound and intelligible creed in that connection to lie in the Moralistic theory that a State develops, not through warfare of all with all, as taught by Hobbes, but through the need of all by all, and the need of each by each, and therefore that an order of State ought to be based, not upon individual right, but upon the individual's obligations towards the State and his fellows. Similarly was the democratic Locke's doctrine that the whole people should share in the work of legislation scarcely likely to commend itself to Golitzin's aristocratic bent, or satisfactorily to answer his questionings. But this much can be said for certain concerning the Prince and his views: that he was one of the most cultured Russians of the eighteenth century. The aim self-propounded by his vigorous intellect was, first and foremost, to form for himself a world-outlook combining compactly (1) his love for the ancient traditions of his native country, (2) the claims not yet abandoned by the old *boyartsvo* of Moscow, and (3) a standard of cultivated political thought in so far as any standard had yet advanced in Western Europe. Nor can there be any doubt that he accomplished what few Russian savants of his time had ever done: he succeeded in educating himself until he came to have an understanding of the whole category of political convictions at the basis of which lies political freedom. Yet whilst he had too great an admiration for the learning and the political systems of Western Europe to be able at any time conscientiously to oppose reforms drawn, as to their ideas, and as to their institutions of State, from that Western quarter, he never succeeded in making himself wholly accept Peter's methods, nor yet the setting and the form of Peter's activity, nor yet the standard of morality observed by Peter's assistants, or in associating himself, even in thought, with the latter. And the result was that, though his austere, upright character always compelled Peter's respect, it never won Peter's liking, or led, during Peter's lifetime, to Golitzin acquiring more than Senatorial status (and even that with difficulty), or to his enjoying any influence in public affairs worth mentioning. For the truth is that the course of public events before, during, and immediately after Peter's day was such as Golitzin could view only with a dour and jaundiced eye, and consider, both as regards the one period and as regards the other, as a menace to and an infringement of ancient tradition, the established order, and common decency. And though he did not stand alone in regretting the two prevalent political maladies of Peter's closing days, the malady that the Supreme Power overrode the law, and the malady that the Supreme Power, as personified in its wielder, was weak, tyrannical, and swayed by favourites, he, more than anyone else in the country, devoted the whole strength of his personality and mental faculties to find a cure for the two ailments, and, to that end, studied all the State institutions of Western Europe, culled from them points suitable for Russia, and discussed the results with Fick. And in this way he who had started from the subjectively, genealogically developed idea that an aristocracy of birth alone can maintain orderliness and equity in a State ended at approval of the aristocratic system of Sweden, and therefore made a Supreme Privy Council his *point d'appui* towards endeavouring to effect further institutional reform.

During the night of 19 January, 1730, Peter II. died of smallpox in the mansion of the Frenchman Lefort, and did so without having nominated his successor. Accordingly there died with Peter's grandson the old dynasty— at all events so far as the male line of the House of Romanov was concerned, and the succession to the throne was left without either a fixed legislative norm or a legal heir. For the Law which Peter I., in the first instance, had enacted, and others, subsequently, had interpreted arbitrarily, or else left altogether inoperative, had now lost its last vestige of norm-creating force, and that much-disputed document, Catherine's will, was not a document to supply the defect. And since things were so, the present Administration's only resource towards filling up the vacant throne was to pass in review all the surviving *personnel* of the Imperial House, and successively con-sider the claims of the Tsaritsa, Peter the Great's first wife (now a nun), of Peter's youngest daughter Elizabeth, of his deceased eldest daughter's two-year-old son, and of Tsar Ivan's three young daughters. But the Administration found itself unable to halt at any of these, for in none of them did there lie a right to the throne that admitted of no dispute—the Law enacted by Peter I. had too hopelessly entangled dynastic ideas and dynastic relations for that to be possible, and all that could be done was to appraise candidates by political considerations, or by personal or family sympathies, rather than by any principle of law. And eventually, to assuage the storm of conflicting interests and rumours, the Privy Council itself assumed, for the time being, the head of affairs, and, as a first step towards closuring the discussion which had been raging ever since the young Emperor's demise, and towards filling up the throne, summoned for the following morning a meeting of all the superior officials of State, whilst intimating to them that when they did assemble they must decide the all-important question forthwith. Meanwhile the Council itself anticipated the meeting by augmenting its own *personnel*: although its members already included three aristocrats (Prince D. M. Golitzin and two Princes Dolgoruki), it invited to its ranks another Golitzin and two more Dolgorukis, and so, with six scions of the two leading *boyarin* families stand-ing ready to take part in its deliberations, acquired a composition so pre-dominantly aristocratic as practically to be aristocratic-oligarchical. Then, when morning arrived, and much had been said in the Council, and "for long," to quote Theofan Prokopovitch, "there had threatened to be a discord of voices," and Prince Dolgoruki, father of Peter II.'s second *fiancée*, had put forth his daughter for the throne on the plea that her late betrothed had expressly bequeathed it to her, and had had his proposal rejected as "inexpedient," and the same had been done with a proposal that the Tsaritsa-Grandmother should be elected to the throne, Prince D. M. Golitzin raised his voice. Russia, he said, had lost the Tsar upon whom all men's hopes had been centred, as a special punishment from God for her adoption of alien vices in addition to her own, but that, though that Tsar's demise had extinguished the male line of the Imperial House, it still remained open for the Convention to pass to the senior female line of the same, to Tsar Ivan's three daughters, whereas the daughters of Peter I. lacked any inherent right through being illegitimate issue born before their parents' legal marriage, and Catherine's testament was the testament of a *parvenu* who had never had any sort of title to sit upon the throne, and still less to dispose of it, and Ivan's eldest daughter, Catherine of Mecklenburg, was ineligible through being the wife of an alien, worthless prince. Hence, concluded Golitzin, the Council had but one course left open to it: which was to elect the only suitable remaining candidate as represented by Anna, the younger of the two Tsarevni, and the Duke of Courland's widow—a woman born of a Russian mother of old and goodly stock, and, at that, a woman gifted with all the right sentiments and qualities for occupation of a throne with dignity. Then unexpectedly, just as there had arisen a general shout of "Agreed! Agreed! Without further exchanging of words, let us choose Anna," Golitzin added to his already sufficiently unexpected proposal the words, "Nevertheless, whilst it lieth with you alone to choose whom ye will, yet would ye do well so to act now as to ease matters for yourselves hereafter." And when Chancellor Golovkin enquired, "What meanest thou by 'Ye would do well to ease matters for yourselves hereafter?'" Golitzin replied, "This: to make easy for yourselves such additions unto your will hereafter as ye may deem good." Upon this one of the Dolgorukis objected, "But how know we for certain that, if thus we begin, thus we shall always be able to maintain?" but Golitzin met him with the firm assurance, "I say that alway ye will so be able." Then Anna received a unanimous vote. Yet for the moment nothing more was said about the proposal to "add unto the Convention's will," about the proposal to effect a subsequent increase of the Council's executive power. No, the proceedings ended with a mere remark from Golitzin that "Now shall your will as to the choosing be fulfilled—albeit, it will be but seemly that also we commit the same unto written *punkti*, [1]

[1] "Points," or clauses.

and present those *punkti* unto her Majesty." Meanwhile the Senators and principal military officers had been awaiting the decision in another hall, and during the time of waiting ex-*Prokurator-General* Yaguzhinski had taken one of the Dolgorukis aside, and said: "How long must we thus suffer this cutting off of our heads? Surely it were time that the Autocracy were ended?" Nevertheless no one opposed the Privy Councillors' decision when they issued from the private conclave to announce that the choice had fallen upon Anna, and Yaguzhinski even ran to one of the Councillors to cry in words almost re-echoing Golitzin's: "My fathers, do ye at the same time add unto your will!"—though of course this was merely a piece of dissimulation on Yaguzhinski's part, seeing that neither he nor his fellows at all relished the Councillors' intelligence, as well as had already been given offence by the omission to invite them to take part in the Councillors' deliberations. In the end, as a matter of fact, the Yaguzhinski party left the hall in dudgeon. The next step was that later during the morning summonses were issued to the Synod, the Senate, the chief officials of State, and the principal military officers to assemble in the Kremlin, where a proclamation informed them that, though the Privy Council proposed to offer the throne of Russia to the Tsarevna Anna, the Council desired first to obtain the "consent of all the land," as expressed through that land's representatives, the high dignitaries there assembled: and upon that the said high dignitaries accorded their approval, and the proceedings terminated. But later there was framed for Anna's benefit, and hastily and secretly despatched to her at Mitau, a letter embodying the *punkti*, or conditions, for limiting her power; and her response to them was an ostensible promise that never, after her assumption of the Russian Crown, would she (1) enter into wedlock, (2) nominate an heir or a successor to herself on her own account, (3) make any exercise of her ruling power save in conjunction with the whole *personnel*, all the eight members, of the Supreme Privy Council, or (4) dispense with that Council's previous consent if at any time she should wish (a) to declare war, (b) to conclude peace, (c) to impose new taxation, (d) to confer any military rank above the rank of colonel, (e) to "assign unto any person any grave matter," (f) to deprive the Privy Council of the control of the Guards or any other State warlike force, (g) to deprive a *shliach* of either life, property, or honour without legal trial, (h) to confer any *otchina* or *derevnia*, (i) to promote any Russian subject or any foreigner to a court post, or (j) to use the State's revenues for her own expenditure. And she clinched these undertakings with the words, "If I should at any time fail to fulfil, or to maintain, any or all of these same, according unto these present promises, be I stripped of the Russian Crown!" Meanwhile, the redoubtable Yaguzhinski, the man who, the night before, had been calling for the Autocracy to be abolished, had become still further incensed on learning that he was not to be given a seat on the Privy Council, and now sent Anna a covert warning that she had better, without placing any trust in the Council's messengers, come to Moscow herself, and personally look into the situation; and the result of this communication was that, though she formally agreed to the *punkti's* conditions before she left Mitau, and confirmed her agreement with her signature and the written words, "By these presents I do vow to maintain these *punkti* without aught of exception," she nevertheless demanded of the Council's messengers a monetary advance of 10,000 roubles for travelling expenses!

CHAPTER XIII

The unrest evoked amongst the *dvorianstvo* by Anna's election—*Proekti* on the subject put forward by the *shliachetstvo*—Prince D. M. Golitzin's novel scheme—The failure of the scheme—The causes of that failure—The connection between the affair of 1730 and anterior events—The Empress Anna and her court—Her foreign policy— An anti-German movement.

IT was not long before the news that the Supreme Privy Council had elected Anna Duchess of Courland became public property: and in Moscow at least the news evoked considerable excitement. The special factor causing the election to be of more than local or Muscovite importance was the coincidence that the very day (19 January) on which the young Emperor died was to have seen him married to the Princess Dolgoruki, and that assembled in Moscow for the festivities was a multitude of provincial *dvoriané*, high military officers, and other persons who had been expecting to take part in a nuptial ceremony, and now found themselves confronted with a funeral. Hence the occasion became a meeting of the political waters, and the more so because the Privy Councillors' scheme at once evoked general murmurings. We can gain our best idea of those murmurings and their accompanying popular movement from the memoirs of Bishop Theofan Prokopovitch, who was at one with the masses in opposing the Council's policy. For in them we read that "throughout the city all things did then become grievous to hear and to behold. No matter whither a man might go, or what company he might attend, nought was to be heard save revilings of the eight conspirators, and harsh blamings and cursings for those conspirators' wondrous and boundless daring and greed and ambition." And very soon the *dvoriané* assembled in Moscow for the expected wedding divided themselves into cliques or "circles," and, says Theofan, held nocturnal meetings at which all the old rumours to the Councillors' detriment were revived. In fact, at least five hundred leading members of the class fell victims to the unrest, until "certain of the most eminent of the *shliachetstvo*," after compounding an "Anti-Privy-Council Union," split themselves, again, into two factions armed with two distinct policies. Of these, the advocates of the liberal or "bolder" policy were for actually assaulting the Councillors, and threatening them with assassination if they did not drop their scheme; whilst the

289

advocates of the conservative or "gentler" policy were merely for waiting upon the Councillors, and intimating to them that it was "inexpedient and most noisome" that any clique should, without the co-operation of the Administration in general, effect so great a change as a recasting of the State's Constitution. However, as Theofan had foreseen, the energies of the two contending parties soon underwent enfeeblement through internal dissension, since the less active and more conservative element amongst the *dvorianstvo* was for continued support of the primordial Autocracy, and the more vigorous and more liberal element found it difficult to sympathise with the Councillors' enterprise after the Councillors' failure to "invite us to partake of their friendship." Nor, at that, was (if we may believe certain foreign ambassadors) the more liberal section unanimous. Magnan, Secretary of the French Embassy, for example, wrote home to his Government that "Here, in streets and in houses alike, is there nought to be heard save words on the English Constitution and the rights of the English Parliament," whilst Mardeveldt, Prussian Ambassador, reported to his superiors that, "though the Russians at large" (by which, however, he meant only the *dvoriané*) "aspire to freedom, they in no wise do agree as to how far they shall restrict the Autocracy, or leave unto it its freedom," and de Liria, the Spanish Ambassador, recorded that "Here are there parties without number, and though all is calm, at any moment may there come an outbreak." Not unnaturally, therefore, certain Russians now began to turn their eyes to the West, and look to see how Europe managed such affairs, and to scan Western constitutions as they might have inspected the stock of a jeweller's shop, and to dispute with one another as to which items had best be selected from the goods displayed, and to vow that each successive item was better than the last. In fact, everyone became fired with a fervent desire to establish new administrative forms in Russia, and the foreign ambassadors whom I have quoted tell us how diverse to infinity was the multiplicity of projects put forward by both influential and petty *dvoriané* as hopelessly they endeavoured to decide which governmental system was most suitable to Russia—some contestants advocating the English manner of limiting the Sovereign's authority with rights of Parliament, and others calling for a Swedish limitation, and others for an elective Administration like the Polish, and others for a purely aristocratic Republic and total elimination of a Sovereign. For, in the absence of any fixed political standard, and in the absence of any marked aptitude for measurement of political points of difference, these thinkers could see no great gulf between an English Parliament and a Russian torture-chamber! At the same time, even this plenitude of political divergencies was not such a plenitude but that all could see looming through the mass a bogey in the face of which even the most irreconcilable political elements were fain to huddle together for protection. Which bogey was that favouritism which ever is the besetting malady of an Autocracy with a wanton and unrestricted will. We have evidence of this from the foreign ambassadors, who write that, after having seen the manner in which, for example, the Dolgorukis had risen to power, the country had become more than ever timorous of time-servers and their influence, and despairingly assured that continuance of an absolute Tsar in being would guarantee a never-failing supply of court favourites like Peter II.'s clique, and, meanwhile, the people's governance as with a rod of iron. The less wonder, therefore, that the *dvoriané* were all for protecting themselves through the method of limiting the Supreme Power. Unfortunately, the Councillors' scheme for doing so was not to their taste—the *dvoriané* considered that scheme to be merely an oligarchical conspiracy designed to replace the authority of the Crown alone with an authority wielded by as many individual despots as the Council contained members, even as was thought by Stchbatov when, during his compilation of some historical notes during the later years of Catherine II., he stated that during the period under review "the Councillors' sole purpose was to supplant one Sovereign with many." And that this view was widely held we have further evidence from a letter sent to a resident of Moscow, in 1730, by a petty provincial *shliachtich*. Says the letter: "In these parts it is being noised abroad that a republic is about to be set up in Moscow: and peradventure it hath been so already. Yet I misdoubt that it hath: I misdoubt that greatly, and in any case may God grant that in place of an Autocrat Emperor we be not given half a score of arrogant and mighty families, since then all we, the *shliachetstvo*, will become undone, and be forced to worship [those families as] idols more even than formerly, and to seek their mercy—which, as of old, will not be easy to obtain." The maximum of the prevailing unrest was reached when, at a solemn convention held on 2 February, the Privy Council read to the Senate, the Synod, the *Generalitet* (Higher Military Staff) and Presidents of Colleges the *punkti* which Anna had subscribed, and with them, a document, couched in letter form, purporting to have come from her direct, but, in reality, framed beforehand in her name, and never submitted to her at all. In this spurious letter Anna was represented as saying that she "duly consented unto" her election, and "solely for the good of the Russian State, and for the satisfaction of Our faithful subjects," had signed the *punkti's* exposition of her proposed methods of government: wherefore it at once became clear that the letter's design was to cause the obligations recently imposed upon her peremptorily, as conditions indispensable if she was to be elected at all, to figure in the people's eyes as sacrifices voluntarily conceded for the Empire's welfare. And, of course, the effect of this mendacious move was at once to throw the conference into a panic. Says Theofan Prokopovitch graphically, when describing the incident: "For a space all present did lay back their ears like unto mules." Meanwhile, amidst the general whispering (for men dared not give their anger more open expression) the Privy Councillors feigned to be conferring together in undertones, and glancing about them as though they were as surprised as anyone else at such an unexpected development: until, intermittently clearing his throat, and harping upon some of his words, and frequently changing his intonation, Prince D. M. Golitzin said: "Truly is our Empress-Tsaritsa a gracious Sovereign! God himself must have moved her unto this writing! And now will Russia for ever be happy and prosperous!" After which, as everyone still sat silent, he continued: "But wherefore speaketh no man a word? Let each, rather, declare what he is thinking, even though nought really remaineth save to thank her Majesty." Someone, thereupon, did venture diffidently to mutter: "It is that I, for my part, being unable to understand how the Empress did come to write thus, am marvelling at it," but the timid words were not re-echoed, and the Councillors went on to propose formulation and inscription of a sessional minute that "all present, having duly heard read" the Empress's letter and imposed *punkti*, "now do stand greatly satisfied with such a favour from her Majesty, and will subscribe unto the same our hands." But here some of the "mules," the end of their tether reached, refused to sign the minute then and there—they said that they could do so "another day." "And thereafter," writes Theofan, "all did sit as though suddenly grown old, or, if moving, did move as though quaking in thought." For the truth is that there was still surviving in these men something of the slave instinct, and that a serious shock had been administered to it—none of them had ever looked to see a limitation of such stringency imposed upon the power of a Russian ruler. Next, the Councillors were asked on what footing the Administration itself was designed to stand, and Golitzin, answering for them (and, incidentally, forbearing to remind his questioners that they stood answered in advance by the Empress's "letter" and by the *punkti*, and to mention that, under those documents, her "will" could not be revised), proposed that each member of the gathering should himself draw up a *proekt*, or "scheme" of administration, and submit that scheme to the Council next day. But the effect of this device was only to expose Golitzin's already badly concealed hand, for whereas the affair had hitherto borne a certain semblance of correctitude, seeing that at the time of its inception the Privy Council had been the only extant organ of the chief administrative system, and therefore qualified, in its own right, to nominate the Tsarevna Anna for the heirless throne, and that, as *ex-officio* representatives of the people (as, to quote Theofan, "men who manifested the country in their own persons"), the other chief officials of State had unanimously bestowed their approval upon the Privy Council's selection, and that the unlooked-for, but seemingly acceptable, nominee had graciously recovered for her people such outworn remnants of the Autocracy as still survived from the times of Peter I., and subscribed *punkti* fixatory of her methods of rule—whereas all this had been so, now, just when the country had accepted these munificent gifts as boons graciously accorded, and not extorted through extortion or barter, and had been preparing to receive them with becoming gratitude, here was this Golitzin demeaning the gifts to the very faces of the State's superior officials "unto the rank of brigadier," and disclosing, thereby, that, after all, the "conditions" represented less gifts from Anna than the outcome of a subterranean compact between her and her Privy Councillors! Yes, all now could see that, though Golitzin had only a set of rickety boards for a stage, and only a counterfeit of loyalty on his part for a setting, he was producing upon those boards a plot with a court intrigue for its *motif*, and was like to increase, rather than to lessen, the complexity of the problem of, firstly, regulating the Unipersonal Supreme Power which at present ruled the State, and secondly, overhauling the subordinate institutions which administered the same. At all events, no matter whether he had had his hand prematurely forced, or whether the incautious disclosure had been his own doing, the fact remains that the proposed new form of administration evoked a storm of protest, and brought upon the proposer a hubbub of suggestions, and of note-takings, and of arguments—the State officials "unto the rank of brigadier," the representatives of the non-official *shliachetstvo*, and everyone else simply beleaguering the Privy Councillors, and begging of them to listen to, and to consider, the many objections to the scheme. Until at last, on the confusion threatening to explode into an open outbreak, the Councillors had to intimidate the objectors by reminding them that at the disposal of the Council lay such resources against brawlers as commanders of military detachments, superintendents of police, and torture-chambers—and, by so doing, converted the opposition party into conspirators pure and simple, and caused its members, even to such men as Theofan describes as "fellows of little potency" (that is to say, not possessing any social ties or obligations), to take to secret conferences, and so fear to sleep in their own homes that, disguised, they had to flit from house to house of their friends.

Hence the net result of the Privy Councillors' resort to their fellow officials of the Superior Administration for assistance in considering the administrative question was to swell an, originally, small oligarchical intrigue into an extensive political movement. For until now the question had been a question confined exclusively to the administrative circle itself, and, in its consideration, the Supreme Privy Council had had to do with none but the superior administrative institutions—with the Senate, with the Synod, with the *Generalitet*, and with the Presidents of Colleges; but Golitzin's latest proposal, his proposal for a general formulation of *proekti*, at once brought into the matter, in addition, the more aristocratic section of the *shliachetstvo*, the section ranked "in *chini*," or otherwise distinguished, and thereby, again, split departmental staffs into cliques, and led to official Church dignitaries being seen hobnobbing with non-official Church dignitaries, and departmental functionaries with sympathisers who did not even belong to the Civil Service, and new interests with interests which belonged to the movement already. As regards the *proekti* which eventually found their way to the Privy Council, or at least were prepared for presentation to that body, they numbered, so far as we know, thirteen; but of them, though all were drawn up by "circles" of *shliachetstvo*, and signed by a total of over a thousand persons, only the *proekt* presented to the Council by the Senate and the *Generalitet* on Tatistchev's behalf really attained the dignity of an historico-political treatise—the rest were but hastily formulated and roughly developed drafts. At the same time, it is precisely because the latter were what they were that we are enabled to gain so plain and unvarnished a view of the then *dvorianstvo's* then political attitude. In the first place, not a single *proekt* refers directly to the *punkti*, or to Anna's election, or to the proposed limitation of her sovereign authority. Hence, seemingly, they looked upon each of those things as an accomplished fact. Tatistchev alone, playing up to his established rôle of historian-publicist, follower of Wolf, and disciple of the Puffendorfian-Moralistic school, so far airs his acquaintance with Russian history and Western political literature as to make State Law his general basis, and set out to prove that only an autocratic form of rule could cope with the special position in which Russia was then placed, and that, the male line of the Imperial dynasty being extinct, the substitute Sovereign should be elected "according unto none save natural law"—through the method of taking the votes, both personally and by proxy, of the whole of that Sovereign's proposed subjects. Apparently Tatistchev had in his mind equally the Western bi-cameral system of government and the seventeenth century's resource of pan-territorial *Zemskie Sobori*, but, whilst not boggling at the proposed limitation of the Sovereign's authority, was troubled by the fact that the proposal for it had emanated from a mere group, without the cognisance of the general people, secretly, straight against the *shliachetstvo's* special rights, and in seeming disregard of the necessity of State-official co-operation as a whole. Wherefore, in substance, Tatistchev's *proekt* calls upon all men like-minded with himself to rise and defend the *shliachetstvo's* privileges *à outrance*. Thus the Tatistchevian scheme. But its fellows strike a more subservient note, and, conceiving discussion of the theory and the structure of the Supreme Power in a State to lie beyond their capacity, concentrate exclusively upon the wider, less specialised question of re-constructing the State's Chief Administration, and refer particularly, in that connection, to the *dvorianstvo's* pet aspiration of procuring exemption from State service. Unfortunately, so vaguely, with such poverty of detail, is the programme of these *proekti* sketched out that all that that programme really said was: Either let the Supreme Privy Council continue to act as our "Supreme Rule," or let the Senate, in its stead, undertake the work. Nevertheless the programme is deeply preoccupied with that "Supreme Rule's" numerical and family composition, and declares that such a "Rule" ought in no case to be confined to a Privy Council of eight members, but to a Council of a membership of from eleven to thirty at the least, and a Council, at that, in which not more than two members should stand drawn from the same family—this last a sign of how sharply the fact that no fewer than four Princes Dolgoruki had participated in the Council of 19 January was still rankling in the *dvorianstvo's* mentality. Also, the whole of the Administra-tion was to be elective, and drawn exclusively from the *dvorianstvo*—though in this connection we must always remember that the latter was far from an integral or homogeneous body, but one made up of "men of family" (the born aristocracy), of the State, of the military *Generaliteten* (the official aristo-cracy), and of the *shliachetstvo* at large. Similarly the *dvorianstvo* alone was to furnish the country with its Privy Council, its Senate, its Presidents of Colleges, and its Governors of Provinces, whilst a few of the *proekti* even proposed to confine the right of voting for those posts exclusively to members of the *Generaliteten* and such *shliachtichi* as belonged to the more "eminent" (aristocratic) section of their corporate class, or had already been elected to either the Privy Council or the Senate, and that the electoral conclave thus formed should be termed "The *Obstchestvo*" or "Union,"[1] and have assigned to it a certain legislative and institutional authority, but that the clergy and the mercantile classes should expressly be excluded from co-operating in any State reform programme save where their own particular interests might be concerned. As regards any lightening of the peasantry's taxatory burden, only a few of the *proekti* expressed a desire to witness such a thing, for what those *proekti* really wanted to see was the *dvorianstvo's*

---

[1] Or "Company," or "Community," or "Association."

shoulders relieved of the responsibility for that burden's discharge. Nor in any instance do we find a *proekt* making any reference to serf-emancipation, or requesting legal definition of the master's dues and exactions. No, every *proekt* confined its essential portion to such points as *dvorianin* exemption from State service and seigniorial obligations, with, alternatively, a fixed term of State service, a right to enter that service as officer from the first, and abolition of sole succession to landed property. Nevertheless, one result of broaching the question of *dvorianin* exemption in this manner was to draw the *rioadovie*, the rank and file members of the *shliachetstvo*, into the movement, even though the movement's active engineers remained, as before, the born and the official aristocracies, since, little though those rank and file had a taste for debates concerning forms of administration, for action on their own account, or for formation of political cliques, they were led to revolve around the movement's outstanding actors by the hope, the illusory hope, that thereby they too would be enabled to obtain exemptions from State obligations, whilst the re-echoing of the words of one or another leader came the easier to them for the reason that most of them were either Guards or line officers, and therefore men broken in to military service, and readily submissive to a superior. In fact, no fewer than a hundred, or more, of the names appended to the *proekti* are seen to be names of military officers. In general, it must be said that although all those *proekti* stood based upon the idea that the *dvorianstvo* was the only plenipotentiary corporation in the realm naturally possessing civil and political rights, and that it alone represented the people in the true juridical sense (as a sort of *pays légal*), and was competent to assist the Supreme Power in administering the State, and that that State ought to be regarded as made up primarily of themselves, and secondarily of a mass of administered, or working, folk having for its one duty the support of the Supreme Power, of the State, and of its own administration, and for its one right the right of performing the labour necessary for that threefold support, the labour necessary to provide the State's sources of vitality—although all this was so, it must also be confessed that not one of the cliques signing the *proekti* either understood or cared to acknowledge the existence of its country's people as we envisage a people to-day.

Whilst the *shliachetstvo* was occupying itself with these expressions of its corporate desires Prince D. M. Golitzin was elaborating, and discussing with the Senate, a plan for a Constitution in the true sense. His plan was that the Empress should control her court independently, but that the supreme authority in the State should be vested in a Privy Council of from ten to twelve members, and that in this Council, which should be drawn exclusively from families of position, and have sole control of the naval and military forces, the Empress should possess the right to exercise two votes as against each member's one. Whence the scheme clearly had for its model the Swedish State Council which had been formed in 1719–20 after the Swedish State Council's conflict with the Diet. Another item in Golitzin's plan was that three new institutions should be organised for operation under the Privy Council, and consist of (1) a Senate of thirty-six members for scrutinising in advance all matters destined for the Council's final decision, (2) a Chamber of two hundred *shliachtichi* elected by the *shliachetstvo*, itself, for defence of the rights of that class against encroachments by the Privy Council, and (3) a Chamber of provincial town representatives for, firstly, supervision of all commercial and industrial matters, and, secondly, maintenance of the rights of the common people. All of which really was tantamount to a proposal that a few leading families should control the Administration in its entirety, and a few representatives of the *shliachetstvo* and the mercantile community stand to defend themselves and the masses from that Administration's doings! Naturally, so far from helping to extinguish the conflagration, the plan added *boyarin* fuel to *dvorianin* flames, and on consideration, and especially in view of his Imperial nominee's imminent arrival from Mitau, our veteran Don Quixote, our veteran champion of the effete Muscovite *boyarstvo*, concluded that concessions must be made, and at least such a chink opened in the Administration's barred and locked portals as to admit of some sort of popular representation, difficult though he knew it would be for the two ruling classes to swallow such a morsel. To balance it, however, he made—of course, in the people's interest!—further concessions still. That is to say, whilst holding to it that the Privy Council's basis must be a purely aristocratic one, and that the Council must have a monoply of legislative authority, he proposed to confer upon the clergy, upon the mercantile community, and, last but not least, upon the superior *shliachetstvo* further privileges and exemptions, and even held out to the latter class a promise of acquisition of the boon which that class's own *proekti* had not dared to request, of the boon of emancipation from liability to compulsory State service, coupled with a right to enter the warlike forces voluntarily, a right to do so as officer from the first, and a right to pass direct into the Guards. And, as a crowning touch to this *shliachtich* charter of concessions, he offered to give the *shliachetstvo* that class's longest and most ardently desired award of all, and undertake that *krestiané* and household serfs (*dvorovie*) should thenceforth cease to be eligible for official appointments—a step which, incidentally, would have inflicted upon a whole bevy of minor administrative and financial officials of Pososhkov's stamp relegation to the status of boyaral serfs whence Peter had freed them, and political exclusion.

Golitzin's sorrily staged, and still more sorrily played, political comedy then moved onwards towards its epilogue more swiftly than ever, for the discord raging in administrative circles joined with the Guards' attitude in encouraging opponents of Crown limitation who had hitherto concealed their opinions, or pretended to see eye to eye with the Opposition, to come out into the open, and form yet another (to use Theofan's term) "company," party, in the State. And in this party, a party fully as *ad hoc* in its principles as the rest, there stood included the Empress's kinsfolk, those kinsfolk's friends, a few functionaries (the Princes Charkasski, Trubetskoi, and others whom the Privy Council had offended by not extending to them an invitation to join its ranks), and a tail of variously hesitant and indifferent members; whilst for its special inspiration there came to life again Chancellor Ostermann, who for long past had seemed to be lying so immediately at death's door that he had had to receive the Sacrament and Extreme Unction! All this, of course, brought about a complete re-classification of interests, inter-relations, and personalities—the new party setting out to encourage its members with an assurance that it would be easier for them to obtain what they wanted from an Autocrat Empress than from an arbitrary Privy Council, and to beguile the Senators with a suggestion that possibly the task of operating the Chief Administration might be converted into a Senatorial monopoly, and to please the *Generalitet* and the Guards with a hint that possibly the party might procure for them riddance from the Privy Council's control, and to please all and sundry with a hint that possibly the party might be able to abolish the Privy Council itself. The sounder of the tocsin for the new party was Theofan Prokopovitch, and he made Moscow so ring with his tales of how the Councillors had browbeaten the Empress—"her guardian dragon" (V. L. Dolgoruki) "oft hath caused her scarce to draw her breath"—that he came near to wearing himself out with his exertions. But those exertions met with success. On one occasion this was so much the case that even he himself became alarmed, for, seemingly, the congregation to which he was preaching began all of a sudden to look as though it "were devising something strange." And the final result of this reputedly "godless" and "German" Synodal President's vigorous, insidious preparation of Moscow's soil was that when Anna set foot upon it from Mitau she found it hold firm beneath her tread, and could unhesitatingly place herself at the head of the conspiracy aimed against herself and her solemnly pledged word. Her first infringement of the *punkti* was that she proclaimed herself Lieutenant-Colonel of the Preobrazhenski Regiment, and

Captain of the Horse Guards, tendered them *vodka* with her own hand, and stirred them into shouting that they would rather have one monarch than several. And her next step in the same direction was that on 15 February, when she made her State entry into Moscow, and the chief administrative officials took the oath of fealty, she, whilst forbearing for the time being to have them swear to her as Autocrat as well as Empress, made them take also the old customary oath "unto all the land." Meanwhile the Privy Council's adherents still remained blind to the swarm of intrigues of which she was the centre—openly they exulted that at last a regularly, clearly defined Administration had come into existence, and even went so far as to have it put about that the amount to be allowed the Empress annually for her personal expenses was not to exceed, by a single *kopek*, 100,000 roubles, and that if she should take from the Treasury so much as the value of a snuff-box without the Council's written consent she should straightway be sent back to her native Courland, and informed that her election had been only so much lip-salve. But upon that, for some reason or another, the Councillors lost faith in their own enterprise, and a rumour spread that Anna was, after all, to be offered the full Autocracy. And the upshot was that on 25 February a gathering of 108 Senators, high military officers, and *dvoriané* assembled in the great hall of the Palace, and then and there requested Anna to appoint a Commission to revise the *punkti* in the direction of establishing some form of administration more calculated to benefit the people as a whole. In other words, this gathering requested Anna to become mediator between her Privy Council and its opponents! True, one solitary Councillor present did venture upon the counter-proposal that the Empress should leave the petition undecided upon until she had taken his and his colleagues' advice, but for the second time she infringed her word of honour, and agreed to, and signed, the document on the spot. This left the Privy Councillors dumbfounded. Yet even if they had had a mind to resist, they would straightway have been overborne by the tumult of the assembled Guards officers, who were better organised than their opponents, and joined the *dvorianin* petitioners in shouting: "Not our will is it that laws be prescribed unto the Empress, but that she be our Autocrat as our Tsars ever before have been." And when Anna feigned to try and quell the demonstrators they went down upon their knees, protested ecstatic devotion, and cried: "Do thou speak the word, and we will lay the heads of thine ill-wishers at thy feet." Also, the same evening, towards the close of a dinner-party given to the Privy Councillors by the Empress, a second deputation of *dvoriané* and others entered, and handed her a petition, signed by a hundred and fifty persons, which set forth that "with all possible devotion do we, thine humble slaves, offer unto thy most gracious Majesty the Autocracy ever pertaining unto thy right glorious and most praiseworthy ancestors, and pray of thee to accept the same whilst setting at nought the *punkti* laid before thee by the Privy Council, and subscribed unto with thine hand." With well-feigned astonishment, with an artless show of ignorance, Anna exclaimed: "What? Then were those same *punkti* not written with the people's will?" and the petitioners replied: "Not so were they." Anna turned to Prince Vasilii Lukitch Dolgoruki, exclaimed, "So thou hast deceived me!" bade the actual document signed at Mitau be brought to her, and publicly tore it into shreds. "Yet," says a foreign ambassador, "had the Privy Councillors spoken so much as a word, straightway the officers of the Guards would have cast them from the windows." In the result, there was carried out, on 1 March, in all the country's churches and cathedrals, a complete new swearing of allegiance—this time to Anna as, practically, Autocrat, whilst those who, accordingly, had to execute a *volte-face* found it the easier to do so, even as regards really devout consciences, because at the same time she received the Church's benediction. Thus expired the one constitutional-aristocratic monarchy of the eighteenth century, after a ten-days' existence secured to it by a four-weeks-old Privy Council. But whilst the *dvoriané* restored the Autocracy, they took good care not to leave themselves out of the Government—to guard against that, they had prayed in their after-dinner petition of 25 February that abolition of the Privy Council should be followed by the creation of a Senate of twenty-one members, and that that Senate should have all its old Senatorial status, and be balloted for by none but members of the *shliachetstvo*, and that the same rule should be applicable to Presidents of Colleges and *Gubernatori* of Provinces, and that the general administrative system should be (as requested also in the before-dinner petition) established on a permanent footing. Wherefore, had these requests been conceded in their entirety, the Central and the Provincial Administrations would in each case have issued as bodies exclusively composed of nominees of *dvorianin* election, of functionaries closely akin to the Captain-Superintendents of Catherine II.'s later days: but, as things turned out, the Russian Empire did not become what Fick had wanted to see her become—"Poland's and Sweden's administrative sister": all that she did in that direction was so far to assimilate herself to *shliachetstvo*-governed Poland as to become a *shliachetstvo*-governed Autocracy.

By contemporary observers this affair of 1730 seems to have been regarded as a struggle confined exclusively to the two ruling classes, the *dvorianstvos* and the born aristocracy, and turning exclusively upon the proposal to limit the Autocracy. The country's remaining classes, those observers considered, had no share in the affair at all, and even Theofan Prokopovitch's strenuous preparatory canvassing of the leading Muscovite families did little to set it on foot. True, the original scope of the task abortively assumed by the Supreme Privy Council was modest enough, for the latter sought, not to limit the Autocracy with any popular-representative, or class-representative, system, but merely to confer the Supreme Power's prerogatives jointly upon the person whom it had invited to assume that Power and upon itself as the institution tendering the invitation. Nor did the Council aim at changing the Supreme Power's form and composition, beyond that that Power was to cease to be unipersonal, or at in any way altering its relation to the community. Nor, lastly, did the Council's *punkti* seek to allot more than one right to anyone, the right of civil freedom. The unfortunate point was that right was to go exclusively to one class. "From the *shliachetstvo* shall there not be taken without trial or stock or property or honour." Not a word about *political* freedom: not a word about popular participation in the task of government. No, the Empress and the Privy Council alone were to administer the State, and to do so with unfettered hands, nor was the Council to represent, in the State, any portion of the people except itself, as a body of members one section of whom had already stood appointed at the time of the Supreme Power's limitation, and the other section had already been co-opted in pursuance of the Council's nocturnal session of 19-20 January! But though the Council's plan for the future working of the State was this and no more, the Opposition subsequently succeeded in forcing that body to summon a general-official conference, and to consider further means towards the desired administrative-reconstructional end. The trouble was that the Council was not representative even of the old aristocracy of birth, since, though many of the official-aristocratic families, such as the Sheremetevs, the Buturlins, the Cherkasskis, the Trubetskois, the Kurakins, the Odoevskis, and the Bariatinskis, were fully equal, from the genealogical standpoint, to families like the Dolgorukis, those official-aristocratic families were in opposition to the Council rather than in its favour, whilst not in every case were members of the Council able to rally to themselves even their own kinsfolk, and we find quite as many signatures of Golitzins and Dolgorukis in the Opposition's *proekti* as in the *proekti* put forward by the Council's partisans. At the same time, it was the latter that constituted the soul of the movement, for it was they who stirred up the petty *shliachetstvo* with illusory promises of exemption from service and seigniorial obligations, and took the lead in the innumerable *shliachtich* cliques, and suggested to those cliques so many points suitable for presentation to the Council as to cause the presenters of the points to look, not like individual actors, but like one of those crowds of supernumeraries which clever marshalling can make seem larger than the reality. And these efforts the Council's aristocratic patrons were the better able to make because the "Table of Ranks" had not yet wholly succeeded in re-shuffling Russian society, or in extinguishing in the *dvorianstvo* that class's natural promptings to the point that its more obscure, impoverished, and slighted section did not still cherish a grudging respect for rank, a slavish veneration for birth. "Certain men of the *shliachetstvo* are as serfs, and serve great families, and so fulfil their will as to gain them enrichment under the authority of the State, and places of command, and weighty interests." This description of the Petrine *dvorianstvo's* attitude towards the aristocracy is quoted from a work by Ivan Filippov, one of Peter's "projectors": and it applies equally well to the post-Petrine period. And since the leaders of the *shliachetstvo* in the affair were men of high position in the Senate or in the *Generalitet* (which had now become something more than a bevy of general officers, and was an institution to itself, a sort of Supreme Army Council or General Staff, and had a special scale of grades and emoluments, and sometimes even was called upon to help the Senate in certain matters—for example, in drafting the first series of *proekti* presented to the Privy Council),—since all this was so, it follows that the affair of 1730 was less a struggle of persons with persons, or of classes with classes, than a struggle of institutions with institutions: we do not see the old aristocracy of birth then warring with the new official aristocracy, or the one or the other warring with the petty *shliachetstvo*, but an alliance of the Senate, the Synod, and the *Generalitet* warring with the Supreme Privy Council, and doing so because the latter was for arrogating to itself the entire control of the administrative machine. And inasmuch as institutions are the wheels of administrative machines, and can be set in motion only by an administrative or a social force, the Privy Councillors designed that the required force in this case should be themselves and the country's leading families. The result was everywhere to set men of family against men of family, and the more so as the Opposition's design was precisely the same as that of the Councillors. Moreover, the ruling classes of the country had so steadily been increasing in genealogical intricacy and complexity ever since the days of the *Oprichnina* that now it was socially difficult to distinguish a man of birth from a man of none, not to mention the precise extent of his ancestral qualifications, whilst also the working of time had caused the aristocratic and the official-aristocratic sections largely to have their members attached to particular administrative institutions, seeing that abolition of the *Miestnichestvo* had broken up the old military-genealogical organisation of the "State servitors," and Peter's subsequent attempts to induce local *dvorianin* associations to take part in the task of administration had proved abortive, and no other social institution remained for the purpose. True, this grouping of families into particular administrative institutions might have acted as a factor towards uniting in one the whole welter of divergent interests and smouldering views, but, as a matter of fact, the welter was such as to keep some of the Council's members themselves sundered by personal hostilities and family considerations, and bring it about that, for all that body's seeming solidarity and unanimity, its power of co-operation depended less upon its sense of co-membership for deliberative purposes than upon its sense of aristocratic solidarity. So what really was needed was that the State's superior administrative institutions should become purely public, elective, and representative bodies. And we see the fact of this need flitting, almost to the exclusion of all other considerations, through the best intellects of the day. Yet it is clear that neither the Privy Councillors (save, perhaps, Prince D. M. Golitzin) nor those Councillors' opponents had any understanding of the real meaning of popular representation. Not even upon the preliminary constructional details to that end could they agree, for to them election of a given number of representatives of the *shliachetstvo* at large meant merely random selection of certain *shliachtichi* from amongst the section of *dvorianstvo* then happening to be serving in the metropolis. Wherefore neither the community's old-established social relations nor the period's political ideas could furnish the necessary facilities for untying the knot of divergent social interests and views. And when eventually the question did attain resolution it did so through the agency of force, through the mechanical stimulus of a blow delivered by a corps which, though *dvorianin* of composition, regarded the matter purely from the barrack-room standpoint, and, instead of attacking the autocratic rule of a few in the name of the rights of all, attacked all in the name of a unipersonal Autocracy. Yet, the blow delivered, the deliverer could not well put the helm about, and ask for popular elective representation as a sequel to their restoration of the Autocracy, for that would have been tantamount to hiding behind the trees. True, directly after the country's swearing of allegiance to her, Anna, now Autocrat, did accord the *shliachetstvo* a partial fulfilment of its wishes by setting up a Senate of twenty-one members; but those members were nominated by herself, and in no sense of the term elected. In general, we shall best discern the causes of the movement's failure by following the movement's course. The truth is that the Golitzin scheme of 1730 lacked sufficient support; it lacked it from within, and it lacked it from without, and instead of aiming at a limitation of the Supreme Power with a permanent Law, sought to limit that Power with an institution both variable in composition and casual in status. And though efforts subsequently were made to remedy these defects, and at least to cause the institution in question to constitute an organ and a bulwark for the aristocracy of birth, the misfortune was that the latter was now practically extinct, and confined to a few mutually hostile families. In fact, all that Golitzin really succeeded in organising was a Monarchy limited by a shadow. Besides, even of the administrative world itself a large proportion became alienated and antagonised by the proposed non-popular and casual elements in the Council's composition, and by the proposed item that that body alone should carry on the working of the Chief Administration, and, owing to these two factors, formed, eventually, such a party of opposition as, backed by the Guards and the *shliachetstvo*, was able completely to change the affair's complexion, and convert the question of limiting the Autocracy into a protest against the Council's attempt itself to assume autocratic powers. On the other hand, the Opposition, in addition to being at odds with the Council, suffered from internal differences, in that, whilst the Council desired to limit the Autocracy, but leave the Chief Administration untouched, and the Opposition demanded reconstruction of the Administration, but no modification of, or reduction of, the Autocracy, there was a large Oppositional clique, a clique made up exclusively of *dvoriané* and Guards officers, whose sole object was class exemptions, and to which the questions of limiting the Supreme Power and reconstructing the administrative system meant little or nothing. And, naturally, the fact that such a divergency of views, added to immaturity of political understanding, severed the Opposition into numerous sections rendered it all the harder for those sections to evolve, in common, a properly conceived and really workable counter-plan, and it was not without reason that, *à propos* of the circumstance, Mardeveldt, the Prussian Ambassador, wrote home to his Government that the Russians did not genuinely understand freedom—that they talked about it a great deal, but never would convert it into a *fait accompli*. Golitzin himself explained his failure with the plea that the enterprise ended by outgrowing the capacity of those whom he had invited to be his helpers in it. At all events, it is difficult to understand his words in any other sense when, in chanting his scheme's requiem after the full re-establishment of the Autocracy, he wrote: "The banquet was spread: but not worthy to partake of it were those bidden unto the same. And though well I know that now I must suffer in that my task hath gone amiss, yet will I accept and bear my lot the more in that I shall know that those sufferings are for my country, and that even yet it may befall that those who now are making my tears to flow shall one day weep longer than I." Yet if this was Golitzin's verdict upon himself, why did he, after constituting himself host, invite to the banquet guests "un-worthy" of what he had to offer, or, if he knew of no guests who were "worthy," prepare a banquet at all? The questions are perplexing, and leave us the more astonished that he should have selected to occupy the throne a person hereditarily disqualified for the post, and that, by resorting to a sophistical electoral act, he should have converted the conditions which he imposed upon the elected into a voluntary gift by the latter. Well, to a certain extent his recourse to the former of those acts leads us to suspect the agency of Swedish influence, for Anna's accession in Russia in 1730 is more than a little reminiscent of the accession of Ulrica Eleanor in Sweden in 1719. In each case the outstanding constituent features were (1) election of a woman over the head of the direct heir (in the Swedish instance, over the head of the Duke of Holstein), (2) limitation of the elected's power, (3) bestowal of sufficient authority upon an aristocratic State Council to enable that Council to develop into a body possessed of plenipotentiary status, and (4) opposition offered to the three foregoing features by the country's *dvorianstvo*. Yet though these similarities have always led Russian students, when examining the events of 1730 in the light of Swedish historiography, to draw the conclusion that the Russian *punkti* of limitation and Golitzin's plan and scope for the Russian oath of allegiance alike were influenced by the then constitutional procedure of Sweden, circumstantial resemblance does not invariably spell identity of condition. True, it is probable that, when selecting Anna, Golitzin remembered and considered the occasion of Ulrica Eleanor's election, and said to himself, "If the affair succeeded in Sweden, why should it not here?"; but, even if that be so, the Swedish case is unlikely to have encouraged him as an example, even as it is unlikely that he looked upon Sweden's then laws and institutions as, at best, anything more pertinent than a set of ready-made forms and *formulæ*. No, the motives, the tactics, and the interests which moved him on this occasion were his own, and not borrowed: and this is shown with particular clearness by evidence connected with the ambiguous feature which I voiced above in the query as to how Golitzin came to falsify his own electoral act. For let us turn to his country's past. That past held a long and obscure record of subterranean intrigue which had had for its purpose, always, alterations in the country's administrative forms; and when in the present year 1730 there once more cropped up the old, deep-rooted question of what should be Russia's order of State, and what her legal composition of Supreme Power, the resurrection came of the extinction of the Rurik-descended dynasty, and represented, therefore, an historical necessity rather than a political demand. Up to 1598 the Tsar of Moscow had been "Lord of the Land" rather than of the people: up to that time the people's conception of Sovereign Right had not been large enough to include the conception that it, the people, was a union of State, nor yet to include any sort of theory of popular freedom, since always the Church had taught that State authority was of God alone, and that the Divine Will could not be subjected to juridical definition, and that therefore any earthly incarnation of that Will stood above right and law, and was comprehensible only as an anomy. But then there had come the year 1598, when Russian political thought had found itself confronted with the difficulty that, though the Church's conception of the Supreme Power in a State might still be applicable to an hereditary "Tsar-Lord of the Land," it was not so easy to make an elected Tsar, a Tsar manifestly sprung of an earthly agency, a Tsar created solely of the "Land's" inhabitants, fit into the theory that a Supreme Power was exclusively a divinely-appointed instrument. With the result that there had come about a duality in the people's political attitude. Perplexed by Boris Godunov's appearance upon the scene, and wondering what had happened to the old-time Tsars, yet still contriving to preserve the Biblical, the purely abstract, conception of the original form of monarchical puissance, even though in the popular mind that conception was indissolubly and inevitably bound up with the idea of how best that puissance's oppression could be evaded, the people of the seventeenth century had come to differ from their predecessors in at all events initiating rebellions against their *boyaré* and superior-departmental officials, and the latter, in their turn, to differ from their predecessors in, at all events, learning, through bitter experience added to observation of neighbouring systems of government, a first notion of the advisability of accepting a Tsar on terms. But since this last-mentioned notion had been a notion emanating exclusively from the ruling class, and not at all from the people as a whole, and since that people had had only too much reason to hold its *boyarstvo* in distrust, the notion in question had shown a constant tendency to fade, and twice had become merged into a form of secret contract which, though figuring outwardly as voluntary bestowal of ruling power, had found inward manifestation in the direction of relaxation of administrative authority. For as a matter of fact the phenomenon had been but an attempt to escape from the position between two fires which inevitably had become imposed upon the country through the latter's involuntary, instinctive attempts to cut down the unhealthy growth of its Supreme Power: and now what we see in the affair of 1730 is a seventh scheme for a clique's extortion, through a covert method, of State freedom on terms, and a fourth attempt by a clique to, for the State's benefit, compel the Sovereign to place upon the Sovereign's power a formal limitation admitting of no ambiguity. The real origin of this unsuccessful experiment we may assign to the people's distrust of ill-trained political authority, no matter what its form, and to a nervousness resultant from a popular loss of faith in the country's ruling class. And the real origin of the experiment's failure we may assign to that ruling class's internal dissensions.

Hence nothing in the way of popular liberty sprang from the movement. For a time, true, it stimulated the *dvorianstvo* to political thought, and even its failure did not wholly damp or extinguish the dominant *motif* of the *dvorianstvo's* policy; but, for all that, its ultimate result was temporarily (until the close of Anna's reign) to place that *motif* in abeyance, and permanently to give it a different bent.

Russia's history contains few murkier pages than Anna's term of rule: and the murkiest blot on that page is Anna herself. Tall and stout, masculine of feature rather than feminine, she was one in whom a naturally hard nature had become still further hardened through the factors of an early widow-hood, of many years spent amongst the diplomatic wiles and amorous gallantries of the Courlander court, and of service as the puppet alternately of Russia, of Prussia, and of Poland. Hence, landed in Moscow, at the age of thirty-seven, with no qualifications whatsoever for her new position, but only a taste for cruelty, an indifferently developed intellect, and an inordinate appetite for the gross pleasures and grosser diversions denied her until her chance transference from obscure Mitau to a throne girt with irresponsible power, she proceeded wholly to surrender herself to the novel delights of banquets and galas, and to mingle barbarism with extravagance so crudely as to make foreign observers absolutely gasp with amazement. Nor ever, even for a single moment, could she dispense with jesters and "gossips," and the Empire would be ransacked from end to end when fresh ones were wanted, so wholly was it the case that their stream of babble alone could deaden in her her sense of isolation in her new country, and, for all that she had had constantly to be on her guard there, her home-sickness for her old land. A peculiarly favourite diversion of hers was to pick out one or more of the male members of her court, and set herself to humiliate them, to gloat over their discomfiture, and to ridicule their mistakes. And that although she herself once commanded that the eleven members of the Holy Synod should be divided into two equal quorums, a Great Russian and a Little! Moreover, such was her distrust of her Russian subjects that con-stantly she had her person guarded by retainers imported from Mitau and other Courlander localities, and thereby caused German officials to accumu-late in Moscow like chaff sprinkled from a leaky sack, so that they overran the court, besieged the throne, and grabbed every administrative post to which any sort of a salary was attached. Nor, in allocating its forces, did this parasitic rabble of immigrants neglect to see that they clung most to the skirts of the period's two most powerful patrons, as represented by Biron, a man commonly known as "the rascally Courlander," and said to be limited, in his abilities, to an expert knowledge of dogs, and by "the rascally Courlander's equally "rascally" Livonian understudy and potential rival, Count Löwenfeld, *Oberstallmeister* (Master of the Horse), a man universally known to be treacherous, venal, and a gambler. So at a court of dissipated surroundings, and of amusements which centred chiefly upon the brilliant galas ably organised by the *Oberstallmeister's* younger brother, the *Oberhofmarschall*, of Anna's establishment, a man even worse than his elder, this Teutonic herd ate and drank to repletion, and had the cost of its festive doings defrayed out of such arrears of taxation as could by any means be wrung from the wretched populace, Thus Anna's court proved fully five or six times as expensive as Peter's court had been, though since Peter's day the State's income had, so far from increasing, diminished to the point of causing a foreign ambassador to record: "So unheard-of is the luxury of this court that the Treasury now standeth bereft of its last groat, and no man can be paid his due." Naturally, the work of administration suffered in proportion. In 1731 the Privy Council was abolished, but upon that even an enlarged Senate was found insufficient to exercise the necessary governmental influence, and Ostermann created a Cabinet of three members (he himself was its president, and under him, silently, all-powerfully inspired by him, sat the insignificant Prince Cherkasski and the equally insignificant Chancellor Golovkin), and then re-created that parody of a Privy Council into a sort of private bureau, an institution which, sitting under the Empress, superintended supremely important legislative matters, arranged for contracts for the supply of game for the court's consumption, and revised her Majesty's bills for furbelows. Which "Cabinet," being, as it was, the organ of an independent, irresponsible Supreme Will, and also a body with no juridical basis, soon threw the competencies and operations of the country's principal institutions into such a state of confusion as thoroughly to typify both the devious mentality of Ostermann, that "Cabinet's" creator, in general, and the character of Anna's sinister reign in particular. With its one hand that body used the Crown's manifestos for purposes of self-advertisement and self-praise, and as excuses for baiting the aristocracy in the people's presence: with its other hand it used the prison and the scaffold for removing prominent Russian nobles like the Golitzins and the Dolgorukis, and *donos* and the Chancellory of Secret Inquisition (an institution descended from the old

Preobrazhenski Prikaz which Peter II. had closed down) for extracting from the general community at least a show of respect for a Power which, without those safeguards, would at once have stood in imminent peril. Whence espionage became the most fashionable of all branches of State employment, and, owing to its working, social exclusion could speedily be inflicted upon anyone who appeared to be growing either inconvenient or dangerous. Even prelates were not spared, and we read of at least one case of a monk undergoing impalement. Banishment too now came into vogue, and was carried out on such a widespread and well-organised system that the number of persons transported during the reign has been estimated at at least 20,000—of whom over a fourth disappeared without trace, since either names were not registered before the victims' dispatch to their Siberian destinations, or the victims were dispatched under changed names, or they were dealt with from the first under none at all, so that even the Secret Chancellory later could not identify them. And, in proportion, the industry alike of State and of people went to pieces: commerce declined rapidly, large areas of land lay unworked for five or six years at a time, and an intolerable system of military service sent so many of the inhabitants of the frontier provinces scurrying across the borders that a foreign observer declares some of those provinces to have looked "as though they had been ravaged by war or a pestilence." All of which factors weakened the people's taxpaying powers, and exhausted the sources of the Treasury's income, until by 1732 the 2,500,000 roubles estimated to accrue from that year's indirect imposts and customs duties were collected to the tune of 187,000 only. At length, therefore, this and other instances did lead Biron to turn his eyes to the many millions of taxatory arrears still owing from previous years, and to add to the already existent misfortunes of bad harvests, wholesale famine, widespread pestilence, and extensive fire losses by enmeshing the people in a network of fiscal deficits the clearing off of which called for fittings out of distraint expeditions, for arrestings of provincial administrators, for leavings of *pomiestchiki* and *starosti* to starve in gaol, and for subjectings of *krestiané* to *pravozh* and seizure of chattels. Practically the system was a repetition of the Tartar raids, save for the fact that now the raiders' base of operations was the raided's own capital city. Groans and lamentations filled the land. A group of soldiers and others, we read, summed up the situation thus: "Biron and Münnich now have gotten unto themselves power, and we are undone, and in the hands of foreigners and tyrants who levy toll upon the blood and the tears of their needy underlings so that they may sate their own drunkenness and gluttony, and rate the Russian *krestianin* at less than a dog. All the State is in ruins. Nowhere is corn growing. And all this because a woman hath gotten herself unto the Tsarship, and leadeth therein—ah, such a life!" But though the people's hatred of the German-staffed Government grew and grew, the Government possessed a sure stay and support in the Guards—and not the less so because during the first year of Anna's rule the Government had added a third corps to the existing Brigade, a corps drawn from the *dvorianin* militia of the Ukraine, and called, according to the system of military nomenclature initiated by Peter I., after the village near Moscow where it had pleased Anna to establish her principal residence. And inasmuch, also, as *Oberstallmeister* Löwenfeld, commander of the new Izmailovski Guards, was allowed at any time to recruit subordinate officers from Livonia, Esthland, and Courland equally with from Russia, the people of the Muscovite Empire thereby found themselves confronted with a fresh fact constituting a challenge to national sentiment, whilst upon it followed the further fact that, since Biron and his following owed much to the Guards for the Guards' assistance in upholding the foreign yoke, it was from the Guards' staff that officers now were selected to lead the detachments charged with recovery of taxatory arrears, and the country had to endure the spectacle of the once cherished flower of Peter's army acting as hangmen and constables for the benefit of an upstart adventurer, and shielding with their loyal bayonets villainies rendered possible only by the impotence of the villainies' victims. But the gang of German Governmental folk had not been indulging in these proceedings for long before the Polish Ambassador overheard talk on the subject, and intimated to Magnan, then Secretary to the French Embassy, that in his opinion the Russians would shortly deal out to Biron and his Germans what once had been dealt out to the false Dmitri and his Poles. And to this opinion the Polish Ambassador held even when Magnan replied: "Not so. Remember that those Poles had not behind them the Russian Guards." Well, as a matter of fact, it was a heavy price that the *dvorianin*-composed Brigade was destined to pay for the "humble petition" presented to Anna on 25 February, the petition "humbly requesting" re-establishment of the Autocracy, and for the splendid banquet accorded it on 4 April, since the German faction had yet to show it in full the rehabilitated Autocracy's reverse side.

Not that Biron shared openly or directly in the administrative rôle which his creatures played. No, he crept to and fro behind the throne like a footpad, and left it to his two most prominent henchmen, Vice-Chancellor Ostermann and Field-Marshal Münnich, to figure before the public with a policy of seeking to stifle the ever-growing popular discontent with home mismanagement, and to keep a Russian Sovereign's Teutonic Government in its place, through resounding announcements of foreign-gained diplomatic achievements and prestige. Not that the latter constituted a task peculiarly difficult of accomplishment, seeing that all that was required was to play France against Austria, to play against one another two Powers mutually hostile, but both anxious to win the favour of Russia, whose magnificent Petrine army still stood untouched by the universal process of Russian internal disruption. Moreover, Münnich and Ostermann, Russia's leading exponents of the arts of war and diplomacy, received, as luck would have it, two particularly good chances of showing how much better they could do these things than could Russia's own native "boors and sluggards." For, in the first place, there died in 1732 August II., King of Poland, Peter I.'s futile ex-friend and ally; and that event gave rise to a struggle for the Polish throne in which Russia took the side of the son of the late king against the French candidate, old Stanislaus Leszczynski. Yet whereas the similar conjunction of circumstances of 1691 had called for transport of the then irregular Russian army no further than to the Lithuanian frontier, with the object merely of enabling August to hold the French Prince temporarily in check, the present case was that 50,000 of Russia's reformed, properly disciplined regulars had to be moved into the very kingdom of Poland itself. And though, when these forces reached their destination, they had the advantage of being placed, not under a German commander this time, but under the Scotch General Lacy, the best of Russia's available foreign leaders, and a man adored by his troops, the enterprise was so badly managed from St. Petersburg, and Ostermann's crony, the "rascally" *Oberstallmeister* Löwenfeld (sent on in advance to prepare the ground) soon placed the Russian army in such an impossible position, and that army was so handicapped through Lacy being replaced with Münnich, that, after four months had been wasted in bottling up Stanislaus within the walls of Dantzig, and over 8000 men had been lost in the process, and Ostermann's Austrian friends had failed to come to the support of their Russian allies, France and her allies took up the cudgels on Poland's behalf, declared war upon Austria, speedily stripped that State of Naples, Sicily, Lotharingia, and most of Lombardy, and compelled the renowned, all-powerful diplomatist of St. Petersburg to dispatch a further force of 20,000 under Lacy before his allies could be rescued from their pitiable position on the Rhine. And as regards the second example of outstanding Ostermann-Münnich talent displayed, we behold it when circumstances of the Polish War, added to raids by the Crimean Turks, compelled hostilities to be declared also against the Ottoman Empire. On this occasion it was hoped that, aided by Austria and Persia, Russia would conduct the campaign with such ease and dispatch as speedily to remove the unpleasant impression caused by Russia's abandonment of Peter the

Great's conquests on the Caspian, and also finally choke off Turkey from interfering further with Polish affairs, and enable Russia to evade fulfilment of the onerous conditions of the Pruth Treaty of 1711: but the truth is that, though overweighted already with his duties as War Minister, added to his functions of scrutiniser of petitions presented to the Crown, the ambitious Münnich advocated entry upon the Turkish venture less for the above-mentioned reasons than for the reason that he hoped to see the affair cleanse his military escutcheon of its lingering stain of Dantzig. And at first he did so far succeed that the Russian arms won a stroke or two—thrice invaded and devastated the hitherto invincible Crimean-Tartar stronghold, captured Azov and Otchakov, proved victorious at Stavukhan, and occupied Khotin and Jassy. Hence, after halting in the latter city to celebrate the overthrow of the Principality of Moldavia, Münnich felt his breast so swell with heroism against Turkey as to spread his wings for further flight—he built, at Briansk-on-Desna, a dockyard which should enable ships to be rapidly constructed for passage down the Dnieper to the Black Sea, and, badly put together though these vessels were, so badly, indeed, that they did not even last out the campaign, took, in 1737, Otchakov, and went on to boast that if only he could blow up the Dnieper rapids meanwhile, the world would, during the following year, see a Russian flotilla sail past the mouths of the Dniester and the Danube, and reach Constantinople, where at once the Turkish Christians would rise, 20,000 Russian troops would be landed on the Bosphorus, and the Sultan would take to flight! But though, at the Austro-Russo-Turkish congress convened at Nemirov in 1737, Russia at first demanded that the Turks should surrender to her the Tartar portions of the Crimea, and the region between Kuban and the mouths of the Danube, and also recognise Moldavia and Wallachia as independent States, the casualties of over 100,000 sustained in the steppe country, the Crimea, and the Turkish forts zone, added to the fact that even his miracles of valour had not prevented Münnich from throwing many millions of roubles to waste, led to Russia's Government eventually entrusting Russia's interests at the conference to the not over-friendly offices of Villeneuve, the French representative in Constantinople, a man whom Russia's own Constantinople representative subsequently declared to be, at best, a negotiator of second-rate ability. However that may be, Villeneuve at least made such hay of Russia's cause that during the peace negotiations (the Treaty finally being signed at Belgrade in 1739) he procured for her, as her reward for her many victories, sacrifices, and exertions, the humiliating conditions, (1) that though Azov was to be ceded to her, it was to be ceded only when its fortifications had been razed to the ground, (2) that she was for ever to be debarred from sailing either warlike or mercantile vessels on the Black Sea, and (3) that the Sultan was still not to be subject to the ruler of Russia as his Emperor. So much for the Briansk flotilla, for the three successful Crimean raids, for the stormings of Otchakov and Stavukhan, and for, in general, Munnich's lighthearted Constantinople throw! Nevertheless, Villeneuve received for his "services" the Order of St. Andrew and 15,000 *thalers* (though at least he had the decency to refuse to accept these emoluments until the "services" in question had been finally completed), whilst to the lady sharer of his fortunes there was apportioned a diamond ring. More than once has Russia concluded an untoward peace; but never has she put her hand to a more comically shameful treaty than the treaty signed at Belgrade in 1739. Possibly never again will she sign a document of the sort.[1] The chief credit for the costly farce must go to the first-rate talents of Ostermann, the then Government's prime diplomatic expert, and of Münnich, the then Government's prime expert in the art of war, and of those two experts' Russian and German sympathisers. And that the two experts received adequate reward at all times for their labours would appear from the fact that the many and various duties performed by Grand-Admiral Ostermann brought him in what would now be equivalent to 100,000 roubles a year.

Meanwhile the highly combustible heap of popular discontent which had been accumulating for the past ten years was still smouldering, even if kept from breaking into open flame by the people's agelong habit of respect for the current wielder of the Supreme Power, and by the fact that certain of the *shliachetstvo's* requests of 1730 had now attained fulfilment, and by a national sense of shame that the German yoke resting upon the nation's neck had been placed there by the nation itself. But on Anna's death all tongues became unloosed, and the more so because Biron acted as he did as soon as he became Regent. The tongues to clamour the loudest of all were those of the Guards, and an officer never could encounter any of his men in the streets without those men at once proceeding to fill his ears with protests that Biron should have been made Regent over the heads of the Emperor's kinsfolk, and with reproaches that the Brigade's officers in general should have failed to forestall such a *dénouement*. And this sort of thing gave rise to such incidents as that one day when the pro-Bironist Cabinet Minister Bestuzhev-Rumin saw a certain Captain Brovtsin arguing with men of his company at a spot on Vasilii Island,[2] the spectacle so enraged the Minister that he converted himself into a temporary constable, drew

---

[1] Of course the author wrote these words before the year 1917.
[2] One of the islands in the Neva on which St. Petersburg is built.

his sword, and pursued Brovstin until the latter was fain to take cover in Münnich's residence hard by; whilst on another occasion, when a lieutenant-colonel who habitually discussed the events of 1730 persuaded some of his colleagues and others to frame a petition saying that the Russian *shliachet-stvo* desired to see the Prince-Father appointed Regent, and asked Cabinet Minister Prince Cherkasski (one of the *shliachetstvo's* leaders in the earlier affair of 1730) to act as the document's presenter to the Empress, the Minister, instead, went and informed Biron of what was going forward. Nevertheless it was seldom that Guards discussions of the sort included any reference to the infant Emperor, and probably this came of the fact that already the officers, even the most junior of them, had seen sufficient of the throne's *de facto* occupant to dismiss the point with the contemptuous comment that no son of a Duke of Brunswick would allow the throne to leave German hands, and the Regency question, therefore, was immaterial. What the throne really needed was a Sovereign capable of dispensing with the Regency and the German element alike, and in time the national sense of anti-Teutonism so affected the whole people as to give rise to a new current in its political motives and turn all men's minds towards Peter I.'s only surviving daughter. We read that in the very act of leaving the ceremony of swearing allegiance to the infant Emperor some Guardsmen fell to discussing the Tsarevna Elizabeth, and a corporal said to his comrades: "To what a shameful pass are we now come! Remember ye, however, what our Emperor Peter did effect in the State, and that even yet we have here amongst us that crowned father's daughter, the Lady Tsarevna." And this political *motif* spread from Guards circles to inferior social circles with which the former were in touch, and brought about such an incident as that when the formal announcement of the accession of Ivan Antonovitch and the appointment of Biron as Regent reached Schlüsselberg, a clerk in the Ladoga canal works-office was seen to smile derisively, and, though reminded by his colleagues that the announcement meant they he and they alike would have to swear allegiance to the persons named, exclaimed: "Never will I do that! Unto Elizabeth, the daughter of Peter I., alone do I owe allegiance." Which incident shows that even the humblest officials now had a mind to form their own political opinions. Also, it explains why the Guards' revolution of the night of 25 November, 1741, brought Elizabeth to the throne with such ease. Yes, clearly that revolution had behind it a passionate ebullition of patriotism, an almost frenzied display of national sentiment. The fact alone can explain why everywhere the men who for years had been chafing under German rule broke into German houses, and even went to the lengths of thrashing Chancellor Ostermann, Field-Marshal Münnich, and others of the type, and, even when Elizabeth so far yielded to their prayers for relief from the German yoke as to banish, not all, but most, of the Teutonic element, remained unsatisfied, and demanded that every German without exception should be cleared out of the country. For the same reason it must have been that during the Finnish period of the war with Sweden such a riot arose in the camp at Viborg that, to quell the outbreak, General Keith had to seize the first rioter encountered, send for a priest, and straightway have the culprit prepared for execution.

CHAPTER XIV

The significance of the Court Revolution Period—The relation of the first few post-Petrine Governments to Peter's reforms—Those Governments' importance—The peasant question—*Oberprokuror* Anisin Maslov—The *dvorianstvo* and serf-right—*Dvorianstvo* service exemptions—The *dvorianstvo's* educational standard and terms of service—Consolidation of *dvorianin* land-ownership—Abolition of sole succession—A *dvorianin* credit bank—The *ukaz* on peasant absconders—Extension of serf-right—Class purification of *dvorianin* land-ownership—Abolition of *dvorianin* compulsory service—The third formation of serf-right—Serf-right in practice.

UNDER the Empress Anna and the infant who succeeded her a change took place in the attitude of the Russian *dvorianstvo*. This was because, under the influences which we have been studying, that class adopted a new political *motif*, and turned its attention to new questions raised in connection with the order of State according as the nation recovered from the shock of the Petrine reforms sufficiently to take stock of things once more, and its more thoughtful members discovered that the existent plethora of legislation lacked the supremely important element of legality. Indeed, it was the resultant quest for that element that enabled all parties, despite their mutual hostility, to unite in at least one common interest even amid the clash of opinions of 1730. Owing to the upper social classes' political amateurishness and inexperience, the events of that year were followed by the retribution of the Biron *régime*, and by the fact that Menshikov's and the Dolgorukis' Russian non-legality gave place to the German non-legality of such men as "the rascally Courlander" and the Löwenfelds; and all this eventually united the Russian *dvorianstvo* sufficiently in spirit to put forth a demand additional to the demand for legality. True, the new demand was less complex than the former one, but it admitted of further expansion, since its source was the fact that *dvorianin* circles began to develop a sense of national honour, and a feeling of resentment that proud hereditary nobles like the Princes Golitzin and Dolgoruki should have had to withdraw from their administrative tasks in favour of chance-come *parvenus*. It was a *motif* which led the few surviving remnants of the born aristocracy, though still clinging to their patrician pride, to draw closer to the general body of the *shliachetstvo*, and so to slough much of their *dvorianin* exclusiveness,

316

There is a story that once when Khrapovitski, the Secretary of Catherine II.'s later days, was discussing with his Imperial mistress "the dread which the *boyaré* of the times of Elizabeth Petrovna inspired in the then ruling authorities," Catherine, who was engaged in paring her finger-nails, replied: "Yes, but since then the *boyaré* have had their claws blunted, and can no longer rend": and the story shows that though, in this conversation concerning the possibility of a revival of the *boyarin* claims of 1730, those claims could, some fifty years later, be spoken of with a smile as a nuisance for ever banished from the State, they still were troubling the State like an uneasy dream. Amongst other results of the Annine-German yoke we must number the fact that there then arose a general prejudice against all and sundry of the Reformer's disciples, and likewise a general sense of nationalist discontent. For the mere fact that Peter's most zealous agents of reform had all of them been foreigners was sufficient, in the eyes of many, to identify the continued reform movement with foreign rule, whilst, *vice versa*, both that movement's advocates and the foreign element looked upon a nationalist *régime* as bound to entail reaction, and to throw back progress to pre-Petrine antiquity. In fact, even Peter II.'s re-transference of the court to Moscow they considered to be a return to the darkness of the old Muscovite *régime*, and Peter II.'s words, "The seas I will not sail as my grandfather did," to foreshadow a whole programme of political retreat. Well, if the foreign element thought to itself, "The grandson is going to set at nought all the devisings of his glorious grandsire," certainly Anna's foreign and domestic policy, plus the doings of her nephew's subsequent Administrations, proved that a German "expert" could undo a Petrine "devising" quite as thoroughly as could any self-taught Russian official. Hence the *dvorianstvo* believed its best hope of avoiding political trouble to lie in legislative settlement of the more important demands and aspirations formulated in some of the *proekti* of 1730. Owing to various exemptions from service and seigniorial obligations which I have still to expound, the *pomiestchik* was largely brought back from the *milieu* of the regiment and the metropolis to the *milieu* of the rural manor, where at last he had leisure to realise what it meant to be a Russian subject, and to develop a national sense, and so, after Peter's death, to go on to further mental stages or attitudes, from a scheme for limiting the Supreme Power through a Council composed of leading aristocrats to an idea of giving the *dvorianstvo* as a whole a larger constitutional share in the working of the Chief Administration. And when the oligarchism of the leading aristocracy and the constitutionalism of the *shliachetstvo* alike proved failures the *pomiestchik* next developed such a sense of true patriotism as educated him to conceive that, though he belonged to the particular class that he did, he must cease to be too ambitious as to that class's State position, and showed him that Russians were better managing their own affairs than letting those affairs be managed by a band of alien administrators. Which reversion from restless, tentative debates on the subject of European constitutions to consideration of the country's real conditions, and to a quest of generally intelligible class interests, created in the *dvorianin* a political incentive destined to hold good for the next seventeen years, to leave definite traces both upon Russia's State order and upon Russia's social system, and both directly and indirectly to stimulate the *dvorianstvo* to take a new view alike of service of the State and of conduct of rural industry. The effect of this change upon the history of our State and our community was all the greater in that, though the political dreams of the men of 1730 faded, the political rôle henceforth played in events by that *dvorianin*-composed force, the Guards, affected Russian history right up to the middle of the nineteenth century.

Hence the State position of the *dvorianstvo* came to be a position closely connected with the political rôle which I have outlined, and with the needs of the State as those needs were understood by the first few post-Petrine Governments. The chief anxiety besetting each such Government was the condition of State and popular industry. Previously, Peter's feverish activity had sufficiently masked the exhaustion of the national resources to mask also the intolerable fiscal burdens imposed upon the people's labour, even though as long as a year before his death certain foreign ambassadors had detected a taxatory decline, and therefore a coming end to the country's power of taxatory production, and decided that the only financial resource capable of further expansion was the Tsar's despotic power over, and disregard of, his subjects' right of property! But as soon as Peter was gone the men who had been his helpers revealed the truth concerning the lamentable results of his over-tension of the popular labour, and told a tale not merely of the people's taxatory exhaustion, but also of impending ruin to the people's State. In particular did *Prokurator-General* Yaguzhinski find himself with no choice but to lay before the Empress a hastily framed, but strongly worded, memorandum which, after painting a gloomy picture of the situations created by bad harvests, mortality through famine, devastating collections of poll-tax, wholesale pauperisation, and wholesale emigration to Poland and the Don basin and the country of the Bashkirs, wound up its review of the imbroglio with the warning that, "should matters thus continue, then will every son of the Russian land have to take thought for that land, lest negligent direction lead our glorious Empire to eternal loss and calamity." In view of this, the Supreme Privy Council considered the questions raised by Yaguzhinski, and, on 9 January, 1727, set forth its opinion in a programmatical *ukaz* which, beginning with the despondent (but none the less positive) statement that Peter the Great's efforts to organise the nation's spiritual and secular affairs had largely come to nothing, "through those matters not having since been actually commanded," and that things were everywhere more or less amiss, went on to call for speedy amendment, and to specify as the first item to be taken in hand a general review of Peter's reforms which might lead to their beginnings being completed, and to their completions being corrected. After which the Council went on to scrutinise the various projects and suggestions outlined therewith in the Council's *ukaz*, and, finally, to issue ordinances for rendering the collection of poll-tax less onerous; for removing the regiments from their present rural quarters, and re-distributing them to urban cantonments; for cheapening the administrative system by annulment both of the College of Manufactures, of the post of *Rechtmeister*,[1] of all chancellories and bureaus found to be superfluous, and of the Aulic Courts; for adding the duties of tax-collection and legal dispensation to the duties already incumbent upon *voevodi* and *gubernatori*; and, "the better to defend from the same our townsfolk," for placing the new urban magistracies under the latter of these two categories of officials. Also, the *ukaz* of 9 January mooted the radical question of the best manner of gathering in the country's taxation, and offsetting it against the existing deficit—whether by collecting it from all revisional souls, or from working-hands alone, or from *dvori*, or from *tiagla* (arable lands attached to certain *dvori*), or from all classes of land without exception: and eventually an Order in Council delegated the matter, for debate and decision, to a Commission of the Council itself and the Senate, with a proportion of upper- and middle-*shliachtich* assessors, and bade those Commissioners bring their labours to a conclusion by the following September. In other words, the Privy Council shuffled off on to others all responsibility for the question, whilst the Commission on to whom the responsibility was shuffled did nothing at all, and scarcely so much as sat. Nor did subsequent post-Petrine Governments do much to delve to the root of things, to probe throughout the principles and the problems of reform, and to tackle the existent difficulties. None the less there had resulted from Peter's costly innovations a chronic deficit in the country's budget, whilst the process of extorting taxes to mask that deficit had, in its turn, caused arrears the attempted recovery of which had increased still further the poverty of the taxpayers and this, again, had increased still further the taxpayers' arrears —the two factors together keeping the deficit in continuous existence. In other words, Peter's reformed institutions had proved powerless to break

[1] See p. 187.

the financial charmed circle—rather, they had augmented the difficulties besetting all ways of escape, and caused affairs to be managed, if not worse than under the old *Prikazi*, at all events no better. In 1726, for instance, when the provincial-administrative system of collecting the Treasury's dues was overhauled, the Senatorial revisor appointed for the purpose discovered that in one case some revenue-and-expenditure registers had been replaced with rough lists made out on mouldy scraps of paper, and that certain "thievings and ravishings in no wise to be understood" had taken place. Well, the revisor took an extreme course. He hanged out of hand both the clerk who had framed the lists and the amanuensis who had copied them out. Even the central institutions failed to set a good accountancy example. True, for a long time the Petrine manner of auditing the Treasury's funds was rigidly adhered to, and observed as a tradition—even as late as 1744 we find a soldier picturesquely commenting upon the manner in which that monarch had been "wont to choke over every *kopek*"; but, for all that, the standard of State accountancy began to decline from Peter's death, and went on doing so until some time after Elizabeth had ascended the throne, even though she tirelessly asserted that she meant to have her father's financial rules preserved intact. A particularly glaring instance of this deterioration is seen in 1748, since, when the Senate then ordered the *Kammer-Collegium* to furnish a revenue-and-expenditure statement for the year 1742, it found the difference between the statement and an earlier one to amount to 1,000,000 roubles, whilst in 1749, on the Senate ordering the *Collegium* similarly to furnish a statement for the years 1743-7, it was long before the statement could be extracted at all, and when it was extracted it was extracted only as the result of informing the *Collegium* that, in case of the return continuing to be not forthcoming, its, the *Collegium's*, president and members would receive a visit from an *Unteroffizier* and a squad of soldiers, and be kept prisoners in the building until the matter had been liquidated. These methods of State book-keeping had for their worst results a periodical perplexity on the part of the Government as to how much cash was available, and even as to where it was. Thus, when, in the year 1726, 30,000 roubles were required for building works at Kronstadt, and enquiry was made, it was not until every single provincial office where there could possibly be any funds existent had been ransacked that the *Kammer-Collegium* was able to forward even as much as 20,000 roubles; whilst in 1748, though the *Staats-Kontora*, or Department of Expenditure, was holding accumulated some unaccounted-for sums amounting to 3,000,000 roubles which, by 1761, had swelled to over 8,000,000, the Department still had to meet every demand with an assertion that sources and means of rectifying the State deficit still were lacking, "in that sendings of money from the *gubernii* have rendered the *gubernii* needy, and despoiled them, until they no longer hold so much as the wherewithal for their own outgoings." And the prime factor, above all others, which helped to maintain the deficit was the Supreme Power, for Elizabeth amassed and hoarded Treasury funds as though she had a mind eventually to flee the country, and take them with her—leaving her Ministers, meanwhile, to make ends meet as best they could, and therefore hastening the time when, every possible source of direct taxation having become exhausted, other, and more stable, sources would need to be sought for. Those sources the Government found in Treasury monopolies of salt and liquor, and the credit for those monopolies' invention is due to Senator Count P. I. Shuvalov, who was practically a reincarnation of the Petrine *pribyltschik-vymishlennik*, as at once a dabbler in finance, a codifier of laws, an organiser of land systems, an authority upon military matters, a farmer of taxes, a master of engineering, an expert in gunnery (he is said to have invented a "secret" *haubitze*, or howitzer, which worked wonders during the Seven Years' War), and a man who had a ready-made answer for every question and every difficulty. Most of all, though, was he always prepared to deal with questions of finance—never, in that connection, was he without an *ad hoc* scheme waiting in his pocket. And now he came forward with such a scheme, a scheme warranted to prove an inexhaustible means of guaranteeing the cost of the army's upkeep, a constant resource towards multiplication of the Treasury's revenue, and a system "applicable in rotation, and for ever, and without any end." And this infinitely-rotary method of acquiring the needed funds lay in a proposed Treasury monopoly of the sales of salt and liquor, with prices of those commodities raised or lowered as circumstances might demand. For, Shuvelov argued, everyone, even the taxpayer, required salt, whilst, as regards enhancing the price of liquor, the spendthrift would always neglect to husband his money, and squander his substance as readily upon dear liquor as upon cheap; and since the price of salt varied according to locality (it ranged from three *kopeki* per *pud* to fifty), the Treasury could always reap an annual profit of 750,000 roubles if it made twenty-one *kopeki* the average, whilst an addition of another fourteen *kopeki*, and a sale of the commodity at thirty-five, would raise the Treasury's profits (provided that the present annual demand of 7,500,000 *pudi* remained unabated) from 700,000 roubles to 1,000,000 roubles, or even to more. So in 1750 Shuvalov's scheme was established, and by 1756, the year when the Seven Years' War broke out, the price of salt had risen to fifty *kopeki* per *pud*, or a price which, when translated into modern values, shows salt to have been sold at six *kopeki* per pound as against the one *kopek* of to-day! Naturally, however, the salt income waxed apace. Yet it did not invariably accord with the estimates—in some years sales fell off, and consumption stopped short at about 1,000,000 *pudi*; and the most likely reason of this is that the years concerned were years of leanness, and that during them the population either largely dispensed with salt or supplemented the Treasury article with contraband stuff, or with a zinc-adulterated mixture—both of these being illegal resources which such a tax was bound, respectively, to encourage and to bring into the market. For his conception of the project (the surplus profits from which went to lighten the poll-tax, and lightened it to the extent of from two to five *kopeki* per soul) Shuvelov received 30,000 (200,000) roubles. As a matter of fact, his device only repeated the old Muscovite financial experiment of 1646,[1] save that, unlike that scheme of Peter's, its aim was once more to make indirect taxation predominate over indirect exactions. A Government notion that was more in harmony with the spirit of the Reformer was the notion of adding a credit element to the currency, a notion born originally of the fact that when the Government intervened in the Seven Years' War in 1757, and found, once again, every available source of State income to have come to an end, the ever-ready Shuvelov presented himself as usual, and this time proposed the minting of some small copper coinage only half as heavy as the ordinary issue, so that the Treasury, for its part, would save some 3,500,000 roubles, and the citizen, for his, would have the comforting reflection that at least the new money was twice as easy to carry in the pocket. But in the main the post-Petrine Governments failed altogether to maintain Peter I.'s high level in any of the spheres of State organisation to which he had given special attention; and though a Commission on Commerce sat under Ostermann's presidency, and long wrestled with fiscal monopolies and tax-farming concessions and so forth, and strove to extend the area of toll-free trade, and to regulate imports and exports, and to support the bill rate, and to frame a bill tariff, it effected little for the reason that Russian merchants exported little, and that the whole of the country's import trade was in the hands of foreigners who, as in Peter's day, and as one of themselves wrote at the time, "sucked the blood of the Russian people as though they had been gadflies, and then departed elsewhither." Again, although Peter had always striven to clothe his army in Russian cloth, and, for the purpose, had conceded exceedingly generous leasehold terms to his cloth factories, it was not until many years after his death that Russia stood competent to dispense with English and Prussian material, and to cease sending out of the country payments of money to the amount annually of hundreds

[1] See vol. iii. p. 230.

of thousands of roubles. Besides, trade had heavy customs dues and petty tolls to bear—the latter came to number, altogether, seventeen, as an ancient Russian heritage retained and re-bequeathed by Peter; whilst of course the usual toll-collectors' tricks and abuses obtained. So in 1753, to remedy this, Shuvalov proposed total abolition of direct imposts, and above all of the excise dues, and replacement of them with an increased *ad valorem* tax upon imports and exports—the tax to be fixed at thirteen *kopeki* per rouble's-worth of goods, instead of at five as heretofore. And, sure enough, the tax, as levied upon the 9,000,000 roubles' worth of goods a year, not only enabled the Treasury to transfer a source of income from one basis to another without incurment of loss, but also so far justified Shuvalov's calculations as to net for that Treasury an annual profit of over 250,000. Moreover, it was a measure which adhered to Peter's rule (little good though that rule had ever done Peter himself) of gaining profit for the Treasury without meanwhile overburdening the people, since in those days the chief item of Russian trade was Russian raw material, and Russia held practically monopolies in her own lines of such material, and therefore, whilst elaboration of that material into valuable finished goods involved only a negligible addition to the export duty, and did not check exportation, the Russian producer or purveyor obtained relief from his burden of tolls without simultaneously having the demand for his merchandise fall off, and the increased import duty in any case affected only the Treasury and the moneyed classes, since it was only to their order that goods were imported at all. In short, the Act constituted the one solitary successful financial measure which the first six reigns after Peter were privileged to behold. At the same time, even this outstanding tribute to the Reformer's memory did not enable his successors to maintain the country's military affairs at anything like the Poltava-Hango level: all writers and documents of the day refer to disorganisation in the post-Petrine army, and declare that its officers were poor in quality, and that the skill both of its infantry, its artillery, and its engineers declined to the point that Field-Marshal Lacy once had to report that the state of the forces was "exceeding sorry and pitiful," whilst "flights" both of trained soldiers from established regiments and of peasants from recruit squads became wholesale. Only the Seven Years' War, a school equalling, in costliness, the Swedish struggle, enabled Russia to re-brace the relaxed tension of her warlike energies. The plight of the fleet became more lamentable yet. In fact, so little attention was paid to that arm that it became the custom, as its Petrine stock of expert officers and men gradually gave out, to fill up the resultant gaps with recruits drawn from *terra firma*, from the military arm, whilst at all times its sixty line-of-battle ships merely ornamented harbours or figured at reviews—barely a score of their number could have put to sea. Hence before Anna had sat long upon the throne such irreparable and acknowledged ruin had come upon Russia's naval force that during the Swedish campaign of 1741 every one of her vessels had to remain in port, and in 1742 a hastily improvised squadron had to decline battle with a numerically weaker enemy flotilla.

Such were the achievements of the first few post-Petrine Governments! Never at any time did those Governments ask themselves what was the proper course to adopt with regard to Peter's reforms—whether those reforms ought to be continued, or whether they ought to be annulled. Not that the authorities left them in abeyance *in toto*. What happened was that the authorites never fitted themselves wholly and radically to complete those reforms, but either cancelled them in part, out of deference to current exigencies and fortuitous considerations, or allowed official diffidence or official neglect to throw their principal bearings out of gear, or permitted Governmental ignorance of the true state of Imperial affairs to delegate their execution to subordinate institutions too incompetent even to frame a correct or a trustworthy return. For example, although an *ukaz* issued by Catherine I. likened the *voevodi* of her day to "wolves breaking into a fold," the same *ukaz* could give those "wolves" charge of the urban magistracies, entrust them with collection of taxes, and commit to their authority the courts of second instance! Again, whereas in 1752 Elizabeth promulgated an *ukaz* beneficently designed to remit 2,500,000 roubles' worth of poll-tax arrears accumulated during the years 1724-47, and seized the occasion to proclaim that the Empire was prosperous beyond precedent, "in that its incomings, with the numbers of its people, do surpass those of late well-nigh by one-fifth," an *ukaz* of 16 August, 1760, had to give a pessimistic review of the Empire's affairs, and invite the Senate's earnest attention to "divers irregularities and illegalities of the foes who are abiding within our borders"; which foes, the document added, were some of the Empire's own administrators and legal dispensers, and particularly the Senators, in spite of the fact that, as the supreme legal authority in the Empire, those Senators "should reverence their land as their own parents, and in all things seek honour as a friend." Nevertheless the choleric, floridly prolix proclamation's hint glided over the Legislature's head with no more effect than if it had been a fine, intangible cloud. It was a period when only one factor could galvanise Russia's somnolent Governments into actual life: and that factor was the chronic deficit, the chronic lack of funds, which periodically did compel the authorities to glance into and probe the national life which they were supposed to be administering. An instance of how true it was (as every clear-sighted man could see) that, to quote the *ukaz* of 16 August, that life "had in it nought but chaos and many a circumstance of evil" is seen from the fact that though the Governments of Russia always had a force of 100,000 men employed in maintaining the balance of power in Europe, those men had not even tailors to make their uniforms, since the country's tailors were craftsmen who produced "only luxuries harmful unto the State," whilst, though countless wagons were built with Russian labour for the army's use, few such wagons ever reached their destination, and lack of public funds forbade foreign labour to be engaged for the purpose. Again, on any outbreak of war the departure of troops from the interior provinces always proved the signal for local outbreaks of brigandage and peasant unrest, and whenever the Senate had to dispatch copies of a decree, say, from Moscow to Saratov, the copies took months to perform the journey, and once when some "singing deacons" were conveyed from Moscow to St. Petersburg in order to participate in a Maundy Thursday performance given "by command" all other traffic between the two capitals had to be stopped until the deacons' journey had been completed. These items show that a foreign observer was well justified when he said that, for all her natural wealth, contemporary Russia stood culturally below all the other European Powers.

Another question which specially troubled and perplexed the statesmen of the day when considering the Empire's position was the peasant question. The first post-Petrine thinker to voice his thoughts on the subject of the *krestianin's* impoverished plight was Yaguzhinski, the Senate's hot-headed *Prokurator-General*: and his example was followed by the Supreme Privy Council, which took to debating the necessity of peasant relief, and actually grew heated as it did so. Yet, though the phrase "our poor peasantry" came to be stereotyped in administrative circles, the Government was anxious, in reality, less for the peasants themselves than because the all-prevalent peasant "flights" had a constant tendency to rob the Government of taxpayers and of military recruits. It was not only that peasants absconded by households. They absconded by whole villages. Any day an estate might find its every *krestianin* gone, and not a trace of the runaways left. In fact, merely during the period 1719–27 the estimated number of such absconders came near to reaching 200,000 (though the figure is an official one, and therefore may be taken as standing at a certain official distance from the facts), and everywhere the areas subject to epidemics of peasant "flights" increased, and whereas, in former times, serfs had usually removed themselves merely from one *pomiestie* estate to another, they now drifted as far as to the Don country, and the region of the Urals, and Siberian towns, and the Bashkir country, and the northern settlements of Old Believers, and

Moldavia and Poland. All this at last brought Catherine's Supreme Privy Council to the conclusion that, at the existing rate, the country would soon find itself without either taxpayers or recruits, and a memorandum framed by Menshikov and his colleagues bluntly voiced the incontrovertible truth that since the State rested upon its army, and the *krestianin* was not being sufficiently cared for, and the one stood bound up with the other as does the body with the soul, a lack of the one would inevitably end in a lack of the other. So for prevention of further peasant "flights" the rate of poll-tax was abated, all arrears were remitted, and runaways were informed that if they at once returned to their localities nothing would be done to them, but that if they returned later they would undergo corporal chastisement. But the evil began again—some of the returned runaways absconded a second time, and, on this occasion, were accompanied by comrades fired by their tales of the free life which could be attained in Poland or on the steppes. Moreover, it increasingly happened that the harshness of landowners or their stewards evoked peasant risings, and Elizabeth's reign proved especially fruitful in this respect—in particular as regards the monasterial peasantry. Constantly had punitive expeditions to be dispatched to the scene of such occurrences. Sometimes the troops beat the rebels; and sometimes the rebels beat the troops, whilst all the time there went on smouldering what, twenty or thirty years later, blazed up into the Pugachev conflagration. Of no effect were successive Governments' police measures, since those Governments only resorted to the methods employed everywhere and at all times by in-competent authorities, to the methods which, whilst seeking to lop away the results of an evil, aggravate continuously that evil's causes. At the same time, thinking administrators were not wholly wanting who discerned the trouble's radical origin. At all events, there came a time when from admini-strative circles there began to be evolved the idea that neither a people nor an individual taxpayer was a mere State industrial chattel, but an entity calling to be developed into an effective, competent union, or member of such a union, and to have its, or his, mutual rights and duties equitably defined. We have seen that Pososhkov's view of the serf was that the latter was a State-owned *krestianin* temporarily loaned to the *pomiestchik*, and that Pososhkov therefore insisted upon regularisation of landowner-peasant relations: and, in general, it was Pososhkov's period that first saw the national mentality turn to the thought of freeing the peasant, and safeguarding his personality, with, as that thought's immediate cause, the social differentia-tions born of the period, and of Peter's reforms. The same period has be-queathed to us a "petition on freedom" which, personally presented to the ruling authorities, it would seem, by a group of employees in *boyarin* households, appears to have had for its purpose a protest against the conduct of certain princes and *boyaré* who had been ill-treating the petitioners "as though we had been dwelling in Sodom and Gomorrah." Indeed, Peter had not been dead a year when the Supreme Privy Council initiated a debate on the advisability of licensing toll-free trading, "seeing that now our *kupeche-stvo* [1] also is demanding liberty"; and finally the straits in which the Treasury found itself brought the new ideas to the surface, and suggested tentative re-formation of the peasant question in general, and resurrection of the item of serf-right in particular. Hence it only remained for Shuvalov to show how the existent excise duties were working to the detriment of trader and peasant alike, and to add that "the State's chief strength doth lie in the persons ascribed unto assessment of poll-tax" (meaning that the principal power in the Russian Empire was, not the non-taxpaying classes as represented by the *dvorianstvo* and the clergy, but the underlying general mass of workers), and at once the Senate approved of the statement, and the Supreme Power openly commended it. All this shows how ripe for establishment upon a socio-political basis the peasant question had now become, and how widely both eminent and lowly social circles now looked upon a settlement of that question as the prime requisite towards equitable social reconstruction.

As a matter of fact, the idea expanded into practical proposals and definite juridical norms earlier even than Shuvalov's day, under the hand of Anisin Maslov, one of those statesmen who are apt to emerge during a darker period of a nation's life, and help to reconcile one, if not to the period, at all events to the country producing him. This was when, in his capacity of *Prokurator-General* to the Senate, Maslov laid before Biron and Anna a series of reports which arraigned the unscrupulous rascality of certain influential administrators, and included in the arraignment even some Senators, and led to Maslov having entrusted to him, as a task equally odious and arduous, a revision of the existent many-millioned arrears. And, again calling attention, during that task's performance, to the *krestianin's* wretched position, he persisted in doing so until the moral influence of his virile, impartial perseverance won over even the Empress and her favourite, moral pot-sherds though both of them were, and enabled his Cabinet, in 1734, to draw up, and to transmit to every *pomiestchik* in the realm, an Injunction commanding all landowners to make a declaration as to "in what condition they are maintaining their villages, and how best, in case of need, they may render aid unto the same." Also, as Maslov could not altogether rely upon the Cabinet's stability, he composed, and submitted to Anna, a *proekt* (draft) for a sternly-worded *ukaz*. That *ukaz* has recently been unearthed from our

---

[1] The merchant class.

archives, and we see that it laid the whole of the blame for the existent arrears of poll-tax upon "divers unscrupulous *pomiestchiki*" who burdened their *krestiané* with labour and tithes beyond capacity. Hence it charged the Senate, with all diligence to devise such a means of tax-collection as should, whilst entailing no arrears at all in future, also inflict no oppression, but establish for all classes of peasant a set standard of labour and tithes renderable to masters. Lastly, the *ukaz* wound up with a threat that a failure to decree "some such useful ordinance" would be visited upon the Senate with the utmost severity. The utterance's net effect was once more to bring rudely into prominence the long-burning question of legal regularisation of serf-right; and inasmuch as the Senate next was ordered to have the matter considered through the medium of calling a conference of such civilian and military officials as best could give the matter their attention, it would almost seem as though Maslov had been reading up Pososhkov, so wholly were the proposals of the two in harmony.[1] However, just as the *shliachetstvo's proekti* of 1730 had treated the matter cautiously, and confined themselves to expressions of a desire to see the peasants' obligations alleviated, so the Senate now converted itself practically into a caucus of conspirators, and kept the suspicions of the restless *Prokurator-General* quiet by intermittently sending him reassuring messages by the hands of its secretaries. And when in 1735 a long and disabling illness caused him to breathe his last the Senate gained, at the same time, a definite breathing-space. On the manuscript of his *proekt* we see a docket, inscribed in the hand-writing of one of the Empress's private secretaries, which reads, "*Obozhdat*," or "Let it stand over." And, sure enough, the matter did stand over—it stood over for the next hundred years. The principal reason why I have thought it well to call attention to this *proekt* is that in Maslov we see a precursor of Speranski, Miliutin, and other Russian thinkers who later, again, took up the bonded peasant question, and imitated him in devoting to it the full force of their powerful and enlightened intellects.

The reason why Maslov's *proekt* met with no acceptance at the time was that the Legislature still stood unprepared to attempt another decision of the problem, whilst the Government, for its part, was out, not so much for a juridical fixation of serf relations, as for a means of doing away with arrears of poll-tax, seeing that the barbarous system of collecting the tax through regimental detachments and "commissaries from the land" introduced by Peter on his first allotment of his army to provincial quarters was a system bound to ruin and scatter the peasantry, and so leave the arrears, if anything, worse than before. But though we have seen that Catherine I.'s

[1] See chap. v.

Government resolved altogether to remove the function of tax-collection from the military, and to impose its performance upon the *voevodi*, and that at the same time the Government voted for collection of the tax, not from the peasantry direct, but through their *pomiestchiki*, the plan worked no better than the earlier one had done, for both *voevodi* and rascally voevodal staffs proved worse than the regimental detachments in venality, and, after temporarily, in 1730, reverting to the military collection method, the Government had, on 23 June of the year following, to send the *Kammer-Collegium* a new *Reglament*. This *Reglament* selected from previous fruitless experiments their more useful points, and, permanently abolishing the local *dvorianin* commissaries, delegated the task of tax-collection to the *pomiestchiki* and their managers, and bade them, half-annually, forward the proceeds to the local *voevoda*, and do so without waiting for an actual tax-call—any *pomiestchik* failing to be punctual in the matter to have an expeditionary detachment from the local regiment dispatched to his estate, and undergo distress upon himself or his manager. This made the person actually responsible for rendition of the tax his own collector, and laid upon the *pomiestchik* an administrative commission over and above his already existent obligation to preside over the local court of justice on his estate, to police his *krestiané*, to act as their surety in legal suits, and to defend them in disputes with outsiders. In fact, he was henceforth to combine the duties of local superintendent of constabulary, local *gubernator*, and local serf attorney. Yet we should be mistaken in thinking that through his new taxatory obligation his right of serf possession gained enlargement as a civil institution. All that the *ukaz* did was to increase his dispositive authority, and extend the area of his jurisdiction as the local police agent. But after a while his duties as local tax-collector had added to them another, an automatically derived, obligation, through the fact that towards the close of 1733 accumulated bad harvests sent so many peasants flocking into the towns in quest of charity that by April a further *ukaz* had to bid the *pomiestchiki* feed their *krestiané* in times of scarcity, and advance them seed corn to prevent the land from falling out of cultivation. Which ordinance yet another *ukaz* of the year following confirmed, whilst adding to the confirmation a threat of, in case of non-compliance, "cruel torture and ruin for always"—a clear sign that, in the authorities' opinion, the person entrusted with such an important State financial resource as the collection of the State's poll-tax must take good care not to allow that resource to become dried up for want of nourishment.

The main outcome of the foregoing was to divert the burning peasant question from the socio-political sphere (a sphere always difficult for eighteenth-century administrative circles to envisage) to the sphere of fiscal-police authority. The same factor also brought about some important changes in the *dvorianstvo's* State position. This was because there met, and coincided, in the peasant question the aspirations of the *dvorianin* and the needs of the Exchequer. The Exchequer's chief need at the moment was a body of reliable agents for conduct of local administration; and inasmuch as colonels, military detachments, *gubernatori*, and *voevodi* had all proved faulty in promoting the Treasury's interests, it was with the idea of making the *pomiestchik* fill that rôle that, as we have seen, he now became invested with the functions of, at one and the same time, collecting his serfs' poll-tax, lending them seed corn in times of scarcity, and acting as their industrial guarantor. More than one circumstance facilitated this reversion of the landowning class to rural industrial pursuits and rural police supervision. Peter I. considered that the cardinal thing was to use the *dvorianstvo* jointly as his chief agency of local administration and as a military service corps for furnishing officers to, and forming the *cadres* and the staff of, his new regular military establishment. In other words, Peter's interest in the industrial position of the *dvorianstvo* was limited to the extent to which he could make that position help to qualify the class for the class's warlike duties. But when the lull which fell upon Russia and Western Europe after the Northern and Spanish-Successional Wars rendered *dvorianin* service a less pressing necessity for the Government, it, the Government, resumed its view that the *dvorianstvo* was a land-owning class pure and simple, and tightened its hold upon that view the more as taxatory arrears and peasant "flights" revealed the *krestianin's* hopeless fiscal exhaustion, and the need of a system of rural administration which should secure the State against fiscal loss. The root idea in the matter was that the *pomiestchik* was his serfs' natural protector, and should be made to act as such; but as he could not well do this without also being made supreme on his estate, and relieved of all official duties not connected with it, post-Petrine legislation reveals a constant fluctuation between two sets of measures—between a set for increasing the powers already inherent in *dvorianin* landownership and a set for lightening the *dvorianin's* compulsory service of State. For one thing, the fact that *pomiestchiki* often had to be away on military duty left their serfs constantly at the mercy of *prikazchiki*, or estate stewards, and of the local *voevodi*, and therefore an ordinance of 1727 relieved two-thirds of the whole body of *dvorianin* officers and men of their service obligations, and bade them return home to protect their estates from "wolves," and generally keep them in good working order. Again, as, in time, the *dvorianstvo* began (as we see from the *proekti* of 1730) to find the indefiniteness of its terms of State service a difficulty, whilst such service also necessitated a *dvorianin* entering upon a military or a naval career in the grade merely of common soldier or of ordinary rating, the year 1731 saw instituted a cadet corps of 200 (later increased to 360) from which the youths were, when fully trained, to become full-blown officers (or full-blown civilian officials of corresponding rank) at once. Next, an *ukaz* of 31 December, 1736, cut down the total term of *dvorianin* service to twenty-five years at most, and allowed *dvorianin* fathers of two or more sons to keep one at home to help in the management of the estate, and thereby added to the two already existing categories of State service *dvoriané* (*dvoriané* in military employ, and *dvoriané* in civilian employ) a third in the shape of young non-service *dvoriané* resident on the paternal estate—rather, of young *dvoriané* liable to service as soon as they reached the age of twenty, but privileged to retire from that service as soon as they were fit to manage an agrarian property. The extent to which the *dvorianin* preferred residence on his rural manor to service away from it is best discerned in the fact that in 1739, at the close of the Turkish War, so many time-expired *dvoriané* applied for leave to retire for good that the stock of available officers threatened to become seriously depleted, and the Law of 1736 had, consequently, to be treated, temporarily, as a dead letter.

Nor was it only that the *pomiestchik* now received permission to return home and indulge, at leisure, in rural-industrial pursuits: he now, because of his newly granted service exemptions, could return home feeling more assured as to his juridical relation to his property. This was due to the fact that, although, in 1714, his class had taken the *ukaz* of that year relating to sole succession to have conferred upon the class its *pomiestia*, as permanently, not temporarily, held estates, but had objected to the *ukaz* still leaving certain restrictions upon succession to such estates, Anna, in 1730, met the class's wishes and objections by abolishing those restrictions, and thereby gave the *dvorianin* legal ground for interpreting the *ukaz* still more in favour of the claims of his caste. From the first Peter's *ukaz* had failed to realise the expectations of its framer, bred a multitude of difficulties, sown such discord as even, in some cases, to lead to parricide, set the landowning class endeavouring by every possible means to evade it, and, in short, made confusion worse confounded. Fathers lacking monetary capital, but desirous of securing their portionless sons' and daughters' position, had taken to selling their estates piecemeal, or to assuming testamentary responsibility for debts which fell upon the sole heir on their death, and forced him to discharge his liability for what was owing by at once alienating his inherited property. Also, through a further artful interpretation of the *ukaz* testators had taken to classifying their grain and stock as movables, devising the bare estate to the eldest son, and dividing the "movables" in question amongst their remaining children—with the result that the eldest son had found himself left with stockless land, and his brothers and sisters with landless stock. Hence in 1731 the Senate compiled a report upon these evils resultant from the sole-successional system, and on 31 March, an *ukaz* abolished it, and ordained, instead, that *pomiestia* and *otchini* should both be "immovable properties of *otchina*," and that all properties should be divided amongst a testator's children as a whole— divided in the sense of the *Ulozhenie's* term "equally and unto each." The result was to cause the whole of the huge aggregate of populated State lands which hitherto had constituted the country's aggregate of *pomiestie* estates to pass, purchase-free and in perpetuity, into private possession, and to convert the *pomiestchik* from an occasional visitor to his property into that property's permanent master and proprietor—into, in fact, the endowed lord of an hereditary manor.

At the same time, it not infrequently happened that a *pomiestchik* encountered difficulties when he assumed the mastership of an estate which had fallen into decay during his absence. Firstly, there might be lack of working capital and, secondly, there might be lawsuits in connection with landmarks, or seizures of his land, or runaway serfs, or complexities of serf relations, and thirdly there might be personal ignorance of such matters. So, to give him a helping hand, and to meet the costliness of private credit (which now stood at about twenty per cent.), the Government, by an *ukaz* of 7 May, 1753, opened a *dvorianin* bank which, based upon a State-funded capital of 750,000 roubles (5,000,000, in modern currency), and backed with the profits from Shuvalov's liquor excise, was designed to enable the *pomiestchik* to borrow of it at six per cent., and, in return, pledge his immovable property—always so long as what he borrowed did not exceed 10,000 roubles, and that the sum was repaid within three years from the loan date. And to put *dvorianin* landownership on a basis sounder still, and release it from the juridical tangle to which the long contest between legal enactment and illegal interpretation had led up, the State took occasion, on 13 May, 1754, to give orders for a general ordnance survey of the country, and, for the purpose, sent out parties of civilian *métayers*, under high military officers instructed strictly to scrutinise all rights of tenure and deeds of enserfment, to abolish the hitherto system of *cherezpolositza* (cultivation in strips), and to see that contiguous estates received separate surveys. And as the area where the first start was to be made the Government selected the *gubernia* of Moscow. Unfortunately, the measure merely succeeded in stirring up the *dvorianin* antheap again, and causing such litigation that the enterprise had to be abandoned. Another source of grave trouble in the agrarian industry both of the State and of private owners was the number of peasant "flights" which occurred, as the scourge merited in equal measure by the State and by the *pomiestchik* for their senseless highhandedness. Hence courts of justice came to be inundated with *donosi* against runaways, and their records to run over with judgments on the same. Yet either inability or indifference left the Senate still unable to devise a system of judicial procedure capable of coping with the development. The ancient *Ulozhenie* had prescribed that runaways should be tracked down and surrendered in accordance with the registers and census lists for the years 1620–40; but what this now led to may be inferred from the following. In 1627 the register of a village in the canton of Kolomna had upon it the name of a runaway serf called Sidorov, and a hundred years later a tracker in the employ of the owner of that village arrested a *krestianin* of the name on the steppes of Voronezh, and haled him before the local court as a descendant of the original runaway. And when the court asked the accused whether in very fact he was descended from the Sidorov of 1627 the accused was led by his confusion to reply that he was, and the court ordered him to be surrendered to his supposed owner. But it happened that another owner of a neighbouring village also had had a serf named Sidorov abscond; and now he seized Sidorov Number One as soon as he was surrendered from the court, and had him arraigned again. The *dénouement* was that when the justices again asked the accused whether he was descended from the original Sidorov, and the man, more than ever confused, replied this time, that he was not, the court awarded him, "for so great a change of speech," torture! The moral of the story, of course, is that one should always be sure of one's ancestors. In 1754, however, the Empress ordered the Senate to arrange for runaways to be surrendered solely on the basis of the lists of the First Revision, which went back to 1719 only. To add to other difficulties experienced by the smaller *dvoriané*, those *dvoriané's* senior brethren, the "*dvoriané* of eminence," developed a practice of abducting the former's *krestiané*, and holding them concealed on their estates. True, in 1722, Peter I. had suspended over the abductors' heads an *ukaz* ordaining "cruel chastisement" and a fine of (in modern currency) 400 roubles for each year that a runaway serf was thus harboured and employed, and so intimidating some of the leading *dvoriané* that they had asked Peter to allow it to become the rule that whenever a member of the petty *dvorianstvo* was discharged on completion of his State service he should be sent to the capital for a conference with themselves before returning to his own estate—the object of the conference being that he might be talked over into desisting from any suits for peasant abductions by his seniors during his absence on service; but with Peter's death the larger landowners began their proceedings of serf removal and harbourage as before, and indulged in them more than ever.

Again, the Legislature not only regularised and confirmed the *dvorianstvo's* privilege of owning land and peasant souls; it also extended the scope of serf-right. Not that, in this respect, it really did more than sanction existing practice, and insert a few norms into a plan of procedure which the *pomiestchik* had, in the course of his collection of his peasantry's taxes and supervision of his peasants' industry, woven into an inextricable web. First of all, by *ukaz* of 6 May, 1736, the *pomiestchik's* local judicial-police authority had added to it the function of actually determining the punishment to be awarded to an absconded serf, whilst, secondly, an *ukaz* of 2 May, 1758, compelled him (rather, empowered him) to act as standing supervisor of his serfs' behaviour in general, and thirdly, an *ukaz* of 13 December, 1760, awarded him the right to banish a serf to Siberia, and have him settled there as a recruit on half-pay, and, fourthly, an *ukaz* of 1765 empowered him to send a serf into "a state of detention" in Siberia—that is to say, to send him there to serve a term of hard labour. Also, the more to obliterate the serf's personality, the law so stripped him of his last surviving rights as to enable the *pomiestchik* to trade in him as a living chattel, and sell him for a recruit apart from the land on which he dwelt, and wrest him from his family circle, and deprive him of (1) his legal means of attaining freedom (through an offer to perform military service), (2) his right to bind himself under a legal deed, and (3) his right to go surety for anyone. Lastly, the reign of Catherine II. reached, we see the serf standing powerless even to complain against his master. Chiefly the Senate's abilities as a social organiser it was that led the *pomiestchik* thus to assume that his new and highly important rights and powers were designed to be corporate privileges, and exercised as such. On issuing from the legislative factory, and entering into workaday life, a legislative norm is apt to derive from life a life-meaning causing it widely to diverge from the legislator's original intention, and to undergo such independent legal interpretation as to evade even the keenest authoritative scrutiny if the authority concerned be not long-sighted. Hence, although, originally, the class privileges which I have mentioned were not local administrative powers in any way connected with right of private land-ownership, since, originally, they were conferred exclusively upon persons having charge of court and Treasury *krestiané*, they ended by so merging with the *dvorianstvo's* already held powers of serf-possession as to develop from mere items of civil right into State-established prerogatives. Another use to which the Government put serf-right was to sweep away all those social classes which it rated as "litter," and *ukazi* of 1729 and 1752 commanded that, in addition to peasant absconders, vagrants and unemployed *tserkovniki*[1] should be placed in serf dependency upon *pomiestchiki* of their localities, and that the latter should pay for them a poll-tax. And the very fact that the Legislature extended serf-right to include police powers for the *pomiestchik* suggested to the Legislature also an idea later abandoned, the idea that precautions ought to be taken to ensure proper usage of a right so far-reaching as the right of serf-possession. And it sought to obtain that ensurance through compulsory *dvorianin* education, and insisted that the class must not only take to study, but show in that regard no slackness whatsoever. At the same time, the Legislature could not make entry into the cadet corps a *sine qua non*, for no corps could be large enough to contain the whole of the *dvorianstvo's* sons, and therefore an *ukaz* of 1737 met the difficulty by establishing for all other young *dvoriané* an educational course requiring minors, the age of seven attained, to present themselves before the *Heroldmeister* or the local *gubernator* as the case might be, and, after registration, repair to some allotted elementary school, under the conditions that, whilst such of them as came of poor parents should receive a "recompense" (a subsidy similar to that awarded to ordinary soldiers' sons) towards doing so, those of them who were allotted to home education were, on attaining the ages successively of twelve, sixteen, and twenty, to present themselves for examination in, on the first of those occasions, reading and writing, and, on the second, Holy Writ, arithmetic, and geometry, and, on the third, fortification, geography, and history; after which they were to be posted to the service, and promoted on the scale of service *chini* strictly in proportion as they continued to advance in their studies, save that students of the sort failing in their second examination were to be posted indefinitely to the Navy only. Lastly, at least the first two of the foregoing examinations were to be undergone by minors retained at home for management of their father's estates. The importance which the authorities ascribed to arithmetic and geometry in the conduct of rural industry is emphasised in the *ukaz*' every line. "Without zeal in those useful and not burdensome exercises," says the document, no youth could hope ever to become a skilled domestic economist.

Throughout the seventeenth century the right to own lands and serfs had belonged to all members of the service class "*po otechestvu*" ("through heredity") without distinction of rank; and the list of service families which

---

[1] "Church persons," or persons attached to or employed in or about churches.

was compiled on the abolition of the *Miestnichestvo*, and entered in the so-called *Barkhatnaia Kniga*, or "Velvet Book," had established the family *personnel* of the hereditary-service class subsequently (in Peter's day) known as the *dvorianstvo*, and dowered with right of personal proprietorship of lands and serfs. Nevertheless it gradually came about, owing to discontinuance of *pomiestie* allotment, to imposition of *dvorianin* hereditary service in the rank of *Oberoffizier*, to fusion of the *pomiestie* with the *otchina*, to fusion of *kholopstvo* (slavery) with *krestianstvo* (peasanthood), to the creation of factory and workshop *krestiané*, and to other measures of class legislation, that there arose a confusion of ideas as to the composition of the *dvorianstvo*, and also as to the extent of that class's right to own populated lands; whilst, owing, on the other hand, to the fact that the *dvorianstvo* succeeded in gaining the important administrative powers and long-desired privileges which it did, there became increasingly felt the need of an exact definition both of the composition and of the extent of the right referred to. Yet always the Legislature declined to elaborate durable norms on the subject. It vacillated between its wish to see serf-right develop into a fiscal resource and its wish to see that right develop into a class privilege. For example, in 1739 it forbade serfs to be acquired apart from land, but in 1743 a Revisional Instruction conceded serf-possession to military officers and to Government officials the right of possessing serfs in return for payment of those serfs' poll-tax: and, in short, there resulted such a babel of *ukazi* speaking in different tongues that at last the Senate took to interlarding such documents with glosses and examples. Unfortunately, the one were arbitrary, and the other were ill-advised, and matters grew worse still. By some *ukazi posadskie* (urban tradesmen) were permitted to own household serfs: by others this procedure was not permitted; and on a particular group of tradesmen petitioning that they might be exempted from assessment on their serfs, the Senate first referred them to the many *ukazi* conceding household serf-possession to such persons, and then rejected the plea so curtly as to convert a licence into a command, and a right into a duty. And yet another example of legislative inconsistency. We have seen that some of the *shliachtich* "schemes" of 1730 referred to the necessity of framing a new list ("canon") of the "original" *shliachetstvo*, and of fixing exact tokens of *shliachtich* membership, and of stating conditions under which a *shliachtich* might acquire a share in full *dvorianin* rights. Up to that period three categories of non-*dvorianin* persons had, in greater or in less measure, and with varying degrees of legality, enjoyed the right to own serfs and lands. Those three categories had been (1) non-free boyaral retainers, with archiepiscopal and monasterial servants, (2) freemen assessed to poll-tax, with merchants, urban tradesmen, Treasury peasants, and *odnovortsi*,[1] and (3) service officials not yet become *Oberoffizieren* — persons known as *lichnie dvoriané*.[2] But *ukazi* of 1730, 1740, and 1758, added to the Survey Instruction of 1754, deprived one and all of these categories both of their right to acquire serfs with land and of their right to acquire serfs without land, and, upon the top of that, ordered their already held lands to be sold by a given date. The effect of these ordinances was juridically to differentiate the hereditary *dvorianstvo* from its contiguous classes, classes hitherto sharing its prerogatives, and to leave it in the position of being the only social category competent to own lands and bonded peasantry. And this differentiation and this monopoly the authorities further confirmed in 1761 by ordering a fresh book of genealogical degrees to be compiled, and no fresh entry in the *dvorianstvo's* registers to be made without previous proof of the would-be *dvorianin's* title to become one. Nevertheless, though the Legislature intended, by the step, to preserve the class's genealogical purity, the solicitude at least did not solidify the class concerned, whether from the genealogical point of view or from the moral, since whilst the *dvorianstvo* of birth, the original *dvorianstvo*, continued, as before, to look down upon the *dvorianstvo* of meritaward, the new *dvorianstvo*, the law so increasingly favoured the elder stepbrother as increasingly to widen the breach between the two. Thus, whereas the ordnance survey "Instruction" of 1754 ordered the lands of *e merito dvoriané* to be registered exclusively to such of their sons as had been brought up in the rank of *Oberoffizier*, an *ukaz* of 1760 enjoined that persons merely promoted to *dvorianin* rank for civilian service should neither take rank with persons promoted for military service nor possess estates in their own right. One reason for this ordinance may have been that by that time the long series of legislative measures on the subject had caused the military rank automatically conferring *dvorianin* rights to approximate so closely to the civilian rank automatically conferring the same that *dvoriané* had taken too much to selecting the service's civilian branch, as the easier and more lucrative road towards worming their way into the coveted class.

Thus the thirty years 1730–60 saw the hereditary *dvorianstvo* acquire, in connection with ownership of peasant souls and lands, the following prerogatives and amenities: (1) ascription of immovable properties tenable as *otchini*, and disposable of at will, (2) a class monopoly of serf-right, (3) an extension of the *pomiestchik's* judicial-police authority to include a power of awarding the criminal code's severer penalties, (4) a right of sale of serfs, even of bonded *krestiané*, apart from land, (5) regularisation of recovery of

---

[1] A category partly landowner, and partly peasant.

[2] "*Dvoriané* apart," or "*dvoriané* unto themselves" (in the sense of "*dvoriané* of a separate class").

peasant absconders, and (6) facilities for obtaining cheap State credit secured upon the borrower's immovable property. The general effect of these privileges was to bring about both a juridical differentiation and a sharp moral estrangement between the hereditary *dvorianstvo* and the other social classes. Meanwhile the *dvorianin's* liability to State service underwent a gradual lightening through (1) acquisition of a right to enter that service as an officer direct if first the necessary educational standard had been attained, and (2) fixation of a definite term for that service. And, finally, all these grants of proprietorial rights and of exemptions from service had placed upon them the crown of emancipation from any service of State save service of a voluntary nature. For around the throne, during Elizabeth's "patriotic" reign, there stood Russian statesmen of hereditary-*dvorianin* or Cossack origin who, though having nothing in common with the ideas of the *boyaré* of 1730, yet jealously watched over the interests of the class to which they had been born, or into which they had become adopted; and the consideration which these men voiced more frequently than any other, and which first had emanated from the brain of Prince D. M. Golitzin, a man absolutely obsessed with his fear of a possible abatement of the *dvorianin* class, was the consideration that the first and foremost necessity of the day was the class's exemption from compulsory service. True, one member of that circle, the young Duke of Holstein, continued to slight the prevailing patriotic spirit of Russia so long as he held the position only of his aunt's heir and nominee; but no sooner had he ascended the throne as Peter III. than he was taken in hand by other members of the circle like Roman Vorontzov, the father of young Peter's favourite light-of-love, and other National Liberals, and "instructed by rote" on the question of emancipating the *dvorianstvo* from both military and civilian service until 18 February, 1762, saw that aspiration attain fulfilment through a Manifesto which conferred "upon all the well-born of Our Russian *dvorianstvo* full freedom from service, and release thence," and, with a touch of the illiteracy of the school-room mingled with a touch of the pompousness of the bureau, ordained that *dvoriané* then in the service of the State need continue in it only so long as they might wish, save that such of them as were in the military branch must not, in case of election to continue in service, apply to retire either during the actual progress of a campaign or when a campaign might ensue within the next three months; that non-service *dvoriané* might at any time migrate to other States of Europe, and enter the service of non-Russian Sovereigns, and, after their return home, retain any rank gained in that service, provided always that "if the need should arise," and the Russian Government recalled them, they obeyed the summons forthwith. But, with that, the Manifesto balanced the items conceded. For one thing, it preserved to the Supreme Power that Power's right to call up *dvoriané* for service "whensoever there shall be a particular necessity for the same." And, for another, it did not repeal the educational obligation, but, on the contrary, commanded that all *dvoriané* should have their sons instructed in a Russian school, or in a foreign school, or through home tuition, and added to the injunction the stern warning that "if any man of the *dvorianstvo* shall rear a son, nor set him to learn the sciences proper unto the born *dvorianstvo*, that man shall be made to undergo Our grievous displeasure." Also, as a further incitement to the *dvorianstvo* to undertake service, the Manifesto remarked that, notwithstanding all that had been said in its pages, it still trusted that no *dvorianin* would wilfully evade the service obligation, but "honourably accept the same," and continue in it "as a true son of the land," seeing that neither the *dvorianin* who would not rally to the help of his country nor the son of a *dvorianin* who would not, for his country's sake, learn his letters was really a man to "be held in aught save contempt and abasement for ever," and to be regarded as a contemner of the common weal, and one unworthy to be received either at court or at public *assemblées*. From this the Manifesto's basic idea is clear: clearly it had for its main desire conversion of what hitherto had been demanded by the law as an imperative obligation into a moral demand which, if disregarded, would automatically bring down upon the defaulter's head censure both from the State and from public opinion. Yet though the idea is logically enough developed in the document, the actual effect of it was to make dishonourable conduct possible for the *dvorianin* who did not mind braving court and social disability. Besides, even as it uttered the words relieving the *dvorianstvo* of the obligation hitherto connected with the class's every interest and pursuit the document overlooked the fact that it ought to have added some practically thought-out directions as to its own fulfilment and probable results. And we can easily guess how the class received the concessions! Indeed, we read in the quaint memoirs of a contemporary writer named Bolotov: "Never could I hope, by any conceiving, to describe the joyfulness instilled into the hearts of the *dvoriané* of our well-beloved country by this Act. For one and all are like to leap with thankfulness unto the Emperor, and ever do continue calling down blessings upon the hour in which he did deign to sign the *ukaz*." Whilst a *dvorianin* poet named Rzhevski, in writing a special ode on the subject, said in reference to the Tsar: "Now at last hath he given unto Russia both freedom and prosperity!"

Also, though the Manifesto of 18 February relieved the *dvorianstvo* of compulsory service, it said not a word concerning *dvorianin* serf-right, despite that the latter was sprung from the former. As a matter of fact, though the demands both of historical logic and of social equity could only have been met with instant abolition of that right, the abolition did not take place until ninety-nine years later. The main effect of the legislative anomaly was to complete the heterogeneous juridical process through which the *dvorianstvo* had attained its present position in the State, the process whereby always, as that class had obtained lightenment of its service obligations, it had obtained also expansion of the rights of seigniorial possession based upon those obligations. In short, we now see serf-ownership in the third phase of its evolution, in the phase prepared for it during the period of the First Revision. That is to say, by now the old *krestianin-pomiestchik* personal contract of the pre-*Ulozhenie* epoch, the contract which, during that epoch, had become converted into an hereditary obligation towards the State, and had been imposed upon all peasantry resident on private lands, with the object of maintaining the military class permanently service-efficient, had acquired, through abolition of *dvorianin* compulsory service, a new formation altogether. True, that formation is not easy to define, since it represented a phenomenon without a political excuse, a result without a cause; but also it was a phenomenon inevitably evolved from Russian history. In it the industrial and the juridical composition of serfdom reached its most complex phase. Like the rest of the tax-paying classes, serfs paid State poll-tax as their contribution towards military upkeep: yet the bulk of what serf toil produced in the form of the *obrok* (monetary tithe) and *barstchina* (forced labour) and dues payable in kind went into the landowner's pocket, and were divided into two theoretically distinct portions consisting of, firstly, payment of rent for a plot of land to the plot's owner—a payment which, if the *krestianin* had not been a serf, he would have rendered, not for the land, but for the industrial assistance of the land's proprietor, and, secondly, a special serf-tax designed originally to indemnify the proprietor against his obligatory rendition of State service, against, that is to say, the expenditure which that rendition necessitated. Moreover, up to the time of abolition of compulsory *dvorianin* service the *pomiestchik* had his judicial-police powers further to help him towards performance of State duties—which, so far as his estate was concerned, consisted only of collecting his serfs' poll-tax, and providing them with assistance in times of scarcity. Hence exemption of the *dvorianin* from compulsory service combined with transference of his position from a military-political basis to a fiscal-police footing to render him and the State co-sharers of the rights in the serf's personality and labour, with the *dvorianin* undertaking, as regards the State, to pay the serf's poll-tax on his, the serf's behalf, and also to supervise the serf's industry at least sufficiently well to ensure that the land should not come to be unproductive, and, therefore, inefficient as a producer of State revenue. And inasmuch as like rights and functions were conferred upon managers of Court and Church *krestiané*, it follows that by the time of the Second Revision some 4,900,000 souls, or 73 per cent. of the whole taxpaying population, had become, for industrial and judicial-police purposes, and in return for a total annual payment to the State of 3,425,000 roubles, transferred to the possession of private persons and institutions. Or, if we state the matter non-juridically, the process was Government redemption of the country's serfs from possession by the hereditary-landowning class in order to convert the serf's labour and personality into assets of Crown revenue. Wherefore, this third formation of serf-right might be termed redemptional, or fiscal-police, serf-right, to distinguish it from the two previous formations represented by personal-contract serf-right and hereditary-military serf-right. But though next there followed secularisation of the Church's lands and *krestiané*, the character of this third formation is best seen on the estates of private owners, since at the time of the Second Revision there were settled on those lands upwards of 3,500,000 registered souls, or over one-half (54 per cent., to be exact) of the whole of the Empire's rural population. The formation was a still more inequitable measure than its predecessors had been, for it caused law and practice alike (law and practice, that is to say, as the authorities acquiesced in them) gradually to annul the few such guarantees of the serf's labour and personality as had been spared to him by the *Ulozhenie*, and to add new abuses to the old, and to give the serf question a new direction (1) through spontaneous migrations of peasantry, (2) through conferment of populated lands upon *dvoriané* without the consent of the resident *krestiané*, (3) through wholesale enserfment and assessment to poll-tax of hitherto unattached persons (vagrants and unemployed, *tserkovniki*) (4) through fusion of peasant plots with seigniorial tillage, a fusion which, during the First Revision, transferred taxation from lands to souls, greatly militated against standardisation of peasant plot - allotments and liabilities, and largely conduced to extension of seigniorial tillage at the expense of peasant plots, and (5) through permission to sell *krestiané* apart from land. During the seventeenth century the general tendency had been for landowners to settle their household serfs upon the land as *krestiané*, to allot them tillage, and so to fuse the two current forms of bondage into one, whilst to this fusion the First Revision's general assessment of non-taxpaying *kholopi* to payment of poll-tax on the same footing as *krestiané* had contributed further; but with Peter's death both the Government and the *dvorianstvo* began to utilise this process, (despite that it had been designed to increase rather than to enserf the people's labour, for converting the bonded *krestianin* into a taxpaying *kholop*, and so compounding the worst form of servitude ever known to Europe, the servitude of attachment, not to land, as in the West, nor to social status, as in the Russia of the *Ulozhenie*, but to the person, and to the unrestricted will, of the landowner. And upon this reinforcement of serf-right Russia entered just at the moment when serf-right was losing its last vestige of historical justification! From two quarters at one and the same time did the movement receive an impetus; and those two quarters were the Government and the *dvorianstvo*. That is to say, after long showing itself exacting towards the *dvorianin*, much as a master might show himself exacting towards a servant who had no choice but to continue in his employ, the Government took to doing everything possible to lighten things for the *dvorianin* class, and, whilst binding the *pomiestchik* always to reside on his estate, and there to maintain law and order, began to treat him in all else as a free agent. The magnitude of this revolution in the theory of the *dvorianin's* status can be seen from the following instance. During the seventeenth century, when the Tsarevna Sophia was in power, Prince V. V. Golitzin found it possible to emancipate the *krestianin* by a mere process of law, and to make over to him the land on which he worked; but some seventy or eighty years later, when a descendant of that Golitzin, in the shape of Prince D. A. Golitzin, Voltaire's friend, proposed the far more modest scheme of emancipating the *krestianin* by merely conceding to him a right to own property, the Prince was accused of advocating that the *krestianin* should have the *krestianin*-worked land actually conveyed to him, and had to exculpate himself by replying that never at any time had he contemplated so gross an impropriety, "in that the lands do belong unto ourselves, and it would be a manifest injustice to deprive us of the same," and that by "bestowal of right of property upon the *krestianin*" he had only meant that the person of the peasant should be emancipated—that "our *krestiané* be granted the possession of their own selves," and receive a right to own chattels, and a right to acquire land in the ordinary course. Hence, how greatly had the *ukaz* of 1731, the *ukaz* ordaining conferment of *pomiestia* for *otchini*, now altered the *pomiestchik's* views with regard to his estate! And how entirely did the Manifesto of 18 February, 1762, confirm that alteration! Formerly the *pomiestchik* appointed to a district-regimental, or a civilian-departmental, post had felt, with the appointment, his estate to cease to be anything but partially, restrictedly, and conditionally his property; but now that compulsory service slipped from his shoulders, and, with it, all need to consider the real origin and meaning of serf-right, he could sit snugly housed on his manor, and look upon his seigniorial *pomiestie* as his State in little, and upon his serfs as his miniature subject population.

And, indeed, that is what administrative documents of the day actually began to call those serfs, for the Government now had reason to feel assured that the *pomiestchik* would give them—or, rather, would give their industry —proper attention, seeing that that would redound to his interest, as of the person responsible for rendition of the serfs' taxes, more than would any decline in their tax-producing capacity. Unfortunately, the Government seems to have overlooked the question of whether State service in the past was a good preparation for direction of rural industry in the present: and in any case we find some of the *dvorianin* petitioners of 1730 suggesting that a band of 50,000 "baser *shliachtichi*" (the estimate was the petitioners' own) who were due soon to complete their terms of service might, after discharge, fail to learn how properly to maintain themselves through agrarian industry, and, resorting to larceny and brigandage instead, convert their manors into dens of thieves.

Thus the third formation of serf-right was not so much a legalised right as a never legalised fact, since *ukazi* on the subject failed to furnish that right with anything more than general definitions so faultily phrased as to leave practice at liberty to fill in the legislative blanks at will. Yet this is not to say that no attempt was ever made to back practice with juridical norms, for, in addition to framing a criminal code and a *proekt* for an ordinance on legal procedure and management, the Commission of 1754 drew up regulations with regard to social statuses, a sort of draft for a second *Ulozhenie*, from whose second portion we can see fairly well the view of serf-right which the ruling classes took for their basis in putting that right into practical working. For one thing, we see that the document does not devote so much as a single section to the rural taxpaying classes, and that in all the sections treating of rural landowning conditions those classes are spoken of as proprietary-taxatory articles rather than as social statuses, and that the statuses of the household serf and the bonded *krestianin* are regarded as juridically identical with one another, and that the bonded *krestianin* ranks as a full *kholop* save that he is not in household service. "The *dvorianin*," the *proekt* says, "shall be free to exercise full authority over his serving-men and his *krestiané*, and over their goods, in all matters save in seizings of their stock, in chastisings of them with the *knut*, and in exercisings of torture." In other words, the *dvorianin* was to have his serfs completely at his disposal—to be able not only to regulate their labour, but also to govern their personalities so completely as to have power to allow them to marry or not, and to "award all save the aforesaid penalties." True, in 1742 the Senate recognised the necessity of a second revision, in order that, amongst other things, it might put a stop to the system of "harsh removals of *krestiané* to other places"; but twelve years later the *proekt* of which I am speaking calmly proposed to let landowners have a right to annex the peasantry of Treasury lands "without restraint," and "if so be that it will work to their better advantage." Never a thought for the interests of the souls thus annexed! Never a thought for the duties to which those souls might subsequently be put! True, also, the *dvorianin* was to be permitted to "release a serf for ever into freedom"—whether with his children or without them; but this was merely a process calculated to break up the serf family, whilst in any case the right stood beset with so many difficulties that manifestly any extensive application of it was impossible. In fact, the *proekt* is permeated throughout with distrust of, and contempt for, the serf's personality, and everywhere hems about that personality with surveillance. It is as though the serf had been a slave perpetually meditating "flight" or a crime, so exclusively is that the only aspect in which he receives attention from the codifiers, and so exclusively are the sections on peasant "flights" the only peasant sections highly developed. Nor is the *proekt's* attitude towards the *krestiané* on Court and State lands much different. Naturally, such a school of civism eventually bred Pugachevists, since that school turned out machines, not men; and, were one solely to base one's judgment upon the *proekt*, Russia was, at that period, purely a slave-owning State, and a State preparing to adopt an obsolete Oriental model just at the time when even such countries as Denmark and Austria were attempting to solve their serf questions, and the *Junker*-ridden Prussian Government was considering how best to defend its bonded peasantry from the highhandedness of its *Junker* landowners. At all events, in turning aside in order to institute serf-right afresh, Russia divorced herself from all the States of Central Europe. And that right, when re-instituted, maintained its validity for the next two and a half centuries.

CHAPTER XV

The Russian Empire at the middle of the eighteenth century—The fate of Peter the Great's reforms under his successors—The Empress Elizabeth—The Emperor Peter III.

ONLY six reigns, or a period of thirty-seven years, were needed to decide the fate of the Petrine reforms. As a matter of fact, could Peter have beheld how his work was continued after his death, he would scarcely have recognised that work for his own, seeing that though he had pursued his policy despotically, and made his person replace the State, and his will the people's, he had at least excelled all his predecessors in his recognition that a State's one and only aim should be the welfare of its inhabitants.

So, as soon as he was gone, every tie of State, moral and juridical alike, began to fall apart, and the idea of State to fade until its last remnants are seen making furtive appearances merely in the casual, formal phraseology of administrative documents. After his death, too, the picture presented to us is that of the most autocratic empire in the world bereft of an established dynasty save for a few stray members of a moribund Imperial House; of an hereditary throne without a legal heir; of a State confined to the walls of a casually, briefly tenanted palace; of a ruling class partly aristocratic and partly high-official of origin, irregular of composition, and constantly being re-shuffled; of a political life of court intrigues, Guards' *émeutes*, and police inquisitions; and of a general system of official highhandedness blunting the popular sense of equity. Which being the phenomena obtaining, we cannot wonder that the spectacle of them moved certain observers attached to the Russian court on behalf of foreign countries to write home to their Governments that at that period the court in question was changing its *personnel* daily, and that no man in the country had confidence in anything, or even knew to which saint he had best pray! Yet Russia's administrative ring still had in it a few thinkers with a clear inkling of the danger threatened by the fact that the State no longer stood based upon law, but was dependent upon chance circumstances and a purely mechanical cohesion liable to fall apart before the first blow dealt it from within or from without. Nor was the general mass of the people altogether blind to the fact that there was a need for a substratum of permanent, legal authority to be laid, and for administerers and administered to be drawn closer together. That was why I. I. Shuvalov presented to the Empress Elizabeth his *proekt* "on Fundamental Laws," and why Count P. I. Shuvalov called the Senate's attention to the State advantages derivable from "a free recognition of popular opinion." But the only fate, for the present, of such suggestions was to find a resting-place in the Senatorial archives, for no eighteenth century Government was competent to tackle so great an institutional task as the task of bringing fundamental statutes into being, or even (though help in this could have been obtained from certain Western authorities), the much simpler task of tabulating the State's existent *ukazi* and ordinances—a task, nevertheless, once accomplished by Alexis' Government.[1] At all events the Commission of 1700 got no further in its attempt to frame a new *Ulozhenie* than a few feeble disputes and a few makeshift appointings of sub-commissions of a composition variously departmental, inter-departmental, and Government-clerical-class-representative, with one such sub-commission (this was Ostermann's arrangement) actually sitting under a German president! At length, on March 11, 1754, the Senate and some members of the Collegiate and Chancellorial staffs held a solemn conference with the Empress Elizabeth, and pointed out to her the confusion that was existent in judicial procedure. Finally, after a remark from the ever-resourceful P. I. Shuvalov that a properly formulated digest of laws was the only remedy, but that that remedy was impossible in view of the fact that amongst the voluminous mass of extant *ukazi* there stood included, nevertheless, not a single ordinance of generally clear import, the Empress took up the tale. First she condoled with her faithful subjects on their lack of jurisprudential equity. Then she observed that the initial step should be a drafting of intelligible laws. Then she went on to argue that, nevertheless, jurisprudential changes were as inevitable as were changes in manners and customs. Then she gave it as a dictum that "no man not possessed of the qualities of an angel" could be familiar with the details of every *ukaz* extant. Then she rose and left the chamber. Upon that the Senate re-fell to its labours, and spent the next eighty years in once more attempting, fruitlessly, to compose "clear and generally understandable laws." Its first step was to appoint yet another sub-commission, of a membership inclusive, this time, of a certain "Professeur de Séances d'Académie"; but though, some twelve months later, this body did evolve two sections of a digest of the sort presumably required, those sections were so wretched as regards the amount of juridical knowledge and acumen which they dis-

[1] Through means of, of course, the *Ulozhenie.*

played that eventually their publication was deemed inadvisable. Impotence and timidity in the face of unlimited authority over the person were features peculiar to all the Russian Governments of the period. Such features could not but exist in a State in which a decorative European façade masked an Eastern-Asiatic-modelled edifice. And evidences of the same feature are seen in the manner in which Peter I.'s successors conducted another of their inherited tasks. The task in question was the task of delimiting inter-class relations, and Peter himself, in grappling with it, had sought to base those relations uniformly upon duties towards the State, and therefore, in some cases, made two or more classes assume liabilities which formerly had fallen only upon one (as when he had imposed the poll-tax upon all forms of *kholopstvo*, and military service upon every single class), and so constructed for himself a basis for equalising also the administrative classes—wherefore his system may be said to have been reached from below, by way, first of all, of legally establishing the *krestianin's* exclusive liability, as a serf, to render to his master certain fixed cash and labour payments; but when, soon after the accession of Catherine I., the nation entered upon the renewed agitation concerning the serf question of which Pososhkov tells us, and Catherine had once more had the question examined by her Privy Council, and Anna's Cabinet of Ministers had done the same (and so, incidentally, given *Ober-prokuror* Maslov his opportunity of coming forth as one of the *krestianin's* stoutest advocates) and officialdom, in its higher ranks, had nearly become spurred to the requisite pitch for really taking action, there occurred the sudden anti-climax of a complete disappearance of the question, and with it, of any chance of seeing any other post-Petrine reform radically considered. No wonder that Yaguzhinski earlier wrote to Catherine: "What though many do speak of our divers needs, and do speak of them as though with sorrow and repining, no man striveth with zeal to exercise labour upon the same." In short, the helplessness of Governments was such that the further course of the matter was merely the course which the ruler of the day happened casually, and from time to time, to indicate to his Ministers that the matter must pursue. Always, if the wielder of an absolute power of authority lacks personal qualifications for that wielder's self-guidance, the authority in question tends either to bow to environment or to truckle to its at once most needed and most feared social class: and in the case of Russia circumstances caused that class to become the Russian *dvorianstvo* headed by the Russian Guards. Hence, no sooner had the *dvorianstvo* won for itself emancipation from service of State, and settled down upon its rustic domains, than most of its members assumed an uncontrolled right— rather, an uncontrolled measure of power—over their serf populations' labour and persons, and were helped in doing so by the fact that they now resided cheek by jowl with their *krestiané*. This still further accentuated the moral estrangement between the two which juridically dated from the seventeenth century, and established it as a permanent bar between master and man, and as a constant drain upon Russia's social life. To this day that estrangement exists: to this day every person in this country is conscious of its influence. Another result of the same eighteenth century process was to deprive Russia's social composition of the balance which rightly should have obtained between the various constituent elements of that composition. At the time of the Second Revision (1742–7) the total population of the *gubernii* was 6,660,000 taxpaying souls; and in a description of the country written thirteen years after Peter's death Fokkerodt, then Secretary to the Russian Embassy, appends to numerical details on the subject of Russia's tax-paying classes during the middle years of Anna's reign [1] (and clearly they are details culled from official sources) a statement that about at the period of writing there were resident in the area of the Russian Empire, less the provinces added to it later, 1,500,000 hereditary *dvoriané* of both sexes, 200,000 departmental officials and "separate *dvoriané*" [2] and 300,000 members of the households of the White and the Black Clergy. And though this estimate may have value for us only as made up of average and approxi-mate data, we shall see, if we compare its figures for the non-taxpaying classes with the total number of persons standing assessed to payment of poll-tax at the time of the Second Revision, that at the period concerned every hundred urban and rural taxpayers were living under a compulsion to support, directly or indirectly, non-taxpayers, male and female, to the number of fifteen. But perhaps the weight of this incubus upon the taxpayers will be better still realised if we compare those taxpayers' burden with the numerical correlation of those classes as that correlation stood 127 years later. Let us leave out the *gubernii* of Finland, Bessarabia, Esthonia, Lith-uania, and the Vistula region, and take only the forty-three *gubernii* of pre-dominantly Russian population. We shall then see that during the two years selected for comparison (1740 and 1867) every hundred male taxpayers had standing against them male and female non-taxpayers in the following proportions:

	1740	1867
Hereditary *dvoriané*	7·5	1·5
"*Dvoriané* apart," and *dvoriané* on State service	3·0	1·0
Clergy	4·5	2·3

[1] It will be remembered that her reign extended from 1730 to 1740, and that Peter I. died in 1725. Fokkerodt therefore was writing in 1738.
[2] See p. 337.

Incidentally, this shows that Russia of the nineteenth century at least, cannot be said to have been poorly endowed with the privileged classes, seeing that, taking, for example, the clergy of the year 1867, there were then six times as many ecclesiastics in the Orthodox *gubernii* of Russia proper as in the Catholic *gubernii* of the Vistula region, and nearly six times as many as in the Protestant *gubernii* of Esthonia. For the rest, though we see from the above that, during the interval included, the natural growth of the nation's means came to relieve taxpaying labour of the burden of having to support some two-thirds of the privileged section of the country's inhabitants, it enables us to understand why the eighteenth century saw the prolonged and arduous toil of the masses for the support of the country's *élite* bring in to those masses so sorry a cultural harvest. And to add to the manner in which the Law of 18 February, 1762, taxatorily overweighted the serf class, the burdens of that class were not even justly and equally distributed within the class itself. For example, although, earlier, the bonded *krestiané* and other taxpaying categories of population had had to maintain both the army, the administrative officials, and the clergy, they at least had received security abroad, good order at home, and individual spiritual peace; whereas, even granting that ever there was a necessity for the serf financially to aid his *pomiestchik* towards the latter's rendition of State service whilst that service remained compulsory (at the time of which I am speaking the ratio of *pomiestchik* individuals and families to male serfs stood as 14 stands to 100, and the exact totals of each, at the time of the Second Revision, and with the *gubernia* of St. Petersburg omitted, at, respectively, 500,000 and 3,449,000), on what ground were those serfs, when *dvorianin* compulsory service had been abolished, still compelled to support their masters with *barstchina*, as well as, in common with all other taxpayers, to pay for the maintenance of the tax-free classes' pensioners? At all events, one effect of laying these excessive burdens upon *pomiestchiki's* serfs was to evoke a dual form of protest. Of that protest the one form found expression in the fact that, though the period between the First and the Second Revision saw the country's taxable population increase by a little over eighteen per cent., that increase took place so as to leave the taxable population very unequally divided as regards its taxable sections, since its urban section increased by a little over twenty-four per cent., and the Treasury peasantry by forty-six per cent., but the serf section only by twelve, even though a contributory factor to this may have been peasant "flights" from serfdom. The other form of protest expressed itself in an ever-growing number of peasant risings, since everywhere the masses of a country are peculiarly sensitive to social injustice; and though, in Elizabeth's time, serf rebellions never became a real danger owing to the comparative prosperity of the period during which she remained seated upon the throne, no sooner was she gone than they did become such a danger, and one increasingly real after the Government's issue of the Manifesto of 18 February. Wherefore, on Catherine II.'s accession, that Sovereign had to make her first step the task of pacifying 100,000 agrarian serfs, and 50,000 serfs in urban-industrial employment.

Peter I. communicated to his reforming activity not only his own personal energy, and his own personal ideas as to the theory of a State and the necessity of making education a permanent State resource, but also attempts to solve problems partly inherited and partly self-propounded. And even if no other tasks than these had confronted him, they would still have formed an extensive programme of self-appointed labour, since his main purpose was to make of his people a nation at once prosperous and cultured, and he sought to attain that end by enlisting foreign skilled knowledge into the service of Russia, and rendering the people's labour sufficiently productive to meet the State's every requirement, and acquiring the Baltic seaboard as a direct, unobstructed outlet whereby that labour's products might reach the markets of the West, and procuring Russia a position amongst her fellow nations of sufficient influence to render them glad to associate with her, and make good her shortcomings with their resources of culture and technique. Yet when his end was approaching even he himself had to admit that his programme had failed, and that though he had strengthened the State, he had neither enriched nor enlightened the people; whilst already, in 1721, when he had been celebrating the peace with Sweden, he had thought it necessary to warn the Senate that the whole of its future efforts must be devoted to ameliorating the people's lot. Again, though Peter effected military-financial reforms which, if continued, might have come to be re-forms also in the socio-economic sphere, and have augmented the country's productive forces through purely social action; and though also he started upon preparations for such a development by entrusting the State's political, military, and financial affairs to a central board of specialists and experts drawn from every social rank and more than one racial source, and attempted to transfer his cares in connection with industry and industrial organisation to a system of local government, and render that system a public concern, and influence the *dvorianstvo* and the upper stratum of the *kupechestvo* towards acting for themselves—although he did all this, things, after his death, went ill, and industry progressed but little, and external trade still rested in the hands of foreigners, and internal trade still declined in consequence of the harm wrought it by the existing clumsy system of recovering taxatory arrears through distress upon mercantile establishments and stock, so that such multitudes of traders had to abandon commerce (in the desperate hope of making good their losses by other means) that by the period of the Second Revision the taxable urban population had diminished by three per cent. And even the administrative reconstruction of Peter's later days did not adhere a whit more closely to the spirit of his self-propounded dual task, for he resorted to armed assistance in carrying out that reconstruction, and so turned inwards the army originally designed to defend the country's external security, and made it seem as though it were a force designed to defend, rather, a set of Governments filled purely with a self-interested view of their authority, and desirous only of using the troops for tax-collection, and for dealing with brigandage, peasant "flights," and outbreaks. The Central Administration of those days was an organisation neither aristocratic of social composition nor bureaucratic of efficiency, but an organisation directed solely by a mixture of superior *shliachtichi* and risen plebeians who, to quote a contemporary phrase, "knew of their calling as little as they knew of the blacksmith's craft." And sometimes even the Senate had to be reprimanded for its stupidity and negligence, whilst the Government's directors under the Crown were such that during the years 1730–56 the Departments under those directors stood powerless to furnish properly itemed accounts of State income and expenditure, or properly detailed statements of Treasury balances and arrears. And the same with provincial administration. Under Elizabeth the urban magistracies subordinated by Catherine I. to the provinces' *gubernatori* and *voevodi* were restored to their old footing, whilst for the councils of *dvoriané-Landräthe* under *gubernatori* abolished by Peter I. there were substituted certain "commissaries from the land" elected by the *dvoriané* of cantons—thereby increasing the localisation of the latter class's share in the task of provincial government, and finally leading to the whole business resting in the hands of a host of lords of rural manors which those lords had converted into so many judicial-police-jurisdictional centres. Nor, even at that, did the system do anything towards a consolidation of the provincial *dvoriané*; it merely caused the *dvoriané* of each *gubernia* (later, also of each canton) to disperse to their several manorial strongholds, and brought it about that, with the aristocractic and the superior-official sections of the *shliachetstvo* ruling at the top, the inferior and intermediate sections of the class sank to the bottom, and there lay grounded upon serfdom. Next, an idea was mooted of re-welding that mass of rural-manorial squires into local class associations, but according them an authority extending beyond the mere limits of their serf villages. So in 1761 the Senate empowered all *pomiestchiki* to elect, and to send to their local capitals in the capacity of *voevodi*, persons owners of estates in the neighbourhood of those capitals, and so made these locally elected representatives of local *dvorianstvo* take the place of the Treasury officials hitherto administering with the aid of elected *dvorianin* "colleges," Also, in time the Commission which had been appointed to frame a new *Ulozhenie* got as far as to plan establishment of "local councils of *dvoriané* according unto *provintzii*"—but, unfortunately, not as far as to draw up regulations for those councils' guidance. And the next thing was a scheme of the administrative ring for so adding *dvoriané* promiscuously to local administrations as to ensure that always there should be ready to hand a reserve stock of skilled legal dispensers and other such officials; and in 1754, with this end in view, Count P. I. Shuvalov, as a man peculiarly alive to the harm hitherto wrought by Treasury-departmental "governors of impotence," composed a script on "caring for the people." In this lengthy document he propounded for the Senate's benefit a scheme whereby administrative tiros should be prepared "until they shall come to be fit to rule the *gubernii*, the *provintzii*, and the towns, and then proceed also unto the Chief Administration," or, in other words, whereby the provincial administrative system should be converted into "a school wherein youths may perfect themselves in Russian jurisprudence," and then figure as "*Junker dvoriané*," or *dvorianin* cadets employed in the *gubernii's* public departments in the capacity of minor officials studying State business, and, lastly, rise, in proportion to efficiency, to successive posts as secretary, *voevoda*, councillor of *gubernia*, full *gubernator*, and member of the central administrative staff. Which plan of Shuvalov's clearly was a development of Peter's idea on the subject, since Peter too had projected "*Junker-dvorianin*" youths, youths destined to be trained, under the Colleges, to public affairs, and to form the only corps eligible to hold the privileged post of a secretaryship. Yet though this project of Peter's would eventually have placed at his disposal an ever-ready reserve of finished administrative material, it was never Peter's intention to make his *dvorianstvo* a monopolist of the State's civilian service, but only, in that connection, to reinforce the *dvorianstvo* with deserving commoners; whereas it was Shuvalov's aim that his galaxy of *dvorianin*-mandarins should re-establish the class-bureaucratic type of government, that the *dvorianstvo* should become an inexhaustible source and supply of trained *chinovniki*, and that the class's existent means of subsistence should have added to them a whole new category of new official posts. The root basis of the plan, however, must be sought in, besides Peter's measures, the *shliachetstvo's* petition to Anna in favour of restoring the Autocracy, a petition designed to secure also for that class things which included amongst their number exclusive tenure of all central and provincial administrative posts. In fact, there is not a single detail in any scheme or *proekt* or measure of the period in any way concerning the *dvorianstvo* in which we do not see groping for a congenial administrative form the main factor to which the confusion of the age had given birth, the factor of the *dvorianstvo's* desire to predominate. Yes, and we see that that was the factor which, after Peter's death, most sent Peter's reforms astray. During his lifetime his work was directed wholly towards increasing the productiveness of his people's labour with the help of the cultural resources of Europe, but after his death men made his work yield to a harsh system of popular exploitation for the benefit of the Treasury, and of subjection of the exploited to a process of police enslavement. And the chief agent in this perversion was the very class which Peter had hoped to see become the introducer into Russia of European enlightenment. To what extent the statesmen of Elizabeth's period realised how far they had diverged from the road pointed out to them by Peter it is difficult to say, but at least that acute and well-educated man of affairs, Count Kiril Razumovski (brother to the Empress's favourite) seems to have voiced some such realisation, when after preaching before the Empress and her court, in the Cathedral of SS. Peter and Paul, a sermon relative to the battle of Chesme,[1] Platon, the celebrated ecclesiastical orator, theatrically descended the steps from the chancel screen, and, striking his staff against the tomb of Peter the Great, called upon the dead monarch to arise and view his cherished creation, the Russian fleet. Razumovski then took advantage of the general emotion caused to whisper to some of those in his vicinity: "Wherefore calleth he upon Peter? If Peter were indeed to come forth, truly would all of us be in sorry case!" Fate, therefore, brought it about that more than anyone else did the Elizabeth who was for ever citing her father's hallowed behests cause the class which until her time had been accustomed to act only as the Government's instrument in the community's administration now to take it into its head itself to become the Government.

At the same time, Elizabeth's twenty years' reign (which lasted from 25 November, 1741, to 25 December, 1761) was not wholly devoid of lustre, and even of benefit, for Russia—yes, despite that her youth had been passed in a far from edifying manner, and that the prying guardianship exercised over her by Peter's second family had not been quite the thing to teach her strict rules of conduct, or give her pleasurable recollections, seeing that the first word which she must have learnt after "Aunt" and "Mamma" must have been "soldier," and that her mother had so dreaded seeing her daughters

[1] A spot on the coast of Asia Minor near which the Russian fleet defeated a Turkish squadron.

become her rivals on their father's death that she had made every effort to have them married off betimes. A little over medium height, Elizabeth was one who, though her education had been acquired in the servants' hall, never could observe the usual hours for arising, for changing her clothes, for dining, or for going to bed, and whose diversions centred chiefly upon the marryings and givings in marriage of her attendants, when sometimes she would deck the bride for the *vienetz* [1] with her own hands, and watch the later revels of the wedding party through a neighbouring doorway. In disposition a woman of great kindness and simplicity, yet prone to fly into passions over the veriest trifles (when she would upbraid her lacqueys and courtiers in the most unseemly language, and treat her maids-of-honour worse still), she had in earlier days been caught between two mutually contradictory cultural tendencies, since, reared, on the one hand, in the vortex of the new intellectual currents then sweeping through Europe, and brought up, on the other, in the pious traditions of an earlier Russia, she had had the imprints of both influences stamped upon her, and combined the tastes and ideas of both. This was why, for example, she could pass with such ease from Vespers to a ball, and from a ball to next morning's Matins, and why, though accustomed daily and reverently to read the Scriptures, and to observe every rite of the Russian Church, she could write long letters from Paris giving joyous descriptions of the galas and court banquets attended by her at Versailles. French gaieties specially appealed to her, yet the fact did not prevent her from having the whole mystery of the culinary art of Russia at her fingers' ends, any more than the fact that she was an apt pupil of her dancing-master, Rambour, prevented her from being a devout "daughter" of her father confessor, Dubinski, and having the fasts observed at court with such stringency, that her Chancellor of the Kitchen, Count A. P. Bestuzhev-Rumin, once found himself faced with nothing but mushroom ketchup for dinner, and had to apply to the Greek Patriarch for a special dispensation. Lastly, she could dance a minuet or a Russian jig better than anyone else in the Empire. Thus she was one in whom a generous instinct for the æsthetic marched with a frigid feeling for religion. Offered, as a girl, to every eligible *parti* in Europe, from the French King to her own nephew, she was, in Anna's time, rescued from a convent by Biron, and, finally, extricated from the squalor of a ducal castle at Saxe-Coburg-Meiningen to bestow her heart, first of all, upon a Cossack of Chernigov, a court singer, and to convert her palace into a "hall of song," and have choristers hired from Little Russia, and minstrels from Italy, and obviate any risk of break in artistic continuity by commanding that the combined troupes

[1] The crown placed upon the head of a Russian bride during the religious ceremony.

should sing both at Mass and at the Opera. Only this duality of cultural tastes can explain the sometimes pleasant, and sometimes unpleasant, but in every case unexpected, contradictions in her character and her mode of life. Cheerful and animated, tall, buxom, handsome, florid, and round-faced, this lady of Russia never became unmindful of her personality, nor ever forwent a chance of making an "impression." And since masculine costume particularly became her, she instituted holdings of mask-less masquerades at which the men disported themselves in the full-skirted feminine costume of the period, and the women in the court dress of the opposite sex. Also, raised to the throne with the help of Guardsmen's bayonets, she soon proved that no one had a better right than she to be looked upon as Peter's legal successor, by proving that she had inherited her mighty sire's energy and forcefulness in their full entirety. Instances are that once she ordered a palace to be built for her within twenty-four hours, and that a couple of days and nights sufficed for her to cover the distance between Moscow and St. Petersburg—compensation being paid for such horses as were galloped to death on the way. Yet, for all her love of peacefulness and gaiety, Elizabeth had to spend a good half of her reign in making war, and to pay, as the price for doing so, the battlefields of Zorndorf and Kunersdorf, with their heaps of Russian dead. On the other hand, she vanquished Frederick the Great, the period's foremost strategist, and then, by taking Berlin, enabled Russian life to re-enter upon such a phase of ease and quietude as it had not known since the days of the Tsarevna Sophia. The only thing to mar this pleasing impression, the most pleasing of its sort that is to be derived from any of the reigns immediately preceding the reign of Catherine II., is the fact that, exhausted though Europe now lay after its two great coalition wars, so that Elizabeth and her surviving army of 300,000 men might well have seized the opportunity to become arbiters of the whole Continent's destinies, Elizabeth let slip the opportunity, and, though often shown the map of Europe, glanced at it so little that to the end of her life she remained convinced that England could be reached by dry land! And this was the Elizabeth who founded our first Russian university, our own University of Moscow! The fact is that she was too capricious, and too mentally lethargic, and too averse to serious thought and strenuous action to be capable, even in the smallest degree, of understanding European international relations in their complexity, or of making head or tail of Chancellor Bestuzhev-Rumin's beloved diplomatic chicaneries. The only thing that she could do in that way was to form for herself a private circle of intriguers and gossips and toadies, and to set over it a "Cabinet" of her more responsible intimates, and, over the "Cabinet," Mavra Egorovna

Shuvalov, wife of the inventor and framer of *proekti*. The "Cabinet" in question was a clique which included amongst its members Anna Karlovna Vorontzov (*née* Skavronski), a kinswoman of the Empress's, and a lady known variously as "Elizabeth Ivanovna" and "The Minister of Foreign Affairs" (since, says a contemporary writer, "matters do reach the Empress through her alone"), whilst for pastime the members of the clique told tales of one another, intrigued, slandered, cavilled, amused Elizabeth by setting her courtiers at loggerheads, formed "circles," arranged who were to hold the more important ranks and the more lucrative posts in the State, and debated (and sometimes even decided) weighty administrative points. With which occupations, naturally, there went festivities. From earliest girlhood Elizabeth had been given to dreaming (once, before the time of her translation from the position of a Grand Duchess to the full dignity of the Imperial status, she appended to a business document connected with her household, instead of her ordinary signature, the pseudonym "Plamen Ogn——" [1] and, therefore, no sooner did she reach the throne than she set to work to convert these girlish fancies into enchanted reality by embarking upon a round of stage pageants, pleasure excursions, reception days, balls, and masquerades so luxurious and glittering as almost to blind the eye. Amongst other things, she once had the whole of the interior of her palace re-arranged to look like a theatrical *foyer*, and for a while made the conversation at court turn upon nothing but French comedies and Italian farces and interludes—an *entrepreneur* named Locatelli meanwhile producing them for the court's diversion. Yet the ordinary living-rooms to which the court customarily retired after its sportings in the Palace's sumptuous *salons* were so cramped, and so niggardly of fitting, and so slatternly of aspect, that their doors would not shut, their windows were draughty, water trickled down their walls so constantly as to keep the hangings in a permanent state of soddenness, the stove in the Grand Duchess Catherine's own bedroom gaped with cracks, there slept huddled into one small attic next door to her as many as seventeen servants, the furniture everywhere was scanty and rickety and broken, and, to meet requirements, mirrors, bedsteads, tables, and chairs had to be carted about between palace and palace in St. Petersburg, and even between the two capitals. Thus Elizabeth lived and reigned amongst gilded squalor. After her death she left behind her 15,000 gowns, two chestfuls of silk stockings, a multitude of unpaid bills, and a huge unfinished Winter Palace begun six years before her demise, and costing, to date, over 10,000,000 (modern) roubles, yet still so largely unpaid for that when, not long before her end, she besought Rastrelli, the builder of the edifice, at least to accelerate

[1] Probably meant to stand for "Plamen Ognia," "Flame of Fire."

the completion of her private apartments, for her immediate occupation, he refused the request on much the same ground that the jewellers of France refused to send her their elegant goods on credit. Nevertheless, there lurked beneath this crust of prejudice and evil habit and perverted taste something of the same touch of humanity which had distinguished her Courlander predecessor. And there were times when this humanity rose to meet the eye, as when she vowed, before her seizure of the throne, that if, that night, she should become Empress, she would never willingly, thenceforth, send a human being to his death, and as when, on 17 May, 1744, she confirmed that vow with an *ukaz* which practically abolished the death penalty, and as when, later, after refusing for a while to sanction the barbarous criminal clauses and disguised re-enactments of capital punishment added to the new *Ulozhenie*, with the Senate's approval, by the Commission of 1754, and after long withstanding the Holy Synod's scandalous representations as to why she ought to renounce her vow, she burst into tears on finding herself at length compelled by those representations' importunity to render the inequitable decision which she did. Hence, though wayward and dissolute, Elizabeth was clever and kind-hearted—in short, a great lady of eighteenth-century Russia, and a Sovereign such as Russia has always reviled whilst alive, and lamented when dead.

Yet one person at least did not lament her: and the reason why he did not lament her was that he was neither Russian nor capable of tears. The person to whom I allude was her appointed heir, and the worst of the several unpleasant legacies which she bequeathed to her country. This son of Elizabeth's elder sister, this young Duke of Holstein, had been left an orphan shortly after his birth, and a freak of fate subsequently ordained not only that he should become known to history as Peter III. of Russia, but that, on reaching that position, he should posthumously reconcile in his person the two greatest rivals of the eighteenth century. This was because, whilst his mother had been daughter to Peter I., he himself was Charles XII.'s grandson through one of that ruler's sisters, and therefore, though only master, previously to his accession to the Russian throne, of the petty German Duchy of Holstein, heir to two of the most important States in Europe, the Empire of Russia, and the Kingdom of Sweden. Originally he was prepared only for the latter, and made to learn, during the preparatory phase, nothing beyond the Lutheran Catechism, the Swedish tongue, and the Latin grammar; but when Elizabeth had become Russia's ruler, and, to secure continuation of her father's line in the person of her nephew, had dispatched a Major Korf to Kiel with orders to remove that nephew thence, and bring him back with him to St. Petersburg, Karl Petrus Ulrich, Duke of Holstein, now become Peter Fedorovitch, Grand Duke of Russia, as well, had likewise to acquire the Russian language and the Orthodox Catechism. Unfortunately, nature had treated him less kindly than had fortune, for with the fact that he had been born heir-expectant to the thrones of two great foreign countries there went the fact that he had been born possessed of qualities bound to prevent him from ever being fit even to be a Russian Grand Duke. Left, at an early age, an orphan, this meagre-talented, puling stripling of Holstein soon had even the few good *traits* not originally denied him by nature annulled by his stupid education on the Holsteiner pattern—his early schooling was so ineffective (it included floggings and other degrading punishments at the hands of an ignorant German tutor) that he ended by having his health impaired, and his spirits humiliated and depressed, and his habits and tastes rendered such as to leave him permanently irritable, stubborn, quarrelsome, underhand, mendacious, and always artlessly convinced that his lies were true (to which amiable qualities, of course, Russia later added an ability constantly to get drunk). In fact, such was his preparatory training in Holstein that when he reached Russia he was found to be phenomenally ignorant even for a lad of fourteen, ignorant to the point of making the Empress herself stand aghast at the completeness of his illiteracy. Upon which followed the sequel that the sudden change of environment and routine deprived his never well-balanced brain of its last trace of equilibrium, and the more so because the joint facts that he had hitherto been compelled to study without any order or sequence, that the settings of Holstein and Russia were wholly dissimilar from one another, and that he had derived none but futile impressions from Kiel, combined to blunt in him a power of forming a just estimate of his new surroundings. Thus his mental development ended sooner than did his physical growth, and in adolescence he was what he had been in boyhood, and, on reaching manhood, he reached it without also reaching intellectual maturity, so that his forms of thought and action made everything that he said or did appear to be said or done without previous consideration or rehearsal. Grave matters he viewed jejunely; jejune matters he treated with the gravity of an adult. It was as though he at one and the same time imagined himself to be a grown-up, though a child, and a child, though a grown-up. Accordingly, even when the married estate had become his he could not be induced to part with his beloved dolls, and was more than once surprised in their society by visitors to the court. Also, the fact that the hereditary domains whence he hailed were contiguous with the domains of Prussia had early brought him under the spell of Frederick II.'s military fame and strategical genius, and now led him, through possession of a miniature intellect unable to expel its native follies in order to find room for a new ideal, to present, in its addiction to military matters, a caricature of Prussia's hero, the spectacle of a youth "playing at soldiers." Of the Russian Army he knew nothing, and cared nothing: but inasmuch as any sort of a puppet warrior seemed to him real, and alive, and of the size of life, he had whole corps of toy soldiers fashioned of wood, wax, and lead, and then moved them about on tables fitted so as to allow of his intermittently plucking a number of strings stretched across their surface, and thereby obtaining what to his ear sounded like the rattle of musketry discharges. Particularly on festival days did he make it his custom, after donning the uniform of a general officer, to muster before him the whole *personnel* of his retinue, and hold a "grand State review"—plucking gleefully at the strings meanwhile, and listening to the din of "battle." Once, too, when his wife entered the room, she could only stand paralysed with astonishment at what she beheld. For, in the presence of all his "troops," her husband had got a large rat suspended from the ceiling, and his reply to her enquiry was that, inasmuch as the rat had committed so grave and daring a military offence as to make its way into a cardboard fortress, and devour two pasteboard sentries, he had had the culprit arrested, brought before a military tribunal, and sentenced to be hanged. Even his aunt used to find herself driven nearly frantic with his conduct and character, and seldom could spend a quarter of an hour in his company without her feelings being hurt, her temper aroused, and her whole being repelled. Sometimes, in fact, it was necessary only for the talk to turn upon him in his absence to reduce her to tears, and leave her lamenting that God had given her such a successor, if not, as sometimes happened, also vociferating such less reverent phrases as "That accursed nephew of mine!" and "The devil take him— he is a sheer monster!" At all events, so Catherine's *Memoirs* tell us. At the same time, those *Memoirs*' writer adds that though, eventually, the Court decided that the nephew had better be banished, and Elizabeth, on the approach of death, induced to appoint Paul, that nephew's six-year-old son, her successor, the proposal ended merely in the Empress's favourites backing out of the venture, executing a *volte-face*, and once more applying themselves to conciliation of the good graces of the Monarch-Expectant.

So in due course, all ignorant of the fate that was speedily to befall him, and impelled to the step by his aunt's bitter taunts, this topsy-turvy creature, this creature whose mentality inextricably confounded the idea of good with the idea of wrong, ascended the Russian Throne, and there retained unchanged the narrowness, the pettiness, of interests and ideas imbibed during his early rearing and training. Never did his cramped Holsteiner intellect find itself able to expand to correspond with the boundless geographical dimensions of the Empire which now (unfortunately for itself) had become his care, and on the throne of Russia he remained more German even than he had been on the throne of his native country. The quality in him which expressed itself out of all proportion to the other qualities with which nature had dowered him was a sort of admixture equally of irresponsibility, of frivolity, and of cowardice: with the result that he stood in fear of every native of his new country, always referred to Russia as "an accursed land," and frequently gave vent to the conviction that ultimately his adopted home would prove his ruin. Yet he never made the slightest effort to adapt himself to that home, or to draw nearer to his people. To the end he remained ignorant of everything in his realm, and shunned that realm's population. It was as though it filled him with the terror often inspired in children by a large and empty room, so that he felt driven both by his fears and by his natural inclinations hastily to surround himself with society of such a type as even the times of Peter I., a monarch by no means squeamish about social affairs, had never beheld, and to cling to that society as though it was a little world of the imagination whither flight could be sought from the horrors of reality. Also, he instituted a "Holsteiner Guard" of international (but strictly non-Russian) riff-raff in which sergeants and corporals from the Prussian Army figured largely, but which was, nevertheless, according to a remark of Princess Dashkov's on its composition, "nought but a rabble of sons of German cobblers." Moreover, to make things harmonise the better with his selection of Frederick II. for his military model, he himself was for assimilating the manners and customs of a Prussian trooper, and took to limitless smoking, and to an endless drinking of bottles of beer, in the fond belief that only through those means could he convert himself into "a veritable and a brave officer." Indeed, after his accession there was scarcely a day when he remained sober until evening, and then could sit down to table in a non-festive condition. Also, during his daily carousals with his German *coterie* he would add to that constellation of Teutonic talent such wandering planets as strolling actors, actresses, and singers, whilst also we know from Bolotov, an observer with many opportunities of observing the Emperor intimately, that at those gatherings Peter would deliver himself of "follies and un-seemlinesses" which made his subjects blush for very shame, especially if a foreign Minister happened to be present, and that usually the *gaffes* began with Peter expounding some impossible scheme of reform which he had devised, and went on to the relation of an equally heroic and imaginary tale concerning a detachment which he had once led against a gipsy camp near Kiel, and attained their conclusion in the indiscreet revelation of some important diplomatic secret. To add to the general misfortune, there were times when he felt moved to play the fiddle, as an instrument on which he believed himself to have attained sheer virtuosity; and at all times he suspected himself to be a great comic actor, seeing that he could not only, at will, pull a number of grimaces, but also give an imitation of a priest in church. For the same reason it was that he abolished the old Russian obeisance in favour of the French curtsey. That done, he could, after the holding of a reception, mimic the *kniksen* [1] which the more elderly of his court dames had executed at it. It was, therefore, at least unfortunate that a lady whom he had been attempting to amuse with a special exhibition of facial contortions blurted out the remark that, whatever else he looked like as he was making them, he did not look like a Tsar. On the other hand, we may offset against all this the fact that, as regards affairs of State, his reign saw published some important and effective *ukazi*—for example, an *ukaz* for annulment of the Secret Chancellory, and an *ukaz* permitting Old Believers to return to Russia without risk of prosecution for their dissent. Not that these two *ukazi* were inspired by abstract principles of tolerance, nor by a desire to protect the individual from *donos*. What really inspired them was the desire of men like the Vorontzovs and the Shuvalovs to consolidate their position in the State, and render themselves and the Emperor popular by instigating the latter to exercise the Imperial clemency. And the same with the *ukazi* whereby the *dvorianstvo* became emancipated from compulsory service. Yet Peter set so little store by his position as soon to evoke murmurings from the community by his behaviour, for he seemed purposely to set himself to arouse resentment amongst the people, and especially amongst the clergy. Never at any time did he trouble to conceal his contempt for the rites of the Orthodox Church. Nay, he would flaunt and defy the religious sense of Russia to the point of actually receiving foreign ambassadors in the Palace chapel, and whilst divine service was going on, and pace up and down the sacred building as though it had been his private cabinet, and talk at the top of his voice, and halt to loll his tongue at the officiating priests. Particularly, one Trinity Sunday, did he seize a moment when the congregation were kneeling down to pray to burst into a peal of laughter, and rush from the building. In the same way, sheer prejudice bade him tell Dmitri Siechenov, Archbishop of Novgorod, and President of the Holy Synod, that "the churches in Russia must be cleansed"—that is to say, that all their *ikoni* save those of the Saviour and the Holy Mother were to be removed, and their priests made to shave the beard, and put on the dress of Lutheran pastors. And even though the authorities temporised with these orders so far as possible, it soon came about that both the clerical

---

[1] Genuflexions, "bobs."

community and the lay were raising a panic cry of "The Lutherans be upon us!" Especially did Peter exasperate the Black Clergy by ordering, as part of his policy of secularising the whole of the Church's immovable property, that the College hitherto charged with the management of the Black Clergy's economy should be placed under the Senate instead of under the Holy Synod, and make over to its peasantry the whole of such monasterial and episcopal lands as those peasantry worked, and devote a portion of its income from ecclesiastical *otchini* towards making a State-assessed contribution towards the maintenance not only of its own ecclesiastical establishments, but of all. True, Peter never succeeded in actually carrying these measures into effect, but the result was the same. The quarter whence, eventually, danger most threatened was the Guards, the community's at once most elegant and most arrogant section, owing, first and foremost, to the fact that Peter never lost an opportunity of proclaiming how greatly he revered Frederick II. For him to imprint pious kisses upon the Prussian hero's bust in public was not sufficient: once he interrupted the progress of a State banquet by rising from his seat, and prostrating himself headlong. From the first, too, he would make public appearances in Prussian uniform, with a Prussian order: and ultimately the same tight, gaudy, antiquated style of military raiment became foisted upon the Guards—it displaced on their forms the loose green *kaftan* in which Peter the Great had vested them. For Peter III. seemed to regard himself as Frederick's understudy, and, as such, again, attempted to make the Prussian stringency of discipline replace the easy-going military practice of Russia, and to organise for his court, each day, martial exercises exemptory neither of rank nor of age, and to force even the most important personages, and persons who had not for years past seen (let alone drilled upon) a parade-ground, and meanwhile had laid up a fine stock of gout, to subject themselves with the best grace they could to Prussia's ballet-dance of a drill under Prussian officers, and see Russia's native military system gradually undone, and even men like old Field-Marshal and ex-*Prokurator-General* Prince Nikita Trubetskoi, honorary Lieutenant-Colonel of the Guards, drilling and marching like a linesman. Contemporary writers stood flabbergasted at these changes. Says Bolotov: "To-day are great men, and small, and the aged alike being made to raise their feet, and march with the young, and stamp with a neatness equal unto theirs, and tread mire like unto common men-at-arms." And the supremely shameful fact was that Peter gave his rabble of a "Holsteiner Guard" precedence over the true Guards of Russia, and dubbed the latter "Janissaries," and let the Prussian Ambassador not only rule the roost in Russia's foreign policy, but regulate every detail of court ceremonial—all because, before Peter's accession, that Ambassador had been, to all intents and purposes, Frederick's Russian correspondent, and kept the Prussian monarch posted as to Russia's military forces, and continued to do so throughout the Seven Years' War. Until, wounded in its sense of national honour, and seeing before it once more the hateful spectre of a *régime* such as Biron's, the community and the Guards—the latter dreading lest the idea of their reduction to the line should be revived—began to realise how weak and hesitant was the Government's policy, how utterly the deliberations of the administrative ring lacked unanimity and a definite purpose. In other words, all now began to perceive that the administrative machine had fallen out of gear, and soon the cliqueish murmurings of the higher social ranges overflowed to lower levels, became common property, loosened tongues, and led to the Tsar being criticised in spite of deterrent police pressure. Until, finally, that popular discontent passed into open street utterance, and that open street utterance budded into a military conspiracy, and that military conspiracy flowered in a military revolution.

CHAPTER XVI

The Revolution of 28 June, 1762.

THE person on whose behalf the movement mentioned at the close of the last chapter was instituted became Empress for the reason that already she enjoyed popularity both amongst the people and amongst the Guards. From the first she had lived on bad terms with the Emperor—more than once he had threatened to divorce her, and to immure her in a convent, in favour of his paramour, Count Vorontzov's niece; and at length, after a long period of relegation to the background during which she bore up against her position as best she could, and without entering into more than indirect relations with the party of malcontents, Catherine came to the conclusion that action outright must be taken. She took it on 24 April, 1762, and the immediate cause of her doing so was the fact that the Emperor had just completed the cup of Russia's humiliation, and fanned the people's murmurings to the point of an outbreak, and nullified all Russia's victories during Elizabeth's reign (though in their time they had nearly reduced Frederick to despair), by making peace with the Prussian monarch. More: he had renounced in Frederick's favour all the territories (including Eastern Prussia) which Frederick had ceded to Russia with his own hand. Lastly, he had joined forces with Prussia against Russia's allies, the Austrians. According to Bolotov, "The Russians then were gnashing their teeth with rage." Previously, on 9 June, at the banquet held to celebrate the ratification of the Treaty, Catherine had failed to follow the Emperor's example by rising and emptying her glass when he had proposed the health of the Imperial Family, and replied to his query that, as she considered the Imperial Family to consist solely of the Emperor, herself, and her son, she had not thought the proceeding necessary. "But what of my uncles, the Princes of Holstein?" Peter had exclaimed, and then bidden Gudovitch, his aide-de-camp, leave his post behind the Imperial chair, and go and apply to the Empress a foul epithet—following that up, lest the messenger should soften down the unmannerly word, by shouting it across the table himself. And Catherine had burst into tears. But though, the same evening, orders had been given for her arrest, one of the Emperor's uncles, who had witnessed the scene, had intervened, and the step had been left in abeyance. From that moment Catherine lent a still more willing ear to the representations which had been reaching her ever since Elizabeth's death, and the social leaders of St. Petersburg (the more so, perhaps, because all of them had, at one time or another, suffered insult at Peter's hands) lent a still more sympathising attention to the enterprise referred to in those representations. One leader of the sort was Count Nikita Panin, the late Elizabeth's diplomatist, and tutor to the Grand Duke Paul; and another one the nineteen-year-old Princess Dashkov, sister to the court favourite, a lady closely connected with the Guards through her husband; and another one the already mentioned Dmitri Siechenov, Arch-bishop of Novgorod—though, in view of his spiritual office, he took only an indirect share in the plot; and another—secretly, it is true, but filling the prime roll—Count Cyril Razumovski, *Hetman* of Little Russia, and President of the Russian Academy of Sciences, a man who already had won over the Izmailovski Regiment by distributing to it bounteous *largesse*. The actively operative spirits in the plot, however, were two officers of the Preobrazhenski Regiment named Passek and Bredikhin, with three officers (including two brothers) of the Izmailovskis named Lasunski and Roslavlev, an officer of the Horse Guards named Khitrovo, an *Unteroffizier* named Potemkin, and, as a general connecting link, the family of Orlov brothers, more especially Grigori and Alexis—fine, strong, handsome fellows, daring and spirited almost to a fault, skilled hands at arranging carousals and pugilistic bouts in St. Petersburg's more fashionable haunts, noted in their several regiments for professional skill, and the social idols of every Guards subaltern. Moreover, though the fact had always been kept concealed, Grigori, the eldest brother, an officer in the artillery, had for some time past been on intimate terms with the Empress. The conspirators, therefore, divided themselves into four groups, under an arrangement that, whilst their leaders should meet periodically for conferences, all the usual ritual of conspiracy should be omitted, no regular meetings—no, not even of the leaders—be held, and nothing be done in the way either of employing definite propagandist methods or of following fixed plans of campaign. For that matter, the latter were needed the less in that by this time the Guards had so good an education in the art of revolution that the only thing needing to be done in this particular instance was to ensure that the popular heroine on whose behalf the rising was to be made should hold herself in readiness for the appointed moment. Thus by the eve of the affair Catherine came to have at her disposal about forty Guards' officers and 10,000 men, all of them adherents safely to be counted upon. As a matter of fact, the revolution came as a more or less generally expected affair—the public had been looking for it for some time past, and especially in view of the fact that during the previous week the ever-growing crowds in the streets had kept being threaded by persons, mostly Guardsmen, who had boldly and openly depreciated the Tsar. Small wonder, therefore, that discerning observers had known that they need but count the hours to an upheaval. True, reports to much the same effect had reached Peter also, but he was too dissolute and careless really to understand the growing dangers of the situation, and, giving the reports scanty heed, philandered at Oranienbaum as before, and adopted no measures of self-defence. Nay, almost as though he had been one of the conspirators against himself, he seized the present juncture to fan further the embers of revolt with a proposal that Russia's already profitless external war should have added to it a war promising to be equally barren of gain. That is to say, he proposed that, in order to restore to his Duchy of Holstein the Province of Schleswig wrested thence by Denmark, war should be declared by Russia against the latter. Incidentally, a curious feature of this sorry scheme to pit mighty Russia against diminutive Denmark in order to re-establish the unity of Peter's native domain was that it led also to a blow being struck for freedom of conscience, in that at the same juncture the Holy Synod received an *ukaz* of 25 June whereby all Christians were thenceforth to rank as equal before the law, and fasts to cease to be insisted upon, and breaches of the Seventh Commandment to stand exempt from censure ("therein even Christ Himself did not condemn"), and the Treasury to have transferred to it the whole of the monasterial *krestiané*: to all of which, the *ukaz* added, the Senate must accord its consent forthwith. Inevitably these crazy dispositions led to credence of the most improbable rumours, such as, for example, that Peter was minded to have all his court ladies divorced, and then re-married to spouses of his own choosing —he himself giving husbands a lead by divorcing his own wife, and then taking unto himself Elizabeth Vorontzov—a *dénouement* which, had things turned out otherwise than as they did, might quite conceivably have come about in reality. Hence it is the more intelligible that all ended by tacitly agreeing that, cost what it might, an Autocrat of that type must be got rid of at the first favourable opportunity. And that opportunity the Emperor furnished, as we have seen, when he declared war against Denmark. The initial incident was that to the Guards, as resentfully they sat awaiting orders to march on the campaign, there arrived an intimation that the Tsar was purposing to pay them a flying visit, and give them a farewell dinner: and upon that Panin realised that the propitious moment was come. Besides, another chance incident happened to hasten on the moment. On 27 June a corporal of the Preobrazhenski Regiment came running to Passek to know whether it was true that the Empress was dead, and the Emperor about to be deposed—both of which fables, of course, had sprung from rumours circulated by the conspirators themselves: and though Passek assured the soldier that nothing of the sort need be believed, the man was not satisfied, but hastened off to another officer, and put to him the same enquiry. Now, it happened that this other officer was not one of the officers who had been made privy to the plot; and when the soldier put to him his question, and also mentioned the interview already held with Passek, the officer considered that he ought at once to report what he had heard to the authorities. The result was that Passek was arrested the same day, and of course this brought all the conspirators to their feet, in alarm lest Passek should be put to the torture in prison, and forced to betray them. The eventual decision was that, that same night, Alexis Orlov should make his way to Peterhof, where Catherine was in residence in readiness for the Emperor's nameday celebrations on the 29th, and acquaint her with what had occurred: and Alexis duly undertook the journey, reached Catherine's private apartments, and fulfilled his mission. At once, though the time was the small hours of the morning, Catherine arose, dressed herself, entered Orlov's carriage (a maid-of-honour in attendance, and Orlov posted on the box-seat) and drove to the quarters of the Izmailovski Regiment, where beat of drum already had mustered the men to the barrack square. Immediately upon her arrival they swore allegiance to her as Empress in independent right of her own, and then spent the time until their colonel, Count Razumovski, appeared in showering kisses upon her hands, feet, and raiment. Next, headed by the cross-bearing priest who had been summoned to administer the oath of fealty, all moved on to the quarters of the Semenovski Corps, where the same ceremony of swearing allegiance was performed: and when that had been done Catherine placed herself at the head of the combined regiments, and, with them and a number of civilians who had now assembled, proceeded to the Kazan Cathedral, where a Te Deum service was sung, and she was proclaimed Autocrat in solemn form. Thence, now created plenipotentiary Empress, she went to the Winter Palace, where the Senate and the Holy Synod were in joint session, and obtained their fealty and sworn allegiance without protest. Presently the movement was swelled by the arrival of the Horse Guards, the Preobrazhenski Regiment, and line details—in all, about 14,000 men: and as these flocked around the Palace, and enthusiastically acclaimed her as she walked to and fro before their ranks, and were re-echoed in their fervour by the civilian spectators who, on the doors of the Palace being flung open, had unhesitatingly, willingly crowded in to swear allegiance, a spectator might have thought that the revolution was accomplishing itself rather than being accomplished. The truth is that the way had been well and secretly prepared, everyone had been previously brought into complete agreement, and the destined hour had been made known. Later Catherine herself, when recalling the universal rapture and applause with which she had been greeted, attributed the unity of popular sentiment to the fact that from the first the movement had won the people's sympathy. Certainly it was a movement in which all seemed to bear their parts with a will, and to act as agents on their own account, and not as police puppets, or as inquisitive spectators. So the next step was that the authorities hastily composed, and as hastily distributed, a manifesto briefly declaring that that day, in pursuance of the clearly expressed and manifestly sincere wishes of her people, the Empress had ascended the throne, and that from that throne she would ever defend the Russian Orthodox Church, Russia's victorious foreign prestige, and Russia's domestic tranquility, and the latter with the more solicitude in that it had suffered recent disturbance. That day was the 28th of June. The same evening, mounted, and with hair unbound, and a helmet and a sprig of oak resting upon it, and figure clad in a Guard's uniform of the old Petrine cut, she rode with Princess Dashkov (similarly attired) to Peterhof at the head of the Brigade, and reached that place shortly before the Emperor and his suite were due to arrive thither from Oranienbaum for the farewell dinner to the Guards. Yet though the ceremony had been planned to be held in the Empress's pavilion, "Mon Plaisir," Peter and his retinue of courtiers found, when they reached the building, that it was empty, and that, in spite of a search of the grounds, Catherine was nowhere to be discovered. Next it was learnt that, nevertheless, the Empress had called there a little earlier, and departed again: and upon that all stood dumbfounded. As a first step, a few dignitaries, including Chancellor Vorontzov (who seems to have had at least an inkling of what was in the wind), were sent on to St. Petersburg, with instructions to find out how things lay and, if possible, obtain access to the Empress, and remonstrate. Well, it may or may not be true— we have only Catherine's own word for the statement—that those dignitaries were instructed also, if such a course should prove necessary, to assassinate her, but at least there is no doubt that the scouts, instead of returning to Peterhof, seized the moment of their arrival in the capital to swear allegiance to the new Empress. This and other such items having been communicated to the Emperor, he and his party next dispatched aides-de-camp and hussars to reconnoitre each of the roads leading from the metropolis, and in the meantime held a further conference. At first they decided to make for

Kronstadt, and seize it, and then, with the aid of the fleet, use it as a base against the capital; but no sooner did the Emperor and his staff draw near to the fortress than they were met with an intimation that if they did not retire forthwith they would be fired upon. Münnich next advised either that they should attempt to land by force on the island of Kronstadt or that, by way of Revel, they should escape to Pomerania, where possibly Peter would be able to assume command of the Russian forces recently dispatched thither; but Peter had not the courage for either course—he could only cower down in his galley amidst the lamentations of his court ladies, and give orders for sail to be set, and Oranienbaum regained. Lastly, after an unsuccess-cessful attempt to enter into peace negotiations with the Empress on con-dition that thenceforth she should be given a share in the Supreme Power, Peter had no choice but to inscribe and sign a document which said: "Of mine own free will do I swear to renounce the throne herewith." Catherine and her troops occupied Peterhof the next morning, but great difficulty was experienced in protecting Peter from the soldiers as he was being removed thither from Oranienbaum, and on his arrival he was almost swooning with terror. Running to meet Panin, and clinging wildly to his hand, he again and again besought his good offices in trying to procure that the petitioner should be allowed to keep his four most cherished possessions—his fiddle, his lap-dog, his negro servant, and Elizabeth Vorontzov: and though permission was refused as regards the last named—she was dispatched to Moscow, and married off to a Pole—Peter's three other treasures were left at his disposal.

Thus Peter, on the throne of Russia, represented merely a chance, transitory tenant: he glimmered for a brief period above the Russian political horizon, and then shot elsewhither across the firmament, and left everyone wondering why he had ever appeared. Later the same day Catherine had him removed to Ropsha, the suburban villa which Elizabeth, his aunt, had given him, and on the morrow made her State entry into St. Petersburg, and, in doing so, rang down the curtain upon the cleanest-handed—at all events the least sombre—of Russia's many revolutions. For at least that revolution had caused no blood to be shed—it had been only a sort of *émeute de salon*. But what it did cost was a vast amount of liquor, for on 30 June, the day of Catherine's State progress from Peterhof to the capital, every drinking-establishment was thrown open to the soldiers free of charge, and throughout the day they and their wives danced frenziedly, and quaffed beer, mead, *vodka*, and champagne out of bottles or buckets or anything else that came handy, and led to it that as long as three years afterwards we find the Senate still debating the question of indemnifying the metropolis' publicans "for all the imbibings of wine by soldiers and others on the occasion of her present Imperial Majesty's Auspicious Accession to the Throne."

Another circumstance which caused this eighteenth-century affair, this culminating item of Russia's long series of *révolutions de palais*, to differ from all others of its sort was that, though it was accomplished with the help of the Guards, it had for its basis such an amount of openly expressed popular sympathy—at all events so far as the capital was concerned—as gave it the appearance of a movement on the part of the nation as a whole. Both in 1725, in 1730, and in 1741 the Guards' method of establishment, or of restoration, of the Supreme Power had been the method of establishment upon the throne, or of restoration to the throne, of some particular individual whom the Guards' officers had previously persuaded their men to accept as the Supreme Power's legal heir: but in 1762 the Guards acted as an independent political force, and, at that, as a revolutionary, not a conservative, one, since the personage whom it overthrew was the Supreme Power's legal holder, and a holder to whom the Guards themselves had sworn allegiance. This was because in the Guards, on the present occasion, there went with a sense of outraged national dignity a sense of conviction that though they were creating, and imposing upon the country, a Ruling Power which, very possibly, had no legal title, that Ruling Power was a ruling power at least better calculated to understand and to oversee its realm's interests than its legal predecessor had been. Later, Catherine too explained the Guards' enthusiasm as due to every member of the corps, even to the humblest, having felt as though the affair were being carried out with his own hands: wherefore she added an acknowledgment of the revolutionary loyalty shown, and commented that there are times when even a usurpation can secure stability for a new order of State, and prosperity for a people. Next, the stir in St. Petersburg having subsided, she amnestied any excesses which might have been born of street patriotism with an Act explanatory of what the late events had meant. In other words, she published the well-known "circumstantial" Manifesto of 6 July, 1762. It is a document which constituted at once a justification of usurpation, a homily, an impeachment of Catherine's predecessor, and a whole political programme. First it laid bare with unsparing frankness the ex-Emperor's many criminal and shameful deeds and machinations. Then it continued that though those deeds might well have led to military mutiny, the Tsar's assassination, and the State's downfall, the Empress had discerned the dissolution threatening the country, straightway "hearkened unto certain of Our faithful subjects chosen of the people, and sent unto Our Presence," offered herself as a sacrifice for her "beloved fatherland,"[1] and delivered that fatherland from the perils confronting it. Yet what the Manifesto really was castigating and impeaching was less the person of the deposed Tsar, that unfortunate accident of State, than the State's very structure. "Any Autocracy," the Manifesto said, "the Autocrat Sovereign of which hath not good and humane qualities for the curbing of that Sovereign tendeth ever towards evil, and causeth many an untoward result." That is to say, the Supreme Power of Russia now proclaimed from the throne, for the first time in Russia's history, the weighty truth that the coping-stone of the Russian people's edifice of State had long been threatening to fall upon that edifice's unstable main structure, and shatter it. Such a catastrophe, the Manifesto concluded, must be averted, and, accordingly, the Empress therewith, and most solemnly, did pledge herself to sanction any and every such legislative scheme as might "preserve unto posterity" the Empire's and the Autocracy's integrity, and "secure unto the faithful subjects of Our Fatherland freedom from all dejection and offence."

Unfortunately, the lightheartedness and the *camaraderie* accompanying the revolution were to have appended to them a painful and an unnecessary epilogue. The Empress, as I have stated, dispatched Peter to Ropsha, and there he was lodged in a single room, nor ever allowed to set foot even upon the terrace or in the garden, but ceaselessly watched by pickets and patrols. Also, his personal attendants treated him rudely: only Alexis Orlov, their head, showed him, according to report, any real kindness, or occasionally entertained and played cards with him, or occasionally lent him money. Which kind of existence was bound to impair the captive's health. Thus things continued until 6 July, the day of the signing of the Manifesto; and late at night, that day, Catherine's hand received a note which, inscribed in the handwriting as of an imperfectly sober correspondent, informed the Empress that at dinner, on the same date, Peter had picked a quarrel with one of his companions, and that, to the writer's sorrow, so much force had had to be used by Orlov and others before they could part the two combatants that the frail ex-Emperor had been left in a dying condition. "Not until he was no more could the twain be put asunder by us. We scarce knew what we were doing." According to Catherine's own account of what next happened, she remained overcome with grief: but, whether or not that was so, we at all events find her writing a month later: "Now must I the more march ahead. Suspicion must not overtake me." One result of the tragedy of 6 July was that on the following day the solemn reading of the Manifesto in the country's cathedrals and churches had to have appended to it the

---

[1] It will be remembered that Catherine was a German.

solemn reading of a Proclamation of the same date, a Proclamation announcing to all men that on the previous day the Emperor had expired suddenly of "colic," and that therefore they must "pray without remembrance of evil" for the salvation of his soul. Nevertheless when Peter arrived from Ropsha for modest burial in the Monastery of Alexander Nevski (where he was laid beside the ex-Regent, Anna Leopoldovna), the Senate for some reason thought well to give Catherine a hint that she had better absent herself from the obsequies.

In reading the Manifesto of 6 July, we feel that we are standing at one of the turning-points in Russian life. For the document promised the nation something new, something never before attained, in the nation's life: it promised the nation a State based upon legislative enactment alone. But for us really to grasp the scantiness of the nation's preparation for seeing such a State evolved, as well as the swiftness of that State's extinction after its first dawning glimmer, we must retrace our steps a little. Towards the close of the sixteenth century the Russian Empire still stood based upon the principle of *otchina*, upon the principle that the State was not so much a union of population as the private, the family, demesne of its Sovereign, and that within its area that Sovereign's subjects owed no obligations to anyone save that Sovereign alone, nor themselves possessed any law-established rights. But then came the Period of Troubles, when the last remnants of the system were cleared away, and the nation, through its own efforts, extricated itself from the condition of disorder into which it had sunk, and elected a new dynasty. That dynasty, as a dynasty which had had no part, as the previous dynasty had, in building up its subject State, stood disqualified from looking upon the State as its private *otchina*, as the previous dynasty had done, and, *nolens volens*, had to participate with its people in the task of State reconstruction, and, in the process, to permit that people to figure as more than merely the State's building material. All of which means that in the life of the Muscovite Empire there now became started two divergent currents, one of which set about carving out for itself a new channel, and the derelict shores of *Prikaz* officialdom. But as time went on, and the new current drew further from its source, that current began to turn and make backward towards the older current again, until the close of the seventeenth century once more saw the two meet, and the new dynasty become enabled to revive the obsolete customs and ideas of the principle that the State was but the *otchina* of that ruler, and that dynasty's founder to word his legislative Acts so as to show his people that once more he looked upon himself, not as a popularly-elected Sovereign, but solely as nephew of the late Tsar Theodor, and one whose *de facto* authority rested upon that kinship, and not upon any choice of the people's. And though the capacity for independent action originally derived by the people from the Period of Troubles attained reconsolidation in the institution of the pan-corporate *Zemski Sobor*, that institution was followed, again, by a decline in that action's natural basis, in local or territorial self-government, which once more nullified the *Zemski Sobor* as a stable and permanent organ of popular expression, and, depriving it of its original all-class composition, left it in such a condition that, on being blown upon with the blast of Peter's reforms, it expired.

Yet Peter's ideas and aspirations came very near to achieving the theory of a State in the true sense, since he at least realised that a State should make its first and foremost aim the weal of that State's contained population, not a dynastic interest, and that the means to that end lay in legality, in assured preservation of "rights, civil and political," and in recognition of the fact that the Sovereign's authority was not the Sovereign's private, hereditary asset, but an obligation to perform his duties as Tsar, and to shape his policy, so that the Empire should be served thereby, and the Empire alone. Unfortunately, circumstances and custom alike intervened to prevent him from wholly making his work agree with his intentions and ideas, since from the first he had to labour more in the sphere of politics than in the sphere of equity, in that his predecessors had bequeathed to him two political prejudices vitally hostile to their and his efforts. Those two political prejudices were a fixed belief in the creative power of the Sovereign's authority, and an absolute reliance upon the maxim that nothing can exhaust either the strength or the patience of a Sovereign's people. Hence Peter never let either a popular right or a popular sacrifice stand in his way, and, despite that he did in very truth become—at all events to a certain extent—a reformer in the European sense, never ceased to be dominated by, and obsessed with, the idea of the old Muscovite, pre-Petrine type of Tsar, and to pay scanty attention to the people's psychology and instinct for fair play. In fact, in his view his power was a power able even to root out agelong customs, and to instil new ideas—to change the national attire as easily as it could change the regulation width of factory-made cloth. Nothing, he considered, could not be effected by force, could not, through compulsory methods, be initiated amongst the masses. Of all of which the net result was to create a system of equity based upon equity's opposite, and to found a State which, though based upon a system of equity, lacked, as much as did Peter's laws and authority, the one indispensable life-giving element, the element producible only of civic and personal freedom.

To the last, therefore, Peter's attempts to consolidate his theory of a

State in the popular mind proved a failure; and no sooner was he gone than the theory so faded out of administrative intellects that the only two of his successors who acceded through legal means, his grandson and his daughter, never so much as learnt its meaning. For, after him, various changes brought to the throne unlooked-for, and even alien, rulers, rulers who were as incapable of looking upon Russia as their fatherland as they stood disqualified from regarding it as their *otchina*, whilst the State became limited to the walls of a palace, and the governing power in that State sank to being a power which clung to its authority, not as a proprietorial chattel, even as a dynastic-proprietorial chattel, but simply and solely as a commodity which, having been seized by force, required to be justified in the people's eyes only so long as, in default of popular support, it lacked a military-police prop.

And this last phase of all ushered in a turbid flood of Court revolutions, of sudden promotions to court favour, and of sudden court banishments, until the Sovereign and the throne stood surrounded not by a true ruling class of any sort, but by a pseudo-ruling class whose social composition was as heterogeneous as its moral-intellectual bent was uniform. For though the class was the same military service class as once had been officered by the old-established *boyarstvo*, and, as such, had constituted the court retinue of the old-time proprietary-Tsars, it was now officiating in a new formation; and though, also, when that retinue had become Ivan IV.'s *Oprichnina*, or the Sovereign's police-bodyguard against the *dvorianstvo's* provincial sections, it had temporarily taken on a political tinge, the seventeenth century had seen the last remnants of its original *boyarin* element absorbed into the *dvorianstvo* of the metropolis, and the latter entrusted with the *Oprichnina's* functions until under Peter I. the whole had emerged as a Household Brigade, a force containing more than a seasoning of foreigners, and specially charged to act as Russia's introducer to the culture and military skill of the West. Throughout, the State rewarded the class liberally for its warlike and administrative services; throughout, the State made special provision for the class's upkeep by increasing the people's taxatory burdens, distributing State lands wholesale, and delivering, binding, into the class's exclusive service two-thirds of the country's rural population. The result was that as soon as Peter was gone the class joined the Guards in the latter's haphazard formation of Governments, in order that it might procure from those Governments, in addition, emancipation from compulsory service, and arrogate to itself rights making it dominant both in the administration of the State and in the management of the popular economy.

I have now expounded the step-by-step formation of the class through the centuries, and the manner in which its *personnel* changed with the needs of the State, and under the influence of casual occurrences. Practically, until Catherine II. ascended the throne, it was, from the political standpoint, the nation. But though it helped the first few of Peter the Great's successors to transform Russia's "Palace State" into a "*Dvorianin* State," Russia was not for a long while yet to become what she is now, a National State.

INDEX

INDEX

END OF VOL. IV.

MADE AT THE
TEMPLE PRESS
LETCHWORTH

GREAT BRITAIN

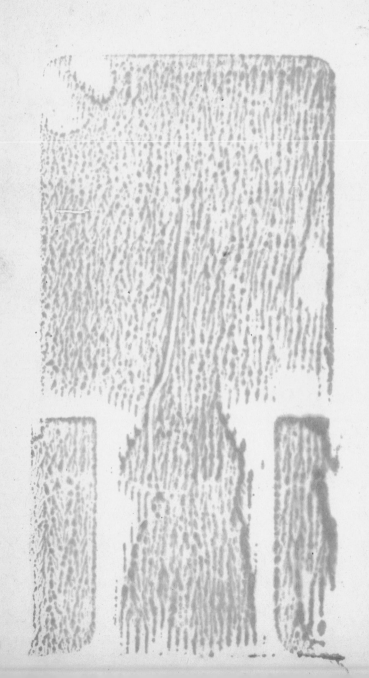